always up to date

The law changes, but Nolo is on top of it! We offer several ways to make sure you and your Nolo products are up to date:

1 **Nolo's Legal Updater**
We'll send you an email whenever a new edition of this book is published! Sign up at **www.nolo.com/legalupdater**.

2 **Updates @ Nolo.com**
Check **www.nolo.com/update** to find recent changes in the law that affect the current edition of your book.

3 **Nolo Customer Service**
To make sure that this edition of the book is the most recent one, call us at **800-728-3555** and ask one of our friendly customer service representatives. Or find out at **www.nolo.com**.

please note

We believe accurate, plain-English legal information should help you solve many of your own legal problems. But this text is not a substitute for personalized advice from a knowledgeable lawyer. If you want the help of a trained professional—and we'll always point out situations in which we think that's a good idea—consult an attorney licensed to practice in your state.

3rd edition

Deduct It!
Lower Your Small Business Taxes

By Attorney Stephen Fishman

NOLO

Third Edition	NOVEMBER 2006
Editor	DIANA FITZPATRICK
Book Design	TERRI HEARSH
Proofreading	ROBERT WELLS
Index	JEAN MANN
Cover photography	TONYA PERME (www.tonyaperme.com)
Printing	DELTA PRINTING SOLUTIONS

Fishman, Stephen.
    Deduct it! : lower your small business taxes / by Stephen Fishman.-- 3rd ed.
       p. cm.
    ISBN 1-4133-0528-8 (alk. paper)
     1. Small Business--Taxation--Law and legislation--United States--Popular works. 2.
Tax deductions--United States--Popular works. I. Title.

    KF6491.Z9F57 2006
    343.7305'268--dc22

                                                                2006046627

Quanity sales: For information on bulk purchases or corporate premium sales, please
contact the Special Sales Department. For academic sales or textbook adoptions, ask for
Academic Sales. 800-955-4775, Nolo, 950 Parker Street, Berkeley, CA 94710.

Acknowledgments

Many thanks to:

Diana Fitzpatrick and Lisa Guerin for their superb editing

Terri Hearsh for her outstanding book design

Table of Contents

Introduction

How to Use This Book

1 Tax Deduction Basics

2 Beating the Hobby Loss Rule

3 Start-Up Expenses

4 Business Operating Expenses

5 Deducting Long-Term Assets

6 Inventory

7 Office Expenses

8 Car and Local Travel Expenses

9 Business Travel

10 Meal and Entertainment Expenses

11 Hiring Workers

12 Retirement Deductions

13 Medical Expenses

14 Additional Deductions

15 Record Keeping and Accounting

16 Claiming Tax Deductions for Prior Years

17 Staying Out of Trouble With the IRS

18 Help Beyond This Book

Index

How to Use This Book

Few of us ever test our powers of deduction, except when filling out an income tax form.

—Laurence J. Peter

If you are truly serious about preparing your child for the future, don't teach him to subtract—teach him to deduct.

—Fran Lebowitz

Anyone who runs a business knows that you have to spend money to make money. This book will show you how to get some of that money back, in the form of tax deductions.

A tax deduction is money on which you don't have to pay income taxes. The government has decided that business owners don't have to pay tax on income they spend for certain business purposes. So, the trick to paying lower taxes—and keeping more of your hard-earned dollars—is to take advantage of every tax deduction available to you.

That's where this book comes in. It shows you how you can deduct all or most of your business expenses from your federal taxes. This book is not a tax preparation guide—it does not show you how to fill out your tax forms. (By the time you do your taxes, it may be too late to take deductions you could have taken if you had planned the prior year's business spending wisely and kept proper records.) Instead, this book gives you all the information you need to maximize your deductible expenses—and avoid common deduction mistakes. You can (and should) use this book all year long, to make April 15th as painless as possible.

Who Can Use This Book

This book is for anyone who is in business, including:

- self-employed business people
- sole proprietors (who own a one-person business)
- professionals who own their own practice, such as doctors, dentists, and (even) lawyers
- those engaged in a part-time or sideline business
- consultants
- freelancers

- independent contractors
- owner-employees of small corporations
- partners in business partnerships, and
- members of limited liability companies.

This book applies only to those who own their own businesses. If you are an employee of a business you do not own, this book does not cover your situation. This book also does not apply to government employees.

Why You Need to Know About Tax Deductions

The United States has two separate and unequal tax systems. One is for wage earners; the other is for business owners. Wage earners—those who work in other people's businesses or for the government—have their income taxes withheld from their paychecks and can take relatively few tax deductions. Business owners live in a different tax universe. The vast majority of small business owners—about 80%—are sole proprietors who have no taxes withheld from their earnings and can take advantage of a huge array of tax deductions available only to business owners.

> **EXAMPLE:** Joe is an employee in a local coffee bar. An avid moviegoer, he spends about $100 a month seeing all the latest films. None of what he spends on movies is deductible from his taxes. Joe's sister, Janice, is a professional screenwriter. She also spends $100 a month going to movies—in fact, she goes with Joe. But, unlike Joe, Janice can deduct every penny she spends on the movies from her income taxes. Why the difference? Janice is in business—the business of being a self-employed screenwriter—and her moviegoing qualifies as a business deduction.

In order to take advantage of the many benefits tax deductions offer, you'll have to figure out which deductions you are entitled to take and keep proper records documenting your expenses. The IRS will never complain if you don't take all the deductions available to you—and it certainly doesn't make a point of advertising ways to lower your taxes. In fact, the majority of small businesses miss out on many deductions every year simply because they aren't aware of them—or because they neglect to keep the records necessary to back them up.

Even if you work with an accountant or another tax professional, you need to learn about business tax deductions. No tax professional will ever know as much about your business as you do, and you can't expect a hired professional to search high and low for every deduction you might be able to take, especially during the busy tax preparation season. The information in this book will help you provide your tax professional with better records, ask better questions, obtain better advice—and, just as important, evaluate the advice you get from tax professionals, websites, and other sources.

If you do your taxes yourself (as more and more small business owners are doing, especially with the help of tax preparation software), your need for knowledge is even greater. Not even the most sophisticated tax preparation program can decide which tax deductions you should take or tell you whether you've overlooked a valuable deduction.

Icons Used in This Book

 This icon alerts you to a practical tip or good idea.

 This is a caution to slow down and consider potential problems.

 This refers you to other sources of information about a particular topic covered in the text.

 This icon means that you may be able to skip some material that doesn't apply to your situation.

Chapter 1

Tax Deduction Basics

The tax code is full of deductions for businesses—from automobile expenses to wages for employees. Before you can start taking advantage of these deductions, however, you need a basic understanding of how businesses pay taxes and how tax deductions work. This chapter gives you all the information you need to get started. It covers:

- how tax deductions work
- how businesses are taxed
- how to calculate the value of a tax deduction, and
- what businesses can deduct.

How Tax Deductions Work

A tax deduction (also called a tax write-off) is an amount of money you are entitled to subtract from your gross income (all the money you make) to determine your taxable income (the amount on which you must pay tax). The more deductions you have, the lower your taxable income will be and the less tax you will have to pay.

Types of Tax Deductions

There are three basic types of tax deductions: personal deductions, investment deductions, and business deductions. This book covers only business deductions—the large array of write-offs available to business owners.

Personal Deductions

For the most part, your personal, living, and family expenses are not tax deductible. For example, you can't deduct the food that you buy for yourself and your family. There are, however, special categories of personal expenses that may be deducted, subject to strict limitations. These include items such as home mortgage interest, state and local taxes, charitable contributions, medical expenses above a threshold amount, interest on education loans, and alimony. This book does not cover these personal deductions.

Investment Deductions

Many people try to make money by investing money. For example, they might invest in real estate or play the stock market. These people incur all kinds of expenses, such as fees paid to money managers or financial planners, legal and accounting fees, and interest on money borrowed to buy investment property. These and other investment expenses (also called expenses for the production of income) are tax deductible, subject to certain limitations. Investment deductions are not covered in this book.

Business Deductions

People in business usually must spend money on their business—for office space, supplies, and equipment. Most business expenses are deductible, sooner or later, one way or another. And that's what this book is about: the many deductions available only to people who are in business (sole proprietors, independent contractors, and small business owners).

You Only Pay Taxes on Your Business Profits

The federal income tax law recognizes that you must spend money to make money. Virtually every business, however small, incurs some expenses. Even someone with a low overhead business (such as a freelance writer) must buy paper, computer equipment, and office supplies. Some businesses incur substantial expenses, even exceeding their income.

You are not legally required to pay tax on every dollar your business takes in (your "gross business income"). Instead, you owe tax only on the amount left over after your business's deductible expenses are subtracted from your gross income (this remaining amount is called your "net profit"). Although some tax deduction calculations can get a bit complicated, the basic math is simple: The more deductions you take, the lower your net profit will be, and the less tax you will have to pay.

EXAMPLE: Karen, a sole proprietor, earned $50,000 this year from her consulting business. Fortunately, she doesn't have to pay income tax on the entire $50,000—her gross income. Instead, she can deduct from her gross income various business expenses, including a $5,000 home office deduction (see Chapter 7) and a $5,000 deduction for equipment expenses (see Chapter 5). She deducts these expenses from her $50,000 gross income to arrive at her net profit: $40,000. She pays income tax only on this net profit amount.

You Must Have a Legal Basis for Your Deductions

All tax deductions are a matter of legislative grace, which means that you can take a deduction only if it is specifically allowed by one or more provisions of the tax law. You usually do not have to indicate on your tax return which tax law provision gives you the right to take a particular deduction. If you are audited by the IRS, however, you'll have to provide a legal basis for every deduction you take. If the IRS concludes that your deduction wasn't justified, it will deny the deduction and charge you back taxes and, in some cases, penalties.

You Must Be in Business to Claim Business Deductions

Only businesses can claim business tax deductions. This probably seems like a simple concept, but it can get tricky. Even though you might believe you are running a business, the IRS may beg to differ. If your small-scale business doesn't turn a profit for several years in a row, the IRS might decide that you are engaged in a hobby rather than a business. This may not sound like a big deal, but it could have disastrous tax consequences: People engaged in hobbies are entitled to very limited tax deductions, while businesses can deduct all kinds of expenses. Fortunately, this unhappy outcome can be avoided by careful taxpayers. (See Chapter 2 for a detailed discussion on how to beat the hobby loss rule.)

How Businesses Are Taxed

If your business earns money (as you undoubtedly hope it will), you will have to pay taxes on those profits. How you pay those taxes will depend on how you have structured your business. So, before getting further into the details of tax deductions, it's important to understand what type of business you have formed (a sole proprietorship, partnership, limited liability company, or corporation) and how you will pay tax on your business's profit.

This section briefly summarizes some fairly complex areas of law. Although it covers the basic tax consequences of each business form, it does not explain how to choose the best structure for your business. If you need to decide how to organize a new business or want to know whether you should change your current business form, you can refer to *LLC or Corporation? How to Choose the Right Form for Your Business,* by Anthony Mancuso (Nolo), or *Choose the Best Legal Structure for Your One-Person Business,* by Stephen Fishman (available on Nolo's website at www. nolo.com, under eProducts).

Basic Business Forms

Every business, from a part-time operation you run from home while in your jammies to a Fortune 500 multinational company housed in a gleaming skyscraper, has a legal structure. If you're running a business right now, it has a legal form even if you made no conscious decision about how it should be legally organized.

The four basic legal structures for a business are sole proprietorship, partnership, limited liability corporation, and corporation. For tax purposes, corporations are either S corporations (corporations that have elected pass-through tax treatment) or C corporations (also called regular corporations). Every business falls into one of these categories—and your category will determine how your business's profits will be taxed.

Sole Proprietorship

A sole proprietorship is a one-owner business. You can't be a sole proprietor if two or more people own the business (unless you own the business with your spouse). Unlike the other business forms, a sole proprietorship has no legal existence separate from the business owner. It cannot sue or be sued, own property in its own name, or file its own tax returns. The business owner (proprietor) personally owns all of the assets of the business and controls its operation. If you're running a one-person business and you haven't incorporated or formed a limited liability company, you are a sole proprietor.

Partnership

A partnership is a form of shared ownership and management of a business. The partners contribute money, property, or services to the partnership; in return, they receive a share of the profits it earns, if any. The partners jointly manage the partnership business. A partnership automatically comes into existence whenever two or more people enter into business together to earn a profit and don't incorporate or form a limited liability company. Although many partners enter into written partnership agreements, no written agreement is required to form a partnership.

Corporation

Unlike a sole proprietorship or partnership, a corporation cannot simply spring into existence—it can only be created by filing incorporation documents with your state government. A corporation is a legal entity distinct from its owners. It can hold title to property, sue and be sued, have bank accounts, borrow money, hire employees, and perform other business functions.

For tax purposes, there are two types of corporations: S corporations (also called small business corporations) and C corporations (also called regular corporations). The most important difference between the two types of corporations is how they are taxed. An S corporation pays no taxes itself—instead, its income or loss is passed on to its owners, who must pay personal income taxes on their share of the corporation's profits. A C corporation is a separate taxpaying entity that pays taxes on its profits. (See "Tax Treatment," below.)

Limited Liability Company

The limited liability company, or LLC, is the newest type of business form in the United States. An LLC is like a sole proprietorship or partnership in that its owners (called members) jointly own and manage the business and share in the profits. However, an LLC is also like a corporation, because its owners must file papers with the state to create the LLC, it exists as a separate legal entity, and the LLC structure gives owners some protection from liability for business debts.

Tax Treatment

Your business's legal form will determine how it is treated for tax purposes. There are two different ways that business entities can be taxed: The business itself can be taxed as a separate entity, or the business's profits and losses can be "passed through" to the owners, who include the profits or losses on their individual tax returns.

Pass-Through Entities: Sole Proprietorships, Partnerships, LLCs, and S Corporations

Sole proprietorships and S corporations are always pass-through entities. LLCs and partnerships are almost always pass-through entities as well— partnerships and multiowner LLCs are automatically taxed as partnerships when they are created. One-owner LLCs are automatically taxed like sole proprietorships. However, LLC and partnership owners have the option of choosing to have their entity taxed as a C corporation or S corporation by filing an election with the IRS. This is rarely done.

A pass-through entity does not pay any taxes itself. Instead, the business's profits or losses are passed through to its owners, who include them on their own personal tax returns (IRS Form 1040). If a profit is passed through to the owner, that money is added to any other income the owner has and the owner pays taxes on the total amount. If a loss is passed through, the owner can generally use it to offset income from other sources—for example, salary from a job, interest, investment income, or a spouse's income (as long as the couple files a joint tax return). The owner can subtract the business loss from this other income, which leaves a lower total subject to tax.

> **EXAMPLE:** Lisa is a sole proprietor who works part time as a personal trainer. During her first year in business, she incurs $10,000 in expenses and earns $5,000, giving her a $5,000 loss from her business. She reports this loss on IRS Schedule C, which she files with her personal income tax return (Form 1040). Because Lisa is a sole proprietor, she can deduct this $5,000 loss from any income she has, including her $100,000 annual salary from her engineering job. This saves her about $2,000 in total taxes for the year.

Although pass-through entities don't pay taxes, their income and expenses must still be reported to the IRS as follows:

- **Sole proprietors** must file IRS Schedule C, *Profit or Loss From Business*, with their tax returns. This form lists all the proprietor's business income and deductible expenses.
- **Partnerships** are required to file an annual tax form (Form 1065, *U.S. Return Partnership of Income*) with the IRS. Form 1065 is

not used to pay taxes. Instead, it is an "information return" that informs the IRS of the partnership's income, deductions, profits, losses, and tax credits for the year. Form 1065 also includes a separate part called Schedule K-1 in which the partnership lists each partner's share of the items listed on Form 1065. A separate Schedule K-1 must be provided to each partner. The partners report on their individual tax returns (Form 1040) their share of the partnership's net profit or loss as shown on Schedule K-1. Ordinary business income or loss is reported on Schedule E, *Supplemental Income or Loss*. However, certain items must be reported on other Schedules—for example, capital gains and losses must be reported on Schedule D and charitable contributions on Schedule A.

- **S corporations** report their income and deductions much like a partnership. An S corporation files an information return (Form 1120S) reporting the corporation's income, deductions, profits, losses, and tax credits for the year. Like partners, shareholders must be provided a Schedule K-1 listing their share of the items listed in the corporation's Form 1120S. The shareholders file Schedule E with their personal tax returns (Form 1040) showing their share of corporation income or losses.

- **LLCs** with only one member are treated like a sole proprietorship for tax purposes. The member reports profits, losses, and deductions on Schedule C—just like a sole proprietor. An LLC with two or more members is treated like a partnership for tax purposes unless the members elect to be taxed like a C corporation (which is rare).

Regular C Corporations

A regular C corporation is the only business form that is not a pass-through entity. Instead, a C corporation is taxed separately from its owners. C corporations must pay income taxes on their net income and file their own tax returns with the IRS, using Form 1120 or Form 1120-A. They also have their own income tax rates (which are lower than individual rates at some income levels).

When you form a C corporation, you have to take charge of two separate taxpayers: your corporation and yourself. Your C corporation must pay tax on all of its income. You pay personal income tax on C corporation income only when it is distributed to you in the form of salary, bonuses, or dividends.

C corporations can take all the same business tax deductions that pass-through entities take. In addition, because a C corporation is a separate tax-paying entity, it may provide its employees with tax-free fringe benefits, then deduct the entire cost of the benefits from the corporation's income as a business expense. No other form of business entity can do this. (Although they are corporations, S corporations cannot deduct the cost of benefits provided to shareholders who hold more than 2% of the corporate stock.)

C corporations may provide their employees (including owners who work in the business) with fringe benefits such as:

- disability insurance
- reimbursement of medical expenses not covered by insurance
- up to $205 per month in parking reimbursements
- the cost of annual medical check-ups
- de minimis fringe benefits (such as small Christmas gifts or occasional meals)
- child and dependent care payments up to $5,000 per year per employee
- $50,000 of group term life insurance
- the cost of a group legal services plan for employees
- up to $5,250 in tuition reimbursements for employee educational expenses, whether or not job-related, and
- death benefit payments of up to $5,000.

Employees do not have to include the cost of premiums or other payments the corporation makes for these benefits in their personal income for income tax purposes. (See Chapter 11 for a detailed discussion.)

The Value of a Tax Deduction

Most taxpayers, even sophisticated businesspeople, don't fully appreciate just how much money they can save with tax deductions. Only part of any deduction will end up back in your pocket as money saved. Because a deduction represents income on which you don't have to pay tax, the value of any deduction is the amount of tax you would have had to pay on that income had you not deducted it. So a deduction of $1,000 won't save you $1,000—it will save you whatever you would otherwise have had to pay as tax on that $1,000 of income.

Federal and State Income Taxes

To determine how much income tax a deduction will save you, you must first figure out your income tax bracket. The United States has a progressive income tax system for individual taxpayers with six different tax rates (called tax brackets), ranging from 10% of taxable income to 35%. (See the chart below.) The higher your income, the higher your tax rate.

You move from one bracket to the next only when your taxable income exceeds the bracket amount. For example, if you are a single taxpayer, you pay 10% income tax on all your taxable income up to $7,550. If your taxable income exceeds $7,550, the next tax rate (15%) applies to all your income over $7,550—but the 10% rate still applies to the first $7,550. If your income exceeds the 15% bracket amount, the next tax rate (25%) applies to the excess amount, and so on until the top bracket of 35% is reached.

The tax bracket in which the last dollar you earn for the year falls is called your "marginal tax bracket." For example, if you have $60,000 in taxable income, your marginal tax bracket is 25%. To determine how much federal income tax a deduction will save you, multiply the amount of the deduction by your marginal tax bracket. For example, if your marginal tax bracket is 25%, you will save 25¢ in federal income taxes for every dollar you are able to claim as a deductible business expense (25% x $1 = 25¢). This calculation is only approximate because an additional deduction may move you from one tax bracket to another and thus lower your marginal tax rate. For example, if you're single and your taxable income is $75,000, an additional $1,000 deduction will lower your marginal tax rate from 28% to 25%. The first $800 of the deduction will save you $224 in tax (28% x $800 = $224); the remaining $200 will save you $50 (25% x $200 = $50). So your total tax saving is $274, instead of the $280 you would get if, say, your taxable income was $76,000.

The following table lists the 2006 federal income tax brackets for single and married individual taxpayers and shows the tax savings for each dollar of deductions.

2006 Federal Personal Income Tax Brackets		
Tax Bracket	**Income If Single**	**Income If Married Filing Jointly**
10%	Up to $7,550	Up to $15,100
15%	From $7,551 to $30,650	$15,101 to $61,300
25%	$30,651 to $74,200	$61,301 to $123,700
28%	$74,201 to $154,800	$123,701 to $188,450
33%	$154,801 to $336,550	$188,451 to $336,550
35%	All over $336,550	All over $336,550

Income tax brackets are adjusted each year for inflation. For current brackets, see IRS Publication 505, *Tax Withholding and Estimated Tax*.

You can also deduct your business expenses from any state income tax you must pay. The average state income tax rate is about 6%, although seven states (Alaska, Florida, Nevada, South Dakota, Texas, Washington, and Wyoming) don't have an income tax. You can find a list of all state income tax rates at www.taxadmin.org/FTA/rate/ind_inc.html.

Self-Employment Taxes

Everyone who works—whether a business owner or an employee—is required to pay Social Security and Medicare taxes. Employees pay one-half of these taxes through payroll deductions; the employer must pony up the other half and send the entire payment to the IRS. Business owners must pay all of these taxes themselves. Business owners' Social Security and Medicare contributions are called self-employment taxes.

Self-employment taxes consist of a 12.4% Social Security tax on self-employment income up to an annual limit; in 2006, the limit was $94,200. Medicare taxes are levied on all self-employment income at a 2.9% rate. This combines to a total 15.3% tax on self-employment income up to the Social Security tax ceiling. However, the effective self-employment tax rate is lower (between 13%–14% for most taxpayers), because you are allowed to deduct half of your self-employment taxes from your net income for income tax purposes.

Like income taxes, self-employment taxes are paid on the net profit you earn from a business. Thus, deductible business expenses reduce the amount of self-employment tax you have to pay by lowering your net profit.

Total Tax Savings

When you add up your savings in federal, state, and self-employment taxes, you can see the true value of a business tax deduction. For example, if you're in the 25% federal income tax bracket, a business deduction can be worth as much as 25% (in federal taxes) + 13% (in self-employment taxes) + 6% (in state taxes). That adds up to a whopping 44% savings. (If you itemize your personal deductions, your actual tax savings from a business deduction is a bit less because it reduces your state income tax and therefore reduces the federal income tax savings from this itemized deduction.) If you buy a $1,000 computer for your business and you deduct the expense, you save about $430 in taxes. In effect, the government is paying for almost half of your business expenses. This is why it's so important to know all the business deductions you are entitled to take—and to take advantage of every one.

Don't buy stuff just to get a tax deduction. Although tax deductions can be worth a lot, it doesn't make sense to buy something you don't need just to get a deduction. After all, you still have to pay for the item, and the tax deduction you get in return will only cover a portion of the cost. If you buy a $1,000 computer, you'll probably be able to deduct less than half of the cost. That means you're still out over $500—money you've spent for something you don't need. On the other hand, if you really do need a computer, the deduction you're entitled to is like found money—and it may help you buy a better computer than you could otherwise afford.

What Businesses Can Deduct

Business owners can deduct four broad categories of business expenses:

- start-up expenses
- operating expenses

- capital expenses, and
- inventory costs.

This section provides an introduction to each of these categories (they are covered in greater detail in later chapters).

⚠️ **You must keep track of your expenses.** You can deduct only those expenses that you actually incur. You need to keep records of these expenses to (1) know for sure how much you actually spent, and (2) prove to the IRS that you really spent the money you deducted on your tax return, in case you are audited. Accounting and bookkeeping are discussed in detail in Chapter 15.

Start-Up Expenses

The first money you will have to shell out will be for your business's start-up expenses. These include most of the costs of getting your business up and running, like license fees, advertising costs, attorney and accounting fees, travel expenses, market research, and office supplies expenses. You may deduct up to $5,000 in start-up costs the first year a new business is in operation. You may deduct amounts over $5,000 over the next 15 years.

> **EXAMPLE:** Cary, a star hairdresser at a popular salon, decides to open his own hairdressing business. Before Cary's new salon opens for business, he has to rent space, hire and train employees, and pay for an expensive preopening advertising campaign. These start-up expenses cost Cary $20,000. Cary may deduct $5,000 of his $20,000 in operating expenses the first year he's in business. He may deduct the remaining $15,000 in equal amounts over the next 15 years.

Operating Expenses

Operating expenses are the ongoing day-to-day costs a business incurs to stay in business. They include such things as rent, utilities, salaries, supplies, travel expenses, car expenses, and repairs and maintenance. These expenses (unlike start-up expenses) are currently deductible—that

is, you can deduct them all in the same year when you pay them. (See
Chapter 4 for more on deducting operating expenses.)

> **EXAMPLE:** After Cary's salon opens, he begins paying $5,000 a
> month for rent and utilities. This is an operating expense that is
> currently deductible. When Cary does his taxes, he can deduct from
> his income the entire $60,000 that he paid for rent and utilities for
> the year.

Capital Expenses

Capital assets are things you buy for your business that have a useful
life of more than one year, such as land, buildings, equipment, vehicles,
books, furniture, machinery, and patents you buy from others. These
costs, called capital expenses, are considered to be part of your investment in your business, not day-to-day operating expenses.

Large businesses—those that buy at least several hundred thousand
dollars of capital assets in a year—must deduct these costs by using
depreciation. To depreciate an item, you deduct a portion of the cost in
each year of the item's useful life. Depending on the asset, this could be
anywhere from three to 39 years (the IRS decides the asset's useful life).

Small businesses can also use depreciation, but they have another
option available for deducting many capital expenses: They can currently
deduct up to $108,000 in capital expenses per year under a provision
of the tax code called Section 179. Section 179 is discussed in detail in
Chapter 5.

> **EXAMPLE:** Cary spent $5,000 on fancy barber chairs for his salon.
> Because the chairs have a useful life of more than one year, they
> are capital assets that he will either have to depreciate over several
> years or deduct in one year under Section 179.

Certain capital assets, such as land and corporate stock, never wear
out. Capital expenses related to these costs are not deductible; the
owner must wait until the asset is sold to recover the cost. (See Chapter
5 for more on this topic.)

Inventory

Inventory includes almost anything you make or buy to resell to customers. It doesn't matter whether you manufacture the goods yourself or buy finished goods from someone else and resell the items to customers. Inventory doesn't include tools, equipment, or other items that you use in your business; it refers only to items that you buy or make to sell.

You must deduct inventory costs separately from all other business expenses—you deduct inventory costs as you sell the inventory. Inventory that remains unsold at the end of the year is a business asset, not a deductible expense. (See Chapter 6 for more on deducting inventory.)

> **EXAMPLE:** In addition to providing hair styling services, Cary sells various hair care products in his salon that he buys from cosmetics companies. In 2007, Cary spent $15,000 on his inventory of hair care product but sold only $10,000 worth of the product. He can only deduct $10,000 of the inventory costs in 2007.

Frequently Asked Questions About Tax Deductions

- **Do I have to pay cash for an item to get a deduction?** No. You may deduct the entire amount you pay for a deductible expense whether you pay by cash, check, credit card, or loan. (See Chapter 4.)
- **Do I need a receipt to take a business expense deduction?** Yes and no. You can claim whatever deductions you want, regardless of whether you have proof of the expense. If you are audited, however, you must be able to prove that you are entitled to the deduction. If you don't have receipts, you may be able to use other records to prove you shelled out those costs. (See Chapter 15.)

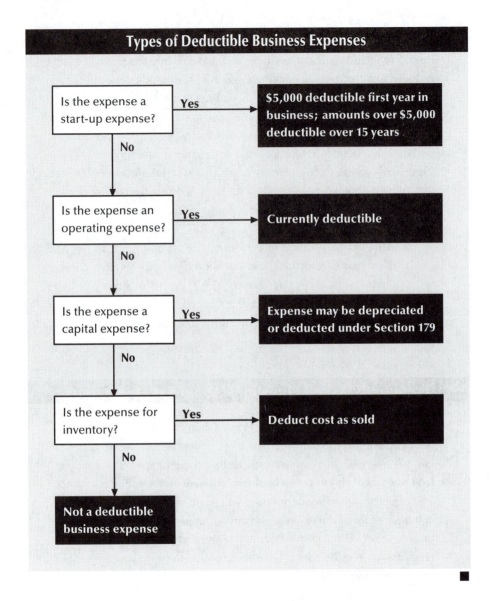

Types of Deductible Business Expenses

Is the expense a start-up expense? → **Yes** → **$5,000 deductible first year in business; amounts over $5,000 deductible over 15 years**

No ↓

Is the expense an operating expense? → **Yes** → **Currently deductible**

No ↓

Is the expense a capital expense? → **Yes** → **Expense may be depreciated or deducted under Section 179**

No ↓

Is the expense for inventory? → **Yes** → **Deduct cost as sold**

No ↓

Not a deductible business expense

Chapter 2

Beating the Hobby Loss Rule

O ne of the most powerful weapons in the IRS arsenal is the hobby loss rule. Under this rule, only taxpayers who operate a bona fide business can take business deductions. To the IRS, a business is a venture operated to make money and run in a professional, businesslike manner. In contrast, the IRS may classify a venture that consistently loses money and/or looks more like a personal pursuit than a business as a "hobby." If the IRS decides that you are indulging a hobby rather than operating a business, you will face some potentially disastrous tax consequences.

> **EXAMPLE:** Jorge and Vivian Lopez thought they found an ideal way to save on their income taxes (and enjoy themselves as well)—they started an Amway distributorship as a sideline business. While they had a lot of fun socializing with family and friends, they never came close to earning a profit. They claimed a loss from this business of over $18,000 a year for two straight years. They deducted this loss from Jorge's salary as a full-time petroleum engineer, which saved them thousands of dollars in income taxes. Things were going great, tax-wise, until the IRS audited the Lopezes' tax returns and concluded that the Amway distributorship was a hobby rather than a business. This meant the Lopezes could no longer deduct their Amway losses from Jorge's salary, and they owed the IRS over $17,000 in back taxes for the deductions they had already taken. (*Lopez v. Commissioner,* TC Memo 2003-142.)

The IRS created the hobby loss rule to prevent taxpayers from entering into losing propositions primarily to incur expenses that they could deduct from their other income. Before the hobby loss rule was enacted in its current form, wealthy people used to do this all the time. For example, they would buy farms, ranches, or other "businesses" they could operate at a loss just to incur expenses to deduct from their other income. The hobby loss rule prevents this form of tax avoidance by allowing taxpayers to take a business expense deduction only if their venture qualifies as a business in the eyes of the IRS.

What Is a Business?

For tax purposes, a business is any activity in which you regularly engage primarily to earn a profit. You don't have to show a profit every year to qualify as a business. As long as your primary purpose is to make money, you should qualify as a business (even if you show a loss some years). Your business can be full time or part time, as long as you work at it regularly and continuously. And you can have more than one business at the same time. However, if your primary purpose is something other than making a profit—for example, to incur deductible expenses or just to have fun—the IRS may find that your activity is a hobby rather than a business.

Crime Doesn't Pay, But It May Be Deductible

Back in the 1970s, Jeffrey Edmondson was a successful drug dealer in the Minneapolis area, selling substantial amounts of marijuana, cocaine, and amphetamines. Unfortunately for him, he got caught, convicted, and sentenced to jail. To add insult to injury, the IRS audited him and concluded that he owed over $17,000 in back taxes on his drug earnings, which he had never declared on his income taxes. Although one would think that a tax assessment would be the least of his problems, Edmondson appealed the audit, claiming that the IRS failed to consider the tax-deductible costs he incurred in conducting his "business." The tax court held that Edmondson was self-employed in the business of selling amphetamines, cocaine, and marijuana. Therefore, he was entitled to deduct the cost of goods sold from his drug-dealing income—and could take a home office deduction as well. (*Edmondson v. Commissioner*, TC Memo 1981-623.)

The tax law was amended in 1982 to bar tax deductions for expenses incurred by drug dealers. (IRC § 280E.) Deductions are still permitted for other illegal businesses, such as prostitution and contract killing. However, people involved in such illegal endeavors rarely file tax returns.

The IRS has established two tests to determine whether someone is in business. One is a simple mechanical test that looks at whether you have earned a profit in three of the last five years. The other is a more complex test designed to determine whether you act like a business.

Profit Test

If your venture earns a profit in three of any consecutive five years, the IRS must presume that you have a profit motive. The IRS can still claim that your activity is a hobby, but it will have to prove you lack a profit motive some other way. In practice, the IRS usually doesn't attack ventures that pass the profit test unless the numbers have clearly been manipulated just to meet the standard.

To show a profit, your gross income from an activity must be more than the tax deductions you took for it. Any profit—no matter how small—qualifies; you don't have to earn a particular amount or percentage. Careful year-end planning can help your business show a profit for the year. If clients owe you money, for example, you can press for payment before the end of the year. You can also put off paying expenses or buying new equipment until the new year.

The presumption that you are in business applies to your third profitable year. It then extends to all subsequent years within that five-year period beginning with your first profitable year.

> **EXAMPLE:** Tom began to work as a self-employed graphic designer in 2001. Due to economic conditions and the difficulty of establishing a new business, his income varied dramatically from year to year. However, as the chart below shows, he managed to earn a profit in three of the first five years that he was in business.

Year	Losses	Profits
2002	$10,000	
2003		$5,500
2004	$6,000	
2005		$9,000
2006		$18,000

If the IRS audits Tom's taxes for 2007, it must presume that he was in business during that year because he earned a profit during three of the five consecutive years ending with 2007. The presumption that Tom is in business extends to 2008, five years after his first profitable year (2003).

Special Rule for Horse Breeders

If you breed, train, show, or race horses, you only need to show a profit in two out of any seven consecutive years for the activity to be presumed a business. Why the special rule for horse breeders? Because it usually takes a long time to make money from horse breeding (and because breeders have an effective lobby in Washington, DC).

The IRS doesn't have to wait for five years after you start your activity to decide whether it is a business or hobby—it can audit you and classify your venture as a business or hobby at any time. However, you can give yourself some breathing room by filing IRS Form 5213, which requires the IRS to postpone its determination until you've been in business for at least five years.

Although this may sound like a good idea, filing the election only alerts the IRS to the fact that you might be a good candidate to audit on the hobby loss issue after five years. It also adds two years to the statute of limitations—the period in which the IRS can audit you and assess a tax deficiency. For this reason, almost no one ever files Form 5213. Also, you can't wait five years and then file the election once you know that you will pass the profit test. You must make the election within three years after the due date for the tax return for the first year you were in business—that is, within three years after the first April 15th following your first business year. So if you started doing business in 2005, you would have to make the election by April 15, 2009 (three years after the April 15, 2006 due date for your 2005 tax return).

There is one situation in which it might make sense to file Form 5213. If the IRS has already told you that you will be audited, you may want to file the election to postpone the audit for two years. However, you can do this only if the IRS audit notice is sent to you within three years after the due date for your first business tax return. If you're notified after this time, it's too late to file the election. In addition, you must file your election within 60 days after you receive an IRS audit notice, whenever it is given, or you'll lose the right to make the election.

Behavior Test

If you keep incurring losses and can't satisfy the profit test, don't panic. Millions of business owners are in the same boat. The sad fact is that many businesses don't earn profits every year or even for many years in a row. Indeed, over four million sole proprietors file a Schedule C tax form each year showing a loss from their business, yet the IRS does not categorize all of these ventures as hobbies.

You can continue to treat your activity as a business and fully deduct your losses, even if you have yet to earn a profit. However, you should take steps to demonstrate that your business isn't a hobby, in case you ever face an audit. You want to be able to convince the IRS that earning a profit—not having fun or accumulating tax deductions—is your primary motive for doing what you do. This will be particularly difficult if you're engaged in an activity that could objectively be considered fun—such as creating artwork, photography, or writing—but it can be done. People who have incurred losses for seven, eight, or nine years in a row have been able to convince the IRS that they were running businesses.

How does the IRS figure out whether you really want to earn a profit? IRS auditors can't read your mind to establish your motives, and they certainly aren't going to take your word for it. Instead, they look at whether you behave as though you want to make money.

Factors the IRS Considers

The IRS looks at the following "objective" factors to determine whether you are behaving like a person who wants to earn a profit (and, therefore, should be classified as a business). You don't have to satisfy all of these factors to pass the test—the first three listed below (acting like a business, expertise, and time and effort expended) are the most important by far. Studies demonstrate that taxpayers who meet these three factors are always found to be in business, regardless of how they do on the rest of the criteria. (See "How to Pass the Behavior Test," below, for tips on satisfying these factors.)

- **Whether you act like a business.** Among other things, acting like a business means you keep good books and other records and carry on your activities in a professional manner.
- **Your expertise.** People who are in business to make money usually have some knowledge and skill relevant to the business.

- **The time and effort you spend.** Businesspeople work regularly and continuously at their businesses. You don't have to work full time, but you must work regularly.
- **Your track record.** Having a track record of success in other businesses—whether or not they are related to your current business—helps show that you are trying to make money in your most recent venture.
- **Your history of profit and losses.** Even if you can't satisfy the profit test described above, earning a profit in at least some years helps show that you're in business. This is especially true if you're engaged in a business that tends to be cyclical—that is, where one or two good years are typically followed by one or more bad years.
- **Your profits.** Earning a substantial profit, even after years of losses, can help show that you are trying to make a go of it. On the other hand, earning only small or occasional yearly profits when you have years of large losses and/or a large investment in the activity tends to show that you aren't in it for the money.
- **Your business assets.** Your profit includes money you make through the appreciation (increase in value) of your business assets. Even if you don't make any profit from your business's day-to-day operations, you can still show a profit motive if you stand to earn substantial profits when you sell your assets. Of course, this rule applies only to businesses that purchase assets that increase in value over time, such as land or buildings
- **Your personal wealth.** The IRS figures that you probably have a profit motive—and are running a real business—if you don't have a substantial income from other sources. After all, you'll need to earn money from your venture to survive. On the other hand, the IRS may be suspicious if you have substantial income from other sources (particularly if the losses from your venture generate substantial tax deductions).
- **The nature of your activity.** If your venture is inherently fun or recreational, the IRS may doubt that you are in it for the money. This means that you'll have a harder time convincing the IRS that you're in business if your venture involves activities such as artwork, photography, or writing; antique or stamp collecting;

or training and showing dogs or horses (for example). However, these activities can still be businesses, if they are carried on in a businesslike manner.

Passive Investing Is Not a Business

Even though you do it to earn a profit, personal investing is not a business for tax purposes. This includes investing in the stock market or real estate, or any other activity in which you are merely a passive investor. You must be engaged in the active, continuous, and regular management or control of a business to qualify as a business owner. The IRS calls passive investing an "income-producing activity." See "Income Producing Activities," below, for a detailed discussion of this topic.

How to Pass the Behavior Test

Almost anyone can pass the behavior test, but it takes time, effort, and careful planning. Focus your efforts on the first three factors listed above. As noted earlier, a venture that can meet these three criteria will always be classified as a business. Here are some tips that will help you satisfy these crucial factors—and ultimately ace the behavior test.

Act Like a Businessperson

First and foremost, you must show that you carry on your activity in a businesslike manner. Doing the things outlined below will not only help you with the IRS, it will also help you actually earn a profit someday (or at least help you figure out that your business will not be profitable).

- **Keep good business records.** Keeping good records of your expenses and income from your activity is the single most important thing you can do to show that you're in business. Without good records, you'll never have an accurate idea of where you stand financially. Lack of records shows that you don't really care whether you make money or not—and it is almost always fatal in an IRS audit. You don't necessarily need an elaborate set of books; a simple record of your expenses and income will usually suffice. (See Chapter 15 for a detailed discussion of record keeping.)

> **EXAMPLE:** A computer consultant who sold software on the side (at a loss) was found not to be in business because he didn't keep adequate records. The tax court found that his failure to keep records meant that he was "unaware of the amount of revenue he could expect and had no concept of what his ultimate costs might be or how he might achieve any degree of cost efficiency." (*Flanagin v. Commissioner*, TC Memo 1999-116.)

- **Keep a separate checking account.** Open up a separate checking account for your business. This will help you keep your personal and business expenses separate—another factor that shows you're running a business.
- **Create a business plan.** Draw up a business plan with a realistic profit and loss forecast: a projection of how much money your business will bring in, your expenses, and how much profit you expect to make. The forecast should cover the next five or ten years. It should show you earning a profit some time in the future (although it doesn't have to be within five years). Both the IRS and courts are usually impressed by good business plans. In one case, for example, a court found that a sailboat chartering operation that incurred losses for three straight years was a business because the owner made a detailed, realistic profit and loss forecast showing that the charter service would be profitable in 12 to 15 years. (*Pryor v. Commissioner*, TC Memo 1991-109.)

Need help drawing up a business plan? If you are really serious about making money, you will need a business plan. A business plan is useful not only to show the IRS that you are running a business, but also to convince others—such as lenders and investors—that they should support your venture financially. For detailed guidance on putting together a business plan, see *How to Write a Business Plan*, by Mike McKeever (Nolo).

- **Get business cards and letterhead.** It may seem like a minor matter, but obtaining business stationery and business cards shows that you think you are in business. Hobbyists ordinarily don't have such things. You can use software programs to create your own inexpensive stationery and cards.
- **Obtain all necessary business licenses and permits.** Getting the required licenses and permits for your activities will show that you are acting like a business. For example, an inventor attempting to create a wind-powered ethanol generator was found to be a hobbyist partly because he failed to get a permit to produce alcohol from the Bureau of Alcohol, Tobacco, Firearms, and Explosives.
- **Obtain a separate phone line for your home office.** If you work at home, obtain a separate phone line for your business. This helps separate the personal from the professional and reinforces the idea that you're in business.
- **Join professional organizations and associations.** Taking part in professional groups and organizations will help you make valuable contacts and obtain useful advice and expertise. This helps to show that you're serious about making money.

Expertise

If you're already an expert in your field, you're a step ahead of the game. But if you lack the necessary expertise, you can develop it by attending educational seminars and similar activities and/or consulting with other experts. Keep records of your efforts (for example, a certificate for completing a training course or your notes documenting your attendance at a seminar or convention).

Work Steadily

You don't have to work full time to show that you're in business. It's fine to hold a full-time job and work at your sideline business only part of the time. However, you must work regularly and continuously rather than sporadically. You may establish any schedule you want, as long as you work regularly. For example, you could work at your business an hour every day, or one day a week, as long as you stick to your schedule.

Although there is no minimum amount of time you must work, you'll have a hard time convincing the IRS that you're in business if you work less than five or ten hours a week. Keep a log showing how much time you spend working. Your log doesn't have to be fancy—you can just mark down your hours and a summary of your activities each day on your calendar or appointment book.

Losing Golfer Scores Hole-in-One in Tax Court

Donald, a Chicago high school gym teacher, decided to become a golf pro when he turned 40. He became a member of the Professional Golfers of America, which entitled him to compete in certain professional tournaments. Donald kept his teaching job but played in various professional tournaments during the summer. His expenses exceeded his income from golfing for five straight years.

Year	Golf Earnings	Golf Expenses	Losses
1978	$ 0	$ 2,538	$ 2,538
1979	148	1,332	1,184
1980	400	4,672	4,272
1981	904	4,167	3,263
1982	1,458	8,061	6,603

The IRS sought to disallow the losses for 1981 and 1982, claiming that golf was a hobby for Donald. Donald appealed to the tax court and won.

The court held that Donald played golf to make a profit, not just to have fun. He carefully detailed the expenses he incurred for each tournament he entered and recorded the prize money available. He attended a business course for golfers and assisted a professional golfer from whom he also took lessons. He practiced every day, up to 12 hours during the summer; he also traveled frequently to Florida during the winter to play. Although his costs increased over the years, his winnings also increased steadily each year. The court concluded that, although Donald obviously enjoyed golfing, he honestly wanted to earn a profit from it as well. (*Kimbrough v. Commissioner*, 55 TC Memo 1988-730.)

⚠️ **You won't find out whether you have a hobby or a business until you get audited.** You may mistakenly presume that you are in business, only to learn five or six years later that the IRS has a different opinion. If that happens, you could owe the IRS for all of the improper deductions you took during those years, as well as miscalculated taxes and penalties. Obviously, these costs can be quite expensive. Be sure to keep good records to bolster your position that you are running a business.

Tax Consequences of Being a Hobbyist

You do not want what you consider business activities to be deemed a hobby by the IRS. Because hobbies are not businesses, hobbyists cannot take the tax deductions to which businesspeople are entitled. Instead, hobbyists can deduct their hobby-related expenses only from the income the hobby generates. If you have no income from the hobby, you get no deduction. And you can't carry over the deductions to use in future years when you earn income—you lose them forever.

> **EXAMPLE:** Charles collects antiques. This year, he spent $10,000 buying antiques and earned no income from the activity. The IRS determines that this activity is a hobby. As a result, his $10,000 in expenses can be deducted only from any income he earned from his hobby. Because he earned no money from antique collecting during the year, he can't deduct any of these expenses this year— and he can't carry over the deduction to any future years.

Even if you have income from your hobby, you must deduct your expenses in a way that is less advantageous (and more complicated) than regular business deductions. Hobby expenses are deductible only as a Miscellaneous Itemized Deduction on IRS Schedule A (the form that you file with your Form 1040 to claim itemized deductions). This means that you can deduct your hobby expenses only if you itemize your deductions instead of taking the standard deduction. You can itemize deductions only if your total deductions are greater than the standard deduction—in 2006, the standard deduction was $5,150 for single people and $10,300 for married people filing jointly. If you do itemize, your hobby expenses can be used to offset your hobby income—but only to the extent that your expenses plus your other miscellaneous itemized deductions exceed 2% of your adjusted gross income (your total income minus business expenses and a few other expenses).

> **EXAMPLE:** Assume that Charles, a single taxpayer, earned $5,000 from his antique collecting hobby this year and had $10,000 in expenses. He could deduct $5,000 of these expenses as an itemized deduction—the amount equal to his antique collecting income. However, Charles can only deduct those expenses that, together with his other miscellaneous itemized deductions, exceed 2% of Charles's adjusted gross income (AGI) for the year. If Charles's AGI was $100,000 and he had no other miscellaneous itemized deductions, he could not deduct the first $2,000 in expenses (2% x $100,000 = $2,000). So Charles can deduct only $3,000 of his antique collecting expenses on his Schedule A.

You don't need to understand all this in great detail. Just be aware that an IRS finding that your activities are a hobby will probably result in tax disaster.

Income-Producing Activities

You can earn money without being in business. Many people do this (or try to) by engaging in personal investing—for example, by earning interest on personal bank accounts or investing in stocks that pay dividends and appreciate in value over time. Activities like these—that are pursued primarily for profit but aren't businesses—are called income-producing activities. They are neither businesses nor hobbies, and they receive their own special income tax treatment. The distinction between a business and an income-producing activity is crucial because income-producing activities generally receive less favorable tax treatment than businesses. Thus, you'll want to avoid this classification whenever possible.

Tax Consequences of Income-Producing Activities

You are entitled to deduct the ordinary and necessary expenses you incur to produce income, or to manage property held for the production of income—for example, real estate rentals. (IRC § 212.) This includes many of the same expenses that businesspeople are allowed (many are covered in later chapters). For example, a person with a real estate rental may deduct maintenance and repair costs; an investor in the stock market may deduct fees for investment advice or accounting services.

However, there are some crucial limitations on deductions for income-producing activities which do not apply to businesses, including:

- **No home office deduction.** You can't take a home office deduction for an income-producing activity. This important deduction is available only for businesses conducted from home. You can, however, still depreciate the cost of equipment and furniture that qualify as ordinary and necessary expenses for your activity.

- **No Section 179 expensing.** Taxpayers engaged in income-producing activities can't take advantage of Section 179 of the tax code. (Section 179 allows businesspeople to deduct up to $105,000 in purchases of long-term personal property in a single year—see Chapter 5.)

- **No seminar or convention deductions.** People with income-producing activities can't deduct their expenses for attending conventions, seminars, or similar events. Thus, for example, you can't deduct the cost of attending a stock market investment seminar.

- **Limit on deducting investment interest.** Interest paid on money borrowed to make an investment is deductible only up to the amount of income you earn from the investment. If you earn no income from the investment, you get no deduction. In contrast, interest on money you borrow to use for a business is fully deductible. (See "Interest on Business Loans" in Chapter 14.)

- **No deduction for start-up expenses.** You get no deduction at all for expenses incurred to start up an income-producing activity. Businesses, on the other hand, can deduct $5,000 of their start-up expenses in the first year they are in business, with any excess deductible over 15 years. (See Chapter 3.)

- **Limit on deductions.** Expenses incurred from an income-producing activity (investing, for example) are miscellaneous itemized deductions. That means you can deduct them only to the extent they exceed 2% of your adjusted gross income—the same standard used for hobbies. If all your itemized deductions don't exceed the standard deductions, you can't itemize and you get no deduction at all.

The only exception is for rents or royalties earned as part of an income-producing activity. With rent and royalty income, you can deduct your related expenses directly from your gross income (just like business expenses). Thus, landlords who earn rent but don't qualify as businesspeople may still fully deduct their expenses. Royalties include income from things like copyrights or patents, or mineral leases.

- **Only individuals can deduct expenses from income-producing activities.** Corporations, partnerships, and limited liability companies cannot deduct these expenses.
- **No self-employment tax.** One positive tax effect of having an income-producing activity instead of a business is that you don't have to pay any self-employment tax on the income from the activity. Only people in business have to pay self-employment taxes. This is a substantial savings, because the self-employment tax is 15.3% of your self-employment income, up to an annual ceiling amount.

> **EXAMPLE:** Jane is a wealthy Florida retiree who invests heavily in the stock market. To help with investment decisions, she subscribes to several very expensive stock market investing newsletters. She creates an office in her home which she uses exclusively for her investing activities and furnishes it with a desk and chair. She also buys a computer that she uses only to track her investments. Because investing in stocks is an income-producing activity rather than a business, and her investing activity does not produce rents or royalties, she can deduct these expenses (the cost of the newsletter, the office furniture, and the computer) only if she itemizes her deductions and only to the extent they exceed 2% of her adjusted gross income for the year. She may not take a home office deduction, and she can't use Section 179 to deduct the cost of the office furniture and computer—instead, she'll have

to depreciate these items over time. (See Chapter 5 for more on depreciation and Section 179.) Had buying stocks been a business instead of an income-producing activity, Jane could have taken a home office deduction, and she could have used Section 179 to deduct the entire cost of the office furniture and computer in one year. Moreover, her total deduction would not have been limited to the amount that exceeds 2% of her AGI.

When you have an income-producing activity, you don't file an IRS Schedule C, *Profit or Loss From Business*, with your tax return. You don't have a business, so that schedule doesn't apply. Instead, you list your expenses on Schedule A, *Itemized Deductions*. However, if your income comes from real estate or royalties, you list it and your expenses on Schedule E, *Supplemental Income and Loss*. Investors who incur capital gains or losses must file Schedule D, *Capital Gains and Losses*.

 **Need more information on investment deductions?** For detailed guidance on tax deductions for investments, refer to IRS Publication 550, *Investment Income and Expenses*. Like all IRS publications, you can download it from the IRS website at www.irs.gov, or obtain it by calling the IRS at 800-829-3676.

Types of Income-Producing Activities

Anything you do primarily to earn a profit is an income-producing activity, unless it constitutes a business. You determine whether an activity is done primarily for profit by applying the same tests as the ones used to determine whether someone is in business—the three-of-five-year profit test or the behavioral test discussed above.

Personal Investing

Personal investing is by far the most common income-producing activity. Investing means making money in ways other than running a business—for example:

- You put your money in a bank and earn interest.
- You buy stocks, bonds, or other securities in publicly traded corporations and earn money from dividends or from the securities' appreciation in value over time.

- You buy commodities like gold or pork bellies and earn money from their appreciation in value over time.
- You buy real estate and earn money from rents or appreciation in the property's value over time.
- You purchase an interest in a privately owned business run by someone else and earn money from the increase in the business's value over time or payments from the business.

What all these activities have in common is that you are not engaged in the active, continuous, and regular management or control of a business. You are passive—you put your money in somebody else's business and hope your investment will increase in value due to their efforts, not yours. Or, you buy an item like gold and then sit and wait for it to increase in value.

Personal investing is always an income-producing activity for tax purposes, not a business. It makes no difference whether you invest from home or an outside office.

Other Activities

Although the most common, investing is by no means the only income-producing activity. Almost any activity can qualify if your primary motive for engaging in it is to make money but you don't work at it enough for it to rise to the level of a business. For example, raising and selling horses or buying and selling rare coins could be income-producing activities. You must work continuously and regularly at the activity for it to be a business.

Professional Trading in Stocks

People who buy stocks, bonds, and other securities as personal investments are engaged in an income-producing activity. Professional securities dealers and traders in securities, on the other hand, are in business, which means they are not subject to the restrictions on deductions that apply to people involved in income-producing activities. (See "Tax Consequences of Income-Producing Activities," above.) Thus, for example, a professional stock trader may take a home office deduction (provided, of course, the other requirements for the deduction are met—see Chapter 7). Because of the difference in how they are treated for tax purposes, it's important to understand the difference between an investor and a professional securities dealer or trader.

Securities Dealers

A securities dealer is someone who maintains an inventory of stocks, bonds, or other securities and offers them for sale to buyers. Dealers make their money from the fees they charge buyers, not from dividends or appreciation in the value of the securities. Dealers include stock brokers and people who buy and sell securities on the floors of stock exchanges. If you're a dealer in securities, you undoubtedly already know it.

Professional Stock Traders

Most people who buy and sell stocks and other securities do it as an investment. Professional stock traders do it as a business. What's the difference between a stock market investor and a professional trader? A trader's profits come from the *very act of trading*; an investor's come from dividends or the increase in value of his or her holdings over time. To qualify as a professional trader, you must be able to show the IRS all of the following:

- You seek to profit from daily market movements in the price of securities, not from dividends, interest, or capital appreciation.
- Your trading is substantial.
- Your trading is continuous and regular.

Key factors the IRS examines are:

- **How long you hold your securities before you sell them.** Professional traders usually don't hold on to stocks for long, often selling them the same day they buy them. You don't have to be a day trader to be in business. But if you have a "buy and hold" portfolio, you are not a professional trader. Indeed, you're probably in trouble if you hold on to your stocks for more than two or three months on average.
- **How often you trade.** Professionals trade frequently. Many accountants use the rule of thumb that a professional investor must execute at least ten trades a day, five days a week; this adds up to at least 3,000 trades a year. However, people who do fewer trades a year may still qualify as professional investors.

- **Whether you pursue trading to earn a living.** Professionals usually trade to make a living (though they may have other sources of income).
- **How much time you devote to trading.** Professional traders spend a lot of time trading, though not necessarily all of their time. Another accountant's rule of thumb is that a professional trader must trade at least five hours a day, five days a week. Moreover, you must trade continuously throughout the year.

> **EXAMPLE:** Martha is a day trader—she buys and sells large numbers of stocks every day (hence the appellation). She holds on to her stocks for a very short time—often only a few minutes or hours, and rarely more than a few days. She makes profits (or incurs losses) based on the daily fluctuations of the stock market. She trades from her home office, using online trading services. She executes her trades herself, without the aid of a stock broker. She works full time at trading—usually seven to eight hours a day, all year round—and earns her livelihood from trading. She does substantial amounts of research, studying market trends and looking for all types of hot investment information. She executes an average of 20 trades per day, and more than 4,000 per year. Martha is a professional stock trader, not an investor. Thus, she may deduct her expenses for her home office as well as other trading-related expenses.

Before the advent of the Internet, few people could afford to engage in the frequent trading required to be a professional trader, because the commissions and other transaction costs were too great. Today, however, with inexpensive online trading, millions of people are making frequent stock trades from their homes. However, simply calling yourself a "day trader" will not make you a businessperson. You must meet the criteria listed above.

Being an investor or a professional trader is not an either/or proposition. You can be both. That is, you can hold on to some stocks as personal investments, while you actively trade others as your business. If you do this, be sure to keep the two categories separate.

Any Type of Buying and Selling Can Be a Business

Buying and selling anything can be a business—it doesn't have to involve stock or other securities. If you earn your money from the activity of buying and selling and you engage in it regularly and continuously, you can qualify as a business. For example, thousands of people now have businesses buying and selling items on eBay. However, sporadic buying and selling is not a business, even though it is profitable—for example, occasionally selling items on eBay won't qualify as a business.

Professional dealers and traders may not deduct the commissions they pay to buy stocks or other securities. These costs are added to the basis (value) of the securities for purposes of calculating gain or loss when they are sold. Traders who are sole proprietors list their expenses on Schedule C, *Profit or Loss From Business*. However, they list their income or loss from trading on Schedule D, *Capital Gains and Losses*.

Real Estate as a Business

Another way people commonly earn money without running a business is by investing in real estate. However, real estate can also qualify as a business if you are actively and regularly involved in it.

Real Estate Dealers

A real estate dealer is anyone who holds property primarily for sale to customers, such as builders or developers. Numerous and frequent sales over an extended time period are the hallmark of a dealer who is engaged in a business, not an income-producing activity.

Being classified as a dealer is often a tax disadvantage, because gains from sales of real property by a dealer are usually subject to ordinary income tax rates. In contrast, gains realized by an investor are usually taxed at capital gains rates, which are lower. However, dealers are better off if real estate proves to be a money-losing proposition: A dealer is typically permitted to deduct the full amount of a loss, while an investor's deductions for losses may be strictly limited.

Managing Rental Property

You don't have to be a big shot developer to be in the business of real estate. You can also run a business by actively managing rental real estate. But the key word here is active. You can't just sit back and collect rent checks while someone else does all the work of being a landlord. You must be actively involved on a regular, systematic, and continuous basis.

> **EXAMPLE 1:** Carolyn Anderson, a nurse, owned an 80-acre farm that she rented to a tenant farmer. She attempted to deduct her home office expenses by claiming that the rental activity was a business. The IRS and tax court disagreed because Carolyn's landlord activities involved little more than depositing rent checks and occasionally talking to her tenant on the telephone. (*Anderson v. Commissioner*, TC Memo 1982-576.)

> **EXAMPLE 2:** Edwin Curphey, a dermatologist, owned six rental properties in Hawaii. He converted a bedroom in his home into an office for his real estate activities. Curphey personally managed his rentals, which included seeking new tenants, supplying furnishings, and cleaning and otherwise preparing the units for new tenants. The court held that these activities were sufficiently systematic and continuous to place him in the business of real estate rental. As a result, Curphey was entitled to a home office deduction. (*Curphey v. Commissioner*, 73 TC 766 (1980).)

Even if managing real estate is a business, you ordinarily don't file Schedule C, *Profit or Loss From Business*, to report your income and expenses. Instead, you file Schedule E, *Supplemental Income and Loss*. However, you must file Schedule C if you run a hotel, motel, or apartment building where you provide hotel-type services to the occupants (such as maid services).

Need more help with real estate taxation? For a detailed guide to tax deductions for residential landlords, refer to *Every Landlord's Tax Deduction Guide*, by Stephen Fishman (Nolo).

Start-Up Expenses

E veryone knows that it costs money to get a new business up and
running or to buy an existing business. What many people don't know
is that these costs (called start-up expenses) are subject to special tax
rules. This chapter explains what types of expenditures are start-up expenses
and how you can deduct these costs as quickly as possible.

What Are Start-Up Expenses?

To have business deductions, you must actually be running a business.
(See Chapter 2 for more about businesses versus hobbies.) This commonsense rule can lead to problems if you want to start or buy a new business.
The money you spend to get your business up and running is not a
business operating expense because your business hasn't yet begun.

Instead, business start-up expenses are capital expenses because
you incur them to acquire an asset (a business) that will benefit you for
more than one year. Normally, you can't deduct these types of capital
expenses until you sell or otherwise dispose of the business. However,
a special tax rule allows you to deduct up to $5,000 in start-up expenses
the first year you are in business, and then deduct the remainder, if any,
in equal amounts over the next 15 years. (IRC § 195.) Without this special
rule for business start-up expenses, these costs (capital expenses) would
not be deductible until you sold or otherwise disposed of your business.

Once your business begins, the same expenses that were start-up
expenses before your business began become currently deductible
business operating expenses. For example, rent you pay for office space
after your business starts is a currently deductible operating expense,
but rent you pay *before* your business begins is a start-up expense.

> **EXAMPLE:** Diana Drudge is sick of her office job. She dreams of
> becoming a whitewater rafting guide. She finally decides to make
> her dream come true and start her own whitewater rafting tour
> company. Diana makes numerous trips to various rafting areas.
> After deciding on a location, she rents a headquarters and rafting
> equipment, hires and trains five employees, and does extensive
> advertising. Her business finally has its grand opening on July 1.
> She spent $15,000 of her life savings to get the business up and
> running. Because these are start-up expenses, she can't deduct them

all in her first year of business. Instead, she can deduct $5,000 of the expenses the first year she's in business and the remaining $10,000 in equal installments over 15 years (assuming she's in business that long). This means she may deduct $667 of the remaining $10,000 for each full year she's in business, starting with the first year she's in business. However, Diana's business is open for only six months her first year, so she may deduct only $333 of the $10,000 that year, plus the initial $5,000 she's entitled to. Her total first year total deduction is $5,333.

Obviously, you want to spend no more than $5,000 on start-up expenses so you don't have to wait 15 years to get all your money back. There are ways you can avoid spending more than the $5,000 threshold amount. These are described in "Avoiding the Start-Up Tax Rule's Bite," below.

Your business must start to have start-up expenses. If your business never gets started, many of your expenses will not be deductible. So think carefully before spending your hard-earned money to investigate starting a new business venture. (See "Organizational Expenses," below.)

Starting a New Business

Most of the funds you spend investigating whether, where, and how to start a new business, as well as the cost of actually creating it, are deductible business start-up expenses. The tax law is much more generous with deductions for start-up costs if you are creating a new business than if you are buying an existing business. (See "Buying an Existing Business," below.)

Common Start-Up Expenses

Here are some common types of deductible start-up expenses:

- the cost of investigating what it will take to create a successful business, including research on potential markets, products, labor supply, and transportation facilities
- advertising costs, including advertising for your business opening
- costs for employee training before the business opens

- travel expenses related to finding a suitable business location
- expenses related to obtaining financing, suppliers, customers, or distributors
- licenses, permits, and other fees
- fees paid to lawyers, accountants, consultants, and others for professional services, and
- operating expenses incurred before the business begins, such as rent, telephone, utilities, office supplies, and repairs.

Costs That Are Not Start-Up Expenses

There are some costs related to opening a business that are not considered start-up expenses. Many of these costs are still deductible, but different rules and restrictions apply to the way they are deducted.

Expenses That Wouldn't Qualify as Business Operating Expenses

You can only deduct as start-up expenses those costs that would be currently deductible as business operating expenses after your business begins. This means the expenses must be ordinary, necessary, directly related to the business, and reasonable in amount. (See Chapter 4 for a discussion of business operating expenses.) For example, you can't deduct the cost of pleasure travel or entertainment *unrelated* to your business. These expenses would not be deductible as operating expenses by an ongoing business, so you can't deduct them as start-up expenses either. (In fact, you can't deduct them at all.)

Inventory

The largest expense many people incur before they start their business is for inventory—that is, buying the goods they will sell to customers. For example, a person opening a florist shop has to buy an inventory of flowers to sell. The cost of purchasing this inventory is not treated as a start-up expense. Instead, you deduct inventory costs as you sell the inventory. (See Chapter 6 for more on deducting inventory costs.)

Long-Term Assets

Long-term assets are things you purchase for your business that will last for more than one year, such as computers, office equipment, cars, and machinery. Long-term assets you buy before your business begins are not considered part of your start-up costs. Instead, you treat these purchases like any other long-term asset you buy *after* your business begins: You must either depreciate the item over several years or deduct the cost in one year under Section 179. (Chapter 5 explains how to deduct long-term assets.) However, you can't take depreciation or Section 179 deductions until after your business begins.

Research and Development Costs

The tax law includes a special category for research and development expenses. These are costs a business incurs to discover something new (in the laboratory or experimental sense), such as a new invention, formula, prototype, or process. They include laboratory and computer supplies, salaries, rent, utilities, other overhead expenses, and equipment rental, but not the purchase of long-term assets. Research and development costs are currently deductible under Section 174 of the Internal Revenue Code, even if you incur them before the business begins operations.

 For a detailed discussion of deductions for research and development, see *What Every Inventor Needs to Know About Business & Taxes*, by Stephen Fishman (Nolo).

Taxes and Interest

Any tax and interest that you pay before your business begins is not a start-up expense. Instead, these costs are currently deductible as business operating expenses once your business begins. There are a few exceptions to this rule. Sales tax you pay for long-term assets for your business is added to the cost of the asset for purposes of depreciation or the Section 179 deduction. (See Chapter 5.) And money you borrow to buy an interest in an S corporation, partnership, or LLC must be allocated among the company's assets. Interest on money you borrow to buy stock in a C corporation is treated as investment interest and may be currently deducted as a personal itemized deduction. (See Chapter 14.)

Organizational Costs

Costs you incur to form a partnership, LLC, or corporation are not part of your start-up costs. However, they are deductible in the same amounts as start-up expenses under a separate tax rule. (See "Avoiding the Start-Up Tax Rule's Bite," below.)

Education Expenses

You cannot deduct education expenses you incur to qualify for a new business or profession. For this reason, courts have held that IRS agents could not deduct the cost of going to law school, since a law degree would qualify them for a new business—being a lawyer. (*Jeffrey L. Weiler*, 54 TC 398 (1970).)

Buying an Existing Business

Different rules apply if you buy an existing business rather than creating a new one. If you are buying a business, you can only deduct as start-up expenses the costs you incur to decide *whether* to purchase a business and *which* business you should buy. The money you pay to actually purchase the existing business is not a start-up expense. Nor is this cost a currently deductible business expense. Instead, it is a capital expense that becomes part of the tax basis of your business. If and when you sell the business, you will be able to deduct this amount from any profit you make on the sale before taxes are assessed. (See "Costs to Start or Acquire a Specific Business," below.)

You don't have to make an offer, sign a letter of intent, or enter into a binding legal agreement to purchase an existing business for your expenses to cease being start-up expenses. You just have to make up your mind to purchase a specific business and focus on acquiring it. (Rev. Rul. 1999-23.)

> **EXAMPLE:** Sean, a wealthy and successful entrepreneur, wants to buy an existing business. He hires Duane, an investment banker, to help him. Duane conducts research on several industries and evaluates publicly available financial information for several businesses. Eventually, Duane focuses on the trucking industry. Duane evaluates several businesses within the industry, including the Acme Trucking Company and several of Acme's competitors. Sean decides he would like to buy Acme and hires accountant Al to conduct an in-depth review of its books and records to determine a fair acquisition price. Sean then enters into an acquisition agreement with Acme to purchase all its assets. The fees Sean paid to Duane are start-up expenses because they were paid to help Sean determine whether

to purchase an existing business and which business to buy. The fees Sean paid to Al are not start-up expenses, because they were incurred to help Sean purchase a specific existing business: the Acme Trucking Company.

Expanding an Existing Business

What if you already have a business and decide to expand your operation? The cost of expanding an existing business is considered a business operating expense, not a start-up expense. As long as these costs are ordinary and necessary, they are currently deductible.

> **EXAMPLE:** Sam runs a dry cleaning store. He pays $2,000 for legal, accounting, licensing, and advertising costs to expand to two new locations. These costs are currently deductible as ordinary and necessary operating expenses.

However, this rule applies only when the expansion involves a business that is the same as—or similar to—the existing business. The costs of expanding into a new business are start-up costs, not operating expenses.

> **EXAMPLE:** Assume that Sam decides to start a Greek restaurant. This business is unrelated to his existing dry cleaning business. Therefore, the ordinary and necessary expenses he incurs before the restaurant begins are start-up costs.

When Does a Business Begin?

The date when your business begins for tax purposes marks an important turning point. Operating expenses you incur once your business starts are currently deductible, while expenses you incur before this crucial date may have to be deducted over many years.

A new business begins for tax purposes when it starts to function as a going concern and performs the activities for which it was organized. (*Richmond Television Corp. v. U.S.*, 345 F.2d 901 (4th Cir. 1965).) The IRS says that a venture becomes a going concern when it acquires all of the assets necessary to perform its intended functions and puts those assets to work. In other words, your business begins when you start doing business, whether or not you are actually earning any money.

This is usually not a difficult test to apply. Here are the rules that apply to some common types of businesses.

Retail Businesses

Retail businesses that sell tangible products to customers begin when the business is ready to offer its product for sale to the public. It is not necessary to actually make any sales. For example, a restaurant owner's business begins when the restaurant's doors open and the restaurant is ready to serve food to customers. If no diners show up and the restaurant doesn't actually sell any food for a week, the start date is not affected. Once the restaurant is ready to offer its food for sale to the public, it's in business.

Manufacturers

A manufacturing or other production-related business begins when it starts using its assets to produce saleable products. The products don't have to be completed, nor do sales have to be solicited or made. For example, a company organized to manufacture bowling trophies would begin when it acquired all the workspace, personnel, material, and equipment it needs to make the trophies and starts using them to manufacture the product. If it takes several days to assemble a completed trophy (and to find someone willing to buy it), that doesn't matter—the company begins when the process of making the trophy starts.

Knowledge Workers

Writers, artists, photographers, graphic designers, computer programmers, and similar knowledge workers might not think of themselves as manufacturers, but the courts do. For example, courts have held that a writer's business begins when he or she starts working on a writing project. (*Gestrich v. Commr.*, 681 F.2d 805 (3d Cir. 1982).) Just like a manufacturing business, a writer's business begins when the necessary materials are in place and the work starts—not when the work is finished or sold. Similarly, an inventor's business begins when he or she starts working on an invention in earnest, not when the invention is completed, patented, or sold.

Service Providers

If your business involves providing a service to customers or clients—for example, accounting, consulting, financial planning, law, medicine, or dentistry—your business begins when you first offer your services to the public. No one has to hire you; you just have to be available for hire. For example, a dentist's business begins when he or she opens a dental office and is ready to perform dental work on patients.

An Existing Business

If you buy an existing business, your business is deemed to begin for tax purposes when the purchase is completed—that is, when you take over ownership.

> **EXAMPLE:** Ben, an amateur taxidermist, has long dreamed of opening a taxidermy business. After extensive investigation and analysis of the taxidermy market, he decides the best way to get into the business is to buy a taxidermy shop with an existing inventory and established customer base. Ben signs a contract to purchase the Acme Taxidermy Shop on October 15, 2006 and completes the acquisition on January 15, 2007. Ben's taxidermy business began on January 15, 2007.

Proving When Your Business Begins

Because your business start date is so important for tax purposes, you should be able to prove to the IRS exactly when it began. There are many ways you can do this. Being able to show the IRS a copy of an advertisement for your business is a great way to prove you were open for business. You can also mail out brochures or other promotional materials. You don't have to advertise to show you are open your business—simply handing out business cards is sufficient. Give your first business cards to friends and associates who could testify for you if you're audited by the IRS. Establish your office to show you are ready to take on clients or customers. Take a photo of it with a digital camera (which will be date-stamped).

If you're selling a product, you can start with a small inventory. Keep invoices and other documents showing the date you purchased the inventory. Take pictures of your equipment and inventory with a digital camera.

If you are making a product, your business begins when you have all the equipment and materials ready to start production. Keep invoices and other documents showing when you obtained these items.

How to Deduct Start-Up Expenses

You can deduct $5,000 in start-up expenses the first year you're in business. Any expenses you have in excess of $5,000, will have to be deducted in equal amounts over the first 180 months (15 years) you're in business. This process is called amortization. One hundred and eighty months is the minimum amortization period; you can choose a longer period if you wish (almost no one does).

If you have more than $50,000 in start-up expenses, however, you are not entitled to the full $5,000 deduction. You must reduce the $5,000 deduction by the amount that your start-up expenditures exceed $50,000. For example, if you have $53,000 in start-up expenses, you may only deduct $2,000 the first year, instead of $5,000. If you have $55,000 or more in start-up expenses, you get no current deduction for start-up expenses. Instead, the whole amount must be deducted over 180 months.

If Your Business Began in 2004

The start-up expense provision of the tax law (IRC § 195) was amended by Congress in 2004 to permit $5,000 of start-up expenses to be deducted the first year a business in is operation. Before the change, all start-up expenses had to be deducted over the first 60 months a business was in operation. The amendment took effect on October 22, 2004. If your business began before this date, the old rule applies to you. Deduct all your start-up expenses in equal monthly installments for the first 60 months you're in business.

EXAMPLE: Tom, a window washer employed by a large window-washing company, decides to start his own window-washing business. He carefully investigates the window-washing businesses in his region, traveling to several cities. He rents equipment, leases vehicles, hires and trains several window washers, and conducts an advertising blitz before his business's grand opening in November of 2006. The start-up expenses he incurred before his business opened amount to $14,000. He may deduct $5,000 of his expenses in 2006. He can deduct the remaining $9,000 over the first 15 years (180 months) he's in business—or $50 per month ($9,000 divided by 180 months equals 50). He was only in business for two months in 2006, so his total start-up expense deduction for 2006 is $5,100. He'll get a $600 deduction in 2007 and each year thereafter until he has deducted the entire $9,000.

Making a Section 195 Election

You must indicate that you want to deduct start-up costs on your tax return by making a Section 195 election. (Section 195 is the tax law governing start-up expenses.) You must attach a statement (called a Section 195 statement) to your tax return listing your start-up expenses, the dates you paid them, the date your business began, and a description of your business. If you have more than $5,000 in start-up expenses, you'll have to deduct the excess over 180 months. You must file IRS Form 4562, *Depreciation and Amortization*, with your return showing how much you're deducting. You must also list the number of months in the amortization period (180) in your Section 195 Statement.

If you forget to list all of your start-up costs in your Section 195 statement, you can file an amended statement later listing any items you omitted. However, you may not list any expenses that you have already claimed were deductible under other tax laws—for example, as ordinary and necessary operating expenses.

> **EXAMPLE:** Tom failed to list a $1,000 accounting fee as a start-up expense in his Section 195 statement. Instead, he deducted the fee as a currently deductible business operating expense. Three years later, he is audited. The auditor says Tom should have listed the fee as a start-up cost, not a currently deductible operating expense, and disallows the deduction. Tom cannot amend his Section 195 statement to add the fee as a start-up expense, because he has already claimed, albeit mistakenly, that the fee was deductible under another tax rule. Even though Tom made an innocent mistake, he won't get any deduction for his accounting fee.

The moral is this: Be very careful when you prepare your first tax return after your business opens. Figure out how to categorize each of your expenses, and make sure to list every start-up expense in your Section 195 election.

You must make a timely election to deduct start-up expenses. If you want to deduct your start-up expenses, you must file your election (IRS Form 4562 and Section 195 statement) on or before the date of your first tax return after you start your business is due. For example, if your business begins in 2006, you must file the election with your 2006 tax return, due April 15, 2007 (or later if you receive an extension). If you miss this deadline, you have one last chance to make your election: You may file an amended return making the election within six months after the date your original return was due. If you fail to do this, you will lose your right to deduct your start-up expenses and you'll have to treat them as capital expenses (as described in "Costs to Start or Acquire a Specific Business," below).

> **EXAMPLE:** Tom's window-washing business began in 2006. He must file his election to deduct his start-up costs with his 2006 tax return, which is due April 15, 2007 (or later, if Tom gets an extension to file). If Tom fails to make the election to file by this deadline, he may file an amended tax return within six months—that is, by October 15, 2007 (or within six months after the end of any filing extension he obtains).

If you decide not to make a Section 195 election, your start-up costs become part of the tax basis of your business. This might be a good idea if you don't expect your business to earn a profit for many years or you want to reduce your deductions in order to show a profit. Deducting your start-up expenses will decrease your business profits for the first 60 months, because they are deducted from your business income. Forgoing the deduction will therefore increase the profit your business earns over that time. This might be advisable, for example, if you fear that the IRS will claim your venture is a hobby instead of a business. Earning profits is the best way to show that an activity is a real business. (See Chapter 2 for more on hobbies versus businesses.)

If Your Business Doesn't Last 15 Years

Not all businesses last for 15 years. In fact, most small businesses don't last this long. If you had more than $5,000 in start-up expenses and are in the process of deducting the excess amount, you don't lose the value of your deductions if you sell or close your business before you have had a chance to deduct all of your start-up expenses. You can deduct any leftover start-up expenses as ordinary business losses. (IRC § 195(b)(2).) This means that you may be able to deduct them from any income you have that year, deduct them in future years, or deduct them from previous years' taxes.

If you sell your business or its assets, your leftover start-up costs will be added to your tax basis in the business. This is just as good as getting a tax deduction. If you sell your business at a profit, the remaining start-up costs will be subtracted from your profits before taxes are assessed, which reduces your taxable gain. If you sell at a loss, the start-up costs will be added to the money you lost—because this shortfall is deductible, a larger loss means lower taxes.

Keep Good Expense Records

Whether you intend to start a new business or buy an existing one, you should keep careful track of every expense you incur before the business begins. Obviously, you should keep receipts and canceled checks. You should also keep evidence that will help show that the money went to investigate a new business—for example, correspondence and emails with accountants, attorneys, business brokers, and consultants; marketing or financial reports; and copies of advertisements. You will need these records to calculate your deductions and to prove your expenses to the IRS (if you face an audit).

Expenses for Businesses That Never Begin

Many people investigate starting a business, but the venture never gets off the ground. While this is no doubt disappointing, you might be able to recoup some of your expenses in the form of tax deductions.

General Start-Up Costs

General start-up costs are expenses you incur *before* you decide to start a new business or acquire a specific existing business. They include all of the costs of doing a general search for, or preliminary investigation of, a business—for example, costs you incur analyzing potential markets. If you never start the business, these costs are personal and not deductible—in other words, they are a dead loss.

EXAMPLE: Bruno is sick of his job and would like to start his own business. An avid gardener, he thinks that opening a flower shop might be a good idea. He buys several books on business start-ups, travels to a florist convention where he stays overnight at a hotel, and attends a class on floral arranging. However, he ultimately decides to keep his day job. None of the expenses he incurred in investigating the florist shop idea are deductible.

One intended effect of this rule is that you can't deduct travel, entertainment, or other "fun" expenses by claiming that you incurred them to investigate a business unless you *actually start the business.* Otherwise, it would be pretty tough for the IRS to figure out whether you were really considering a new venture or just having a good time.

EXAMPLE: Kim spends $5,000 on a two-week Hawaii vacation. While there, she attends a four-hour seminar on how to make money buying a franchise. However, she never starts a franchise business. The cost of her trip is not a start-up expense.

Corporations can deduct general start-up costs. A corporation can deduct general start-up expenses as a business loss, even if the business never gets going.

Costs to Start or Acquire a Specific Business

The expenses you incur to actually start or acquire a particular business (that ultimately never begins operations) are start-up expenses. This includes any of the more common start-up expenses listed in "Common Start-Up Expenses," above—for example, legal or accounting fees you incur to start a new business or acquire an existing business.

These costs are deductible, but only as capital expenses. The cost of any property you acquire during your unsuccessful attempt to go into business becomes part of your basis in the asset. You get no direct tax deduction for these costs, but you may recover these costs when you dispose of the asset. (See "Costs That Are Not Start-Up Expenses," above, to learn how this works.) Other costs may be deducted as investment expenses, which are generally deductible only as itemized miscellaneous deductions. (IRC § 165.) (See Chapter 2.)

> **EXAMPLE:** Bruno takes concrete steps to start his florist shop. He puts down a $2,000 nonrefundable deposit to lease a storefront and spends $2,000 for refrigeration equipment. However, he decides at the last minute that the business is not for him. These expenses were made after Bruno decided to start a specific business, so they are deductible. He may deduct the $2,000 lost deposit as an investment expense. He must take it as a miscellaneous itemized deduction on his tax return, but the deduction is limited to the amount by which it (plus his other miscellaneous deductions) exceeds 2% of his adjusted gross income. He can deduct his $2,000 expense for the refrigeration equipment as a capital expense. However, he can't simply deduct the $2,000 from his income for the year or depreciate the equipment. Instead, the $2,000 is added to the tax basis of the equipment when he disposes of it. If he sells the refrigerator for $1,000, he has a $1,000 capital loss that he may deduct from his income for the year ($2,000 tax basis − $1,000 sales price = $1,000). If he sells the refrigerator for $3,000, he has a $1,000 capital gain on which he must pay tax.

Organizational Expenses

If you decide to go into business, you may want to form some type of business entity, such as a corporation, partnership, or limited liability corporation. (See Chapter 1 for a discussion of different possible business structures.) The costs of forming an entity to run your business are deductible. These organizational expenses are not considered start-up expenses, although they are deducted in much the same way.

If you form a corporation, you can deduct the cost of creating the corporation, including legal fees for drafting articles of incorporation, bylaws, minutes of organizational meetings, and other organizational documents, and accounting fees for setting up the corporation and its books. You can also deduct state incorporation fees and other filing fees. However, you may not deduct the cost of transferring assets to the corporation or fees associated with issuing stock or securities—for example, commissions and printing costs. These are capital expenses.

If you form a partnership or LLC with two or more members, you may deduct the cost of negotiating and drafting a partnership or LLC agreement, accounting services to organize the partnership, and LLC filing fees.

Organizational expenses are deducted in the same way as start-up costs. You may deduct the first $5,000 the first year you are in business, and any excess over the first 180 months. However, your $5,000 deduction is reduced by the amount by which your organizational expenditures exceed $50,000. You must file IRS Form 4562 with your tax return (along with a statement listing the cost).

Avoiding the Start-Up Tax Rule's Bite

You will only be adversely affected by the start-up tax rule if you spend more than $5,000 on start-up costs before your business begins. If you spend $5,000 or less, you can deduct all your start-up expenses during the first year you are in business. You will need to keep track of what you spend and, if you get near the $5,000 threshold amount, cut back on your spending until your business begins. If you are at or near the $5,000 amount and need to keep spending, you could try to postpone paying for an item until after your business begins. Deductible start-up costs always qualify as currently deductible business operating expenses once a business begins. Postponing payment will only work, though, if you're a cash basis taxpayer—someone who reports income and expenses on the date they are actually paid, not on the date when an agreement to pay is made.

If you need to spend more than $5,000, go ahead and do it—you will still be able to deduct those expenses. You'll just have to deduct them over 15 years instead of one. Try to keep your total start-up expenses below $50,000, though. If you go above $50,000, your first-year $5,000 deduction will be reduced by the amount you exceed $50,000 (or wiped out if your total expenses are $55,000 or more).

Chapter 4

Business Operating Expenses

This chapter covers the basic rules for deducting business operating expenses—the bread and butter expenses virtually every business incurs for things like rent, supplies, and salaries. If you don't maintain an inventory or buy expensive equipment, these day-to-day costs will probably be your largest category of business expenses (and your largest source of deductions).

Requirements for Deducting Operating Expenses

There are so many different kinds of business operating expenses that the tax code couldn't possibly list them all. Instead, if you want to deduct an item as a business operating expense, you must make sure the expenditure meets certain requirements. If it does, it will qualify as a deductible business operating expense. To qualify, the expense must be:

- ordinary and necessary
- a current expense
- directly related to your business, and
- reasonable in amount. (IRC § 162.)

Your Business Must Have Begun

You must be *carrying on* a business to have deductible operating expenses. Costs you incur before your business is up and running are not currently deductible operating expenses, even if they are ordinary and necessary. However, up to $5,000 in start-up expenses may be deducted the first year you're in business, with the remainder deducted over the next 15 years. (See Chapter 3 for a discussion of start-up expenses.)

Ordinary and Necessary

The first requirement is that the expense must be ordinary and necessary. This means that the cost is common and "helpful and

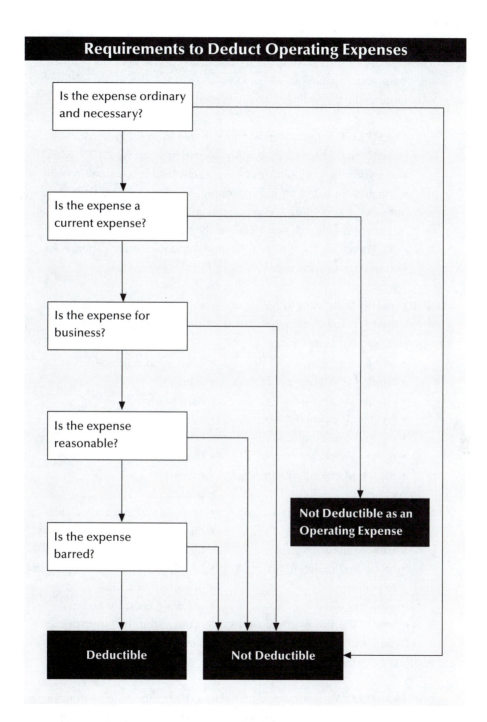

appropriate" for your business. (*Welch v. Helvering*, 290 U.S. 111 (1933).) The expense doesn't have to be indispensable to be necessary; it need only help your business in some way—even if it's minor. A one-time expenditure can be ordinary and necessary.

> **EXAMPLE:** Connie, a dentist, buys a television set and installs it in her dental office waiting room so patients can watch TV while waiting for their appointments. Although having a TV set in her waiting room is not an indispensable item for Connie's dental business, it is helpful; some patients might prefer to see Connie instead of another dentist because they can watch TV while they wait. Therefore, the TV is an ordinary and necessary expense for Connie's dental practice.

It's usually fairly easy to figure out whether an expense passes the ordinary and necessary test. Some of the most common types of operating expenses include:

- rent for an outside office
- employee salaries and benefits
- equipment rental
- legal and accounting fees
- car and truck expenses
- travel expenses
- meal and entertainment expenses
- supplies and materials
- publications
- subscriptions
- repair and maintenance expenses
- business taxes
- interest on business loans
- licenses
- banking fees
- advertising costs
- home office expenses
- business-related education expenses
- postage
- professional association dues
- business liability and property insurance
- health insurance for employees
- office utilities, and
- software used for business.

Generally, the IRS won't second-guess your claim that an expense is ordinary and necessary, unless the item or service clearly has no legitimate business purpose.

> **EXAMPLE:** An insurance agent claimed a business deduction for part of his handgun collection because he had to go to "unsafe job

sites" to settle insurance claims, and there was an unsolved murder in his neighborhood. The tax court disallowed the deduction explaining, "A handgun simply does not qualify as an ordinary and necessary business expense for an insurance agent, even a bold and brave Wyatt Earp type with a fast draw who is willing to risk injury or death in the service of his clients." (*Samp v. Commissioner*, TC Memo 1981-1986.)

The following chart lists the 15 most common operating expenses claimed in 2001 by sole proprietor business owners who earned $25,000 to $100,000 that year.

15 Most Common Operating Expenses for Small Businesses	
Expense	Percentage of Business Owners Who Claimed the Expense
1. Car and truck expenses	81%
2. Utilities	68%
3. Supplies (other than office supplies)	60%
4. Office supplies	60%
5. Legal and professional services	60%
6. Insurance	54%
7. Taxes	51%
8. Meals and entertainment	47%
9. Advertising	43%
10. Repairs	40%
11. Travel	31%
12. Rent on business property	26%
13. Home office	21%
14. Rent on equipment and machinery	21%
15. Interest	18%

(Source: *Information on Expenses Claimed by Small Business Sole Proprietorships*, General Accounting Office (GAO-04-304; January 2004).)

Current Expense

Only current expenses are deductible as business operating expenses. Current expenses are for items that will benefit your business for less than one year. These are the costs of keeping your business going on a day-to-day basis, including money you spend on items or services that get used up, wear out, or become obsolete in less than one year. A good example of a current expense is your business's monthly phone bill, which benefits your business for one month. In contrast, buying a telephone for your business would be a capital expense (not a current expense) because the phone will benefit your business for more than one year. Other common capital expenses include cars, business equipment, computers, and real estate.

Current expenses are currently deductible—that is, they are fully deductible in the year in which you incur them. Because all business operating expenses are current expenses, they are also all currently deductible. However, the annual deductions for some operating expenses (notably home offices) are limited to the amount of profits you earn from the business in that year. (See Chapter 7 for more on the home office deduction.) Items you buy for your business that last for more than one year (capital expense items) must be depreciated over several years or deducted in one year under Section 179. (See Chapter 5 for more on deducting long-term assets.)

Business-Related

An expense must be directly related to your business to be deductible as a business operating expense. This means that you cannot deduct personal expenses. For example, the cost of a personal computer is a deductible operating expense only if you use the computer for business purposes; it is not deductible if you use it to pay personal bills or play computer games. If you buy something for both personal and business use, you can deduct only the business portion of the expense. For example, if you buy a cellular phone and use it half of the time for business calls and half of the time for personal calls, you can deduct only half of the cost of the phone as a business expense.

A business expense for one person can be a personal expense for another, and vice versa. For example, a professional screenwriter could probably deduct the cost of going to movies—he needs to see movies for his screenwriting business. But a salesperson could not deduct this type of expense.

The chart below provides some examples of expenses that courts have found to be (and not to be) business-related.

Deductible Business Expenses	Nondeductible Personal Expenses
Dental expenses a professional actor incurred when his teeth were knocked out while making a boxing movie. (*Denny v. Commissioner*, 33 BTA 738 (1935).) **Reason:** *The expense was directly attributable to his occupation as an actor.*	Money an author paid to prostitutes while researching a book on legal brothels. (*Vitale v. Commissioner*, TC Memo 1999-131.) **Reason:** *The expenditures were "so personal in nature as to preclude their deductibility."*
Flowers the president of a loan company sent to employees while they were in the hospital. (*Blackwell v. Commissioner*, TC Memo 1956-184.) **Reason:** *The expense benefited the company, not the president personally.*	A bar mitzvah reception for a rabbi's son. (*Feldman v. Commissioner*, 86 TC 458 (1986).) **Reason:** *The reception was a personal, family event, not a business meeting or business entertainment.*
High-protein foods a person with a rare blood type ate to maintain the quality of her blood so she could regularly sell it to a serological company. (*Green v. Commissioner*, 74 TC 1229 (1980).) **Reason:** *The expenses were incurred for her business as a seller of blood plasma.*	Parking fees a college professor paid to park on campus. (*Greenway v. Commissioner*, TC Memo 1980-97.) **Reason:** *The fees were part of the professor's commuting expenses and therefore were personal.*

Many expenses have both a personal and business component, which can make it difficult to tell if an expense is business-related. Because of this, the business-related requirement is usually the most challenging factor in determining whether an expense qualifies as a deductible business operating expense.

Even the most straightforward costs can present difficulties. For example, it's usually easy to tell whether postage is a personal or business expense. If you mail something for your business, it's a business expense; if you mail something unrelated to your business, it's a personal expense. But even here, there can be questions. For example, should a doctor be allowed to deduct the postage for postcards he sends to his patients while he is on vacation in Europe? (Yes—the tax court said the postage was deductible as an advertising expense; *Duncan v. Commissioner*, 30 TC 386 (1958).)

The IRS has created rules and regulations for some of the more common operating expenses that often involve a difficult crossover of personal and business. Some of these rules help by laying out guidelines for when an expense is and isn't deductible. Others impose record-keeping and other requirements to prevent abuses by dishonest taxpayers. Most of the complexity in determining whether an expense is deductible as a business operating expense involves understanding and applying these special rules and regulations.

The expenses that present the most common problems (and are subject to the most comprehensive IRS rules and regulations) include:

- home office expenses (see Chapter 7)
- meals and entertainment (see Chapter 10)
- travel (see Chapter 9)
- car and truck expenses (see Chapter 8)
- business gifts (see Chapter 14)
- bad debts (see Chapter 14)
- employee benefits (see Chapter 12)
- interest payments (see Chapter 14)
- health insurance (see Chapter 13)
- casualty losses (see Chapter 14)
- taxes (see Chapter 14), and
- education expenses (see Chapter 14).

Through these rules and regulations, the IRS provides guidance on the following types of questions:

- If you rent an apartment and use part of one room as a business office, should you be allowed to deduct all or a portion of the rent as a business operating expense? How much of the room has to be used as an office (and for what period of time) for it to be considered used for business rather than personal purposes? (See Chapter 7 for information on the home office deduction.)

• Can you deduct the money you spend on a nice suit to wear to your office? (See Chapter 14 for information about deducting business clothing.)

• Can you deduct the cost of driving from home to your business office? (See Chapter 8 for rules about deducting commuting expenses.)

• Can you deduct the cost of a lunch with a former client or customer? Does it matter whether you actually talk about business at the lunch? (See Chapter 10 for rules about deducting meals and entertainment.)

Reasonable

Subject to some important exceptions, there is no limit on how much you can deduct, as long as the amount is reasonable and you don't deduct more than you spend. As a rule of thumb, an expense is reasonable unless there are more economical and practical ways to achieve the same result. If the IRS finds that your deductions were unreasonably large, it will disallow them or at least disallow the portion it finds unreasonable.

Whether a deduction is reasonable depends on the circumstances. In one case, the IRS found that it was unreasonable for an aircraft controller to spend over $17,000 to buy a plane to learn to fly, when she could have learned to fly just as well (but far more cheaply) by renting a plane. (*Behm v. Commissioner*, 53 TC 427 (1987).) On the other hand, it was reasonable for a shopping center developer to pay to keep a charter plane on 24-hour standby when the plane had to be available at a moment's notice to transport prospective tenants to a building site. (*Palo Alto Town & Country Village, Inc. v. Commissioner*, 565 F.2d 1388 (9th Cir. 1977).)

Certain areas are hot buttons for the IRS—especially car, entertainment, travel, and meal expenses. There are strict rules requiring you to fully document these deductions. (See Chapters 8, 9, and 10 for more on car, travel, and meal and entertainment expenses.) The reasonableness issue also comes up when a business pays excessive salaries to employees to obtain a large tax deduction. For example, a business owner might hire his 12-year-old son to answer phones and pay him $50 an hour—clearly an excessive wage for this type of work.

For a some types of operating expenses, the IRS limits how much you can deduct. These include:

- the home office deduction, which is limited to the profit from your business (although you can carry over and deduct any excess amount in future years) (see Chapter 7)
- business meals and entertainment, which are only 50% deductible (see Chapter 10)
- travel expenses, which are limited depending on the length of your trip and the time you spent on business while away (see Chapter 9), and
- business gifts, which are subject to a $25 maximum per individual per year (see Chapter 14).

Operating Expenses That Are Not Deductible

Even though they might be ordinary and necessary, some types of operating expenses are not deductible under any circumstances. In some cases, this is because Congress has declared that it would be morally wrong or otherwise contrary to sound public policy to allow people to deduct these costs. In other cases, Congress simply doesn't want to allow the deduction. These nondeductible expenses include:

- fines and penalties paid to the government for violation of any law—for example, tax penalties, parking tickets, or fines for violating city housing codes (IRC § 162(f))
- illegal bribes or kickbacks to private parties or government officials (IRC § 162(c))
- lobbying expenses or political contributions; however, a business may deduct up to $2,000 per year in expenses to influence local legislation (state, county, or city), not including the expense of hiring a professional lobbyist (such lobbyist expenses are not deductible)
- two-thirds of any damages paid for violation of the federal antitrust laws (IRC § 162(g))
- bar or professional examination fees

A Deductible Day in the Life of a Business Owner

Gina is a full-time suburban mom who runs a part-time baby photography business from her home office. On a particular day, she gets up, makes breakfast, and drives her two kids to school. On the way, she drops off some photos at the home of a client. Later that morning, she drives to the grocery store, where she buys food and a box of envelopes for her business. She then drives to a fancy restaurant where she has lunch with an old friend who recently had a baby. Along with personal chitchat, they arrange a date for Gina to photograph the friend's baby. Gina pays for the lunch. That afternoon, Gina enrolls in a class on photographic printmaking at a local college. She plans to use this skill to expand her photography business. Later that day, the maid comes to clean the house, including Gina's home office (which takes up 20% of her home). That evening, Gina and her husband go to a baby photo exhibition at a local art gallery, where they pay for parking.

Here are her tax deductions for business operating expenses.

Activity	Type of Business Expense	Amount of Business Expense
Driving to drop off photos to clients	Business transportation	5 miles at 44.5 cents per mile = $2.23
Driving to grocery store	Business transportation	7 miles at 44.5 cents per mile = 3.12
Buying envelopes	Business supplies	5.00
Lunch	Business meal	50% of cost of lunch = 25.00
Driving to lunch	Business transportation	3 miles at 44.5 cents per mile = 1.34
Registering for photography class	Business-related education	200
Cleaning home office	Business operating expense	20% of $75 house-cleaning fee = 15.00
Parking fee to visit photo exhibition	Business-related transportation costs	10.00
Total Deductions		$261.69

As this example shows, you should get into the habit of looking for possible operating expense deductions whenever you spend money on anything related to your business.

- charitable donations by any business other than a C corporation (these donations are only deductible as personal expenses; see Chapter 14)
- country club, social club, or athletic club dues (see Chapter 14)
- federal income taxes you pay on your business income (see Chapter 14)
- certain interest payments (see Chapter 14).

Tax Reporting

It's very easy to deduct operating expenses from your income taxes. You simply keep track of everything you buy (or spend money on) for your business during the year, including the amount spent on each item. Then you record the expenses on your tax return. If you are a sole proprietor, you do this on IRS Schedule C, *Profit or Loss From Business*. To make this task easy, Schedule C lists common current expense categories—you just need to fill in the amount for each category. For example, if you spend $1,000 for business advertising during the year, you would fill in this amount in the box for the advertising category. You add up all of your current expenses on Schedule C and deduct the total from your gross business income to determine your net business income—the amount on which you are taxed.

If you are a limited liability company owner, partner in a partnership, or S corporation owner, the process is very similar, except you don't use Schedule C. LLCs and partnerships file IRS Form 1065, and their owners' share of expenses is reported on Schedule K-1. S corporations use Form 1120S. Each partner, LLC member, and S corporation shareholder's share of these deductions passes through the entity and is deducted on the owner's individual tax return on Schedule E. Regular C corporations file their own corporate tax returns.

■

Chapter 5

Deducting Long-Term Assets

Do you like to go shopping? How would you like to get a 45% discount on what you buy? Sound impossible? It's not. Consider this example: Sid and Sally each buy the same $2,000 computer at their local computer store. Sid uses his computer to play games and balance his personal checkbook. Sally uses her computer in her graphic design business. Sid's net cost for his computer—that is, his cost after he pays his taxes for the year—is $2,000. Sally's net cost for her computer is $1,100.

Why the difference in cost? Because Sally uses her computer for business, she is allowed to deduct its cost from her income, which saves her $900 in federal and state taxes. Thanks to tax laws designed to help people who own businesses, Sally gets a 45% discount on the computer.

This chapter explains how you can take advantage of these tax laws whenever you purchase long-term property for your business. You will need to be aware of, and follow, some tax rules that at times may seem complicated. But it's worth the effort. After all, by allowing these deductions, the government is effectively offering to help pay for your equipment and other business assets. All you have to do is take advantage of the offer.

Long-Term Assets

This chapter explains how to deduct long-term assets: business property that you reasonably expect to last for more than one year. Long-term assets are also called capital expenses—the terms are used interchangeably in this book. There are two methods for deducting long-term business property:

- Section 179, and
- regular depreciation.

Each is covered in the sections that follow.

Long-Term Assets Versus Current Expenses

Whether an item is a long-term asset (a capital expense) or not depends on its useful life. The useful life of an asset is not its physical life, but rather the period during which it may reasonably be expected to be useful in your business—and the IRS, not you, makes this call. Anything you buy that will benefit your business for more than one year is a capital expense. For businesses, this typically includes items such as buildings, equipment, vehicles, books, furniture, machinery, and patents you buy from others. These are all long-term assets. Anything you purchase that will benefit your business for less than one year is a current expense, not a long-term asset.

> **EXAMPLE:** Doug pays $15,000 for a car to use in his business. Because a car can reasonably be expected to be useful for several years, it is a capital expense. The $100 per month that Doug spends on gas for his car, however, is a current expense.

Are Paperclips Long-Term Assets?

Are paperclips and other inexpensive items that you buy for your business long-term assets for tax purposes? No. Although things like paperclips might be expected to last more than one year, you can treat these and other similar items as a current expense for tax purposes. Most businesses establish a minimum an asset must cost before they will treat it as a long-term asset. The IRS has no rules on the amount of the limit, except that it must be reasonable. For a small business, a reasonable limit would be $100 to $250. Thus, for example, you would treat a $50 bookcase you buy for your business as an operating expense, while a $500 bookcase would be a long-term asset. For larger businesses, a $1,000 limit may be more appropriate.

Deducting Capital Expenses

There are two basic ways to deduct capital expenses: You can depreciate them, deducting some of the cost each year over the asset's useful life, or you may be able to deduct all or most of the cost in one year under Section 179 of the Internal Revenue Code (IRC). Deducting the entire amount in one year is usually economically advantageous because of the time value of money—the sooner you get your money, the sooner you can start using it to make more money.

Because depreciation forces you to spread out your deduction over several years or more, many small business owners choose to deduct their capital expenses under Section 179 of the IRC instead. Using Section 179, you can currently deduct up to $108,000 in long-term assets purchased each year. Because of the size of the Section 179 deduction (which was increased substantially in recent years), many small and medium-sized businesses no longer need to depreciate long-term assets they purchase for their businesses. This enormous change in the tax law could greatly benefit you.

Repairs and Improvements

When you make repairs or improvements to long-term assets, it can be hard to tell if the cost is a capital or an operating expense. The rule is that ordinary repairs and maintenance for long-term assets are operating expenses that can be currently deducted. However, you must treat a repair or replacement as a capital expense if it:

- increases the value of your property
- makes it more useful, or
- lengthens its useful life.

EXAMPLE 1: Doug spends $100 to repair the carburetor on his company car. This is a current expense because the repair doesn't increase the value of his car or lengthen its useful life. The repair merely allows the car to last for a normal time.

EXAMPLE 2: Doug spends $1,500 on a brand-new engine for his car. This is a capital expense because the new engine increases the car's value and useful life.

This rule can be difficult to apply because virtually all repairs increase the value of the property being repaired. A repair becomes a capital improvement when it makes the property *more valuable, long-lived, or useful* than it was before the repair. Individual repairs made as part of a general plan of improvement are also capital expenses.

EXAMPLE: Doug buys an old house and fixes up one of the bedrooms to use as the office for his architecture business. He pays to repaint and replaster the walls and ceilings, repair the floor, put in new wiring, and install an outside door. Ordinarily, plastering, painting, and floor work are repairs. However, because they are part of a general plan to alter the home for business use, they are capital expenses.

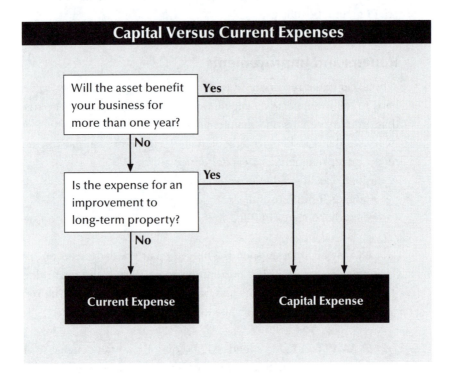

Inventory is not a business expense. This chapter covers the tax treatment of things you buy to use in your business. It does not cover the cost of items you buy or make to sell to others. Such items are called inventory. Inventory is neither a current nor a capital expense. Rather, businesses deduct the cost of inventory as it is sold. (See Chapter 6 for more on inventory).

Section 179 Deductions

If you learn only one section number in the tax code, it should be Section 179. This humble piece of the tax code is one of the greatest tax boons ever for small business owners. Section 179 doesn't increase the total amount you can deduct, but it allows you to get your entire depreciation deduction in one year, rather than taking it a little at a time over the term of an asset's useful life—which can be up to 39 years. This is called first-year expensing or Section 179 expensing. (Expensing is an accounting term that means currently deducting a long-term asset.)

> **EXAMPLE:** In 2007, Ginger buys a $4,000 photocopy machine for her business. Under the regular depreciation rules (using the straight-line depreciation method—see "Depreciation," below), Ginger would have to deduct a portion of the cost each year over its five-year useful life as follows:

Year	Depreciation Deduction
2007	$500
2008	$1,000
2009	$1,000
2010	$1,000
2011	$500

By deducting the copier under Section 179 instead, Ginger can deduct the entire $4,000 expense from her income taxes in 2007. So she gets a $4,000 deduction in 2007 under Section 179, instead of the $500 deduction she gets using depreciation.

Should you take deductions now or later? Because of inflation and the time value of money, it is often better to use Section 179 if you can, to get the largest possible deduction for the current year. There are some circumstances, however, when it may be more advantageous to use depreciation instead. (See "When to Use Depreciation," below.)

Property You Can Deduct

You qualify for the Section 179 deduction only if you buy long-term, tangible personal property that you use in your business more than 50% of the time. Let's look at these requirements in more detail.

Tangible Personal Property

Under Section 179, you can deduct the cost of tangible personal property (new or used) that you buy for your business, if the IRS has determined that the property will last more than one year. Examples of tangible personal property include computers, business equipment and machinery, and office furniture. Although it's not really tangible property, computer software can also be deducted under Section 179. (See "Computer Software," below, for more on deducting software.)

You can't use Section 179 to deduct the cost of:

- land
- permanent structures attached to land, including buildings and their structural components, fences, swimming pools, or paved parking areas
- inventory (see Chapter 6)
- intangible property such as patents, copyrights, and trademarks
- property used outside the United States, or
- air conditioning and heating units.

However, nonpermanent property attached to a nonresidential, commercial building is deductible. For example, refrigerators, grocery store counters, printing presses, testing equipment, and signs are all deductible under Section 179. Structures such as barns and greenhouses that are specifically designed and used for agriculture or horticulture are also deductible, as is livestock (including horses). Special rules apply to cars. (See Chapter 8 for more about deducting car expenses.)

Property Used Primarily (51%) for Business

To deduct the cost of property under Section 179, you must use the property primarily for your business. The deduction is not available for property you use solely for personal purposes or to manage investments or otherwise produce nonbusiness income.

EXAMPLE: Jill bought a computer for $3,000. She used it to play games, manage her checkbook, and surf the Internet for fun. In other words, she used it only for personal purposes. The computer is not deductible under Section 179.

You can take a Section 179 deduction for property you use for both personal and business purposes, as long as you use it for business *more than half of the time.* The amount of your deduction is reduced by the percentage of your personal use. (See "Calculating Your Deduction," below.) You'll need to keep records showing your business use of the property. If you use an item for business less than half the time, you will have to use regular depreciation instead and deduct the cost of the item over several years.

There is another important limitation regarding the business use of property. You must use the property over half the time for business in *the year in which you buy it.* You can't convert property you previously used for personal use to business use and claim a Section 179 deduction for the cost.

EXAMPLE: Kim bought a $2,000 digital camera in 2006 and used it to take family and other personal pictures. In 2008, Kim decides to start her own wedding photography business and uses her digital camera 75% of the time for business. She may not deduct the cost under Section 179 because she didn't use the camera for business until two years after she bought it.

The Section 179 rules also require that you *actually be in business* to take the deduction. Property that you buy before you start your business is not deductible under Section 179. This is one reason why it's a good idea to postpone large purchases until your business is up and running.

EXAMPLE: Andre decides to quit his job as a marketing executive and start a deep sea fishing business. While still employed and before he actually starts his fishing business, he buys and outfits a boat at a cost of $100,000. This amount is not deductible under Section 179 because he had not yet started his new business.

There are other ways to deduct start-up costs. Business start-up expenses not deductible under Section 179 might be deductible under other tax law provisions. See Chapter 3 for information on deducting business start-up expenses.

Property That You Purchase

You can use Section 179 expensing only for property that you purchase—not for leased property or property you inherit or receive as a gift. You also can't use it for property that you buy from a relative or a corporation or an organization that you control. The property you purchase may be used or new.

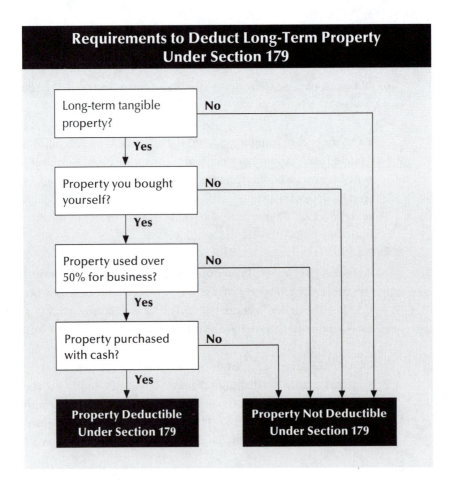

Requirements to Deduct Long-Term Property Under Section 179

- Long-term tangible property? — **No**
- **Yes** → Property you bought yourself? — **No**
- **Yes** → Property used over 50% for business? — **No**
- **Yes** → Property purchased with cash? — **No**
- **Yes** → **Property Deductible Under Section 179**

Property Not Deductible Under Section 179

Calculating Your Deduction

There are several limitations on the amount you can deduct under Section 179 each year. The total you can deduct under Section 179 annually will depend on:

- what you paid for the property
- how much you use the property for business
- how much Section 179 property you buy during the year, and
- your annual business income.

Let's look at each of these factors more closely.

Cost of Property

The amount you can deduct for Section 179 property is initially based on the property's cost. The cost includes the amount you paid for the property, plus sales tax, delivery, and installation charges. It doesn't matter if you pay cash or finance the purchase with a credit card or bank loan. However, if you pay for property with both cash and a trade-in, the value of the trade-in is not deductible under Section 179. You must depreciate the amount of the trade-in.

> **EXAMPLE:** Stuart buys a $10,000 taxi for his taxi fleet. He pays $6,000 cash and is given a $4,000 trade-in for an older taxi that he owns. He may deduct $6,000 of the $10,000 purchase under Section 179; he must depreciate the remaining $4,000.

Percentage of Business Use

If you use Section 179 property solely for business, you can deduct 100% of the cost (subject to the other limitations discussed below). However, if you use property for both business and personal purposes, you must reduce your deduction by the percentage of the time that you use the property for personal purposes.

> **EXAMPLE:** Max buys a $4,000 computer. The year he buys it, he uses it for his consulting business 75% of the time and for personal purposes 25% of the time. He may currently deduct 75% of the computer's cost (or $3,000) under Section 179. The remaining $1,000 is not deductible as a business expense.

You must continue to use property that you deduct under Section 179 for business at least 50% of the time for as many years as it would take to depreciate the item under the normal depreciation rules. For example, computers have a five-year depreciation period. If you deduct a computer's cost under Section 179, you must use the computer at least 50% of the time for business for five years.

If you don't meet these rules, you'll have to report as income part of the deduction you took under Section 179 in the prior year. This is called recapture, which is discussed in more detail below.

Annual Deduction Limit

There is a limit on the total amount of business property expenses that you can deduct each year under Section 179. In 2003, the limit was increased from $24,000 to $100,000 and has been increased each year since then to account for inflation. The Section 179 limit was scheduled to go down to $25,000 in 2008. However, this reduction has been delayed for two years.

Congress could decide to make the higher limit permanent, but at this point no one knows what will happen. If you're planning on buying over $25,000 worth of property for your business in one year and you want to deduct the whole amount under Section 179, your best bet is to make your purchases before 2010.

The annual deduction limit applies to all of your businesses combined, not to each business you own and run.

> **EXAMPLE:** Britney, a highly successful entrepreneur, owns a catering business, a recording studio, and a used car dealership, all as a sole proprietor. Because the Section 179 limit applies to all her businesses together, in 2006 she may expense a total maximum of $108,000 in long-term asset purchases for all three businesses.

You don't have to claim the full amount—it's up to you to decide how much to deduct under Section 179. Whatever amount you don't claim under Section 179 must be depreciated instead. (See "Depreciation," below—depreciation is *not* optional.)

Because Section 179 is intended to help smaller businesses, there is also a limit on the total amount of Section 179 property you can purchase each year. You must reduce your Section 179 deduction by one dollar for every dollar your annual purchases exceed the applicable limit. For 2006 through 2009, the limit is $430,000, plus an amount to be added to account for inflation through 2009. In 2010 and later, the limit is scheduled to go down to $200,000.

> **EXAMPLE:** Acme, Inc. purchases $480,000 in equipment in 2006—$50,000 over the $430,000 total limit. As a result, Acme's $108,000 annual deduction limit is reduced by $50,000, which means that Acme can only deduct $58,000 of its asset purchases under Section 179. It must depreciate the remaining $422,000 over several years.

Year	Section 179 Deduction Limit	Property Value Limit
2006	$108,000	$430,000
2007–2009	$108,000 + annual inflation adjustment	$430,000 + annual inflation adjustment
2010 and later	$25,000	$200,000

The $108,000 Section 179 limit is so high that most small and even medium-sized businesses won't have to worry about ever reaching it. However, if you purchase enough business property in one year to exceed the limit, you can divide the deduction among the items you purchase in any way you want, as long as the total deduction is not more than the Section 179 limit. It's usually best to apply Section 179 to property that has the longest useful life and, therefore, the longest depreciation period. This reduces the total time you will have to wait to get your deductions, which usually works to your financial benefit.

> **EXAMPLE:** In 2006, Acme Printing, LLC, a printing company, buys a substantial amount of equipment, including two new printing presses for $40,000 each, two $15,000 copiers, and a custom computer system for $25,000. This totals $135,000 in business property purchases, $27,000 over the Section 179 limit for 2006. Acme can divide its Section 179 deduction among these items in any way that it wants. Under IRS depreciation rules, the copiers and computer system would

have to be depreciated over five years and the printing presses over seven years. Acme should use Section 179 for the printing presses first ($80,000), and then the remainder ($28,000) for the copiers and computer system. The portion of the cost of the copiers or computers that exceeds the Section 179 limit ($27,000) can be depreciated over five years. This way, Acme avoids having to wait seven years to get its full deduction for the printing presses.

Business Profit Limitation

You can't use Section 179 to deduct more in one year than your total annual business income. Your business income is the total profit you earn from business during the year—whether you have one business or more than one. If you're a sole proprietor, you also add the income you make from your salary, if you have a job in addition to your business. If you're a married sole proprietor and file a joint tax return, you can include your spouse's salary and business income in this total as well. You can't count investment income—for example, interest you earn on your personal savings account—as business income. But you can include interest you earn on your business working capital—for example, interest you earn on your business bank account.

You can't use Section 179 to reduce your taxable income below zero. But you can carry to the next tax year (or any other year in the future) any amount you cannot currently take as a Section 179 deduction.

> **EXAMPLE 1:** In 2007, Amelia earned $5,000 in profit from her engineering consulting business and $10,000 in salary from a part-time job. She spent $17,000 for computer and office equipment. She can use Section 179 to deduct $15,000 of this expense for 2007. She can deduct the remaining $2,000 the following year.

> **EXAMPLE 2:** In 2007, James purchased $100,000 of recording equipment for his fledgling commercial voiceover business but earned only $5,000 from the venture. James's wife, however, earned $75,000 from her job as a college professor. Because James and his wife file a joint return, they may take a Section 179 deduction for up to $80,000 for 2007 ($5,000 + $75,000 = $80,000). Thus, James may

deduct $80,000 of his equipment purchases in 2007 under Section 179 and deduct the remaining $20,000 in a future year.

If you're a partner in a partnership, member of a limited liability company (LLC), or shareholder in an S corporation, the Section 179 limit applies both to the business entity and to each owner personally.

EXAMPLE: Dean, a builder, is a partner in the ABC Partnership and also runs his own part-time home repair business as a sole proprietor. In 2006, ABC purchases $100,000 in construction equipment that it elects to expense under Section 179. Its business income for the year is $120,000, so it can deduct the full $100,000. ABC allocates $50,000 of its purchases and $50,000 of its income to Dean; Dean also purchases $10,000 of equipment for his sole proprietor business that he would like to expense under Section 179 as well. However, Dean's home repair business incurs a $5,000 loss for the year. Dean's total permissible Section 179 deduction for 2006 is $108,000. His total business income for the year is $45,000 ($50,000 from the partnership minus the $5,000 loss from his home repair business). Thus, Dean may only expense $45,000 of the equipment purchases in 2006. He must carry over the remaining $15,000 to deduct in future years.

Date of Purchase

As long as you meet the requirements, you can deduct the cost of Section 179 property up to the limits discussed above, no matter when you place the property in service during the year (that is, when you buy the property and make it available for use in your ongoing business). This differs from regular depreciation rules, by which property bought later in the year may be subject to a smaller deduction for the first year. (See "First-Year Depreciation," below, for more on regular depreciation rules about placing property in service). This is yet another advantage of the Section 179 deduction over regular depreciation.

EXAMPLE: John buys a $5,000 lathe for his machine tool business on January 1, 2007 and $5,000 of office furniture on December 31, 2007. Both purchases are fully deductible under Section 179 in 2007.

Use It or Lose It—Make Your Section 179 Claims

Section 179 deductions are not automatic. You must claim a Section 179 deduction on your tax return by completing IRS Form 4562, Part I, and checking a specific box. If you neglect to do this, you may lose your deduction. If you filed your return for the year without making the election, you can file an amended return within six months after your tax return was due for the year—April 15 plus any extensions you receive. Once this deadline passes, however, you lose your right to a Section 179 deduction forever—you can't file an amended return in a later year to claim the deduction. (See "Tax Reporting and Record Keeping for Section 179 and Depreciation," below.)

Special Rules for Listed Property

The IRS imposes special rules on certain items that can easily be used for personal as well as business purposes. These items, called listed property, include:

- cars and certain other vehicles
- motorcycles, boats, and airplanes
- computers
- cellular phones, and
- any other property generally used for entertainment, recreation, or amusement—for example, VCRs, cameras, stereos, and camcorders.

The IRS fears that taxpayers might use listed property for personal reasons but claim a business deduction for it. For this reason, you're required to document your business use of listed property. You can satisfy this requirement by keeping a logbook showing when and how the property is used. (See Chapter 15 for more on record keeping.)

Exception for Computers

You generally have to document your use of listed property even if you use it 100% for business. However, there is an exception to this rule for computers: If you use a computer or computer peripheral (such as a printer) only for business and keep it at your business location, you need not comply with the record-keeping requirement. This includes computers that you keep at your home office if the office qualifies for the home office deduction. (See Chapter 7 for more on the home office deduction.)

> **EXAMPLE:** John, a freelance writer, works full time in his home office that he uses exclusively for writing. The office is clearly his principal place of business and qualifies for the home office deduction. He buys a $4,000 computer for his office and uses it exclusively for his writing business. He does not have to keep records showing how and when he uses the computer.

This exception does not apply to items other than computers and computer peripheral equipment—for example, it doesn't apply to calculators, copiers, fax machines, or typewriters.

Deducting Listed Property

If you use listed property for business more than 50% of the time, you may deduct its cost just like any other long-term business property. For example, you may deduct the cost in one year using Section 179 or depreciate it over several years under the normal depreciation rules.

However, if you use listed property 50% or less of the time for business, you may not deduct the cost under Section 179 or use accelerated depreciation. Instead, you must use the slowest method of depreciation: straight-line depreciation. (See "Listed Property," below)

Recapture Under Section 179

Recapture is a nasty tax trap an unwary business owner can easily get caught in. It requires you to give back part of a tax deduction that you took in a previous year. You may have to recapture part of a Section 179 tax deduction if, during the property's recovery period, either of the following occurs:

- Your business use of the property drops below 51%.
- You sell the property.

The recovery period is the property's useful life as determined under IRS rules. The IRS has determined the useful life of all types of property that can be depreciated. The useful life of an asset is the time period over which you must depreciate the asset. For personal property that can be expensed under Section 179, the useful life ranges from three years for computer software to seven years for office furniture and business equipment. If you deduct property under Section 179, you must continue to use it in your business at least 51% of the time for its entire useful life—this is the IRS recovery period. For example, if you buy office furniture, you must use it over half of the time for business for at least seven years.

If your business use falls below 51% or you sell the property before the recovery period ends, you become subject to recapture. This means that you have to give back to the IRS all of the accelerated deductions you took under Section 179. You get to keep the amount you would have been entitled to under regular depreciation, but you must include the rest of your Section 179 deduction in your ordinary income for the year.

> **EXAMPLE:** In 2006, Paul purchases office equipment worth $10,000 and deducts the entire amount under Section 179. He uses the property 100% for business during 2006 and 2007, but in 2008 he uses it only 40% for business. The equipment has a seven-year recovery period, so Paul is subject to recapture. He figures the recapture amount as follows.
>
> First, he figures all the annual depreciation he would have been entitled to during 2006 through 2008 had he depreciated the property under the regular depreciation rules:
>
> | | |
> |---|---|
> | 2006 | $1,666 |
> | 2007 | 2,222 |
> | 2008 | 297 ($740.50 x 40% business use) |
> | Total | $4,185 |

He then deducts this amount from the $10,000 Section 179 deduction he claimed in 2006: $10,000 − $4,185 = $5,815.

Thus, Paul's 2008 recapture amount is $5,815. Paul must add $5,815 to his income for 2008. He can continue to depreciate the equipment for the next four years.

You eventually get back through depreciation any recapture amount you must pay. But recapture can spike your tax bill for the year, so it's best to avoid the problem by making sure that you use property you deduct under Section 179 at least 51% for business during its entire recovery period.

You can maximize your Section 179 deduction by keeping your percentage of business use of Section 179 property as high as possible during the year that you buy the property. After the first year, you can reduce your business use—as long as it stays above 50%—and avoid recapture.

> **EXAMPLE:** Paul buys $10,000 of office equipment and uses it 90% for business in 2006. He would have been entitled to currently deduct $9,000 of the cost under Section 179 (90% business use x $10,000 cost = $9,000 deduction). In 2007 and 2008, he uses the equipment for business only 60% of the time. Nevertheless, he need not recapture any of his Section 179 deduction because his business use is still above 50%.

Depreciation

The traditional method of getting back the money you spend on long-term business assets is to deduct the cost a little at a time over several years (exactly how long is determined by the IRS). This process is called depreciation.

Depreciation is a complicated subject. The IRS instruction booklet on the subject (Publication 946, *How to Depreciate Property*) is over 100 pages long. For a comprehensive discussion of depreciation, read Publication 946. In this section, we cover the depreciation basics that all business owners should know.

 Depreciation is not optional. Unlike the Section 179 deduction, depreciation is not optional. You must take a depreciation deduction if you qualify for it. If you fail to take it, the IRS will treat you as if you had taken it. This means that you could be subject to depreciation recapture when you sell the asset—even if you never took a depreciation deduction. This would increase your taxable income by the amount of the deduction you failed to take. (See "Depreciation Recapture," below.) So if you don't expense a depreciable asset under Section 179, be sure to take the proper depreciation deductions for it. If you realize later that you failed to take a depreciation deduction that you should have taken, you may file an amended tax return to claim any deductions that you should have taken in prior years. (See Chapter 16 for information about filing amended returns).

When to Use Depreciation

Do you ever buy more than $100,000 worth of stuff for your business in a year? For most small and many medium-sized businesses, the answer is "no." With the Section 179 deduction at $108,000 plus inflation adjustments (at least through the end of 2009), you may never have to use depreciation.

However, you may need to use depreciation to write off the cost of long-term assets that don't qualify for Section 179 expensing. Also, under some circumstances, it may be better to use depreciation and draw out your deduction over several years instead of getting your deductions all at once under Section 179.

Assets That Don't Qualify Under Section 179

You must meet strict requirements to use Section 179 to currently deduct long-term business property. You will not be able to expense an item under Section 179 if any of the following are true:

- You use the item less than 51% of the time for business.
- It is personal property that you converted to business use.
- It is a structure, such as a building or building component.
- You financed the purchase with a trade-in (the value of the trade-in must be depreciated).
- It is an intangible asset such a patent, copyright, or trademark.
- You bought it from a relative.
- You inherited the property or received it as a gift.
- It is an air conditioning or heating unit.

For any items that fall within one or more of these categories, you will have to use regular depreciation instead of Section 179.

You will also have to use depreciation instead of Section 179 to the extent you exceed the Section 179 annual limit. This limit is $108,000 in 2006; however, it is scheduled to go down to $25,000 in 2010 (unless Congress makes the higher limit permanent). In addition, Section 179 expensing is not available if you spend more than $500,000 in long-term assets in a year during 2005 through 2009, or more than $300,000 in 2010 or later.

Sometimes Depreciation Is Better

Even if you can deduct an asset under Section 179, you may not always want to. There are some circumstances where depreciation is more advantageous than Section 179.

You Expect to Earn More in Future Years

Section 179 expensing lets you take your total deduction up front and in one year, while depreciation requires you to deduct the cost of an asset a little at a time over several years. The slower depreciation method isn't always a bad thing. In some circumstances, you may be better off using depreciation instead of Section 179.

Remember: The value of a deduction depends on your income tax bracket. If you're in the 15% bracket, a $1,000 deduction is worth only $150 of federal income tax savings. If you're in the 28% bracket, it's worth $280. (See Chapter 1 for more on the value of a tax deduction.) If you expect to earn more in future years, it may make sense to spread out your deductions so you save some for later years when you expect to be in a higher tax bracket.

> **EXAMPLE:** Marie, a self-employed consultant, buys a $5,000 computer system for her business in 2006. She elects to depreciate the computer instead of using the Section 179 deduction. That way, she can deduct a portion of the cost from her gross income each year for the next six years. Marie is only in the 15% tax bracket in 2006 but expects to be in the 28% bracket by 2008.

The following chart shows how much more money Marie may deduct by using depreciation to deduct a portion of the computer's cost over six years, instead of taking a Section 179 deduction for the entire cost in the first year. Marie is using the straight-line depreciation method, under which she gets the same deduction every year, except for the first and last.

	Comparison of Deductions: Section 179 and Depreciation		
Year	Marie's Marginal Federal Income Tax Rate	Federal Income Tax Saving Using Section 179 Deduction	Federal Income Tax Savings Using Depreciation Deduction
2006	15%	$750 (15% x $5,000 (total cost))	$ 75 (15% x $500 of total $5,000 cost)
2007	25%	0	250 (25% x $1,000)
2008	28%	0	280 (28% x $1,000)
2009	28%	0	280 (28% x $1,000)
2010	28%	0	280 (28% x $1,000)
2011	28%	0	140 (28% x $500)
Total		$750	$1,305

Of course, money grows in value over time because it earns interest or can otherwise be invested. So it's possible that Marie would be better off using Section 179 and getting $750 all at once, rather than waiting six years to collect a total of $1,305 through depreciation. However, $750 today will be worth more than $1,305 six years from now only if Marie earns at least 10% on her money each year—substantially more than she could get by putting it in the bank.

Your Income Is Too Low

The Section 179 deduction may not exceed your business income. If you're a sole proprietor, this includes your wage income from a job, if any. If you're married and file a joint return, your spouse's income can be included. If your business is making little or no money and you have little or no income from wages or your spouse, you may not be able take a Section 179 deduction for the current year and will have to use it (if possible) in a future year.

In contrast, there is no income limitation on depreciation deductions. You can deduct depreciation from your business income; if this results in a net loss for a year, you can deduct the loss from income taxes you paid in prior years.

> **EXAMPLE:** Marvin made no money from his Internet start-up company in 2007 but incurred $100,000 in expenses for depreciable property. He has no other income for the year, but he earned $100,000 in 2006 from a prior job, on which he paid $25,000 in federal taxes. By depreciating the $100,000 expense, his business ends up with a net loss of $10,000 in 2007. He can file an amended tax return for 2006 and deduct this amount from his income for the year, resulting in a $2,500 tax refund. Had he deducted the $100,000 under Section 179 instead, he would have had to carry forward his $100,000 loss to the next year and use it then or in subsequent years.

You Want to Show a Profit

You may also prefer to use depreciation instead of Section 179 if you want to puff up your business income for the year. This can help you get a bank loan or help your business show a profit instead of incurring a loss—and, therefore, avoid running afoul of the hobby loss limitations. (See Chapter 2 for more on the hobby loss rule.)

> **EXAMPLE:** Larry began his home design business in 2002. His business expenses exceeded his income in 2003 and 2004. He earned a small profit in 2005 and 2006. In 2007, he purchased $10,000 worth of long-term property. If he expenses the whole amount under Section 179, his business income for the year will be reduced by $10,000, which will cause him to incur a $2,000 loss for the year. Larry doesn't want to have another losing year for his

business, because he will have lost money in three of the first five years he was in business. This could cause the IRS to determine that his venture is a hobby, not a real business. So Larry decides to depreciate his 2007 asset purchases. This way, he only gets a $1,000 deduction in 2007, instead of the full $10,000. This enables his business to show a profit for the year. He'll be able to deduct the remaining $9,000 over the next five years.

Some Depreciation Basics

Depreciation is a tax deduction for the decline in value of long-term property over time due to wear and tear, deterioration, or obsolescence. Unless the Section 179 deduction applies, depreciation is the only way you can deduct the cost of long-term property—that is, property that lasts for more than one year, such as buildings, computers, equipment, machinery, patents, trademarks, copyrights, and furniture. You can also depreciate the cost of major repairs or improvements that increase the value or extend the life of an asset—for example, the cost of a major upgrade to make your computer run faster. (See "Repairs and Improvements," above.)

Property You Cannot Depreciate

You cannot depreciate:

- property that doesn't wear out, including land (whether un-developed or with structures on it), stocks, securities, or gold,
- property you use solely for personal purposes
- property purchased and disposed of in the same year
- inventory, or
- collectibles that appreciate in value over time, such as antiques and artwork.

If you use nondepreciable property in your business, you get no tax deduction while you own it. But if you sell it, you get to deduct its tax basis (see below) from the sales price to calculate your taxable profit. If the basis exceeds the sales price, you'll have a deductible loss on the property. If the price exceeds the basis, you'll have a taxable gain.

You also may not depreciate property that you do not own. For example, you get no depreciation deduction for property you lease. The person who owns the property—the lessor—gets to depreciate it. (However, you may deduct your lease payments as current business expenses—see Chapter 4.) Leasing may be preferable to buying and depreciating equipment that wears out or becomes obsolete quickly.

Harrah's Craps Out in Tax Court

Harrah's Club in Reno, Nevada, has one of the world's greatest collections of antique automobiles. Harrah's tried to depreciate the cost of restoring 94 of its vintage vehicles. Both the IRS and the tax court held that the cars were not depreciable because they didn't wear out or become obsolete. Noting that the vehicles were kept in a humidity-controlled environment and needed remarkably little repair or maintenance beyond occasional mending of a crack in a wood part, the court reasoned that, although the vehicles would not last forever, no definite time limit could be put on their use as museum objects. (*Harrah's Club. v. U.S.*, 661 F.2d 203 (9th Cir. 1981).)

When Depreciation Begins and Ends

You begin to depreciate your property when it is placed in service—that is, when it's ready and available for use in your business. As long as it is available for use, you don't have to actually use the property for business during the year to take depreciation.

> **EXAMPLE:** Tom bought a planter for his farm business late in 2007, after the harvest was over. Tom may take a depreciation deduction for the planter for 2007, even though he didn't actually use it, because it was ready and available for use.

You stop depreciating property either when you have fully recovered your cost or other basis or when you retire it from service, whichever occurs first. Property is retired from service when you stop using it for business, sell it, destroy it, or otherwise dispose of it.

EXAMPLE: Tom depreciates the $10,000 cost of his planter a portion at a time over seven years. At the end of that time, he has recovered his $10,000 basis and depreciation ends. He is free to continue using the planter, but he can't get any more depreciation deductions for it.

You must actually be in business to take depreciation deductions. In other words, you cannot start depreciating an asset until your business is up and running. This is one important reason why it is a good idea to postpone large property purchases until your business has begun. (See Chapter 3 for a detailed discussion of tax deductions for business start-up expenses.)

EXAMPLE: In 2007, Julia buys $10,000 worth of kitchen equipment for a new restaurant she plans to open. However, the restaurant does not open its doors for business until 2008. Julia may not take a depreciation deduction for the equipment in 2007, but she may in 2008 and later years.

Calculating Depreciation

How to calculate depreciation is one of the more confusing and tedious aspects of the tax law. In the past, most people had accountants perform the calculations for them. Today, you can use tax preparation software to calculate your depreciation deductions and complete the required IRS forms.

Although a tax preparation program can do the calculations for you, you still need to make some basic decisions about how you will depreciate your property. A computer can't do this for you. To make the best decisions, you'll need to have a basic understanding of how depreciation works.

In a nutshell, your depreciation deduction is determined by the following factors:

- your basis in the property (usually the asset's cost)
- the depreciation period
- the depreciation convention that determines how much depreciation you get in the first year, and
- the depreciation method.

Let's look at each of these factors.

Figuring Out Your Tax Basis

Depreciation allows you to deduct your total investment in a long-term asset you buy for your business over its useful life. In tax lingo, your investment is called your basis or tax basis. Basis is a word you'll hear over and over again when the subject of depreciation comes up. Don't let it confuse you; it just means the amount of your total investment in the property.

Usually, your basis in depreciable property is whatever you paid for it. This includes not only the purchase price, but also sales tax, delivery charges, installation, and testing fees, if any. You may depreciate the entire cost, no matter how you paid for the property—in cash, on a credit card, or with a bank loan.

> **EXAMPLE:** Victor, an inventor, buys an electron microscope for his business. He pays $9,000 cash, $500 in sales tax, and $500 for delivery and installation. His basis in the property is $10,000.

Adjusted Basis

Your basis in property is not fixed. It changes over time to reflect the true amount of your investment. Each year, you must deduct from the property's basis the amount of depreciation allowed for the property— this is true regardless of whether you actually claimed any depreciation on your tax return. This new basis is called the adjusted basis, because it reflects adjustments from your starting basis. Eventually, your adjusted basis will be reduced to zero and you can no longer depreciate the property.

> **EXAMPLE:** Victor (from the above example) bought the microscope in 2007. His starting basis was $10,000. He depreciates the cost over the next six years using the double declining balance method. (See "Depreciation Methods," below.) The following chart shows his adjusted basis for each year.

Year	Depreciation Deduction	Adjusted Basis
2006	$2,000	$8,000
2007	3,200	4,800
2008	1,920	2,880
2009	1,152	1,728
2010	1,152	576
2011	576	0

Your starting basis in property will also be reduced by:
- Section 179 deductions you take for the property
- casualty and theft losses, and
- manufacturer or seller rebates you receive.

If you sell depreciable property, your gain or loss on the sale is determined by subtracting its adjusted basis from the sales price.

> **EXAMPLE:** If Victor sells his microscope for $7,500 in 2008 when its adjusted basis is $2,880, his taxable gain on the sale will be $4,620 ($7,500 – $2,880 = $4,620). If he sells the microscope for $1,000 instead, he will incur a $1,880 loss that he can deduct from his business income.

If you abandon business property instead of selling it, you may deduct its adjusted basis as a business loss. You abandon property when you voluntarily and permanently give up possessing and using it with the intention of ending your ownership and without passing it on to anyone else. Loss from abandonment of business property is deductible as an ordinary loss, even if the property is a capital asset.

> **EXAMPLE:** Victor's microscope breaks down three years after he buys it. He decides it's not worth the money to fix it and throws it away. He has abandoned it and may deduct the microscope's adjusted basis as a business loss.

For more information on the tax implications of selling or otherwise disposing of business property, refer to IRS Publication 544, *Sales and Other Dispositions of Assets.*

Property Not Bought Entirely With Cash

Of course, not all business property is bought with cash. You may pay for it wholly or partly with a trade-in, inherit it, receive it as a gift, or convert personal property to property used for your business. In these cases, basis is not determined according to the property's cost.

If you buy property with a trade-in, your starting basis is equal to the adjusted basis in the trade-in property, plus any cash you pay for the property. Trading in old business property for new property is a great tax strategy. When you sell business property, you have to pay taxes on any gain you receive. If you use old property for a trade-in, you defer any tax on the gain until you sell the newly acquired property.

> **EXAMPLE:** Phil, an independent trucker, buys a new truck. He trades in the truck he already owns, which has a $50,000 basis, and pays $30,000 cash. His starting basis in the new truck is $80,000. This is true even though the sticker price on the truck is only $75,000. Had he sold his old truck for a $5,000 profit, he would have had to pay tax on the amount.

If you convert personal property to business use, your starting basis is equal the lesser of the property's fair market value or adjusted depreciable basis *when you started using it for business.* The fair market value will be lower than the property's adjusted basis unless it's gone up in value since you bought it.

> **EXAMPLE:** In 2007, Miranda decides to become a professional photographer and converts a camera she bought two years earlier to business use. She bought the camera for $1,000 in 2005, which is its adjusted basis when she started using it for business. However, the fair market value of the camera in 2007 is $400, so this is her starting basis.

How do you determine your property's fair market value? By figuring out how much someone would be willing to pay for it. Look at classified ads and listings for similar property on eBay, or call dealers in the type of property involved. If you think the property is extremely valuable, get an appraisal from an expert. Keep records of how you figured out the property's value.

It's not likely that most personal property that you convert to business use will be worth much. You can't claim inflated values for old property just to take depreciation deductions.

> **EXAMPLE:** Kunz, the owner of a cement company, bought out a competitor for $60,000. Included in the purchase were 19 old trucks and cement mixers. Kunz claimed on his tax return that these were worth $32,900 and used this amount as his tax basis to figure out his depreciation deduction. The IRS found that the value Kunz assigned the equipment was "absurd" and "grossly excessive." In reality, the equipment was so old that it had no substantial value except as scrap or junk. This was shown by the fact that Kunz had resold one of the mixers for only $25. The IRS concluded that the items were worth only $2,700. (*Kunz v. Commissioner*, 333 F.2d 556 (6th Cir. 1964), affg TC Memo 1962-276.)

The starting basis of inherited property is its fair market value on the day the owner died. Your starting basis in gifted property is its fair market value at the time of the gift.

Mixed-Use Property

You may take a depreciation deduction for property you use for both business and personal purposes. However, your depreciable basis in the property will be reduced by the percentage of your personal use. This will, of course, reduce the amount of your depreciation deduction.

> **EXAMPLE:** Assume that Miranda in the above example uses her $400 camera 75% of the time for business and 25% for personal use. Her depreciable basis in the camera is reduced by 25%, so her basis is only $300 instead of $400 (75% x $400 = $300). Miranda can depreciate only $300 over the asset's depreciation period.

You can take a depreciation deduction even if you use an asset only 1% of the time for business. This is one advantage of depreciation over the Section 179 deduction, which is only available for property you use more than 50% of the time for business.

If you use property for both business and personal purposes, you must keep a diary or log with the dates, times, and reasons the property was used to distinguish business from personal use. Moreover, special rules apply if you use cars and other types of listed property less than 50% of the time for business.

Depreciation Period

The depreciation period (also called the recovery period) is the time over which you must take your depreciation deductions for an asset. The tax code has assigned depreciation periods to all types of business assets, ranging from three to 39 years. These periods are somewhat arbitrary. However, property that can be expected to last a long time generally gets a longer recovery period than property that has a short life—for example, nonresidential real property has a 39-year recovery period, while software has only a three-year period. Most of the property that you buy for your business will probably have a five- or seven-year depreciation period.

The major depreciation periods are listed below. These periods are also called recovery classes, and all property that comes within a period is said to belong to that class. For example, computers have a five-year depreciation period and thus fall within the five-year class, along with automobiles and office equipment.

First-Year Depreciation

Sid and Sam are identical twins who have competing horse breeding businesses. Sid buys a horse on January 2, 2007 and Sam buys one on December 30, 2007. How much depreciation should each be allowed for the first year they own their horses? Should Sid get a full year and Sam just a day?

The IRS has established certain rules (called "conventions") that govern how many months of depreciation you can take for the first year that you own an asset.

Depreciation Periods	
Depreciation Period	**Type of Property**
3 years	Computer software
	Tractor units for over-the-road use
	Any race horse over 2 years old when placed in service
	Any other horse over 12 years old when placed in service
5 years	Automobiles, taxis, buses, and trucks
	Computers and peripheral equipment
	Office machinery (such as typewriters, calculators, and copiers)
	Any property used in research and experimentation
	Breeding cattle and dairy cattle
	Appliances, carpets, furniture, and so on used in a residential rental real estate activity
7 years	Office furniture and fixtures (such as desks, files, and safes)
	Agricultural machinery and equipment
	Any property that does not have a class life and has not been designated by law as being in any other class
10 years	Vessels, barges, tugs, and similar water transportation equipment
	Any single-purpose agricultural or horticultural structure
	Any tree or vine bearing fruits or nuts
15 years	Improvements made directly to land or added to it (such as shrubbery, fences, roads, and bridges)
	Interior improvements to leased nonresidential property and certain restaurant property placed in service during October 22, 2004 through December 31, 2005
	Any retail motor fuels outlet, such as a convenience store
20 years	Farm buildings (other than single-purpose agricultural or horticultural structures)
27.5 years	Residential rental property—for example, an apartment building
39 years	Nonresidential real property, such as a home office, office building, store, or warehouse

Half-Year Convention

The basic rule is that, no matter what month and day of the year you buy an asset, you treat it as being placed in service on July 1—the midpoint of the year. This means that you get one-half year of depreciation for the first year that you own an asset.

> **EXAMPLE:** If Sam buys one horse in January, one in March, and one in December, he treats them all as having been placed in service on July 1.

Midquarter Convention

You are not allowed to use the half-year convention if more than 40% of the long-term personal property that you buy during the year is placed in service during the last three months of the year. The 40% figure is determined by adding together the basis of all the depreciable property you bought during the year and comparing that with the basis of all of the property you bought during the fourth quarter only.

If you exceed the 40% ceiling, you must use the mid-quarter convention. You group all the property that you purchased during the year by the quarter it was bought and treat it as being placed in service at the midpoint of that quarter. (A quarter is a three-month period: The first quarter is January through March; the second quarter is April through June; the third quarter is July through September; and the fourth quarter is October through December.)

> **EXAMPLE:** Sam buys one horse in January, one in October, and one in December. Each horse costs $25,000, so the basis for all the horses he bought during the year is $75,000. He bought $50,000 of this amount during the fourth quarter, so more than 40% of his purchases were made in the fourth quarter of the year. Sam must use the mid-quarter convention. He must treat the first horse he bought as being placed in service on February 15—the midpoint of the first quarter. The second and last horses must be treated as being placed in service on November 15—the midpoint of the fourth quarter.

As a general rule, it's best to avoid having to use the midquarter convention. To do this, you need to buy more than 60% of your total depreciable assets before September 30 of the year. Assets you currently deduct using Section 179 do not count toward the 40% limitation, so you can avoid the midquarter convention by using Section 179 to deduct most or all of your purchases in the last three months of the year.

Depreciation Methods

There are several ways to calculate depreciation. However, most tangible property is depreciated using the Modified Accelerated Cost Recovery System, or MACRS. (A slightly different system, called ADS, applies to certain listed property (see "Listed Property," below), property used outside the United States, and certain farm property and imported property.)

You can ordinarily use three different methods to calculate the depreciation deduction under MACRS: straight-line or one of two accelerated depreciation methods. Once you choose your method, you're stuck with it for the entire life of the asset.

In addition, you must use the same method for all property of the same class that you purchase during the year. For example, if you use the straight-line method to depreciate a computer, you must use that method to depreciate all other property in the same class as computers. Computers fall within the five-year class, so you must use the straight-line method for all other five-year property you buy during the year, such as office equipment.

Straight-Line Method

The straight-line method requires you to deduct an equal amount each year over the useful life of an asset. However, if the midyear convention applies, you deduct only a half-year's worth of depreciation in the first year. You make up for this by adding an extra one-half year of depreciation at the end. You can use the straight-line method to depreciate any type of depreciable property.

> **EXAMPLE:** Sally buys a $1,000 printer-fax-copy machine for her business in 2006. It has a useful life of five years. (See the chart above.) She bought more than 60% of her depreciable property for the year before September 30, so she can use the midyear convention. Using the straight-line method, she can depreciate the asset over six years. Her annual depreciation deductions are as follows:

2006	$ 100
2007	200
2008	200
2009	200
2010	200
2011	100
Total	$1,000

If the midquarter convention applies, you don't get one-half year's worth of depreciation the first year. Instead, your first year depreciation amount depends on the month of the year when you bought the property. For example, if Sally bought her machine in September, she would only get $75 deprecation in 2006, $200 in 2007 through 2010, and then $125 in 2011. If she bought it in December, she would get $25 in 2006 and $175 in 2011. If she bought it in January, she would get $175 in 2004 and $25 in 2011.

Accelerated Depreciation Methods

There is nothing wrong with straight-line depreciation, but the tax law provides an alternative that most businesses prefer: accelerated depreciation. As the name implies, this method provides faster depreciation than the straight-line method. It does not increase your total depreciation deduction, but it permits you to take larger deductions in the first few years after you buy an asset. You make up for this by taking smaller deductions in later years.

The fastest and most commonly used form of accelerated depreciation is the double declining balance method. This is a confusing name, but all it means is that you get double the deduction that you would get for the first full year under the straight-line method. You then get less in later years. However, in later years, you may switch to the straight-line method (which will give you a larger deduction). This is built into the IRS depreciation tables. This method may be used to depreciate all property within the three-, five-, seven-, and ten-year classes, excluding farm property. This covers virtually all the tangible personal property you buy for your business.

The following table prepared by the IRS shows you the percentage of the cost of an asset that you may deduct each year using the double declining balance method.

200% Declining Balance Depreciation Method
Convention: Half-year

Year	If the recovery period is:					
	3-year	5-year	7-year	10-year	15-year	20-year
1	33.33%	20.00%	14.29%	10.00%	5.00%	3.750%
2	44.45%	32.00%	24.49%	18.00%	9.50%	7.219%
3	14.81%	19.20%	17.49%	14.40%	8.55%	6.677%
4	7.41%	11.52%	12.49%	11.52%	7.70%	6.177%
5		11.52%	8.93%	9.22%	6.93%	5.713%
6		5.76%	8.92%	7.37%	6.23%	5.285%
7			8.93%	6.55%	5.90%	4.888%
8			4.46%	6.55%	5.90%	4.522%
9				6.56%	5.91%	4.462%
10				6.55%	5.90%	4.461%
11				3.28%	5.91%	4.462%
12					5.90%	4.461%
13					5.91%	4.462%
14					5.90%	4.461%
15					5.91%	4.462%
16					2.95%	4.461%
17						4.462%
18						4.461%
19						4.462%
20						4.461%
21						2.231%

EXAMPLE: Sally decides to use the double declining balance method to depreciate her $1,000 printer-fax-copier machine. Her annual depreciation deductions are as follows:

2006	$ 200.00
2007	320.00
2008	192.00
2009	115.20
2010	115.20
2011	57.60
Total	$1,000.00

By using this method, she gets a $200 deduction in 2006, instead of the $100 deduction she'd get using straight-line depreciation. But starting in 2008, she'll get smaller deductions than she would using the straight-line method. An alternative to the double declining method is the 150% declining balance method. This method gives you one and one-half times the deduction in the first year that you would otherwise get using the straight-line method. The 150% method may be used for three-, five-, seven-, ten-, 15-, and 20-year personal property, including farm property.

The following table prepared by the IRS shows you the percentage of the cost of an asset you may deduct each year using the 150% declining balance method.

150% Declining Balance Depreciation Method
Convention: Half-year

| Year | If the recovery period is: | | | | | | |
	3-year	5-year	7-year	10-year	12-year	15-year	20-year
1	25.00%	15.00%	10.71%	7.50%	6.25%	5.00%	3.750%
2	37.50%	25.50%	19.13%	13.88%	11.72%	9.50%	7.219%
3	25.00%	17.85%	15.03%	11.79%	10.25%	8.55%	6.677%
4	12.50%	16.66%	12.25%	10.02%	8.97%	7.70%	6.177%
5		16.66%	12.25%	8.74%	7.85%	6.93%	5.713%
6		8.33%	12.25%	8.74%	7.33%	6.23%	5.285%
7			12.25%	8.74%	7.33%	5.90%	4.888%
8			6.13%	8.74%	7.33%	5.90%	4.522%
9				8.74%	7.33%	5.91%	4.462%
10				4.37%	7.32%	5.90%	4.461%
11					7.33%	5.91%	4.462%
12					3.66%	5.90%	4.461%
13						5.91%	4.462%
14						5.90%	4.461%
15						5.91%	4.462%
16						2.95%	4.461%
17							4.462%
18							4.461%

EXAMPLE: Sally decides to use the 150% declining balance method to depreciate her printer-fax-copier. This gives her a smaller deduction in the first two years than the double declining balance method, but larger deductions in later years.

2006	$ 150.00
2007	250.50
2008	178.50
2009	166.60
2010	166.60
2011	83.30
Total	$1,000.00

Using accelerated depreciation is not necessarily a good idea if you expect your income to go up in future years. There are also some restrictions on when you can use accelerated depreciation. For example, you can't use it for cars, computers, and certain other property that you use for business less than 50% of the time. (See "Listed Property," below.)

Depreciation Tables

Figuring out your annual depreciation deduction might seem to require some complicated math, but actually it's not that difficult. Of course, if you use a tax preparation computer program, it will do the math for you. However, if you want to do it yourself, you can use depreciation tables prepared by the IRS. These tables factor in the depreciation convention and method. They are all available in IRS Publication 946, *How to Depreciate Property*.

EXAMPLE: In 2006, Joe buys a $9,600 lathe for his machinist business. He wants to depreciate it using the double declining balance method so he can get the largest possible deduction during the first year. He uses the property 100% for business, and the half-year convention applies because he didn't buy more than 40% of his business property during the last three months of 2006. To figure his depreciation, he can use the applicable IRS depreciation table from Publication 946 ("200% Declining Balance Depreciation Method"), which is reprinted above.

You can see from the table that for five-year property (like the lathe), you get 20% of your total depreciation deduction in the first year. To figure the deduction for the lathe, you multiply $9,600 by 20%, resulting in a $1,920 deduction in 2006. In 2007, the deduction will be $3,072 (32% x $9,600 = $3,072). For 2006, the deduction is smaller than for 2007 because of the midyear convention—that is, you only get half of the first year's depreciation because the property is assumed to have been purchased on July 1. This is factored into the table.

Publication 946 contains 18 different depreciation tables—one for each type of depreciation you can take. These are all included in Appendix A of Publication 946.

Listed Property

The IRS imposes special rules on listed property—items that can easily be used for personal as well as business purposes. (See "Special Rules for Listed Property," above.) If you use listed property for business more than 50% of the time, you may deduct its cost just like any other long-term business property (under Section 179, the normal depreciation rules).

However, if you use listed property 50% or less of the time for business, you may not deduct the cost under Section 179 or use accelerated depreciation. Instead, you must use the slowest method of depreciation: straight-line depreciation. In addition, you are not allowed to use the normal depreciation periods allowed under the MACRS depreciation system. Instead, you must use the depreciation periods provided for by the Alternative Depreciation System (ADS for short). These are generally longer than the ordinary MACRS periods. However, you may still depreciate cars, trucks, and computers over five years. The main ADS depreciation periods for listed property are provided in the following chart.

ADS Depreciation Periods	
Property	**Depreciation Period**
Cars and light trucks	5 years
Computers and peripheral equipment	5 years
Communication equipment	10 years
Personal property with no class life	12 years

If you start out using accelerated depreciation and/or bonus depreciation and in a later year your business use drops to 50% or less, you have to switch to the straight-line method and ADS period for that year and subsequent years. In addition, you are subject to depreciation recapture for the prior years—that is, you must calculate how much more depreciation you got in the prior years by using accelerated depreciation and/or bonus depreciation and count that amount as ordinary taxable income for the current year. This will, of course, increase your tax bill for the year.

Computer Software

Most businesses buy computer software; some also create it themselves. The tax law favors the latter group.

Software You Buy

The software you buy comes in two basic types for tax purposes: software that comes already installed on a computer that you buy and software you purchase separately and install yourself (often called "off-the-shelf" software).

Software that comes with a computer you buy and is included in the price—for example, your operating system—is depreciated as part of the computer, unless you're billed separately for the software.

Off-the-shelf software must be depreciated over three years using the straight-line method.

In the past, Section 179 expensing was not available for computer software, because it is intangible property. However, Congress temporarily changed the law in 2003 to permit off-the-shelf software to be currently deducted under Section 179. However, this exception applies only to software placed in service from January 1, 2003 through December 31,

2009. Starting in 2010, Section 179 will once again be prohibited for off-the-shelf software (unless, of course, the law is changed again).

If you acquire software that is not off-the-shelf software by buying another business or its assets, the rules discussed above don't apply. This software must be depreciated over 15 years using the straight-line method; this type of depreciation is called amortization. (IRC § 197.)

Software You Create

If, instead of buying off-the-shelf software, you create it yourself, you can currently deduct the cost under Section 174 of the Internal Revenue Code. This section allows deductions for research and experimentation expenses incurred in developing an invention, patent, process, prototype, formula, technique, or similar product.

You may currently deduct the costs under Section 174 whether the software is developed for your own use or to sell or license to others. (Rev. Proc. 2000-50.) For a detailed discussion of Section 174, see *What Every Inventor Needs to Know About Business & Taxes*, by Stephen Fishman (Nolo).

Real Property

Land cannot be depreciated because it never wears out. However, this doesn't mean you don't get a tax deduction for land. When you sell it, you may deduct the cost of the land from the sale price to determine your taxable gain, if any. The cost of clearing, grading, landscaping, or demolishing buildings on land is not depreciable. It is added to the tax basis of the land—that is, to its cost—and subtracted from the money you get when you sell the land.

Unlike land, buildings do wear out over time and therefore may be depreciated. This means that when you buy property with buildings on it, you must separate out the cost of the buildings from the total cost of the property to calculate your depreciation.

As you might expect, the depreciation periods for buildings are quite long (after all, buildings usually last a long time). The depreciation period for nonresidential buildings placed in service after May 12, 1993 is 39 years. Nonresidential buildings include office buildings, stores, workshops, and factories. Residential real property—an apartment building, for example—is depreciated over 27.5 years. Different periods apply to property purchased before 1993. For detailed guidance on how to depreciate residential real property, refer to *Every Landlord's Tax Deduction Guide*, by Stephen Fishman (Nolo).

You must use the straight-line method to depreciate real property. This means you'll only be able to deduct a small fraction of its value each year—1/39th of its value each year if the 39-year period applies.

If you have an office or other workplace you use solely for your business in your home, you are entitled to depreciate the business portion of the home. For example, if you use 10% of your home for your business, you may depreciate 10% of its cost (excluding the cost of the land). In the unlikely event your home has gone down in value since you bought it, you must use its fair market value on the date you began using your home office as your tax basis. You depreciate a home office over 39 years—the term used for nonresidential property. A home office is non-residential property because you don't live in it.

Intangible Assets

Tangible things like equipment and computers aren't the only business assets that wear out or get used up. Intangible assets can also get used up or become obsolete. Intangible assets are things you can't see or touch. They include intellectual property—patents, copyrights, trade secrets, and trademarks—and business goodwill.

The cost of intangible assets that get used up may be deducted over the useful life of the asset. This process is called amortization, but it is the same as straight-line depreciation. You deduct an equal amount of the cost of the asset each year over its useful life.

If you buy an intangible asset from someone else, you may deduct its cost over its useful life. Except for trademarks, which are amortized over 15 years, the IRS has not established any set time periods for the useful lives of intangible assets. The taxpayer determines the useful life, subject to review by the IRS. The useful life of an invention or copyright for tax purposes can be complex to determine: It could be the entire legal duration of the copyright or patent (at least 70 years for copyrights, and up to 20 years for patents) or a shorter time if the asset will become valueless or obsolete more quickly.

However, patents and copyrights that you obtain through the purchase of another business or its assets are depreciated over 15 years using the straight-line method. (IRC § 197.)

Generally, if you create an intangible asset (such as an invention or copyrighted work of authorship like a book or film) yourself, you may currently deduct the cost. Any costs that you can't currently deduct may be amortized as described above.

Amortization can be tricky. This is a complex area of taxation. Consult with a knowledgeable tax pro if you need to amortize an intangible asset.

For a detailed discussion of the tax deductions involved in creating inventions, see *What Every Inventor Needs to Know About Business & Taxes*, by Stephen Fishman (Nolo).

Natural Resources

You can also take depreciation deductions for oil and gas wells, coal deposits, timber, and other natural resources that get used up by mining, quarrying, drilling, or felling. This form of depreciation is called depletion. Anyone who owns an economic interest in these resources is entitled to a depletion deduction. You don't have to own the land containing a natural resource to have an economic interest. You just need to have a legal interest in the resource and the right to receive income from its exploitation. For example, people who lease oil wells are entitled to a depletion deduction.

Depletion is a complex and specialized form of depreciation. If you own natural resources, you should seek an accountant's help to figure out your depletion deduction.

Depreciation Recapture

To currently deduct long-term property under Section 179 or depreciate listed property using accelerated depreciation, you must use the property for your business at least 51% of the time. If you stop using the property at least 51% of the time for business, you'll have to give back part of the

Section 179 or accelerated depreciation deductions you received. This is called "recapture" because the IRS is getting back—recapturing—part of your deduction. (See "Recapture Under Section 179," above, for more on recapture.)

Recapture is required only for listed property (personal use property) when your business use falls below 51% and for any property for which you took a Section 179 deduction. It is not required for nonlisted property for which you took no Section 179 deduction. For example, it is not required for a building or factory machine.

Recapture may be triggered when you sell any long-term, nonlisted asset for a gain—that is, for more than your adjusted basis.

> **EXAMPLE:** Sam buys a lathe for his machine shop for $5,000 in 2006. By 2008, he has taken $3,470 in depreciation deductions, leaving an adjusted basis of $1,530. He resells the lathe in 2008 for $2,500. This gives Sam a gain of $970. This $970 gain is taxable as ordinary income.

You can't avoid recapture by not taking a Section 179 or depreciation deduction to which you were entitled. The IRS will treat you as though you took the deduction for recapture purposes, even if you really didn't.

> **EXAMPLE:** If Sam fails to depreciate his lathe and then sells it in 2008 for $2,500, the IRS will figure that his adjusted basis is $1,530, because he could have taken $3,470 in depreciation for it. So, he still has a taxable gain of $970.

Tax Reporting and Record Keeping for Section 179 and Depreciation

Depreciation and Section 179 deductions are reported on IRS Form 4562, *Depreciation and Amortization*. If you have more than one business for which you're claiming depreciation, you must use a separate Form 4562 for each business. If you're a sole proprietor, you carry over the amount of your depreciation and Section 179 deductions to your Schedule C and subtract them from your gross business income along with your other business expenses.

Form 4562 is one of the most complex and confusing IRS forms. If you want to complete it yourself, do yourself a favor and use a tax preparation program.

You need to keep accurate records for each asset you depreciate or expense under Section 179, showing:

- a description of the asset
- when and how you purchased the property
- the date it was placed in service
- its original cost
- the percentage of time you use it for business
- whether and how much you deducted under Section 179 and/or bonus depreciation
- the amount of depreciation you took for the asset in prior years, if any
- its depreciable basis
- the depreciation method used
- the length of the depreciation period, and
- the amount of depreciation you deducted for the year.

If you use tax preparation software, it should create a worksheet containing this information. Be sure to check these carefully and save them. You can also use an accounting program such as *QuickBooks* to keep track of your depreciating assets. Simple checkbook programs like *Quicken* and *MSMoney* are not designed to keep track of depreciation. You may also use a spreadsheet program to create your own depreciation worksheet. Spreadsheet templates are available for this purpose. Of course, you can also do the job by hand. The Instructions to IRS Form 4562 contain a worksheet you can use. Here's an example of a filled-out worksheet prepared by the IRS.

Depreciation Worksheet

Description of Property	Date Placed in Service	Cost or Other Basics	Business/Investment Use Percentage	Section 179 Deduction and Special Allowance	Depreciation in Prior Years	Basis for Depreciation	Method/Convention	Recovery Period	Rate or Table Percentage	Depreciation Deduction
Used Equipment —Transmission Jack	1-3	3,000	100%	—	—	3,000	200 DB/HY	7	14.29%	$ 429
Used Pickup Truck	1-3	8,000	100%	—	—	8,000	200 DB/HY	5	20%	1,600
Used Heavy Duty Tow Truck	1-3	30,000	100%	—	—		200 DB/HY	5	20%	6,000
Used Equipment —Engine Hoist	1-3	4,000	100%	—	—	4,000	200 DB/HY	7	14.29%	572
										$8,601

For listed property, you'll also have to keep records showing how much of the time you use it for business and personal uses. You should also keep proof of the amount you paid for the asset: receipts, canceled checks, and purchase documents. You need not file these records with your tax return, but you must have them available to back up your deductions if you're audited.

Leasing Long-Term Assets

When you're acquiring a long-term asset for your business, you should consider whether it makes more sense to lease the item rather than purchase it. Almost everything a business needs can be leased—computers, office furniture, equipment. And leasing can be an attractive alternative to buying. However, it's important to understand the tax consequences of leasing when making your decision.

Leasing Versus Purchasing

So which is better, leasing or buying? It depends. Leasing equipment and other long-term assets can be a better option for small business owners who have limited capital or who need equipment that must be upgraded every few years. Purchasing equipment can be a better option for businesses with ample capital or for equipment that has a long usable life. Each business's situation is unique and the decision to buy or lease must be made on a case-by-case basis. The following chart summarizes the major tax and nontax differences between leasing and buying equipment.

	Leasing	Buying
Tax Treatment	Lease payments are a currently deductible business operating expense. No depreciation or Section 179 deductions.	Up to $108,000 in equipment purchases can be deducted in one year under Section 179 (if requirements satisfied). Otherwise, cost is depreciated over several years (usually 5 to 7). Interest on loans to buy equipment is currently deductible.
Initial Cash Outlay	Small. No down payment required. Deposit ordinarily required.	Large. At least a 20% down payment usually required. Bank loan may be required to finance the remaining cost.
Ownership	You own nothing at end of lease term.	You own the equipment.
Costs of Equipment Obsolescence	Borne by lessor because it owns equipment. Lessee may lease new equipment when lease expires.	Borne by buyer because buyer owns equipment, which may have little resale value.

Before deciding whether to purchase or lease an expensive item, it's a good idea to determine the total actual costs of each option. This depends on many factors, including:

- the cost of the lease
- the purchase price for the item

- the item's useful life
- the interest rate on a loan to purchase the item
- the item's "residual value"—how much it would be worth at the end of the lease term
- whether you will purchase the item at the end of the lease and how much this would cost
- how much it would cost to dispose of the item
- your income tax bracket
- whether the item qualifies for one-year Section 179 expensing or must be depreciated, and
- if the item must be depreciated, the length of the depreciation period.

There are several lease versus buy calculators on the Internet that you can use to compare the costs of leasing versus buying:

- www.lease-vs-buy.com
- www.chooseleasing.org

Commercial software and computer spreadsheets can also be used for this purpose.

Leases Versus Installment Purchases

An installment purchase (also called a conditional sales contract) is different from a lease—although the two can seem very similar. With an installment purchase, you end up owning all or part of the property, whereas with a lease you own nothing when the lease ends.

The distinction between a lease and an installment purchase is important because installment purchases are treated very differently for tax purposes. Payments for installment purchases are not rent and cannot be deducted as a business operating expense. The purchaser may deduct installment purchase payments under Section 179 (if applicable) or depreciate the property's value over several years, except that any portion of the payments that represent interest may be currently deducted as an interest expense.

You can't simply label a transaction a lease or installment purchase depending on which is more advantageous. A lease must really be a lease (often called a "true lease" or "tax lease") to pass muster with the IRS. A lease that is really just a way of financing a purchase is a "financial lease," not a true lease, and will be treated as an installment purchase by the IRS.

Whether a transaction is a lease or installment purchase depends on the parties' intent. The IRS will conclude that a conditional sales contract exists if *any of the following* are true.

- The agreement applies part of each payment toward an ownership interest that you will receive.
- You get title to the property upon the payment of a stated amount required under the contract.
- The amount you pay to use the property for a short time is a large part of the amount you would pay to get title to the property.
- You pay much more than the current fair rental value for the property.
- You have an option to buy the property at a nominal price compared to the value of the property when you may exercise the option.
- You have an option to buy the property at a nominal price compared to the total amount you have to pay under the lease.
- The lease designates some part of the payments as interest, or part of the payments are easy to recognize as interest.

A transaction will also look like an installment purchase to the IRS (even if it's labeled a lease) if:

- the lease term is about equal to the functional or economic life of the property
- the lease may not be canceled, and
- the lessee is responsible for maintaining the property.

■

Chapter 6

Inventory

Barbee owns a crafts business—she makes her own crafts and buys finished products from others, which she then sells at her store, at crafts fairs, and on her website. This year, she spent $28,000 on inventory. You might think that she would be able to deduct all of these costs because she is a business owner. Well, think again—Barbee can deduct only a portion of her expenses because of the way the tax code treats inventories.

➡️ If your business makes or buys any goods to sell to customers—even if your primary business is to provide services—you need to read this chapter and learn about inventories. If you only provide services to clients or customers, then you don't need to worry about inventories. You can skip ahead to Chapter 7.

What Is Inventory?

Inventory (also called merchandise) is the goods and products that a business owns to sell to customers in the ordinary course of business. It includes almost anything a business offers for sale, not including real estate. It makes no difference whether you manufacture the goods yourself or buy finished goods from others and resell them to customers. Inventory includes not only finished merchandise, but also unfinished work in progress, as well as the raw materials and supplies that will become part of the finished merchandise.

Only things you hold title to—that is, things you own—constitute inventory. Inventory includes items you haven't yet received or paid for, as long as you own them. For example, an item you buy with a credit card counts as inventory, even if you haven't paid the bill yet. However, if you buy merchandise that is sent C.O.D., you acquire ownership only after the goods are delivered and paid for. Similarly, goods that you hold on consignment are not part of your inventory because you don't own them.

> **EXAMPLE:** Barbee's inventory consists of the finished crafts she has for sale, the unfinished crafts she is working on, and the raw material she will eventually use to create finished crafts. Raw materials that she has on order are not inventory. Neither is Barbee's craft-making equipment, such as her leather hole punch and

jewelry tools, nor the computer she uses to keep track of sales and maintain her website. These items are part of her business assets, not merchandise that she is offering for sale to customers. Jewelry items made by other craftspeople that Barbee is selling in her store on consignment are also not inventory because Barbee doesn't own them.

Supplies Are Not Inventory

Materials and supplies that do not physically become part of the merchandise a business sells are not included in inventory. Unless they are incidental supplies as described below, the cost of these supplies must be deducted in the year in which they are used or consumed, which is not necessarily the year when you purchase them. This means that you must keep track of how many materials you use each year.

> **EXAMPLE:** Barbee decides to tan her own leather that she will use to create leather pouches to sell to customers. She orders large amounts of various expensive chemicals needed for the tanning process. In 2007, she spent $5,000 for the tanning chemicals but used only half of them. She may deduct $2,500 of the cost of the chemicals for 2007. She may not deduct the cost of the unused chemicals until she uses them.

Incidental Supplies

There is an important exception to the rule that the cost of materials and supplies may be deducted only as they are used or consumed. The entire cost of supplies that are incidental to a taxpayer's business may be deducted in the year they are purchased. Supplies are incidental if all of the following are true:

- They are of minor or secondary importance to your business (see "Maintaining an Inventory," below)—if you treat the cost of supplies on hand as an asset for financial reporting purposes, they are not incidental. (Private Letter Ruling 9209007.)

- You do not keep a record of when you use the supplies.
- You do not take a physical inventory of the supplies at the beginning and end of the tax year. (Private Letter Ruling 8630003 and 9209007.)
- Deducting the cost of supplies in the year you purchase them does not distort your taxable income. (Treas. Reg. 1.162-3; Private Letter Ruling 9209007.)

EXAMPLE: In 2007, Barbee purchases $100 worth of light bulbs to light her workspace. She does not keep a record of how many light bulbs she uses each year or take a physical inventory of how many she has on hand at year's end. The light bulbs are incidental supplies and Barbee may deduct their entire $100 cost in 2007, regardless of whether she used up all the light bulbs she bought that year.

Long-Term Assets

Long-term assets are things that last for more than one year—for example, equipment, tools, office furniture, vehicles, and buildings. Long-term assets that you purchase to use in your business are not a part of your inventory. They are deductible capital expenses that you may depreciate over several years or, in many cases, deduct in a single year under Section 179. (See Chapter 5 for more on deducting long-term assets.)

EXAMPLE: Barbee buys a new computer to help her keep track of her sales. The computer is not part of Barbee's inventory, because she bought it to use in her business, not to resell to customers. Because it will last for more than one year, it's a long-term asset, which she must either depreciate or expense under Section 179. (See Chapter 5 for more on long-term assets.)

Merchandise to Include in Inventory	
Include the following merchandise in inventory:	**Do not include the following items in inventory:**
Purchased merchandise if title has passed to you, even if the merchandise is in transit or you do not have physical possession of it for some other reason.	Goods you have sold, if title has passed to the buyer.
Merchandise you've agreed to sell but have not separated from other similar merchandise you own to supply to the buyer.	Goods consigned to you. Goods ordered for future delivery, if you do not yet have title.
Goods you have placed with another person or business to sell on consignment.	Assets such as land, buildings, and equipment used in your business.
Goods held for sale in display rooms, merchandise mart rooms, or booths located away from your place of business.	Supplies that do not physically become part of the item intended for sale.

Deducting Inventory Costs

You cannot deduct inventory costs in the same way as other costs of doing business, such as your office rent or employee salaries. A business may deduct only the cost of goods actually sold during a tax year—not the cost of its entire inventory. Inventory that remains unsold at the end of the year is a business asset, not a deductible expense.

Unsold inventory can be deducted in later years as you sell it or in the year it becomes worthless (as a business loss). In contrast, business expenses (such as rent and salaries) may be deducted entirely in the year in which they are incurred—in other words, they are currently deductible.

To figure out how much you can deduct for inventory, you must calculate the cost (to you) of the goods you sold during the year. You can then deduct this amount from your gross income when you do your taxes.

Computing the Cost of Goods Sold

The easiest way to calculate your inventory costs is to work backwards. Rather than trying to add up everything sold during the year, most businesses figure out how much inventory they had available for sale during the year and how much they have left at the end of the year. The difference between these two numbers is the inventory sold that year.

To figure out the cost of goods sold, start with the cost of any inventory on hand at the beginning of your tax year. Add the cost of inventory that you purchased or manufactured during the year. Subtract the cost of any merchandise you withdrew for personal use. The sum of all this addition and subtraction is the cost of all goods available for sale during the tax year. Subtract from this amount the value of your inventory at the end of your tax year. The cost of all goods sold during the year—and, therefore, the amount you can deduct for inventory expenses on your taxes—is the remainder. This can be stated by the following formula:

	Inventory at beginning of year
Plus:	Purchases or additions during the year
Minus:	Goods withdrawn from sale for personal use
Equals:	Cost of goods available for sale
Minus:	Inventory at end of year
Equals:	Cost of goods sold

EXAMPLE: Barbee had $1,000 in inventory at the beginning of the year and purchased another $28,000 of inventory during the year. She removed $500 of inventory for her own personal use (to give away as Christmas presents). The cost of the inventory she had left at the end of the year is $10,500. She would calculate her cost of goods sold as follows:

Inventory at beginning of year	$ 1,000
Purchases or additions during the year	+ 28,000
Goods withdrawn from sale for personal use	– 500
Cost of goods available for sale	= 28,500
Inventory at end of year	– 10,500
Cost of goods sold	= $18,000

Note that all of these costs are based on what Barbee paid for her inventory, not what she sold it for (which was substantially greater).

IRS Reporting for Cost of Goods Sold

You must report the cost of goods sold on your tax return. If you're a sole proprietor, the amount goes directly on your Schedule C. Part III of Schedule C tracks the cost of goods formula provided above. LLCs and partnerships report their cost of goods sold on Schedule A of IRS Form 1065, *U.S. Partnership Return of Income.* S corporations report cost of goods sold on Schedule A of Form 1120, *U.S. Income Tax Return for an S Corporation.* C corporations report this information on Schedule A of Form 1020, *U.S. Corporation Income Tax Return.*

Technically speaking, the cost of goods sold is not a business expense. Rather, it is deducted from a business's gross income to determine its gross profit for the year. Business expenses are then subtracted from the gross profit to determine the business's taxable net profit, as shown by the following formula:

	Gross income
Minus:	Cost of goods sold
Equals:	Gross profit
Minus:	Deductible business expenses
Equals:	**Net profit**

As a practical matter, this is a distinction without a difference—both cost of goods sold and business expenses are subtracted from your business income to calculate your taxable profit. However, you cannot deduct the cost of goods sold to determine your gross profit and then deduct it again as a business expense—this would result in deducting it twice.

> **EXAMPLE:** Barbee subtracts her $18,000 cost of goods sold from her gross income (all the money she earned from selling her crafts) to determine her gross profit. She earned $50,000 in total sales for the year and had $10,000 in business expenses, including rent, advertising costs, and business mileage. She calculates her net profit as follows:

Gross income		$ 50,000
Cost of goods sold	–	18,000
Gross profit	=	32,000
Business expenses	–	10,000
Net profit	=	$ 22,000

Barbee need pay tax only on her $22,000 in net profit.

Obviously, the larger the cost of goods sold, the smaller your taxable income will be and the less tax you'll have to pay.

Maintaining an Inventory

A business is said to "maintain an inventory" when it must carry unsold inventory items as an asset on its books. It can deduct the cost of these items only when they are sold or become worthless. A business is required to maintain an inventory if the production, purchase, or sale of merchandise produces income for the business—that is, if these activities account for a substantial amount of the business's revenues. How much is substantial? There is no exact figure. But many tax experts believe that any business that derives less than 8% of its revenue from the sale or production of merchandise need not maintain inventories. Anything over 15% probably is substantial, while anything in the 9% to 14% range is a gray area.

Often, it's perfectly obvious when a business must maintain inventories. Barbee's crafts business is a perfect example. Barbee obtains all of her income from the manufacture and sale of crafts to customers, so she must maintain an inventory. On the other hand, a taxpayer who only provides a service to customers ordinarily doesn't need to maintain inventories. For example, an accountant who provides accounting services to clients need not maintain an inventory of the paper he uses, nor does he need to compute the cost of goods sold each year for his taxes.

When You Provide Services and Sell Merchandise

Many businesses that provide services to customers also sell merchandise. For example, a plumber who provides plumbing services to customers may also supply various plumbing fixtures and materials. Separately billing clients or customers for an item tends to show it is merchandise that should be carried as inventory. However, this factor is not determinative in and of itself. The key is whether the sale of the merchandise is a substantial income producing factor for the business. Thus, for example, a plumber who earns 15% or more of his business income from selling plumbing fixtures should probably treat the items as inventory.

 The standards are far from clear in this area. If you sell services and goods, talk to a tax professional for advice on dealing with inventory.

Supplies for Providing a Service

Materials and property consumed or used up while providing services to customers or clients are supplies, not merchandise that must be included in inventory. Good examples are rubber gloves and disposable syringes used by doctors and nurses to provide medical services.

The same item can constitute supplies for one business and inventory for another. It all depends on whether the item is furnished to the customer or consumed in performing a service. For example, the paper used to prepare blueprints is inventory in the hands of a paper manufacturer but supplies in the hands of an architect.

Determining the Value of Inventory

If you are required to maintain an inventory, each year you must calculate how much you spent on inventory and how much of it you sold to determine the cost of goods sold on your tax return. There is no single way to do this—standard methods for tracking inventory vary according to the type and size of business involved. As long as your inventory methods are consistent from year to year, the IRS doesn't care which method you use.

This section provides only a small overview of a large subject. For more information on valuing inventory, refer to:

- *The Accounting Game,* by Darrell Mullis and Judith Orloff (Sourcebooks, Inc.)
  - *Small Time Operator,* by Bernard B. Kamoroff (Bell Springs Publishing)
  - IRS Publication 538, *Tax Guide for Small Businesses* (Chapter 7), and
  - IRS Publication 970, *Accounting Periods and Methods.*

Taking Physical Inventory

You need to know how much inventory you have at the beginning and end of each tax year to figure your cost of goods sold. If, like most businesses, you use the calendar year as your tax year, this means that you need to figure out your inventory each December 31. Unless you hold a New Year's Eve sale, your inventory on January 1 will usually be the same as the prior year's ending inventory—your inventory on December 31. Any differences must be explained in a schedule attached to your return.

Until recently, the IRS required all businesses that sold or manufactured goods to make a physical inventory of the merchandise they owned—that is, to actually count it. This process, often called "taking inventory," is usually done at the end of the year, although it doesn't have to be. Nor is it necessary to count every single item in stock. Businesses can make a physical inventory of a portion of their total merchandise, then extrapolate their total inventory from the sample.

The IRS no longer requires small businesses to take physical inventories. (Small businesses are those that earn less than $1 million in gross receipts per year, and service businesses that earn up to $10 million per year.) But even small businesses must keep track of how much inventory they buy and sell to determine their cost of goods sold for the year. With modern inventory software, it is possible for a business to keep a continuous record of the goods on hand during the year. Keep copies of your invoices and receipts to prove to the IRS that you correctly accounted for your inventory, in case you are audited.

Identifying Inventory Items Sold During the Year

The second step in figuring out your cost of goods sold is to identify which inventory items were sold during the year. There are several ways to do this. You can specifically track each item that is sold during the year. This is generally done only by businesses that sell a relatively small number of high-cost items each year, such as automobile dealers or jewelry sales companies.

If you don't want to identify specific items with their invoices, you must make an assumption about which items were sold during the year and which items remain in stock. Small businesses ordinarily use the first-in first-out (FIFO) method. The FIFO method assumes that the first items you purchased or produced are the first items that you sold, consumed, or otherwise disposed of.

> **EXAMPLE:** Barbee purchased three leather pouches to sell to customers during 2007. She bought the first pouch on February 1 for $5, the second on March 1 for $6, and the third on April 1 for $7. At the end of the year, Barbee finds that she only has one of these pouches left in stock. Using the FIFO method, she assumes that the first two pouches that she bought were the first ones sold. This means that in 2007, she sold two pouches that cost her $11 and has one pouch left in inventory that cost her $7.

Purchases During the Year

February 1, 2007 for:	$5
March 1, 2007 for:	$6
April 1, 2007 for	$7

December 31, 2007

First sale assumed to be:		$ 5
Second sale assumed to be:	+	6
Cost of goods sold	=	$11
Remaining inventory valued at:		$7

Another method of identifying inventory makes the opposite assumption. Under the last-in first-out (LIFO) method, you assume that the last items purchased or produced were the first to go. This method is not favored by the IRS and may not be used by small businesses that don't use the accrual method of accounting or take physical inventory. To use the LIFO method, you must file IRS Form 970 and follow some very complex tax rules.

Valuing Your Inventory

You must also determine the value of the inventory you sold during the year. The value of your inventory is a major factor in figuring out your taxable income, so the method that you use is very important. The two most common methods are the cost method and the lower of cost or market method. A new business that doesn't use LIFO to determine which goods were sold (see above) may choose either method to value its inventory. You must use the same method to value your entire inventory, and you cannot change the method from year to year without first obtaining IRS approval.

Cost Method

As the name indicates, when you use the cost method, your inventory cost is the amount that you paid for the merchandise. Note that this is not the same as what you sold it for, which will ordinarily be higher.

Using the cost method is relatively easy when you purchase goods to resell. To calculate the value of each item, start with the invoice price. Add the cost of transportation, shipping, and other money you had to spend to acquire the items. Subtract any discounts you received.

Things get much more complicated if you manufacture goods to sell. In this situation, you must include all direct and indirect costs associated with the goods. This includes:

- the cost of products or raw materials, including the cost of having them shipped to you
- the cost of storing the products you sell, and
- direct labor costs (including contributions to pension or annuity plans) for workers who produce the products; this does not include your own salary unless you are a corporate employee.

In addition, larger business (those with more than $10 million in gross receipts) must include an amount for depreciation on machinery used to produce the products and factory overhead expenses. Calculating these amounts is complicated and is best done with an accountant's help.

Lower of Cost or Market Method

What if the retail value of your inventory goes down during the year? This could happen if, for example, your inventory becomes obsolete or falls out of fashion. In this event, you may use the lower of cost or market method to value your inventory. Under this method, you compare the market (retail) value of each item on hand on the inventory date with its cost and use the lower value as its inventory value. By using the lower of these two numbers, your inventory will be worth less and your deductible expenses will be greater, thereby reducing your taxable income.

> **EXAMPLE:** Barbee purchased a jeweled belt in 2007 for $1,000. Due to a change in fashion, Barbee finds she can sell the belt for only $500. Using the lower of cost or market method, she may value the belt at $500.

However, you can't simply make up an inventory item's market value. You must establish the market value of your inventory through objective evidence, such as actual sales price for similar items.

Consider donating excess inventory to charity. One way to get rid of inventory you can't sell is to donate it to charity. You'll benefit a worthwhile charity and, by removing the items from your shelves, generate a tax deduction as well. How your business is organized affects the deductions that you can claim for donations like these. (See Chapter 14 for a detailed discussion of charitable deductions.)

By dishonestly manipulating inventories, a business can disguise theft, evade taxes, or falsely enhance its financial position.

EXAMPLE: Back in the 1950s, Anthony "Tino" DeAngelis, a former Bronx butcher, controlled a company called Allied Crude Vegetable Oil and Refining Corp. Allied borrowed $175 million to speculate in vegetable oil futures. The loans were secured by warehouse receipts for millions of pounds of salad oil Allied claimed it had stored in huge petroleum tanks in Bayonne, N.J. However, it turned out that Tino had vastly overreported the amount of his oil inventory by creating fake inventory records with forged warehouse receipts. When financial auditors visited the company's oil storage sites to verify the physical inventory, they found that the tanks contained mostly water with just a small amount of oil floating on top. Not only that, but the company claimed to own more storage tanks than it really did. As the auditors moved from tank to tank, company employees repainted the numbers on the tanks in a desperate effort to have them counted twice. The banks lost their money and Tino went to prison for seven years.

Chapter 7

Office Expenses

E veryone who has a business needs to work someplace. A great many small business owners work from home, while others have an outside office. Either way, your office expenses are usually deductible. If you work from your home, you may be able to use the home office deduction. This deduction allows you to deduct many of the costs associated with running a business from your home. This chapter focuses on the home office deduction, since it is subject to many complex tax rules. If you have an outside office, your expenses will be deductible as well, and you won't have to worry about the home office rules.

Qualifying for the Home Office Deduction

Rich, a professional musician and freelance writer, uses the basement of his San Francisco rental home as his writing office and recording studio. He can deduct his home office expenses, including a portion of his rent, from his business income. This saves him over $2,000 per year on his income and self-employment taxes.

If you're like Rich and you work from home, the federal government will help you out by letting you deduct your home office expenses from your taxable income. This is true whether you own your home or apartment or are a renter. Although this tax deduction is commonly called the home office deduction, it is not only for space in your home devoted to office work. You can also use it for a workshop, lab, studio, or any other home workspace that you use for your business.

If you've heard stories about how difficult it is to qualify for the home office deduction, you can breathe more easily. Changes in the tax law that took effect in 1999 make it much easier for businesspeople to qualify for the deduction. So even if you haven't qualified for the deduction in the past, you may be entitled to take it now.

Some people believe that taking the home office deduction invites an IRS audit. The IRS denies this. But even if taking the deduction increases your audit chances, the risk of an audit is still low. (See Chapter 17 for more on audits.) Moreover, you have nothing to fear from an audit if you're entitled to take the deduction and you keep good records to back it up.

However, if you plan on taking the deduction, you need to learn how to do it properly. There are strict requirements you must follow to qualify for the home office deduction. You are entitled to the home office deduction if you:

- are in business
- use your home office exclusively for business (unless you store inventory or run a day care center), and
- use your home office for business on a regular basis.

These are the three threshold requirements that everyone must meet. If you get past this first hurdle, then you must also meet any one of the following requirements:

- Your home office is your principal place of business.
- You regularly and exclusively use your home office for administrative or management activities for your business and have no other fixed location where you perform such activities.
- You meet clients or customers at home.
- You use a separate structure on your property exclusively for business purposes.
- You store inventory or product samples at home.
- You run a day care center at home.

These rules apply whether you are a sole proprietor, partner in a partnership, limited liability company (LLC) owner, or S corporation owner. If you have formed a regular C corporation that you own and operate and you work as its employee, then there are additional requirements you must meet. (See "Corporation Employees," below, for more on C corporations.)

Threshold Requirement: Regular and Exclusive Business Use

To take the home office deduction, you must have a home office—that is, an office or other workplace in your home that you use regularly and exclusively for business. Your "home" may be a house, apartment, condominium, or mobile home, or even a boat. You can also take the deduction for separate structures on your property that you use for business, such as an unattached garage, studio, barn, or greenhouse.

You Must Be in Business

You must be in business to take the home office deduction. You can't get the deduction for a hobby or other nonbusiness activity that you conduct out of your home. Nor can you take it if you perform invest-ment activities at home—for example, researching the stock market. (See Chapter 2 for information on what constitutes a business for tax purposes.)

You don't have to work full time in a business to qualify for the home office deduction. If you satisfy the requirements, you can take the deduction for a side business that you run from a home office. However, you must use your home office regularly, and the total amount you deduct cannot exceed your profit from the business. (See "What Expenses Can You Deduct?" below, for more on the profit limitation.)

> **EXAMPLE:** Barbara works full time as an editor for a publishing company. An avid bowler, she also spends about 15 hours a week writing and publishing a bowling newsletter. She does all the work on the newsletter from an office in her apartment. Barbara may take the home office deduction, but she can't deduct more than she earns from the newsletter.

If you have more than one business, each business must qualify for the home office deduction. Depending on where you do your work, it's possible that one of your businesses will qualify while the other does not.

> **EXAMPLE:** Jim has two businesses: He runs a bookkeeping service and also works as a professional magician, performing at birthdays, conventions, and similar events. He performs all of his bookkeeping work at home, so he can take a home office deduction for his bookkeeping business. However, because he does not work on his magic business at home, he gets no home office deduction for that income.

This rule can be important because of the profit limit on the amount of the home office deduction—that is, your deduction may not exceed the net profit you earn from your home office business or businesses. You'll want to make sure that your most profitable enterprises qualify for the deduction.

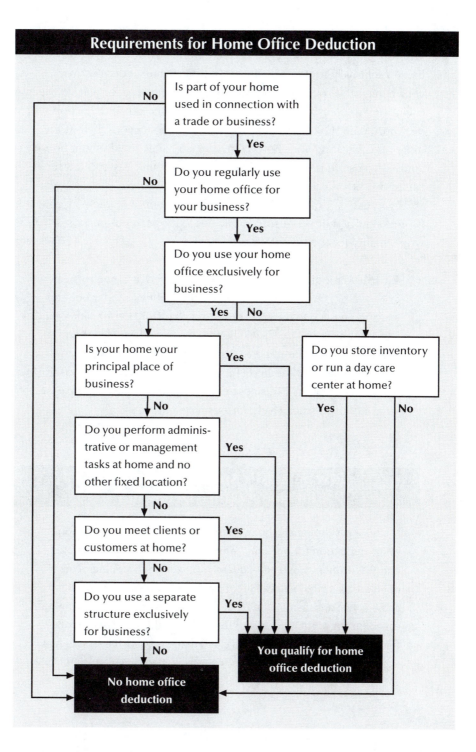

Requirements for Home Office Deduction

You Must Use Your Home Office Exclusively for Business

You can't take the home office deduction unless you use part of your home exclusively for your business. In other words, you must use your home office only for your business. The more space you devote exclusively to your business, the more your home office deduction will be worth. (See "Calculating the Home Office Deduction," below, for more on calculating your home office space.) This requirement doesn't apply if you store inventory at home or run a home day care center (discussed below).

If you use part of your home—such as a room or studio—as your business office, but you also use that space for personal purposes, you won't qualify for the home office deduction.

> **EXAMPLE:** Johnny, an accountant, has a den at home furnished with a desk, chair, bookshelf, and filing cabinet, and a bed for visiting guests. He uses the desk and chair for both business and personal reasons. The bookshelf contains both personal and business books, the filing cabinet contains both personal and business files, and the bed is used only for personal reasons. Johnny can't claim a business deduction for the den because he does not use it exclusively for business purposes.

Psychologist's Apartment Too Small for Home Office Deduction

Mullin, a psychologist who lived in San Francisco, claimed a home office deduction for one-quarter of her apartment. However, the entire apartment was a 400-square-foot studio, consisting of an open area (approximately 13 feet by 15 feet) furnished with a desk and a couch and a small dining area and kitchen (each approximately seven feet by eight feet). Given the layout of this tiny apartment, the court wouldn't buy Mullin's claim that she used 100 square feet exclusively for business. (*Mullin v. Commissioner*, TC Memo 2001-121.)

The easiest way to meet the exclusive use test is to devote an entire room in your home to your business—for example, by using a spare bedroom as your office. However, not everybody has an extra room to spare—and the IRS recognizes this. You can still claim the deduction even if you use just part of a room as your office, as long as you use that part exclusively for business.

> **EXAMPLE:** Paul, a software engineer, keeps his desk, chair, bookshelf, computer, and filing cabinet in one part of his den and uses them exclusively for business. The remainder of the room— one-third of the space—is used to store a bed for houseguests. Paul can take a home office deduction for the two-thirds of the room that he uses exclusively as an office.

If you use the same room (or rooms) for your office and for other purposes, you'll have to arrange your furniture and belongings so that a portion of the room is devoted exclusively to your business. Place only your business furniture and other business items in the office portion of the room. Business furniture includes anything that you use for your business, such as standard office furniture like a desk and chair. Depending on your business, it could include other items as well—for example, a psychologist might need a couch, an artist might need work tables and easels, and a consultant might need a seating area to meet with clients. One court held that a financial planner was entitled to have a television in his home office because he used it to keep up on financial news. Be careful what you put in this space, however. In another case, the IRS disallowed the deduction for a doctor because he had a television in the part of his living room that he claimed as his home office. The court wouldn't buy the doctor's claim that he only watched medical programs.

The IRS does not require you to physically separate the space you use for business from the rest of the room. However, doing so will help you satisfy the exclusive use test. For example, if you use part of your living room as an office, you could separate it from the rest of the room with room dividers or bookcases.

As a practical matter, the IRS doesn't have spies checking to see whether you're using your home office just for business. However, complying with the rules from the beginning means you won't have to worry if you are audited.

IRS Can't Enter Your Home Without Permission

IRS auditors may not enter your home unless you or another lawful occupant gives them permission. The only exception is if the IRS obtains a court order to enter your home, which is very rare. In the absence of such a court order, an IRS auditor must ask permission to come to your home to verify your home office deduction. You don't have to grant permission for the visit. But, if you don't, the auditor will probably disallow your deduction.

The exclusive use requirement can easily trip you up if you don't think things through ahead of time. Use your common sense when you set up your home office. For example, if you live in a one-bedroom apartment and claim the entire bedroom as a home office, you'll have to be able to explain to the IRS where you sleep.

Don't Mix Business With Pleasure

You're not allowed to use your business computer—that is, the computer in your business office—for personal purposes, such as playing games or keeping track of your personal finances. It's best to have two computers, one that you use for business and one for personal use. It's also wise to set aside another place in your home to do personal business tasks and store personal files and other records.

You Must Use Your Home Office Regularly

It's not enough to use a part of your home exclusively for business—you must also use it regularly. For example, you can't place a desk in a corner of a room and claim the home office deduction if you almost never use the desk for your business.

Unfortunately, the IRS doesn't offer a clear definition of regular use. The agency has stated only that you must use a portion of your home for business on a continuing basis—not just for occasional or incidental business. One court has held that 12 hours of use a week is sufficient. (*Green v. Comm'r.*, 79 TC 428 (1982).) There is a good chance that you could also qualify with less use—for example, at least one hour a day—but no one knows for sure.

Additional Requirements

Using a home office exclusively and regularly for business is not enough by itself to qualify for the home office deduction: You also must satisfy at least one of the additional five tests described below.

Home as Principal Place of Business

The most common way to satisfy the additional home office deduction requirement is to show that you use your home as your principal place of business. How you accomplish this depends on where you do most of your work and what type of work you do at home.

If you only work at home: If, like many businesspeople, you do all or almost all of your work in your home office, your home is clearly your principal place of business and you'll have no trouble qualifying for the home office deduction. This would be the case, for example, for a writer who writes only at home or a salesperson who sells by phone and makes sales calls from home.

If you work in multiple locations: If you work in more than one location, your home office still qualifies as your principal place of business if you perform your most important business activities—those activities that most directly generate your income—at home.

> **EXAMPLE:** Charles is a self-employed author who uses a home office to write. He spends 30 to 35 hours per week in his home office writing and another ten to 15 hours a week at other locations conducting research, meeting with publishers, and attending promotional events. The essence of Charles's business is writing—this is how he generates his income. Therefore, his home qualifies as his principal place of business, because it is where he writes.

If you perform equally important business activities in several locations, your principal place of business is where you spend more than half of your time. If there is no such location, you don't have a principal place of business.

> **EXAMPLE:** Sue sells costume jewelry over eBay from her home office and at crafts fairs and consignments to craft shops. She spends 25 hours per week in her home office and 15 hours at fairs and crafts shops. Her home office qualifies as her principal place of business.

You Do Administrative Work at Home

Of course, many businesspeople spend the bulk of their time working away from home. This is the case, for example, for:

- building contractors who work primarily on building sites
- doctors who work primarily in hospitals
- traveling salespeople who visit clients at their places of business, and
- house painters, gardeners, and home repair people who work primarily in their customers' homes.

Fortunately, legal changes that took effect in 1999 make it possible for these people to qualify for the home office deduction. Under the rules, your home office qualifies as your principal place of business, even if you work primarily outside your home, if both of the following are true:

- You use the office to conduct administrative or management activities for your business.
- There is no other fixed location where you conduct substantial administrative or management activities.

Administrative or management activities include, but are not limited to:

- billing clients or patients
- keeping books and records
- ordering supplies
- setting up appointments, and
- writing reports.

This means that you can qualify for the home office deduction even if your home office is not where you generate most of your business income. It's sufficient that you regularly use it to administer or manage your business—for example, to keep your books, schedule appointments, do research, write reports, forward orders, or order supplies. As long as you have no other fixed location where you regularly do these things— for example, an outside office—you'll get the deduction.

EXAMPLE: Sally, a handyperson, performs home repair work for clients in their homes. She has a home office that she uses regularly and exclusively to keep her books, arrange appointments, and order supplies. Sally is entitled to a home office deduction.

You don't have to perform all the administrative or management activities your business requires at home to qualify for the home office deduction. Your home office can qualify for the deduction even if you:

- have others conduct your administrative or management activities at locations other than your home—for example, another company does your billing from its place of business
- conduct administrative or management activities at places that are not fixed locations for your business, such as in a car or a hotel room
- occasionally conduct minimal administrative or management activities at a fixed location outside your home, such as your outside office.

EXAMPLE: Sally is a solo practitioner attorney with a flourishing criminal defense practice. She has a small office she shares with several other attorneys but spends most of her work time in court, at local jails, and in her car. Sally employs an outside firm to bill her clients and perform other bookkeeping for her business. She has a home office she uses to perform most of the administrative and management tasks she does herself, such as setting up appointments, writing briefs and memos, and ordering supplies. Sally also performs some of these tasks, such as making appointments, while in court or in her car on the way to or from court. She rarely uses her outside office for these tasks.

Sally's home office qualifies as her principal place of business for purposes of the home office deduction. She conducts administrative or management activities for her business there and has no other fixed location where she conducts substantial administrative or management activities. The fact that she occasionally performs some administrative tasks in her car or in court does not disqualify her for the deduction because they are not fixed locations for her law practice. Likewise, she doesn't lose the deduction because she has an outside company do her billing.

Moreover, you can qualify for the deduction even if you have suitable space to conduct administrative or management activities outside your home but choose to use your home office for those activities instead.

> **EXAMPLE:** Paul is a self-employed anesthesiologist. He spends the majority of his time administering anesthesia and postoperative care in three local hospitals. One of the hospitals provides him with a small shared office where he could conduct administrative or management activities, but rarely does. Instead, he uses a room in his home that he has converted to an office. He uses this room exclusively and regularly to contact patients, surgeons, and hospitals regarding scheduling; prepare for treatments and presentations; maintain billing records and patient logs; satisfy continuing medical education requirements; and read medical journals and books.
>
> Paul's home office qualifies as his principal place of business for deducting expenses for its use. He conducts administrative or management activities for his business as an anesthesiologist there and has no other fixed location where he conducts substantial administrative or management activities for this business. His choice to use his home office instead of the one provided by the hospital does not disqualify it from being his principal place of business. The fact that he performs substantial nonadministrative or non-management activities at fixed locations outside his home—that is, at hospitals—also does not disqualify his home office from being his principal place of business.

Meeting Clients or Customers at Home

Even if your home office is not your principal place of business, you may deduct your expenses for any part of your home that you use exclusively to meet with clients, customers, or patients. You must physically meet with others in this home location; phoning them from there is not sufficient. And the meetings must be a regular part of your business; occasional meetings don't qualify.

It's not entirely clear how often you must meet clients at home for those meetings to be considered regular. However, the IRS has indicated that meeting clients one or two days a week is sufficient. Exclusive use means you use the space where you meet clients only for business. You are free to use the space for business purposes other than meeting clients—for example, doing your business bookkeeping or other paperwork. But you cannot use the space for personal purposes, such as watching television.

> **EXAMPLE:** June, an attorney, works three days a week in her city office and two days in her home office, which she uses only for business. She meets clients at her home office at least once a week. Because she regularly meets clients at her home office, it qualifies for the home office deduction even though her city office is her principal place of business.

If you want to qualify under this part of the rule, encourage clients or customers to visit you at home, and keep a log or appointment book showing all of their visits.

Using a Separate Structure for Business

You can also deduct expenses for a separate freestanding structure, such as a studio, garage, or barn, if you use it exclusively and regularly for your business. The structure does not have to be your principal place of business or a place where you meet patients, clients, or customers.

Exclusive use means that you use the structure only for business— for example, you can't use it to store gardening equipment or as a guesthouse. Regular use is not precisely defined, but it's probably sufficient to use the structure ten or 15 hours a week.

> **EXAMPLE:** Deborah is a freelance graphic designer. She has her main office in a downtown office building but also works every weekend in a small studio in her back yard. Because she uses the

studio regularly and exclusively for her design work, it qualifies for the home office deduction.

Storing Inventory or Product Samples at Home

You can also take the home office deduction if you're in the business of selling retail or wholesale products and you store inventory or product samples at home. To qualify, you can't have an office or other business location outside your home. And you must store your inventory in a particular place in your home—for example, a garage, closet, or bedroom. You can't move your inventory from one room to the other. You don't have to use the storage space exclusively to store your inventory to take the deduction—you just have to regularly use it for that purpose.

> **EXAMPLE:** Lisa sells costume jewelry door to door. She rents a home and regularly uses half of her attached garage to store her jewelry inventory and also park her Harley Davidson motorcycle. Lisa can deduct the expenses for the storage space even though she does not use her entire garage exclusively to store inventory.

Operating a Day Care Center at Home

You're also entitled to a home office deduction if you operate a day care center at home. This is a place where you care for children, people who are at least 65 years old, or people who are physically or mentally unable to care for themselves. Your day care must be licensed by the appropriate licensing agency, unless it's exempt. You must regularly use part of your home for day care, but your day care use need not be exclusive—for example, you could use your living room for day care during the day and for personal reasons at night.

Corporation Employees

If you form a corporation to own and operate your business, you'll probably work as its employee. You'll be entitled to deduct your home office expenses only if you meet the requirements discussed above in "Qualifying for the Home Office Deduction," and you maintain your home office for the convenience of your employer—that is, your corporation. An employee's home office is deemed to be for an employer's convenience if it is:

- a condition of employment
- necessary for the employer's business to properly function, or
- needed to allow the employee to properly perform his or her duties.

When you own the business that employs you, you ordinarily won't be able to successfully claim that a home office is a condition of your employment—after all, as the owner of the business, you're the person who sets the conditions for employees, including yourself. But, if there is no other office where you do your work, you should be able to establish that your home office is necessary for your business to properly function and/or for you to perform your employee duties.

It will be more difficult to establish convenience if you have separate corporate offices. Nevertheless, business owners in this situation have successfully argued that their home offices were necessary—for example, because their corporate offices were not open or not usable during evenings, weekends, or other nonbusiness hours or were too far from home to use during off-hours.

If you've incorporated your business as a C corporation and you can't meet the convenience of the employer test or the other requirements for the home office deduction, you have another option: Forget about the home office deduction and rent your home office to your C corporation. You won't save any income tax this way, but you can still save on Social Security and Medicare taxes.

Here's how it works.

- You rent your home office to your C corporation for a fair market rental.
- Your C corporation deducts the rent as a business expense on its tax return (Form 1120).
- You report the rent you receive as ordinary income on your personal tax return, and pay income tax on it.

Ordinarily, a landlord may deduct his rental expenses such as mortgage interest, depreciation, and utilities. However, a special tax rule prohibits an employee who rents part of his home to his employer from deducting such expenses. (IRC § 280A(c)(6).) So, you can forget about taking any deductions for your rental expenses to reduce your income taxes.

However, you still save on Social Security and Medicare taxes because the rental income you receive is not subject to these taxes. For the rent to be deductible by the corporation, however, there must be a legitimate business reason for this rental arrangement. This would be the case if your home office was your only office, or if you could otherwise show a legitimate need for it.

> **EXAMPLE:** Rod, an accountant who works out of his home, formed a C corporation. Rod does not qualify for the home office deduction because he does not use his office exclusively for his accounting business. He charges his corporation $10,000 per year for the use he makes of his office for his accounting business. Rod gets no home office deduction, but his corporation deducts the rent on its own tax return. He reports the $10,000 on his personal tax return as rental income, but takes no deductions for rental expenses such as depreciation and utilities. Rod saves nothing on his income taxes, but he and his corporation need not pay Social Security and Medicare taxes on the $10,000 rental payment. This saves $1,530 in taxes that he would have had to pay if the $10,000 were paid to him as employee salary.

This strategy only works for C corporations because they are not subject to the home office deduction rules (although their employees are). It won't work with an S corporation because the home office rules apply to pass-through entities. As a result, an S corporation can't deduct rent paid for a home office that doesn't satisfy all the rules discussed above.

You need to be careful not to charge your corporation too much rent. Amounts the IRS deems excessive may be recharacterized as constructive dividends that are not deductible by the corporation. They will, therefore, be subject to corporate income tax which professional corporations usually pay at a 35% rate. To avoid this, the rent you charge your corporation should be the same as what you would charge a stranger.

Calculating the Home Office Deduction

This is the fun part—figuring out how much the home office deduction will save you in taxes. Whether you own or rent the space you're claiming, the home office deduction can result in substantial savings for you each year.

> ⚠️ **The day care center deduction amount is calculated differently.**
> If you operate a day care center at home but you don't devote a portion of your home exclusively to day care, your home office deduction is calculated differently from what is described here. You need to compare the time you use the space for day care with the time you use it for personal purposes—for example, if you use 50% of your house as a day care center for 25% of the hours in a year, you can claim a deduction for 12.5% of your housing costs (50% x 25% = 12.5%). See IRS Publication 587, *Business Use of Your Home*, for more information.

How Much of Your Home Is Used for Business?

To calculate your home office deduction, you need to determine what percentage of your home you use for business. The law says you can use "any reasonable method" to do this. Obviously, you want to use the method that will give you the largest home office deduction. To do this, you want to maximize the percentage of your home that you claim as your office. There is no single way to do this for every home office. Try both methods described below and use the one that gives you the largest deduction.

Square Footage Method

The most precise method of measuring your office space is to divide the square footage of your home office by the total square footage of your home. For example, if your home is 1,600 square feet and you use 400 square feet for your home office, 25% of the total area is used for business. Of course, you must know the square footage of your entire home and your office to make this calculation. Your home's total square footage may be listed on real estate documents or plans; you'll have to measure your office space yourself.

Square Footage Method
(Total Area)

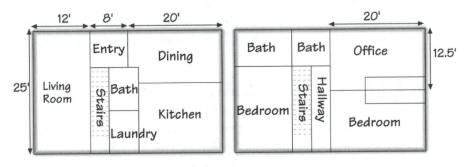

Square Footage Method
(Excluding Common Areas)

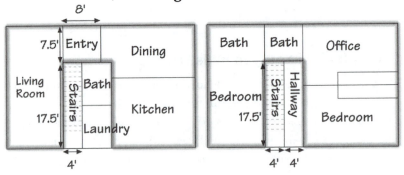

Room Method

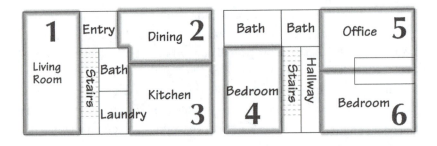

You are allowed to subtract the square footage of common areas—such as hallways, entries, stairs, and landings—from the total area that you are measuring. You can also exclude attics and garages from your total space if you don't use them for business purposes. You aren't required to measure this way, but doing so will give you a larger deduction because your overall percentage of business use will be higher.

Room Method

Another way to measure is the room method. You can use this method only if all of the rooms in your home are about the same size. With this method, you divide the number of rooms used for business by the total number of rooms in the home. Don't include bathrooms, closets, or other storage areas. You may also leave out garages and attics if you don't use them for business. For example, if you use one room in a five-room house for business, your office takes up 20% of your home.

The room method usually yields a larger deduction. Even though IRS Form 8829 (the form sole proprietors file to claim the home office deduction) seems to require you to use the square footage method, this isn't the case. As long as all of the rooms in your home are about the same size, you can use the room method. And unless you live in a rabbit warren, using the room method will almost always result in a larger deduction.

EXAMPLE: Rich (from the example at the beginning of this chapter) rents a six-room house in San Francisco and uses one bedroom as his home office.

Using the square footage method, Rich measures his entire house and finds it is 2,000 square feet. His home office is 250 square feet. Using these figures, his home office percentage is 12.5% (250 divided by 2,000 = 12.5%). However, he wants to do better than this, so he measures his common areas, such as hallways and stairways, which amount to 200 square feet. He subtracts this amount from the 2,000 total square feet, which leaves 1,800 square feet. This gives him a home office percentage of 14% (250 divided by 1,800 = 14%.)

Rich then tries the room method to see whether this provides a better result. His house has six rooms—three bedrooms, a living room, a dining room, and a kitchen. He doesn't count the bathroom, garage, or attic. Because he uses one entire room as his home office, he divides one by six, leaving 16.7% as his home office percentage. Rich uses this amount to figure his home office deduction.

What Expenses Can You Deduct?

The home office deduction is not one deduction, but many. Most costs associated with maintaining and running your home office are deductible. However, because your office is in your home, some of the money you spend also benefits you personally. For example, your utility bill pays to heat your home office, but it also keeps the rest of your living space warm. The IRS deals with this issue by dividing home office expenses into two categories: direct expenses, which benefit only your home office, and indirect expenses, which benefit both your office and your home.

Direct Expenses

You have a direct home office expense when you pay for something just for the home office portion of your home. This includes, for example, painting your home office, carpeting it, or paying someone to clean it. The entire amount of a direct home office expense is deductible.

> **EXAMPLE:** Jean pays a housepainter $400 to paint her home office. She may deduct this entire amount as a home office deduction.

Virtually anything you buy for your office that wears out, becomes obsolete, or gets used up, is deductible. However, you may have to depreciate permanent improvements to your home over 39 years, rather than deduct them in the year that you pay for them. Permanent improvements are changes that go beyond simple repairs, such as adding a new room to your home to serve as your office. (See Chapter 5 for more on improvements versus repairs.)

Indirect Expenses

An indirect expense is a payment for something that benefits your entire home, including both the home office portion and your personal space.

You Can Deduct Expenses Even If You Don't Qualify for the Home Office Deduction

Many business owners believe that they can't deduct any expenses they incur while working at home unless they qualify for the home office deduction. This is a myth that has cost many taxpayers valuable deductions. Even if you don't qualify for or take the home office deduction, you can still obtain tax deductions for various expenses you incur while doing business at home. These include:

- **Telephone expenses.** You can't deduct the basic cost of a single telephone line into your home, but you can deduct the cost of long distance business calls and special phone services that you use for your business (such as call waiting or message center). You can also deduct the entire cost of a second phone line that you use just for business.

- **Business equipment and furniture.** The cost of office furniture, copiers, fax machines, and other personal property you use for your business and keep at home is deductible, whether or not you qualify for the home office deduction. These items can be expensed (deducted in one year) under Section 179 or depreciated over several years. If you're a sole proprietor, these costs are deducted directly on Schedule C, *Profit or Loss From Business*. You don't have to list them on the special tax form used for the home office deduction. If you use the property for both business and personal reasons, the IRS requires you to keep records showing when the item was used for business or personal reasons—for example, a diary or log with the dates, times, and reasons the item was used.

You may deduct only a portion of this expense—the home office percentage of the total.

> **EXAMPLE:** Instead of just painting her home office, Jean decides to paint her entire home for $1,600. She uses 25% of her home as an office so she may deduct 25% of the cost, or $400.

Most of your home office expenses will be indirect expenses, including:

- **Rent.** If you rent your home or apartment, you can use the home office deduction to deduct part of your rent—a substantial expense that is ordinarily not deductible. Your tax savings will be particularly great if you live in a high-rent area.

> **EXAMPLE:** Sam uses 20% of his one-bedroom Manhattan apartment as a home office for his consulting business. He pays $2,000 per month in rent and may therefore deduct $400 of his rent per month ($4,800 per year) as a home office expense. This saves him over $2,000 in federal, state, and self-employment taxes.

- **Mortgage interest and property taxes.** Whether or not you have a home office, you can deduct your monthly mortgage interest and property tax payments as a personal itemized income tax deduction on your Schedule A (the tax form where you list your personal income tax deductions). But, if you have a home office, you have the option of deducting the home office percentage of your mortgage interest and property tax payments as part of your home office deduction. If you do this, you may not deduct this amount on your Schedule A (you can't deduct the same item twice). The advantage of deducting the home office percentage of your monthly mortgage interest and real estate tax payments as part of your home office deduction is that it is a business deduction, not a personal deduction; as such, it reduces the amount of your business income subject to self-employment taxes, as well as reducing your income taxes. The self-employment tax is 15.3%, so you save $153 in self-employment taxes for every $1,000 in mortgage interest and property taxes you deduct as part of your home office deduction.

EXAMPLE: Suzy, a sole proprietor medical record transcriber, uses 20% of her three-bedroom Tulsa home as a home office. She pays $10,000 per year in mortgage interest and property taxes. When she does her taxes for the year, she may deduct $2,000 of her interest and taxes as part of her home office deduction (20% of $10,000). She adds this amount to her other home office expenses and decreases her business income for both income tax and self-employment tax purposes. The extra $2,000 business deduction saves her $306 in self-employment tax (15.3% x $2,000). She may deduct the remaining $8,000 of mortgage interest and property tax as a personal deduction on her Schedule A.

- **Depreciation.** If you own your home, you're also entitled to a depreciation deduction for the office portion of your home. (See Chapter 5 for a detailed discussion of depreciation.)
- **Utilities.** You may deduct your home office percentage of your utility bills for your entire home, including electricity, gas, water, heating oil, and trash removal. If you use a disproportionately large amount of electricity for your home office, you may be able to deduct more.

EXAMPLE: Sheila, a pottery maker, works out of a home workshop that takes up 25% of the space in her home. Her pottery making requires that she use a substantial amount of electricity. About 50% of her monthly electricity bill is for her home workshop. She may deduct 50% of her electricity costs as a home office expense, instead of just 25%. However, to prove her deduction isn't too big, she should keep electricity bills for her home before she began using the workshop, or for periods when she doesn't use the workshop—for example, while she is on vacation—to show that her bills for these months are about 50% lower than the bills for her working months.

- **Insurance.** Both homeowners' and renters' insurance are partly deductible as indirect home office expenses. However, special insurance coverage you buy just for your home office—for example, insurance for your computer or other business equipment—is fully deductible as a direct expense.

- **Home maintenance.** You can deduct the home office percentage of home maintenance expenses that benefit your entire home, such as housecleaning of your entire house, roof and furnace repairs, and exterior painting. These costs are deductible whether you hire someone or do them yourself. If you do the work yourself, however, you can only deduct the cost of materials, not the cost of your own labor. Termite inspection, pest extermination fees, and snow removal costs are also deductible. However, the IRS won't let you deduct lawn care unless you regularly use your home to meet clients or customers. Home maintenance costs that don't benefit your home office—for example, painting your kitchen—are not deductible at all.

- **Casualty losses.** Casualty losses are damage to your home caused by such things as fire, floods, or theft. Casualty losses that affect your entire house—for example, a leak that floods your entire home—are deductible in the amount of your home office percentage. Casualty losses that affect only your home office—for example, a leak that floods only the home office area of the house—are fully deductible direct expenses. Casualty losses that don't affect your home office at all are not deductible—for example, if only your kitchen is flooded. (See Chapter 14 for a detailed discussion of casualty losses.)

- **Condominium association fees.** These fees (often substantial) are partly deductible as an indirect expense if you have a home office.

- **Security system costs.** Security system costs are partly deductible as an indirect expense if your security system protects your entire home. If you have a security system that protects only your home office, the cost is a fully deductible direct expense.

- **Computer equipment.** Computers and peripheral equipment (such as printers) are deductible whether or not you qualify for the home office deduction. However, if you don't qualify for the home office deduction, you must prove that you use your computer more than half of the time for business by keeping a log of your usage. (See Chapter 4 for more on deducting business expenses). If you qualify for the home office deduction, you don't need to keep track of how much time you spend using your computer for business.

- **Supplies and materials.** Office supplies and materials you use for your business are deductible whether or not you qualify for the home office deduction.

Mileage Deductions for Leaving the House

If your home office is your principal place of business, you can deduct the cost of traveling from your home to other work locations for your business. For example, you can deduct the cost of driving to perform work at a client's or customer's office. The value of this deduction often exceeds the value of the home business deduction itself. If you don't have a home office, these costs are not deductible. See Chapter 8 for a detailed discussion of the business mileage deduction.

Profit Limit for Deductions

Unfortunately, there is an important limitation on the home office deduction: You cannot deduct more than the net profit you earn from your home office. If you run a successful business out of your home office, this won't pose a problem. But if your business earns very little or is losing money, the limitation could prevent you from deducting part or even all of your home office expenses in the current year.

If your deductions exceed your profits, you can deduct the excess in the following year and in each succeeding year until you deduct the entire amount. There is no limit on how far into the future you can deduct these expenses; you can claim them even if you are no longer living in the home where they were incurred.

So, whether or not your business is making money, you should keep track of your home office expenses and claim the deduction on your tax return. You do this by filing IRS Form 8829. (See "IRS Reporting

Requirements," below, for more on tax reporting.) When you complete the form by plugging in the figures for your business income and home office expenses, it will show you how much you can deduct in the current year and how much you must carry over to the next year.

The profit limitation applies only to the home office deduction. It does not apply to business expenses that you can deduct under other provisions of the tax code. To figure out your home office deduction, you need to know what portion of your total income is from your home office work. Tax preparation software can perform the calculations for you, but it's a good idea to understand the principles involved.

First, start with your gross income from your business—if you sell goods, this is the total sales of your business minus the cost of goods sold; if you sell services, it's all the money you earn. Next, figure out how much money you earn from using your home office. If you do all of your work at home, this will be 100% of your business income. But if you work in several locations, you must determine the portion of your gross income that comes from working in your home office. To do this, consider how much time you spend working in your home office and the type of work you do at home.

Then, subtract from this amount:

- the business part of your mortgage interest and real estate taxes (you'll have these expenses only if you own your home), plus any casualty losses, and
- all your business expenses that are not part of the home office deduction—for example, car expenses, depreciation of business equipment, business phone, advertising, or salaries. (You must deduct these separately from the home office deduction, even if you incurred them while doing business at home.)

The remainder is your net profit—the most you can deduct for using your home office.

> **EXAMPLE:** Sam runs a part-time consulting business out of his home office, which occupies 20% of his home. In one year, his gross income from the business was $4,000. He had $1,000 in expenses other than his home office deduction and he paid $10,000 in mortgage interest and real estate taxes for the year. His home

office deduction for the year is limited to $1,000. He calculates this as follows:

Gross income from business:	$ 4,000
Minus business portion of mortgage interest and taxes ($10,000 x 20% = $2,000)	– 2,000
Balance:	2,000
Minus direct business expenses	– 1,000
Home office deduction limitation:	$ 1,000

Sam's total home office expenses for the year are $6,000. This includes $2,000 in mortgage interest and real estate taxes, plus $4,000 in other expenses, such as utilities and depreciation of his home. Sam first deducts the expenses that are not deductible as personal itemized deductions (everything other than mortgage interest, real estate taxes, and casualty losses). These expenses (utilities and depreciation) were $4,000, but he can deduct only $1,000 of this amount because his home office deduction profit limit is $1,000. Sam can't deduct any portion of his $2,000 mortgage interest and real estate tax expenses because he has reached his home office deduction profit limit. However, he may deduct these entire amounts as personal itemized deductions on Schedule A. The $3,000 in unused home office expenses that Sam couldn't deduct this year he may deduct the following year, if he has sufficient income from his business.

If your business is organized as a partnership, LLC, or corporation, the income limit still applies to your home office deduction. Your income when computing your allowable deduction is based on the gross income from your business allocable to your home office, minus all other deductions of the LLC, partnership, or corporation. IRS Publication 587, *Business Use of Your Home*, contains a worksheet you can use to calculate this amount.

Special Concerns for Homeowners

Until recently, homeowners who took the home office deduction were subject to a special tax trap: If they took a home office deduction for more than three of the five years before they sold their house, they had to pay capital gains taxes on the profit from the home office portion of their home. For example, if you made a $50,000 profit on the sale of your house, but your home office took up 20% of the space, you would have had to pay a tax on $10,000 of your profit (20% x $50,000 = $10,000).

Fortunately, IRS rules no longer require this. As long as you live in your home for at least two out of the five years before you sell it, the profit you make on the sale—up to $250,000 for single taxpayers and $500,000 for married taxpayers filing jointly—is not taxable. (See IRS Publication 523, *Selling Your Home.*)

However, you will have to pay a capital gains tax on the depreciation deductions you took after May 6, 1997 for your home office. This is the deduction you are allowed for the yearly decline in value due to wear and tear of the portion of the building that contains your home office. (See Chapter 5 for more on deducting a long-term asset.) These "recaptured" deductions are taxed at a 25% rate (unless your income tax bracket is lower than 25%).

> **EXAMPLE:** Sally bought a $200,000 home in the year 2002 and used one of her bedrooms as her home office. She sold her home in 2006 for $300,000, realizing a $100,000 gain (profit). Her depreciation deductions for her home office from 2002 through 2006 totaled $2,000. She must pay a tax of 25% of $2,000, or $500.

Having to pay a 25% tax on the depreciation deductions you took in the years before you sold your house is actually not a bad deal. This is probably no more—and is often less—tax than you would have to pay if you didn't take the deductions in the first place and instead paid tax on your additional taxable income at ordinary income tax rates.

Additional Limitations for Corporation Employees

If you form a regular corporation to own and operate your business, you will probably be its employee. In this event, you can take home office deductions only as miscellaneous itemized deductions on Schedule A of your tax return. This means you may deduct home office expenses only to the extent that they, along with your other miscellaneous deductions (if any), exceed 2% of your adjusted gross income (AGI). For example, if your AGI was $100,000, you would get a tax benefit only on the amount of your miscellaneous deductions that exceed $2,000. This rule greatly reduces the value of the home office deduction for corporation employees.

Make Your Corporation Reimburse You

There is a better way to recoup your office expenses if you're a corporate employee. Instead of claiming these expenses as miscellaneous itemized deductions, get your C corporation to reimburse you directly for your home office expenses. The corporation can then deduct this amount as an ordinary business expense.

The reimbursement will not be taxable to you personally if all of the following are true:

- You keep careful track of your home office expenses and can prove them with receipts or other records.
- Your corporation formally approves reimbursement of your home office expenses and the approval is documented in its corporate minutes.
- You have an "accountable reimbursement plan"—a written agreement in which the corporation agrees to reimburse you if you provide proper substantiation for your expenses.

For more information, see *Tax Deductions for Professionals,* by Stephen Fishman (Nolo), and IRS Publication 334, *Tax Guide for Small Business.*

IRS Reporting Requirements

IRS reporting requirements for the home office deduction differ depending on how you've legally organized your business.

Sole Proprietors

If you are a sole proprietor, you deduct your business operating expenses by listing them on IRS Schedule C, *Profit or Loss from Business*. You also list your home office deduction on Schedule C, but, unlike any other operating expense deduction, you must file a special tax form to show how you calculated the home office deduction. This form, Form 8829, *Expenses for Business Use of Your Home*, tells the IRS that you're taking the deduction and shows how you calculated it. You should file this form even if you can't currently deduct your home office expenses because your business has no profits. By filing, you can apply the deduction to a future year in which you earn a profit. For detailed guidance on how to fill out Form 8829, see IRS Publication 587, *Business Use of Your Home*.

LLCs and Partnerships

If you organize your business as a partnership or LLC, you don't have to file Form 8829. Instead, you deduct your unreimbursed home office expenses (and any other unreimbursed business expenses) on IRS Schedule E (Part II) and attach it to your personal tax return. You must attach a separate schedule to Schedule E listing the home office and other business expenses you're deducting.

Any home office expense for which your partnership or LLC reimbursed you must be listed on the partnership or LLC tax return, IRS Form 1065, *U.S. Partnership Return of Income*. These deductions pass through to you along with other partnership deductions.

Corporations

If you are an employee of a corporation and have deductible home office expenses for which you have not been reimbursed, you list the amount as an employee business expense on Schedule A of your Form 1040. This is the schedule where you list your personal itemized deductions. You don't have to file Form 8829 with your tax return.

If your corporation reimburses you for some, but not all, of your home office expenses, you must file Form 2106, *Employee Business Expenses,* to deduct the unreimbursed amount. Any home office expenses paid by your corporation must be listed on the corporate tax return—they do not go on your personal tax return. If you have an S corporation, your share of its deductible expenses will be passed on to your personal return. If you have a C corporation, you get no personal deduction for its deductible expenses.

Filing 1099s

If you're a renter and take the home office deduction, you should file an IRS Form 1099-MISC each year, reporting the amount of your rental payments attributable to your home office.

> **EXAMPLE:** Bill rents a house and takes the home office deduction. He spends $12,000 per year on rent and uses 25% of his house as a home office. He should file Form 1099, reporting $3,000 of his rental payments.

You should file three copies of Form 1099:
- file one copy with the IRS by February 28
- give one copy to your landlord by January 31, and
- file one copy with your state tax department, if your state imposes income taxes.

Your landlord may not appreciate receiving a Form 1099 from you, but it will definitely be helpful if you're audited by the IRS and your home office deduction is questioned. It helps to show that you were really conducting a business out of your home.

You don't have to file Form 1099 if your landlord is a corporation. Form 1099 is also not required in the unlikely event that your rental payments for your home office total less than $600 for the year.

Audit-Proofing Your Home Office Deduction

If you are audited by the IRS and your home office deduction is questioned, you want to be able to prove that you:
- qualify for the deduction, and
- have correctly reported the amount of your home office expenses.

If you can do both those things, you should be home free.

Show You're Following the Rules

Here are some ways to convince the IRS that you qualify for the home office deduction:

- Take a picture of your home office and draw up a diagram showing your home office as a portion of your home. Do not send the photo or diagram to the IRS. Just keep it in your files to use in case you're audited. The picture should have a date on it—this can be done with a digital camera, or you can have your film date-stamped by a developer.
- Have all of your business mail sent to your home office.
- Use your home office address on all of your business cards, stationery, and advertising.
- Obtain a separate phone line for your business and keep that phone in your home office.
- Encourage clients or customers to regularly visit your home office, and keep a log of their visits.
- To make the most of the time you spend in your home office, communicate with clients by phone, fax, or electronic mail instead of going to their offices. Use a mail or messenger service to deliver your work to customers.
- Keep a log of the time you spend working in your home office. This doesn't have to be fancy; notes on your calendar will do.

Keep Good Expense Records

Be sure to keep copies of your bills and receipts for home office expenses, including:

- IRS Form 1098 (sent by whoever holds your mortgage), showing the interest you paid on your mortgage for the year
- property tax bills and your canceled checks as proof of payment
- utility bills, insurance bills, and receipts for payments for repairs to your office area, along with your canceled checks paying for these items, and
- a copy of your lease and your canceled rent checks, if you're a renter.

Deducting an Outside Office or Workplace

If you have an outside office or other workplace, your tax life is simpler than if you use a home office. The expenses you can deduct depend on whether you rent or own your workspace.

Renting an Outside Workplace

Virtually all the expenses you incur for an outside office, lab, workshop, studio, or other workspace that you rent for your business are deductible, including:

- rent
- utilities
- insurance
- repairs
- improvements
- real estate broker fees and commissions to obtain the lease
- fees for option rights, such as an option to renew the lease
- burglar alarm expenses
- trash and waste removal
- security expenses
- parking expenses
- maintenance and janitorial expenses
- lease cancellation fees, and
- attorneys' fees to draft a lease.

If you sign a net lease, you'll have to pay part (or all) of the landlord's maintenance expenses, property taxes, insurance, and maybe even mortgage payments. These payments are treated the same as rent.

A rental deposit is not deductible in the year it is made if it is to be returned at the end of the lease. However, if the landlord applies the deposit to pay rent you owe, make repairs, or because you've breached the lease, you may deduct the amount in that year.

None of the rules applicable to the home office deduction covered above apply to outside offices. Thus, unlike the home office deduction, there is no profit limit on deductions for outside rental expenses—you get your entire deduction even if it exceeds the profits from your business. You report rental expenses for an outside office just like any other business expense. You don't have to file IRS Form 8829, which is required when sole proprietors take the home office deduction.

Because you will ordinarily be in your office for more than one year, some of the expenses you pay may benefit your business for more than a single tax year. In this event, you may have to deduct the expense over more than one year instead of currently deducting it all in a single year. (This discussion assumes that you, like most professionals, are a cash basis taxpayer and use the calendar year as your tax year.)

Current Versus Multiyear Deductions

You may currently deduct any expense you pay for use of your office during the current tax year.

> **EXAMPLE:** In 2007, Leona paid $800 rent each month for the outside office she uses for her import-export business. The $9,600 she paid in 2007 is fully deductible on Leona's 2007 taxes. The rental payments were a current expense because they only benefited Leona for a single tax year—2007.

But if an expense you pay applies beyond the current tax year, the general rule is that you can deduct only the amount that applies to your use of the rented property during the current tax year. You can deduct the rest of your payment only during the future tax year to which it applies.

> **EXAMPLE:** Last January, Steve leased an outside office for three years for $6,000 a year. He paid the full lease amount up front: $18,000 (3 x $6,000). Each year, Steve can deduct only $6,000—the part of the rent that applies to that tax year.

Subject to the exceptions noted below, these rules apply to office expenses, not just rent you pay in advance. For example, they apply to all expenses you pay to get a lease.

> **EXAMPLE:** Maxine pays $2,000 in attorney fees to draft her office lease. The lease has a five-year term, so the payment was for a benefit that lasts beyond the end of the following tax year. Thus,

Maxine may not currently deduct the entire $2,000 in one year. Instead, she must deduct the $2,000 in equal amounts over five years (60 months). This comes to $33.33 per month. Her lease began on March 1, 2007, so she can deduct $333.33 for 2007 (10 months x $33.33).

12-Month Rule

There is an important exception to the general rule that you may be able to use. Under the "12-month rule," cash basis taxpayers may currently deduct any expense in the current year so long as it is for a right or benefit that extends no longer than the earlier of:

- 12 months, or
- until the end of the tax year after the tax year in which you made the payment.

EXAMPLE: Stephanie leased an office for five years beginning July 1, 2007. Her rent is $12,000 per year. She paid the first year's rent ($12,000) on June 30. Under the general rule discussed above, Stephanie may deduct in 2007 only the part of her rent payment that applies to 2007. Her lease started July 1, 2007 (which is 50% of 2007), so she may deduct 50% of the $12,000, or $6,000. However, if Stephanie uses the 12-month rule, her entire $12,000 payment is deductible in 2007. The fact that 50% of her payment was for 2007 doesn't matter because the benefit she obtained—the use of her office—lasted for only 12 months: from July 1, 2007 to July 1, 2008.

EXAMPLE: Steve paid three years of rent in advance. He may not use the 12-month rule because the benefit he obtained from his payment lasted for three years, which is both more than 12 months and beyond the end of tax year after the tax year in which he made the payment.

EXAMPLE: Assume that Maxine (from the example in the previous section) paid $2,000 in attorney's fees to draft a lease that lasts for one year, starting March 1, 2007. She may currently deduct the whole amount under the 12-month rule.

To use the 12-month rule, you must apply it when you first start using the cash method for your business. You must get IRS approval if you haven't been using the rule and want to start doing so. Such IRS approval is granted automatically. (See "Accounting Methods," in Chapter 15.)

Determining Your Lease Term

How long a lease lasts is important because it can determine whether you can currently deduct an expense or have to deduct it over the entire lease term. If you have to deduct an expense over the entire lease term, the length of the lease will determine the amount of your deduction each year. It might seem simple to tell how long a lease lasts: just look at the lease term in the lease agreement. However, things are not so simple if your lease includes an option to renew.

The IRS says that the term of the lease for rental expense deductions includes all renewal options plus any other period for which you and the lessor reasonably expect the lease to be renewed. For example, a one-year lease with an option to renew for five years would be a six-year lease for deduction purposes.

However, this rule applies only if less than 75% of the cost of getting the lease is for the term remaining on the purchase date (not including any period for which you may choose to renew or extend the lease). Sound confusing? It is.

> **EXAMPLE 1:** You paid $10,000 to get a lease with 20 years remaining on it and two options to renew for five years each. Of this cost, you paid $7,000 for the original lease and $3,000 for the renewal options. Was 75% of the cost of the lease paid for the initial 20-year lease term? No. $7,000 is less than 75% of the total $10,000 cost of the lease. Thus, the IRS rule discussed above applies. The lease term for deduction purposes is the remaining life of your present lease plus the renewal periods—30 years in all. The $10,000 will have to be amortized (deducted in equal amounts) over 30 years.

> **EXAMPLE 2:** Assume the same facts as in Example 1, except that you paid $8,000 for the original lease and $2,000 for the renewal options. The $8,000 cost of getting the original lease was 80% of

the total cost of the lease, not less than 75%. Thus, the IRS rule doesn't apply and you can amortize the entire $10,000 over the 20-year remaining life of the original lease.

The crucial question is how you figure out how much of the cost of the lease was for the original lease term and how much was for the renewal term or terms. The IRS only says that the lease costs should be allocated between the original and renewal terms based on the facts and circumstances. The IRS also says that in some cases it may be appropriate to make the allocation using a present value computation. In such a computation, a present value—a value in today's dollars—is assigned to an amount of money in the future, based on an estimated rate of return over the long-term. You'll probably want an accountant to do this for you.

Improvements and Repairs

It's very common for commercial tenants to make permanent improvements to their offices—for example, they may install new carpeting or new walls. Landlords often give these tenants an allowance to make improvements before they move in. You get no deduction in this event. The landlord gets to depreciate improvements it paid for, not you

However, if you pay for improvements with your own money, you may deduct the cost as a business expense. You can depreciate the improvements, or treat the money you spent for the improvements as rent.

Improvements may be depreciated over several years as described in Chapter 5. They are depreciated over their recovery periods assigned by the IRS, not over the whole term of the lease. For example, the cost of installing new carpeting would be depreciated over five years, even if the lease term is ten years.

If you treat your expenses for improvements as rent, you deduct the cost the same as any other rent. Rent is deductible in a single year (unless it is prepaid in advance). This means you'll get your deduction much more quickly than if you depreciated the improvements over several years. However, if the cost of the improvement is substantial, part of the cost may have to be treated as prepaid rent and deducted over the whole lease term as described above.

Whether an improvement must be depreciated or treated as rent depends on what you and your landlord intended. Your intent should be written into your lease agreement.

In contrast to improvements, repairs may be currently deducted. The key difference between a repair and an improvement is that *a repair merely returns property to more or less the state it was in before it stopped working properly.* The property is not substantially more valuable, long-lived, or useful than it was before the need for the repair arose. In contrast, an improvement makes property *substantially* more valuable and/or long-lived or useful than it was before the improvement. Good examples of repairs include repainting your property, fixing gutters or floors, fixing leaks, plastering, and replacing broken windows. Examples of improvements include installing a new heating system, or putting on a new roof.

Modifying or Canceling a Lease

You may have to pay an additional "rent" amount over part of the lease period to change certain provisions in your lease. You must ordinarily deduct these payments over the remaining lease period. You cannot deduct the payments as additional rent, even if they are described as rent in the agreement.

> **EXAMPLE:** The ABC Medical Corporation signs a 20-year lease to rent part of a building starting on July 1. However, before it occupies the building, ABC decides it really needs less space. The lessor agrees to reduce ABC's rent from $60,000 to $50,000 per year and to release the excess space from the original lease. In exchange, ABC agrees to pay an additional rent amount of $25,000, payable in 60 monthly installments of $417 each. The extra payments must be deducted over the 20-year lease term. ABC's amortization deduction each year will be $1,250 ($25,000 ÷ 20 years), but it may deduct only half this amount the first year because the lease began on July 1. ABC cannot deduct the $5,004 (12 × $417) that it will pay during each of the first five years as rent.

The only exception to this rule is where the 12-month rule can be used. The lease will have to have a short term for the rule to apply.

EXAMPLE: Assume that ABC Medical Corporation (from the example above) signed a nine-month lease starting on July 1, instead of a 20-year lease. It can currently deduct its lease modification expense under the 12-month rule because the benefit it obtains from the expense lasts less than 12 months and doesn't extend beyond the end of the following tax year.

Unlike the cost of modifying a lease, you can ordinarily deduct as rent an amount you pay to cancel a business lease.

Buying an Outside Workplace

If you buy an outside workplace, you may currently deduct as ordinary and necessary business expenses your mortgage interest, real estate taxes, and expenses associated with the purchase. In addition, you may depreciate the value of the real estate (not including the land) over 39 years. The cost of repairs can be currently deducted, but permanent improvements to the property must be depreciated. (See Chapter 5 for more on depreciation.) As with rental expenses, there is no profit limit on these deductions.

■

Chapter 8

Car and Local Travel Expenses

T hat expensive car parked in your garage not only looks great—it could also be a great tax deduction. If, for example, you drive 10,000 miles per year for business, you can get a deduction of at least $4,450 (based on 2006 rates). You might be able to deduct even more, depending on how you choose to deduct your car expenses.

This chapter shows you how to deduct expenses for local transportation—that is, business trips that don't require you to stay away from home overnight. These rules apply to local business trips using any means of transportation, but this chapter focuses primarily on car expenses, the most common type of deduction for local business travel.

Overnight trips (whether by car or other means) are covered in Chapter 9.

Different rules apply for corporate employees. This chapter covers local transportation deductions by business owners—sole proprietors, partners in partnerships, or LLC members—not by corporate employees. If you have incorporated your business and work as its employee, there are special rules you must follow to deduct local transportation expenses. Those rules are covered in Chapter 11.

Transportation expenses are a red flag for the IRS. Transportation expenses are the number-one item that IRS auditors look at when they examine small businesses. These expenses can be substantial—and it is easy to overstate them—so the IRS will look very carefully to make sure that you're not bending the rules. Your first line of defense against an audit is to keep good records to back up your deductions. This is something no tax preparation program or accountant can do for you—you must develop good record-keeping habits and follow them faithfully to stay out of trouble with the IRS.

Deductible Local Transportation Expenses

Local transportation costs are deductible as business operating expenses if they are ordinary and necessary for your business, trade, or profession. The cost must be common, helpful, and appropriate for your business. (See Chapter 4 for a detailed discussion of the ordinary and necessary requirement.) It makes no difference what type of transportation you use to make the local trips—car, van, pick-up, truck, motorcycle, taxi, bus, or train—or whether the vehicle you use is owned or leased. You can deduct these costs as long as they are ordinary and necessary and meet the other requirements discussed below.

Travel Must Be for Business

You can only deduct local trips that are for business—that is, travel to a business location. Personal trips—for example, to the supermarket or the gym—are not deductible as business travel expenses. A business location is any place where you perform business-related tasks, such as:

- the place where you have your principal place of business, including a home office
- other places where you work, including temporary job sites
- places where you meet with clients or customers
- the bank where you do business banking
- a local college where you take work-related classes
- the store where you buy business supplies, or
- the place where you keep business inventory.

Starting a New Business

The cost of local travel you do before you start your business, such as travel to investigate starting a new business, is not a currently deductible business operating expense. It is a start-up expense subject to special deduction rules. (See Chapter 3 for more on start-up expenses.)

You don't have to do all the driving yourself to get a car expense deduction. Any use of your car by another person qualifies as a deductible business expense if any of the following are true:

- It is directly connected with your business.
- It is properly reported by you as income to the other person (and, if you have to, you withhold tax on the income)—for example, where an employee uses your car (see Chapter 11).
- You are paid a fair market rental for use of your car.

Thus, for example, you can count as business mileage a car trip your employee, spouse, or child takes to deliver an item for your business or for any other business purpose.

Commuting Is Not Deductible

Most business owners have an office, workshop, store, lab, or other principal place of business where they work on a regular basis. Unfortunately, you can't deduct the cost of traveling from your home to your regular place of business. These are commuting expenses, which are a nondeductible personal expense item.

> **EXAMPLE:** Sue lives in a Chicago suburb and drives 15 miles each day to her office in a downtown Chicago building. These trips are nondeductible commuting expenses.

Even if a trip from home has a business purpose—for example, to haul tools or supplies to your office or other work location—it is still considered commuting and is not deductible. (You may, however, deduct the cost of renting a trailer or any other extraordinary expenses you incur to haul the tools or supplies from your home.)

Nor can you deduct a commuting trip because you make business calls on your cell phone, listen to business-related tapes, or have a business discussion with an associate or employee during the commute. Also, placing an advertising display on your vehicle won't convert a commute to a business trip.

Because commuting is not deductible, where your business office or other principal workplace is located has a big effect on the amount you can deduct for business trips. You will get the fewest deductions if you work solely in an outside office—that is, your principal workplace is away from home in an office building, industrial park, or shopping mall. You lose out on many potential business miles this way because you can't deduct any trips between your home and your office.

> **EXAMPLE:** Kim, a marketing consultant, runs her business from an office in a downtown office building. Every day, she drives 20 miles to and from her suburban home to her office. None of this

commuting mileage is deductible. But she may deduct trips from her office to a client's office, or any other business-related trip that starts from her office.

As explained below, you can get the most deductions for local business trip expenses if you have a home office.

You Have a Home Office

If you have a home office that qualifies as your principal place of business, you can deduct the cost of any trips you make from home to another business location. You can get a lot of travel deductions this way. For example, you can deduct the cost of driving from home to a client's office or to attend a business-related seminar. The commuting rule doesn't apply if you work at home because, with a home office, you never commute to work (you're there already).

Your home office will qualify as your principal place of business if it is the place where you earn most of your income or perform most of your business administrative or management tasks. (See Chapter 7 for more on the home office deduction.) If your home office qualifies as your principal place of business, you can vastly increase your deductions for business trips.

> **EXAMPLE:** Kim (from the above example) maintains a home office where she does the administrative work for her consulting business; she also has an outside office where she does her other work. She can deduct all her business trips from her home office, including the 20-mile daily trip to her outside office. Thanks to her home office, she can now deduct 100 miles per week as a business trip expense, all of which was a nondeductible commuting expense before she established her home office.

You Have No Regular Workplace

If you have no regular office—whether inside or outside your home— the location of your first business contact of the day is considered your office for tax purposes. Transportation expenses from your home to this first business contact are nondeductible commuting expenses. The same is true for your last business contact of the day—your trip home is nondeductible commute travel. You can deduct the cost of all your other trips during the day between clients or customers.

> **EXAMPLE:** Jim is a Bible salesman who works in the Houston metropolitan area. He works out of his car, with no office at home or anywhere else. One day, he makes ten sales calls by car. His trip from home to his first sales contact of the day is a nondeductible commuting expense. His next eight trips are deductible, and his trip home from his last sales contact is a nondeductible personal commuting expense.

There is an easy way to get around this rule about the first and last trip of the day: Open a home office. That way, all of your trips are deductible.

> **EXAMPLE:** Jim creates an office at home where he performs the administrative tasks for his sales business, such as bookkeeping. He may now deduct the cost of all of his business trips during the day, including driving from home to his first business contact and back home from his last contact of the day.

You Go to a Temporary Business Location

Commuting occurs when you go from home to a permanent work location—either:

- your office or other principal place of business, or
- another place where you have worked or expect to work for more than one year.

If you have a regular place of business, travel between your home and a temporary work location is not considered commuting and is therefore deductible. A temporary work location is any place where you realistically expect to work less than one year.

> **EXAMPLE:** Sally is a computer trainer with a regular office in a downtown office building; she does not have a home office. She is hired by Acme Corporation to teach their employees how to use a new computer system. The job is expected to last three months. Sally may deduct the cost of driving from home to Acme Corporation's offices to conduct the training.

Temporary work locations are not limited to clients' offices. Any place where you perform business-related tasks for less than one year is a temporary work location. This may include a bank, post office, office supply store, or school, and similar places.

> **EXAMPLE:** Jim owns a florist shop and has no home office. One day he travels from home to his local flower wholesaler to pick up flowers for his shop. This is not commuting and is deductible.

However, a place will cease to be a temporary work location if you continue to go there for more than one year.

> **EXAMPLE:** Jim goes from his house to the flower wholesaler to pick up flowers every day year after year. The flower wholesaler is no longer a temporary work location, and his trips there from home are nondeductible commuting expenses.

You can convert a nondeductible commute into a deductible local business trip by making a stop at a temporary work location on your way to your office. Stopping at a temporary work location converts the entire trip into a deductible travel expense.

> **EXAMPLE:** Eleanor's business office is in a downtown building. She has no home office. One morning, she leaves home, stops off at a client's office to drop off some work, and then goes to her office. The entire trip is deductible because she stopped at a temporary work location on her way to her office.

Keep in mind, though, that making such stops is necessary only if you don't have a home office. If Eleanor had a home office, the commuting rule wouldn't apply and the trip would be deductible with or without the stop.

If you don't have a regular office, the rules about travel to temporary work locations are more restrictive. Without a regular office, you can deduct the cost of going from home to a temporary work location only if the temporary work location is outside your metropolitan area.

EXAMPLE: Artie is a cosmetics salesman with no regular office. He lives in Boston and regularly visits customers in and around the Boston area. He can't deduct any expenses for his local travel around Boston. One day he travels from his Boston home to New Haven, Connecticut, to see a customer. He goes back home that same day. Artie can deduct this trip because he traveled outside of his metropolitan area.

What constitutes a "metropolitan area" is not defined in the tax law, which leads to confusion and uncertainty. The U.S. Census Bureau has divided the country into various metropolitan areas for its own purposes, but these vary greatly in size and not every town is located in one. When the IRS attempted to use these Census Bureau areas to deny a taxpayer travel expense deductions, it was shot down by the tax court, which elected to use a commonsense definition of metropolitan area instead.

EXAMPLE: Corey L. Wheir, a union boilermaker who lived and worked in Wisconsin Rapids, Wisconsin, was assigned to temporary jobs all over the state ranging from one day to several months. Wheir deducted his travel costs for jobs farther than 35 miles from his home. The IRS disallowed his deductions on the ground that Wisconsin Rapids was not a metropolitan area as defined by the U.S. Census Bureau. The IRS said that the entire state of Wisconsin should be considered Wheir's normal work area for purposes of travel expense deductions.

Wheir appealed to the tax court and won. The judge decided that the U.S. Census Bureau's definition of metropolitan area should not be used because these areas varied greatly in size and tax-payers in rural areas would be at a disadvantage to those in more-populated areas. Rather, the court adopted the dictionary definition of a metropolitan area: "a region including a city and the densely populated surrounding areas that are socially and economically integrated with it." The judge held that Wheir's conclusion that he was "out of town" whenever he was more than 35 miles away from his home was reasonable. (*Wheir v. Comm'r.*, TC Summary Opinion 2004-117.) Unfortunately, the judge's ruling is not binding on the

IRS. But it should still provide you with useful ammunition if the IRS claims that your metropolitan area extends more than 35 to 40 miles from your home.

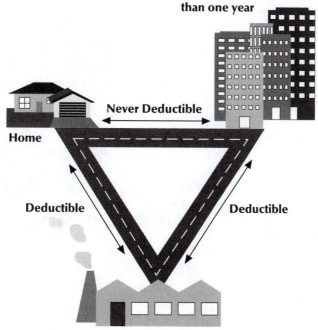

1. **Office**
2. **First and last business stops of the day** (if no regular office)
3. **Place you expect to work for more than one year**

Never Deductible

Home

Deductible   Deductible

Temporary Work Location
If you have regular outside or home office, trips to and from home are deductible only if temporary work location is outside metropolitan area of home.

Business Mileage Self-Test

See if you can figure out how many business miles were driven in each of the following examples.

1. John, a salesman with no home office, drives 25 miles to his downtown office in the morning, works all day, and then drives 25 miles back home. After dinner, he drives 30 miles to meet a client and then drives directly back home that night. Total business miles _____.

   Answer: 60. The trip to and from home to his office is nondeductible commuting, but the trip from home to the client and back is deductible because the client's office is a temporary work location for John.

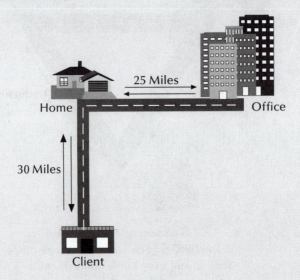

2. Sue is a freelance writer who works from home. She drives five miles to the grocery store and then heads off to the library five miles away to do research for an article. She then drives from the library back home, a distance of ten miles. Total business miles _____.

Business Mileage Self-Test (continued)

Answer: 20. This is a good example of how you can convert a personal trip into a business trip. Sue's trip to the grocery store isn't deductible, but her journey to the library is. Because the grocery store is en route to the library, she gets to deduct all ten miles (five to the grocery store; five to the library). It's ten miles back to her house from the library, so she gets a total of 20 business miles.

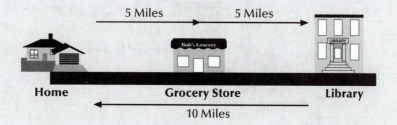

| Home | Grocery Store | Library |

5 Miles → 5 Miles →

Bob's Grocery — LIBRARY

← 10 Miles

3. Nick is a bookie who works out of his car. One day he drives 20 miles from home to the racetrack. He then drives 15 miles from the track to the homes of three customers to make collections. At the end of the day, he drives ten miles to get back home. That evening, he drives 15 miles from home to the house of an associate for a business meeting and then drives back home. Total business miles _____.

Answer: 15. Because Nick has no fixed business location, he may not deduct travel from home to his first business location or back to home from his last business location. Thus, he cannot deduct the 20-mile trip to the track or the ten miles back home from the customer's house. Nor could he deduct the 30 miles round-trip later that night from home to the business meeting. He can only deduct the mileage for the two middle collection calls that he made.

Business Mileage Self-Test (continued)

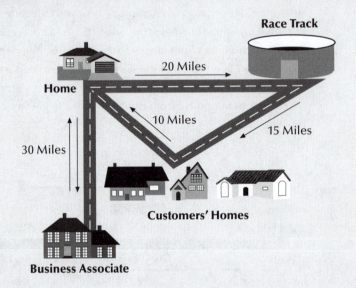

4. Gloria runs her home construction business from an outside office. She has no home office. One day she drives from home to a site 30 miles away where her company is building a house and then drives back home at the end of the day. The project is expected to last six months. Total business miles _____.

Answer: 60. Gloria is working at a temporary work location. Her travel from home to the building site is not considered commuting.

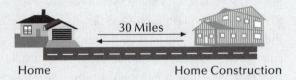

The Standard Mileage Rate

If you drive a car, SUV, van, pick-up, or panel truck for business (as most people do), you have two options for deducting your vehicle expenses: You can use the standard mileage rate, or you can deduct your actual expenses.

Let's start with the easy one: the standard mileage rate. This method works best for people that don't want to bother with a lot of record keeping or calculations. But this ease comes at a price—it often results in a lower deduction than you might otherwise be entitled to using the actual expense method. However, this isn't always the case. The standard mileage rate may give you a larger deduction if you drive many business miles each year, especially if you drive an inexpensive car. (See "How to Maximize Your Car Expense Deduction," below.) But, even if the standard mileage rate does give you a lower deduction, the difference is often so small that it doesn't justify the extra record keeping you will have to do using the actual expense method.

How the Standard Mileage Rate Works

Under the standard mileage rate, you deduct a specified number of cents for every business mile you drive. The IRS sets the standard mileage rate each year—in 2006, the rate is 44.5 cents per mile. To figure out your deduction, simply multiply your business miles by the standard mileage rate for the year. The rate is the same whether you own or lease your car.

> **EXAMPLE:** Ed, a self-employed salesperson, drove his car 10,000 miles for business in 2006. To determine his car expense deduction, he simply multiplies the total business miles he drove by 44.5 cents. This gives him a $4,450 deduction (44.5 cents x 10,000 = $4,450).

The big advantage of the standard mileage rate is that it requires very little record keeping. You only need to keep track of how many business miles you drive, not the actual expenses for your car, such as gas, maintenance, or repairs.

If you choose the standard mileage rate, you cannot deduct actual car operating expenses—for example, maintenance and repairs, gasoline and its taxes, oil, insurance, and vehicle registration fees. All of these items are factored into the rate set by the IRS. And you can't deduct the cost of the car through depreciation or Section 179 expensing, because the car's depreciation is also factored into the standard mileage rate (as are lease payments for a leased car).

The only expenses you can deduct (because these costs aren't included in the standard mileage rate) are:

- interest on a car loan
- parking fees and tolls for business trips (but you can't deduct parking ticket fines or the cost of parking your car at your place of work), and
- personal property tax that you paid when you bought the vehicle based on its value—this is often included as part of your auto registration fee.

Auto loan interest is usually the largest of these expenses. Unfortunately, many people fail to deduct it because of confusion about the tax law. Taxpayers are not allowed to deduct interest on a loan for a car that is for personal use, so many people believe they also can't deduct interest on a business car. This is not the case. You may deduct interest on a loan for a car you use in your business. But there is one exception: If you're an employee, you may not deduct interest on a car loan even if you use the car 100% for your job.

If you use your car for both business and personal trips, you can only deduct the business use percentage of interest and taxes.

> **EXAMPLE:** Ralph uses his car 50% for his printing business and 50% for personal trips. He uses the standard mileage rate to deduct his car expenses. He pays $3,000 a year in interest on his car loan. He may deduct 50% of this amount, or $1,500, as a business operating expense in addition to his business mileage deduction.

Requirements to Use the Standard Mileage Rate

Not everyone can use the standard mileage rate. You won't be able to use it (and will have to use the actual expense method instead) if you can't meet the following requirements.

First-Year Rule

You must use the standard mileage rate in the first year you use a car for business, or you are forever foreclosed from using that method for that car. If you use the standard mileage rate the first year, you can switch to the actual expense method in a later year, and then switch back and forth between the two methods after that, provided the requirements listed below are met. For this reason, if you're not sure which method you want to use, it's a good idea to use the standard mileage rate the first year you use the car for business. This leaves all your options open for later years. However, this rule does not apply to leased cars. If you lease your car, you must use the standard mileage rate for the entire lease period if you use it in the first year.

There are some restrictions on switching back to the standard mileage rate after you have used the actual expense method. You can't switch back to the standard mileage rate after using the actual expense method if you took accelerated depreciation, a Section 179 deduction, or bonus depreciation on the car. You can switch back to the standard mileage rate only if you used the straight-line method of depreciation during the years you used the actual expense method. This depreciation method gives you equal depreciation deductions every year, rather than the larger deductions you get in the early years using accelerated depreciation methods.

However, these restrictions on depreciation are often academic. Because of the severe annual limits on the depreciation deduction for passenger automobiles, it often makes no difference which depreciation method you use—you'll get the same total yearly deduction. So using straight-line depreciation poses no hardship. Keep in mind, however, that if you switch to the actual expense method after using the standard mileage rate, you'll have to reduce the tax basis of your car by a portion of the standard mileage rate deductions you already received. This will reduce your depreciation deduction. (See "Vehicle Depreciation Deductions," below.)

Five-Car Rule

You can't use the standard mileage rate if you have five or more cars that you use for business simultaneously. (Before 2004, the IRS prohibited the standard mileage rate for business owners who used more than one car at the same time. The change to five or more cars allows an additional 800,000 businesses to use the standard mileage rate.) When the IRS says "simultaneously," it means simultaneously. You're barred from using the standard mileage rate only if you operate five or more cars for business *at the exact same time*

> **EXAMPLE 1:** Maureen owns a car and five vans that are used in her housecleaning business. Her employees use the five vans, and she uses the car to travel to customer's houses. Maureen can't use the standard mileage rate for her vehicles because all six cars are used in her business at the same time.

> **EXAMPLE 2:** Paul used four cars at the same time for his business from January to June. One car broke down in July and he bought another and used it for business. In September, he sold one of his cars and bought another which he also used for business. Paul used a total of six cars for his business during the year, but he never used more than four cars for business at the same time so he can still use the standard mileage rate.

Corporation Employees

If you've incorporated your business and work as its employee, you can't use the standard mileage rate if:

- your corporation supplies you with a car, or
- you use your own car for business and your corporation reimburses you for your business mileage.

This rule applies to any employee who owns more than 10% of the company stock or is a close relative of a 10% or more owner—a brother, sister, parent, spouse, grandparent, or other lineal ancestor or descendent. In these instances, the employee must keep receipts for all business-related car expenses.

You may use the standard mileage rate if you own your own car and your corporate employer does not reimburse you for your business driving; however, this is not advantageous for you tax-wise—see "Reimbursing Employees for Business-Related Expenditures" in Chapter 11.

Stop That Cab!

Taxi drivers and others who hire out their vehicles for business can't use the standard mileage rate. They must use the actual expense method as described in the following section.

The Actual Expense Method

Instead of using the standard mileage rate, you can deduct the actual cost of using your car for business. This requires more record keeping, but it also gives you a big advantage—it usually results in a higher deduction.

Business Travel by Motorcycle

You must use the actual expense method if you ride a motorcycle—the standard mileage rate is only for passenger vehicles. However, the limits on depreciation for passenger automobiles discussed in "Vehicle Depreciation Deductions," below, do not apply to bicycles or motorcycles. You may depreciate these items just like any other business property. Or, if you wish, you can deduct the full cost of a motorcycle or bicycle in the year that you purchase it under Section 179. (See Chapter 5 for more on Section 179.)

How the Actual Expense Method Works

As the name implies, under the actual expense method, you deduct the actual costs you incur each year to operate your car, plus depreciation. If you use this method, you must keep careful track of all the costs you incur for your car during the year, including:

- gas and oil
- repairs and maintenance

- depreciation of your original vehicle and improvements
- car repair tools
- license fees
- parking fees for business trips
- registration fees
- tires
- insurance
- garage rent
- tolls for business trips
- car washing
- lease payments
- interest on car loans
- towing charges, and
- auto club dues.

Watch Those Tickets

You may not deduct the cost of driving violations or parking tickets, even if you were on business when you got the ticket. Government fines and penalties are never deductible as a matter of public policy.

When you do your taxes, add up the cost of all these items. For everything but parking fees and tolls, multiply the total cost of each item by the percentage of time you use your car for business. For parking fees and tolls that are business-related, include (and deduct) the full cost. The total is your deductible transportation expense for the year.

EXAMPLE: In one recent year, Laura, a salesperson, drove her car 8,000 miles for her business and 8,000 miles for personal purposes. She can deduct 50% of the actual costs of operating her car, plus the full cost of any business-related tolls and parking fees. Her expenses amount to $10,000 for the year, so she gets a $5,000 deduction, plus $500 in tolls and parking for business.

If you have a car that you only use for business, you may deduct 100% of your actual car costs. Be careful, though. If you own just one car, it's usually hard to claim that you use it only for business. The IRS is not likely to believe that you walk or take public transportation everywhere except when you're on business. Your argument might be more persuasive if you live in a city with a developed transportation system, such as Chicago, New York City, or San Francisco, and drive your car only when you go out of town on business. But be prepared for the IRS to question your deduction. And if you're a sole proprietor, the IRS will know how many cars you own, because sole proprietors who claim transportation expenses must provide this information on their tax returns.

Record-Keeping Requirements

When you deduct actual car expenses, you must keep records of all the costs of owning and operating your car. This includes not only the number of business miles and total miles you drive, but also gas, repair, parking, insurance, tolls, and any other car expenses. Record keeping for car expenses is covered in Chapter 15.

Vehicle Depreciation Deductions

Using the actual expense method, you can deduct the cost of your vehicle. However, you can't deduct the entire cost in the year when you purchase your car. Instead, you must deduct the cost a portion at a time over several years, using a process called depreciation. (For more on depreciation generally, see Chapter 5.) Although the general concept of depreciation is the same for every type of property, special rules apply to depreciation deductions for cars. These rules give you a lower deduction for cars than you'd be entitled to using the normal depreciation rules. Because of these rules, it can take a very long time to fully depreciate an automobile—as much as 20 years or more in the case of an expensive car. As a result, few people ever fully depreciate an automobile—they usually sell it or trade it in first.

This section focuses on the depreciation rules for passenger automobiles, as defined by the IRS. To understand the depreciation rules discussed in this section, you will need to be familiar with the general depreciation rules covered in Chapter 5.

Is Your Vehicle a Passenger Automobile?

First, you must figure out whether your vehicle is a passenger automobile as defined by the IRS. A passenger automobile is any four-wheeled vehicle made primarily for use on public streets and highways that has an unloaded gross weight of 6,000 pounds or less. The vehicle weight includes any part or other item physically attached to the automobile, or usually included in the purchase price of an automobile. This definition includes virtually all automobiles.

However, if your vehicle is a truck, SUV, or van, or has a truck base (as do most SUVs), it is a passenger automobile only if it has a gross loaded vehicle weight of 6,000 pounds or less. The gross loaded weight is based on how much the manufacturer says the vehicle can carry and is different from unloaded weight—that is, the vehicle's weight without any passengers or cargo.

You can find out your vehicle's gross loaded and unloaded weight by looking at the metal plate in the driver's side door jamb, looking at your owner's manual, checking the manufacturer's website or sales brochure, or asking an auto dealer. The gross loaded weight is usually called the Gross Vehicle Weight Rating (GVWR for short). The gross unloaded weight is often called the "curb weight."

Vehicles that would otherwise come within the passenger automobile definition are excluded if they are not likely to be used more than a minimal amount for personal purposes—for example, moving vans, construction vehicles, ambulances, hearses, tractors, and taxis and other vehicles used in a transportation business. Also excluded are trucks and vans that have been specially modified so they are not likely to be used more than a minimal amount for personal purposes—for example, by installation of permanent shelving, or painting the vehicle to display advertising or a company's name. The restrictions on depreciation discussed in this section don't apply to these vehicles.

Passenger Automobiles Are Listed Property

All passenger automobiles are "listed property": property that is often used for personal purposes. As explained in Chapter 5, the IRS imposes more stringent requirements on deductions for listed property to discourage fraudulent deduction claims. Because passenger automobiles are listed property, you must keep mileage records showing how much you use your car for business and personal purposes and you must file IRS Form 4562, *Depreciation and Amortization*, with your annual tax return. (See "Records Required for Specific Expenses" in Chapter 15.)

Other Vehicles That Are Listed Property

Passenger automobiles are not the only vehicles that are listed property. Trucks, buses, boats, airplanes, motorcycles, and any other vehicles used to transport persons or goods are also listed property. The listed property rules apply to these vehicles even if they weigh more than 6,000 pounds and therefore don't qualify as passenger automobiles. However, some types of vehicles are not subject to the listed property rules, including vehicles not likely to be used more than a minimal amount for personal purposes (as described in "Is Your Vehicle a Passenger Automobile?" above) and any vehicle with a loaded gross vehicle weight of over 14,000 pounds that is designed to carry cargo.

What You Can Depreciate

You can depreciate your entire investment in a car (also called your basis). If you buy a passenger automobile and use it for business that same year, your basis is its cost. You may depreciate the entire cost, even if you financed part of the purchase with a car loan. The cost also includes sales taxes, destination charges, and other fees the seller charges. It does not, however, include auto license and registration fees. This assumes you use the car 100% for business. If you use it less than 100%, you may only depreciate an amount equal to your percentage of business use. For example, if you use your car 50% for business, you may depreciate only 50% of the cost.

If you trade in your old car to a dealer to purchase a new car, your basis in the car you purchase is equal to the adjusted basis of the trade-in car, plus the cash you pay (whether out of your own pocket or financed with a car loan).

EXAMPLE: Brenda buys a new pick-up for her construction business. The pick-up has a $20,000 sticker price. She trades in her old pick-up and pays the dealer $15,000, all of which she finances with a car loan from her bank. Her trade-in has an adjusted basis of $3,000. Her basis in the new pick-up is $18,000 ($3,000 + $15,000), even though the sticker price on the new pick-up was $20,000.

If you convert a car that you previously owned for personal use to a business car, your basis in the car is the lower of what you paid for it (at the time you purchased it for personal use) or its fair market value at the time you convert it to business use. Your basis will usually be its fair market value, as this is usually the lower number. You can determine the fair market value by checking used car value guides, such as the *Kelley Blue Book*.

Used car price guides often give more than one value—for example, the *Kelley Blue Book* gives a private party value and a retail value. Using the highest value will give you the largest deduction. The best known used car price guides (available free on the Internet) are:

- *Kelley Blue Book*: www.kbb.com
- Edmunds: www.edmunds.com
- NADAguides: www.nadaguides.com.

Look at more than one guide, because the prices can vary.

Depreciation Limits for Passenger Automobiles

Passenger automobiles have a five-year recovery period (but it takes six calendar years to depreciate a car; see "Depreciation Methods" in Chapter 5). As a result, you'd think it would take at most six years to fully depreciate a car. Unfortunately, this is usually not the case. Depreciating a passenger automobile is unique in one very important way: The annual depreciation deduction for automobiles is limited to a set dollar amount each year. The annual limit applies to all passenger vehicles, no matter how much they cost. Because the limits are so low, it can take many years to fully depreciate a car, far longer than the six years it takes to depreciate other assets with a five-year recovery period.

Starting in 2003, the IRS established two different sets of deduction limits for passenger automobiles: one for passenger automobiles, other than trucks and vans, and slightly higher limits for trucks and vans that qualify as passenger automobiles (based on their weight) and are built on a truck chassis. This includes minivans and sports utility vehicles built on a truck chassis (as long as they meet the weight limit).

The charts below show the maximum annual depreciation deduction allowed for passenger automobiles and trucks and vans placed in service in 2006. (You can triple these limits if you buy an electric car after 5/6/03.) The second chart shows the limits for passenger automobiles that are trucks and vans as defined above. Both charts assume 100% business use of the vehicle. You can find all the deduction limits in IRS Publication 946, *How to Depreciate Property,* and Publication 463, *Travel, Entertainment, Gift, and Car Expenses.*

Depreciation Limits for Passenger Automobiles Placed in Service During 2005	
1st tax year	$2,960
2nd tax year	$4,800
3rd tax year	$2,850
Each succeeding year	$1,775

Depreciation Limits for Trucks and Vans Placed in Service During 2005	
1st tax year	$3,260
2nd tax year	$5,200
3rd tax year	$3,150
Each succeeding year	$1,875

The depreciation limits are not reduced if a car is in service for less than a full year. This means that the limit is not reduced when the automobile is either placed in service or disposed of during the year.

EXAMPLE: Mario pays $50,000 for a new passenger automobile on June 1, 2006 and uses it 100% for his sales business. He may deduct a maximum of $2,960 in 2006; $4,800 in 2007; $2,850 in 2008; and $1,775 thereafter.

The deduction limits in the above table are based on 100% business use of the vehicle. If you don't use your car solely for business, the limits are reduced based on your percentage of personal use.

> **EXAMPLE:** Mario uses his new car 60% for business. His first-year deduction is limited to $1,776 (60% x $2,960 = $1,776).

Determining Your Business Miles for Depreciation

Your total depreciation deduction depends on the percentage of the time you use your car for business. For example, if you drive 5,000 miles for business and 5,000 for personal purposes in a year, you'll have 50% business use and you'll only qualify for 50% of the total allowable depreciation deduction for that year. For example, if the total allowable deduction was $2,960, you'd only get $1,480. Obviously, you want to have as many business miles as possible. A little-known IRS rule can help you rack up more business mileage. When you determine your business mileage for purposes of your depreciation deduction, you may include miles you drove for investment or other income-producing purposes—for example, to visit a rental property or attend an investment seminar. This rule applies only when you figure your total allowable automobile depreciation deduction. (See Chapter 2 for a detailed discussion of investment or other income-producing activities.)

Depreciation Methods

You may use regular depreciation or Section 179 expensing (provided certain requirements are met), or both, to deduct the cost of a passenger automobile used for business. However, your total deduction cannot exceed the annual limits listed in the charts in the previous section. Because the dollar limits on automobile depreciation are so low, there is usually no advantage gained by using Section 179 to take this deduction instead of regular depreciation. It won't increase your deduction and will count against the $108,000 annual Section 179 limit. The only exception is when you are depreciating an extremely inexpensive car.

The following table shows how much of the cost of an automobile may be depreciated each year using the three different depreciation methods and applying the half-year convention. (If more than 40% of all the depreciable property you placed in service during the year was placed in service during the last quarter of the year, you'll have to use the midquarter convention; see "Depreciation" in Chapter 5.) You must use the slower straight-line method if you use your car less than 51% for business, and you must continue to use this method even if your business use rises over 50% in later years. Although automobiles have a five-year recovery period, they are depreciated over six calendar years.

Automobile Depreciation Table

Year	200% Declining Balance Method (midyear convention)	150% Declining Balance Method (midyear convention)	Straight-Line Method (midyear convention)
1	20%	15%	10%
2	32%	25.5%	20%
3	19.2%	17.85%	20%
4	11.5%	16.66%	20%
5	11.5%	16.66%	20%
6	5.76%	8.33%	10%

Restrictions on Section 179

You may use Section 179 to expense a passenger automobile's cost only if you use it at least 51% of the time for business. In addition, you cannot use Section 179 if you convert a personal passenger automobile to business use. The Section 179 deduction is also subject to an income limit—you can't deduct more than your total business income for the year. (See Chapter 5.) If you elect to use Section 179, you must use it before you take regular depreciation.

EXAMPLE 1: Mario buys a $20,000 car in February 2006 and uses it 80% of the time for his sales business. The maximum 2006 depreciation deduction for his car is $2,960. However, because he only uses the car 80% for business, his deduction is limited to $2,368 (80% x $2,960). He may use regular depreciation, Section 179 expensing, or both, to deduct the $2,368. Using the fastest form of depreciation—the 200% declining balance method—results in a $4,000 deduction (20% x $20,000 tax basis in the car). However, Mario may only deduct $2,368 of this amount. He decides not to use Section 179 because it won't increase his deduction and will count against the $108,000 annual Section 179 limit. (See "Section 179 Deductions" in Chapter 5.)

EXAMPLE 2: Billie buys a used Yugo in February 2005 and uses it 100% for business. The car cost $5,000—her tax basis for depreciation purposes. Using the fastest form of regular depreciation (200% declining balance method), the most Billie could deduct the first year is $1,000 (20% x $5,000), which is far less than the $2,960 annual limit for auto depreciation. She decides to combine depreciation with Section 179 expensing instead. First, she deducts $1,960 using Section 179, then she deducts the remaining $1,000 using regular depreciation. This way, she gets to use the full $2,960 auto depreciation deduction, instead of just $1,000.

How Long Do You Depreciate an Auto?

Because of the annual limits on depreciation and Section 179 deductions for passenger automobiles, you won't be able to deduct the entire cost of a car worth more than $15,935 over the six-year recovery period. Don't worry: As long as you continue to use your car for business, you can keep taking annual deductions after the six-year recovery period ends, until you recover your full basis in the car. The maximum amount you can deduct each year is determined by the date you placed the car in service and your business use percentage.

EXAMPLE: In 2006, Kim pays $30,000 for a car she uses 100% for business. Her depreciable basis in the car is $30,000. Her maximum depreciation deductions for the car over the next six years are as follows:

2006	$ 2,960
2007	4,800
2008	2,850
2009	1,775
2010	1,775
2011	1,775
Total	$ 15,935

At the end of the depreciation period, she has $14,065 in unrecovered basis. Even though the depreciation period is over, she may continue to deduct $1,775 each year until she recovers the remaining $14,065 (assuming she continues to use the car 100% for business). This will take another eight years.

Heavy Deductions for Heavy Metal: Expensing Weighty Vehicles

The limits discussed above apply only to passenger automobiles (including trucks, SUVs, and vans that fall within the definition of a passenger automobile because of their weight). They don't apply to trucks, pickups, RVs, vans, and other vehicles that don't come within the passenger automobile definition—that is, vehicles with a gross loaded weight of more than 6,000 pounds. (See "Is Your Vehicle a Passenger Automobile?" above.) So the owners of these vehicles can take a full depreciation deduction—and, if they meet the requirements, a Section 179 deduction for the first year they own the vehicle. If both are used, the first year deduction can be enormous, since the Section 179 deduction alone can go up to a total of $108,000 (except for SUVs; see below).

EXAMPLE: In 2006, Phil purchases a new 9,000-pound truck for $125,000 that he uses 100% for his hauling business. He may deduct the following amounts in 2005:

Section 179 deduction	$108,000
Regular depreciation	2,960
Total	$ 110,960

Phil may depreciate the remaining $14,040 using regular depreciation over the next several years.

To qualify for Section 179 expensing and bonus depreciation, the vehicle must be used more than 50% of the time for business for the full recovery period. You can't get around this rule by using it over 50% for business in the first year and less in subsequent years. If your use goes below 50% during any year in the six-year recovery period, you'll have to repay the Section 179 and bonus depreciation deductions to the IRS—a process called recapture. (See Chapter 5 for more about recapture.)

Until recently, people who purchased SUVs that weighed over 6,000 pounds could use the full Section 179 deduction if the SUV was used 100% for business. However, allowing these huge deductions for Hummers and other SUVs bought for business purposes caused such an uproar that Congress limited the Section 179 deduction for SUVs to $25,000. The limit applies to any SUV placed in service after October 22, 2004.

For these purposes, an SUV is any four-wheeled vehicle primarily designed or used to carry passengers over public streets, roads, or highways that has a gross vehicle weight of 6,000 to 14,000 pounds. However, the $25,000 limit does not apply to any vehicle:

- designed to have a seating capacity of more than nine persons behind the driver's seat,
- equipped with a cargo area of at least six feet in interior length that is an open area or designed for use as an open area, but is enclosed by a cap and not readily accessible directly from the passenger compartment, or
- that has an integral enclosure, fully enclosing the driver compartment and load carrying device, does not have seating rearward of the driver's seat, and has no body section protruding more than 30 inches ahead of the leading edge of the windshield.

Thus, for example, the $25,000 limit does not apply to the large truck in the example above (because it is designed primarily to carry cargo—not passengers), or to most pick-ups or vans that weigh more than 6,000 pounds. (It doesn't apply to any vehicle that weighs more than 14,000 pounds.)

Although the Section 179 deduction for SUVs weighing over 6,000 pounds is limited to $25,000, this is still a very good deal compared to the allowable deduction for passenger automobiles. For example, a person who buys a $50,000 SUV that weighs 6,000 pounds and is used

100% for business can deduct $35,000 of the cost the first year ($25,000 Section 179 deduction + $10,000 regular depreciation using the 200% declining balance method and half-year convention). But, a person who buys a $50,000 passenger automobile can only deduct $2,960 the first year. If the SUV was used only 60% for business, $21,000 could still be deducted the first year (60% of $35,000 amount for 100% business use). The first-year deduction for a 60% business-use passenger automobile is only $1,776. Note that an SUV must be used at least 51% of the time for business to take any Section 179 deduction.

Auto Repairs and Improvements

Auto repairs and maintenance costs are fully deductible in the year they are incurred. You add these costs to your other annual expenses when you use the actual expense method. (You get no extra deduction for repairs when you use the standard mileage rate.) If you fix your car yourself, you may deduct the cost of parts and depreciate or deduct tools, but you get no deduction for your time or labor.

Unlike repairs, improvements to your car must be depreciated over several years, not deducted all in the year when you pay for them. What's the difference between a repair and an improvement? Good question. Unlike a repair, an improvement:

- increases the value of your car
- makes the car more useful, or
- lengthens your car's useful life.

EXAMPLE 1: Doug spends $100 to repair the carburetor for his company car. This is a current expense, because the repair doesn't increase the value of his car or lengthen its useful life. The repair merely allows the car to last for a normal time.

EXAMPLE 2: Doug spends $2,000 on a brand-new engine for his car. This is a capital expense because the new engine increases the car's value and useful life.

This rule can be difficult to apply because virtually all repairs increase the value of the property being repaired. Just remember that an improvement makes your vehicle more valuable than it was before it was worked on, while a repair simply restores the car's value to what it was worth before it broke down.

Improvements are depreciated separately from the vehicle itself—that is, they are treated as a separate item of depreciable property. The same rules, however, apply to depreciating improvements as for regular auto depreciation. Depreciation of the original automobile and the later improvements are combined for purposes of the annual depreciation limits. The recovery period begins when the improvement is placed in service.

Deduct Your Car Repair Tools

If you work on your car yourself, you may deduct the cost of your car repair tools. Your tools must be deducted separately from your auto expenses. If they are only worth $100 or so, you can currently deduct them as a business operating expense. If they are worth more, you must depreciate them or expense them under Section 179. If your tools are older or you haven't kept your receipts for tools you bought this year, you'll have to estimate their fair market value. Take a look in your garage and see what you have to deduct.

Should You Trade In or Sell Your Car?

Whether you sell or trade in a car you use for business can have a big effect on your taxes. The general rule is:

- sell the car if the sale results in a loss for tax purposes (as it usually does)
- trade in the car instead of selling it if you'd earn a profit on the sale.

To determine whether you would earn a profit or incur a loss on a sale of a business car, you subtract the car's adjusted basis from its sales price. For example, if your car has an adjusted basis of $15,000 and you sell it for $20,000, you will earn $5,000 in profit. If you sold the car for $10,000, you'd have a $5,000 loss. The depreciation allowed on a business vehicle reduces its tax basis; thus, it has a major effect on whether you earn a profit or incur a loss when the vehicle is sold. Usually, a car is sold at a loss because its true resale value is less than the depreciation allowed by the IRS.

A loss on the sale of a business car is good tax-wise because you can deduct it from your other income. So you should sell your car instead of trading it in if the sales price is less than your adjusted basis.

> **EXAMPLE:** Adolf purchased a $30,000 car in 2005 and used it 100% for business every year. In 2007, his adjusted basis is $22,400 ($30,000 − $7,600 depreciation). The most he can sell the car for is $15,000. He should sell the car rather than trade it in, because the sale will result in a $7,400 business loss that he can deduct from his income.

The above example assumes you use the car 100% for business. If you use it less than 100%, you may deduct only the business portion of your loss. To do this, you treat your car as if it were two separate vehicles: a business car and a personal car. You'll have two different basis numbers: one for your business use of the car, and one for your personal use. You separately determine your business and personal profit or loss when you sell the car. A business loss is deductible, a personal loss is not. However, both business and personal profit on an auto sale are taxed.

> **EXAMPLE:** Assume that Adolf from the above example used his $30,000 car for business only 75% of the time. His starting business basis is $22,500 (75% x $30,000 = $22,500). His starting personal basis is $7,500 (25% x $30,000 = $7,500). He took a total of $7,600 in depreciation during the years he used the car for business. Depreciation is a business deduction, so it is only subtracted from his business basis. This leaves him with a $14,900 business basis ($22,500 − $7,600 = $14,900). He still has his original $7,500 personal basis. If he sells the car, he must deduct his $14,900 business basis from 75% of the sales price and deduct his personal basis from the remaining 25%. If the sales price is $15,000, he must deduct $14,900 from $11,250 (75% of the $15,000 sales price), leaving him with a $3,650 business loss. He also deducts his $7,500 personal basis from 25% of the sales price ($3,750), leaving him with a $3,750 personal loss. He may deduct the $3,650 business loss, but he may not deduct the $3,750 personal loss.

If, like most people, you don't use your car the same amount for business each year, you'll have to calculate your business use percentage for the entire time you used the car. You do this by adding up all your business and personal miles and then dividing the business miles by the total of all your miles.

EXAMPLE: Shoshona purchased a car in 2003 and used it for both business and personal driving as follows:

Year	Business Miles	Personal Miles	Total Miles
2003	8,543	4,260	12,803
2004	9,288	3,702	12,990
2005	11,684	4,633	16,317
2006	7,307	5,953	13,260
Total	36,822	18,548	55,370

36,822 business miles divided by 55,370 total miles =0.67. Thus, Shoshona used her car a total of 67% of the time for business during 2003 through 2006.

A profit on a sale is bad tax-wise because you'll have to pay tax on it. If you use your car for both business and personal driving, you must pay tax on both your business and personal profit. You'll avoid earning a taxable profit if you trade in your car instead of selling it. Instead of ending up with money in your pocket you have to pay tax on, the adjusted basis of your trade-in car becomes part of the tax basis of the new car. (See "What You Can Depreciate," above.) In addition, if you owe sales tax on the purchase of a new car, many states make you pay tax only on the purchase price less the value of the trade in. If, instead, you sell the old car and apply the proceeds to the purchase of a new car, you would have to pay sales tax on the full purchase price.

EXAMPLE: Eva purchased a car in 2005 and used it 100% for her business every year. She paid $20,000 for the car and had taken $7,660 in depreciation by 2007. Her car's adjusted basis is $12,340 ($20,000 – $7,660 = $12,340). A friend offers her $15,000 for the car. Should she sell it? No! If she sells the car for $15,000, she'll have a $2,660 gain she'll have to pay tax on ($15,000 – $12,340 = $2,660). Instead of selling the car, she should trade it in for another car (assuming she gets a decent value on her trade-in). This way she'll have no profit she'll have to pay tax on. Instead, her $12,340 adjusted basis in the old car will become part of the basis of the new car. If the new car costs $25,000 and she pays $10,000 cash plus her trade-in, the new car's basis will be $22,340: the cash she paid for the new car plus the basis of her old car.

In the above example, the amount Eva received on her trade-in was equal to what she would have received if she sold her car to her friend. However, if you can get substantially more selling your car than on a trade-in, you may be better off selling it. Why? The tax benefits of the trade-in may not equal the extra amount received on the sale.

Selling Your Car

Subject to two exceptions, you can sell your old car to anyone and deduct the business portion of your loss. You may sell to a car dealer, but you cannot purchase another car from the dealer at the same time—this would be considered a trade-in by the IRS.

Exception #1: You cannot sell your old car to a close relative and deduct your loss. For these purposes, a close relative is any lineal descendent or ancestor, such as parents, children, siblings, or grandparents. However, aunts, uncles, nieces, nephews, and cousins are not included in this exception.

Exception #2: You cannot sell your car to a business entity, such as a corporation or LLC in which you are the majority owner, and deduct your loss. Thus, you can't form an LLC, sell your car to it at a loss, and then deduct the loss from your taxes.

If you've taken the standard mileage deduction for your car for any year, you won't have a separate depreciation deduction because it is included in the single standard mileage rate. To determine how much depreciation you've taken, multiply the total business miles you drove the car by the amount of the standard mileage rate that accounts for depreciation. These amounts are shown in the following table.

Year	Amount of Depreciation Included in Standard Mileage Rate (Per Business Mile)
2005–2006	17 cents
2003–2004	16 cents
2001–2002	15 cents
2000	14 cents
1994–1999	12 cents
(For earlier years, see IRS Publication 463, *Travel, Entertainment, Gift, and Car Expenses*.)	

EXAMPLE: Reginald drove his car 10,000 miles for business in 2004, 2005, and 2006. His annual depreciation was $1,700 in 2005 and 2006 (17 cents x 10,000 = $1,700). He had $1,600 depreciation in 2004, giving him $5,000 total depreciation. He must reduce the basis of the car by this amount to determine its adjusted basis. He paid $15,000 for the car, so its adjusted basis is $10,000.

Leasing a Car

If you lease a car that you use in your business, you can use the actual expense method to deduct the portion of each lease payment that reflects the business percentage use of the car. You cannot deduct any part of a lease payment that is for commuting or personal use of the car.

EXAMPLE: John pays $400 a month to lease a Lexus. He uses it 50% for his dental tool sales business and 50% for personal purposes. He may deduct half of his lease payments ($200 a month) as a local transportation expense for his sales business.

Leasing companies typically require you to make an advance or down payment to lease a car. You can deduct this cost, but you must spread the deduction out equally over the entire lease period.

With the standard mileage method, you don't deduct any portion of your lease payments. Instead, this cost is covered by the standard mileage rate set by the IRS.

Is It Really a Lease?

Some transactions that are called "auto leases" are really not leases at all. Instead, they are installment purchases—that is, you pay for the car over time, and by the end of the lease term you own all or part of the car. You cannot deduct any payments you make to buy a car, even if the payments are called lease payments. Instead, you have to depreciate the cost of the car as described in "Vehicle Depreciation Deductions," above.

Should You Lease or Buy Your Car?

When you lease a car, you are paying rent for it—a set fee each month for the use of the car. At the end of the lease term, you give the car back to the leasing company and own nothing. As a general rule, leasing a car instead of buying it makes economic sense only if you absolutely must have a new car every two or three years and drive no more than 12,000 to 15,000 miles per year. If you drive more than 15,000 miles a year, leasing becomes an economic disaster because it penalizes you for higher mileage.

There are numerous financial calculators available on the Internet that can help you determine how much it will cost to lease a car compared to buying one. Be careful when you use these calculators— they are designed based on certain assumptions, and different calculators can give different answers. For a detailed consumer guide to auto leasing created by the Federal Reserve Board, go to the Board's website at www.federalreserve.gov/pubs/leasing.

Leasing Luxury Cars

If you lease what the IRS considers to be a luxury car for more than 30 days, you may have to reduce your lease deduction. The purpose of this rule is to prevent people from leasing very expensive cars to get around the limitations on depreciation deductions for cars that are purchased. (See "Vehicle Depreciation Deductions," above.) A luxury car is currently defined as one with a fair market value of more than $15,200.

The amount by which you must reduce your deduction (called an "inclusion amount") is based on the fair market value of your car and the percentage of time that you use it for business. The IRS recalculates it each year. You can find the inclusion amount for the current year in the tables published in IRS Publication 463, *Travel, Entertainment, Gift, and Car Expenses*. For example, if you leased a $40,000 car in 2006 and used it solely for business, you would have to reduce your car expense deduction by $168 for the year. If you used the car only 50% for business, the reduction would be $84. The inclusion amount for the first year is prorated based on the month when you start using the car for business.

How to Maximize Your Car Expense Deduction

Sam and Sue both drive their cars 10,000 miles for business each year. This year, Sam got a $4,450 auto deduction, while Sue got $5,500. Why the difference? Sue took some simple steps to maximize her deduction. You can get the largest deduction possible by following these tips.

Use the Method That Gives the Largest Deduction

Many taxpayers choose the standard mileage rate because it's easier—it requires much less record keeping than the actual expense method. However, you'll often get a larger deduction if you use the actual expense method. The American Automobile Association estimated that the average cost of owning a car in 2006 was 62 cents per mile. This is substantially more than the 44.5 cents per mile the IRS allows you to deduct under the standard mileage rate in 2006. Of course, this is just an average; your expenses could be lower, depending on the value of your car and how much you spend for repairs, gas, and other operating costs. The only way to know for sure which method gives you the largest deduction is to do the numbers.

> **EXAMPLE:** In January 2006, Vicky buys a $20,000 car. During the year, she drives it 10,000 miles for her sales business and 5,000 miles for personal purposes. She keeps track of all of her car expenses during the year. When she does her taxes, she compares the deduction she would receive using the actual expense method and the standard mileage rate. To do so, she completes the table shown below.

Actual Expense Method Worksheet

Business/Personal Use

Total Mileage for Business		$ 10,000
Total Mileage for Year	÷	15,000
Business %	=	67%

Actual Annual Expenses

Gas and Oil		$ 2,400
Insurance	+	1,500
Repairs and Maintenance	+	500
Registration	+	50
Wash and Wax	+	200
Other	+	50
Total Actual Expenses	=	$ 4,700
Business %	X	67%
Business Total		= $ 3,149
Depreciation Deduction (67% x $2,960)		+ 1,983
Interest (total x business %)		+ 500
Personal Property Taxes (total x business %)		+ 350
Parking and Tolls		+ 1,800
Total Auto Deduction		= $ 7,782

Standard Mileage Rate Worksheet

Total Business Mileage		$10,000
Total Mileage for Year	÷	15,000
Business %	=	67%
Standard Mileage Rate Deduction (44.5 x 15,000 x 67%)	= $	4,450
Interest (total x business %)	+	500
Personal Property Taxes (total x business %)	+	350
Parking and Tolls	+	1,800
Total Auto Deduction	= $	7,100

There are circumstances when the standard mileage rate might give you a better deduction than the actual expense method. If you drive a car that's not worth much, either because it's old or an inexpensive model, you might come out ahead. Why? Because you get the same fixed deduction rate no matter how much the car is worth. Seventeen cents of the 44.5 cent rate for 2006 is for depreciation. With an inexpensive car, you might benefit from using the standard mileage rate, because the car's actual depreciation will be less than the 17-cent fixed amount.

> **EXAMPLE:** Max buys a $1,000 used car in January 2006 and uses it exclusively in his photocopier repair business. He drives it 20,000 miles in 2006. Using the standard mileage rate, he gets an $8,900 deduction (20,000 x 44.5 cents = $8,900). Using the actual expense rate, he could get a $1,000 deduction for depreciation the first year (assuming he used Section 179 to deduct the entire purchase price of the car). This is $2,400 less than the $3,400 depreciation deduction he can get using the standard mileage rate (17 cents x 20,000 miles = $3,400). Because his other actual expenses are less than $7,900, he's better off using the standard mileage rate. He'll do even better in 2007 and later—he would get no depreciation at all under the actual expense method, but he still gets 17 cents a mile using the standard mileage rate.

Use Two Cars for Business

If you use the actual expense method, you might think you would get a larger deduction by using one car 100% of the time for business instead of having two cars that you use less than 100% for business. This is usually not the case—two cars are usually better than one, because you can get a larger total depreciation deduction by depreciating two cars.

> **EXAMPLE:** Biff owns two cars. He needs to drive 20,000 miles for business during the year and 10,000 miles for personal purposes. Let's see how big a deduction he gets using one car versus two.

One Business Car		
	Car 1	Car 2
Total Miles	20,000	10,000
Business Miles	20,000	0
Business %	100%	0
Total Costs	$6,500	$5,000
Total Auto Deduction	$6,500	0

Two Business Cars		
	Car 1	Car 2
Total Miles	20,000	10,000
Business Miles	15,000	5,000
Business %	75%	50%
Total Costs	$6,500	$5,000
Total Auto Deduction	$4,875	$2,500

By using two cars instead of one, but driving the same total number of miles, Biff gets a $7,375 deduction, compared with only a $6,500 deduction for one car.

The IRS requires you to have a good reason for using two cars instead of one for your business. It shouldn't be hard to come up with one—for example, you don't want to put too many miles on each car, or one car carries more cargo and the other gets better gas mileage.

Of course, if you use the standard mileage rate, it makes no difference how many cars you drive—your deduction is based solely on your total business mileage.

Keep Good Records

More than anything else, keeping good records is the key to the local transportation deduction. The IRS knows that many people don't keep good records. When they do their taxes, they make wild guesses abut how many business miles they drove the previous year. This is why IRS auditors are more suspicious of this deduction than almost any other.

Record keeping for the transportation deduction doesn't have to be too burdensome. If keeping records of gas, oil, repairs, and all your other car expenses is too much trouble (and it can be a pain in the neck), use the standard mileage rate (assuming you qualify for it). That way, you'll only need to keep track of how many miles you drive for business. Indeed, you might not even have to keep track of your business miles for the entire year; instead, you may be able to use a sample period of three months or one week a month. Remember that keeping track of your actual expenses often gives you a larger deduction. It's up to you to decide which is more important: your time or your money.

See Chapter 15 for a detailed discussion of how to keep car and mileage records.

Other Local Transportation Expenses

You don't have to drive a car or other vehicle to get a tax deduction for local business trips. You can deduct the cost of travel by bus or other public transit, taxi, train, ferry, motorcycle, bicycle, or any other means. However, all the rules limiting deductions for travel by car discussed in "Commuting is Not Deductible," above, also apply to other transportation methods. This means, for example, that you can't deduct the cost of commuting from your home to your office or other permanent work location. The same record-keeping requirements apply as well.

When Clients or Customers Reimburse You

Some small business owners have their local travel expenses reimbursed by their clients or customers. This is especially common for professionals such as lawyers. You need not include such reimbursements in your income if you provide an adequate accounting of the expenses to your client and comply with the accountable plan rules. Basically, this requires that you submit all your documentation to the client in a timely manner, and return any excess payments. Accountable plans are covered in detail in Chapter 11. Record-keeping rules for business driving are covered in Chapter 15.

EXAMPLE: Erica, a sole proprietor accountant, is hired by Acme Corp. to handle an audit. She keeps a complete mileage log showing that she drove 500 miles while working on the audit. Acme reimburses Erica $250 for the business mileage. Erica need not include this amount in her income for the year. Acme may deduct it as a business expense.

If you do not adequately account to your client for these expenses, you must include any reimbursements or allowances in your income. They should also be included in any 1099-MISC form the client provides to the IRS reporting how much you were paid. The client can still deduct the reimbursement as compensation paid to you. You may deduct the expenses on your own return, but you'll need documentation to back them up in the event of an audit.

EXAMPLE: Assume that Erica doesn't keep proper track of her mileage. At the end of the year, she estimates that she drove 500 miles on Acme's behalf. Acme reimburses Erica $250, but concludes she didn't adequately account for her expenses under the IRS rules. It deducts the $250 on its tax return as compensation paid to Erica, and includes the $250 on the 1099-MISC form it sends the IRS the following February reporting how much it paid her. Erica deducts the $250 on her return as a business expense. Two years later, Erica is audited by the IRS. When the auditor asks her for her records showing how many miles she drove while representing Acme, Erica tells him she doesn't have any. The auditor disallows the deduction.

Reporting Transportation Expenses on Schedule C

If you're a sole proprietor, you will list your car expenses on Schedule C, *Profit or Loss From Business*. Schedule C asks more questions about this deduction than almost any other deduction (reflecting the IRS's general suspicion about auto deductions).

Part IV of Schedule C is reproduced below. If you answer "no" to question 45, you cannot claim to use your single car 100% for business. If you answer "no" to questions 47a or 47b, you do not qualify for the deduction.

Part IV | **Information on Your Vehicle.** Complete this part **only** if you are claiming car or truck expenses on line 9 and are not required to file Form 4562 for this business. See the instructions for line 13 on page C-4 to find out if you must file Form 4562.

43   When did you place your vehicle in service for business purposes? (month, day, year) ▶ ..../......../........ .

44   Of the total number of miles you drove your vehicle during 2004, enter the number of miles you used your vehicle for:

a   Business ....   b Commuting ....   c Other ....

45   Do you (or your spouse) have another vehicle available for personal use?. . . . .   ☐ **Yes**   ☐ **No**

46   Was your vehicle available for personal use during off-duty hours?   . . . .   ☐ **Yes**   ☐ **No**

47a Do you have evidence to support your deduction?   . . . .   ☐ **Yes**   ☐ **No**

b   If "Yes," is the evidence written? . . . .   ☐ **Yes**   ☐ **No**

How to Reduce Your Schedule C Auto Deduction

If you deduct the interest you pay on a car loan, you have the option of reporting the amount in two different places on your Schedule C: You can lump it in with all your other car expenses on line 9 of the schedule titled "Car and truck expenses," or you can list it separately on line 16b as an "other interest" cost. Reporting your interest expense separately from your other car expenses reduces the total car expense shown on your Schedule C. This can help avoid an IRS audit.

You must also file IRS Form 4562, *Depreciation and Amortization*. This form is used to report your Section 179 and depreciation deductions for the vehicle.

Corporations, LLCs, and Partnerships

If your business is legally organized as a corporation, LLC, or partnership, there are special complications when it comes to deducting car expenses. Moreover, you have the option of having your business own (or lease) the car you use, instead of using your personal car for business driving.

Using Your Own Car

If you use your own car for business driving, how your expenses may be deducted depends on whether your business is a corporation, LLC, or partnership.

LLCs and Partnerships

If you have organized your business as an LLC (with more than one member), you'll usually seek reimbursement for your deductible car and other local travel expenses from your business entity. You can use either the standard mileage rate or actual expense method to calculate your expenses.

As long as you comply with the record-keeping rules for car expenses and your reimbursement is made under an accountable plan, any reimbursement you receive will not be taxable income. Basically, you must submit all your documentation to the business in a timely manner and return any excess payments. Accountable plans are covered in detail in Chapter 11.

The business can deduct the amount of the reimbursed car expenses on its tax return (Form 1065) and reduce its taxable profit for the year. Or, in many cases, the business will obtain reimbursement from the client on whose behalf you did your local business travel.

> **EXAMPLE:** Rick, a partner in a CPA firm organized as an LLC, uses his personal car for local business driving. He uses the standard mileage rate and keeps careful track of all of his business mileage. He submits a request for reimbursement to the firm, along with his mileage records. He was entitled to a $4,050 reimbursement from his firm. This money is not taxable income to Rick, and the firm may list it on its tax return as a business expense or seek reimbursement from Rick's clients.

Instead of seeking reimbursement, you can deduct car expenses on your personal tax return, provided either of the following is true:

- You have a written partnership agreement or LLC operating agreement which provides that the expense will *not* be reimbursed by the partnership or LLC.
- Your business has an established routine of not reimbursing the expense.

Absent such a written agreement or established business, *no personal deduction may be taken*. You must seek reimbursement from the partnership or LLC instead. If you take a personal deduction for your car expenses, your business does not list them on its tax return and they do not reduce your business's profits. But they will reduce your taxable income. (See Chapter 11 for a detailed discussion.)

You deduct your unreimbursed car expenses (and any other unreimbursed business expenses) on IRS Schedule E (Part II) and attach it to your personal tax return. You must attach a separate schedule to Schedule E listing the car and other business expenses you're deducting.

> **EXAMPLE:** Assume that Rick's CPA firm has a written policy that all the partners must personally pay for their own car expenses. Instead of seeking reimbursement, Rick lists his $4,050 car expense on his own tax return, Schedule E, reducing his taxable income by that amount. The law firm does not list the expense on its return, thus it does not reduce the firm's income.

Corporations

If your business is legally organized as a corporation (whether a C or S corporation), you are probably working as its employee. Special rules govern all business expense deductions by employees. Your best option is to have your corporation reimburse you for your car expenses. You get reimbursement in the same way as described above for LLCs and partnerships. You must comply with all the documentation rules for car expenses and the accountable plan requirements. If you do, your corporation gets to deduct the expense and you don't have to count the reimbursement as taxable income. If you fail to follow the rules, any reimbursements must be treated as employee income subject to tax (but you may deduct your expenses as described below). (See Chapter 11.)

Using a Company Car

If your business entity buys a car that you use (that is, your business holds the title to the car, not you personally), the dollar value of your business driving is a tax-free working condition fringe benefit provided to you by your business. In addition, the business gets to deduct all of its actual car expenses on its tax return—for example, depreciation, interest on a car loan, maintenance, fuel it pays for, and insurance costs.

You get no personal deduction for these expenses; but, of course, if your business is a pass-through entity, the deduction on its return will reduce the amount of taxable profit passed on to your tax return. However, you can personally deduct the actual cost of fuel or maintenance you pay for yourself, and the cost of anything else you buy for the car. You can't use the standard mileage rate to figure your costs. You must keep track of your mileage using one of the methods described above; and, if you personally buy fuel or other items for the car, you must comply with all the documentation rules for car expenses covered in Chapter 15.

> **EXAMPLE:** John, a veterinarian, is a one-third owner of a group business organized as an LLC. The LLC buys a $20,000 car that John uses 100% for business driving. He keeps careful track of his mileage. In 2005, he drove the car 6,000 miles. The LLC may deduct on its tax return all the expenses it incurs from owning the car:

Interest on car loan	$ 1,100
Depreciation	2,960
Fuel	1,200
Maintenance	1,000
Insurance	1,000
Total	$ 7,260

> John's LLC lists the $7,260 as a deduction on its tax return. As a result, instead of reporting a $300,000 annual profit, it has a $292,740 profit. John pays income and self-employment tax on his distributive share of this amount, which is one-third. John gets no personal deduction for these expenses, but he may personally deduct as a business expense the cost of fuel he paid for using his own money. This gives him a $400 deduction. John need not pay any tax on the value of having the car because it is a tax-free working condition fringe benefit provided to him by the LLC.

Things get more complicated if, as is often the case, you use a company car for both business and personal driving. The dollar value of your personal use of the car is treated as a taxable fringe benefit. The amount must be added to your annual compensation and income, Social Security, and Medicare taxes must be paid on it.

> **EXAMPLE:** Assume that John from the above example uses his company car 60% for business driving and 40% for personal driving. His LLC still gets the $7,260 deduction for its car expenses. However, the dollar value of John's personal driving is a taxable fringe benefit that must be added to his annual compensation. If the value of his personal driving was $5,000, he has to pay income and self-employment tax on this amount. He still gets to deduct the cost of fuel he paid for when he drove the car for business.

Here's a key question: How do you place a dollar value on your personal use of a company car? This determines how much money must be added to your income for such use. You may be able to use any of three different methods to figure this out, and they may yield very different results. The easiest way is to use the IRS Annual Lease Value Table contained in IRS Publication 15-B, *Employer's Tax Guide to Fringe Benefits*.

If your company leases a car it provides you, all the rules above still apply. But it's much easier to figure out the value of your personal use of the car—simply multiply the annual lease payments by the percentage of personal use.

Chapter 9

Business Travel

f you travel overnight for business, you can deduct your airfare, hotel bills, and other expenses. If you plan your trip right, you can even mix business with pleasure and still get a deduction. However, IRS auditors closely scrutinize these deductions. Many taxpayers claim them without complying with the copious rules the IRS imposes. To avoid unwanted attention, you need to understand the limitations on this deduction and keep proper records.

What Is Business Travel?

For tax purposes, business travel occurs when you travel away from your tax home overnight for your business. You don't have to travel any set distance to get a travel expense deduction. However, you can't take this deduction if you just spend the night in a motel across town. You must travel outside your city limits. If you don't live in a city, you must go outside the general area where your business is located.

You must stay away overnight or at least long enough to require a stop for sleep or rest. You cannot satisfy the rest requirement by merely napping in your car.

> **EXAMPLE 1:** Phyllis, a self-employed salesperson based in Los Angeles, flies to San Francisco to meet potential clients, spends the night in a hotel, and returns home the following day. Her trip is a deductible travel expense.

> **EXAMPLE 2:** Andre, a self-employed truck driver, leaves his workplace on a regularly scheduled round trip between San Francisco and Los Angeles and returns home 18 hours later. During the run, he has six hours off at a turnaround point where he eats two meals and rents a hotel room to get some sleep before starting the return trip. Andre can deduct his meal and hotel expenses as travel expenses.

If you don't stay overnight, your trip will not qualify as business travel. However, this does not necessarily mean that you can't take a tax deduction. Local business trips, other than commuting, are deductible.

However, you may only deduct your transportation expenses—the cost of driving or using some other means of transportation. You may not deduct meals or other expenses like you can when you travel for business and stay overnight.

> **EXAMPLE:** Philip drives from his office in Los Angeles to a business meeting in San Diego and returns the same day. His 200-mile round trip is a deductible local business trip. He may deduct his expenses for the 200 business miles he drove, but he can't deduct the breakfast he bought on the way to San Diego.

 For a detailed discussion of tax deductions for local business travel, see Chapter 8.

Where Is Your Tax Home?

Your tax home is the entire city or general area where your principal place of business is located. This is not necessarily the place where you live.

> **EXAMPLE:** Tim is a political lobbyist who maintains his office in Washington, DC. However, his family lives in New York City. He spends weekends with his family in New York and stays in a hotel during the week when he works in Washington. Tim's tax home is in Washington, DC. This means that when he travels back and forth between his Washington office and his New York home, his trips are nondeductible commuting. In addition, he gets no travel expense deductions while staying in Washington—for example, he can't deduct his hotel room or meals as a business travel expense. Because Washington, DC, is his tax home, he's not traveling while staying there.

The IRS doesn't care how far you travel for business. You'll get a deduction as long as you travel outside your tax home's city limits and stay overnight. Thus, even if you're just traveling across town, you'll qualify for a deduction if you manage to stay outside your city limits.

EXAMPLE: Pete, a tax adviser, has his office in San Francisco. He travels to Oakland for an all-day meeting with a client. At the end of the meeting, he decides to spend the night in an Oakland hotel rather than brave the traffic back to San Francisco. Pete's stay qualifies as a business trip even though the distance between his San Francisco office and the Oakland business meeting is only eight miles. Pete can deduct his hotel and meal expenses.

If you don't live in a city, your tax home covers the general area where it is located. This general area is anywhere within about 40 miles of your tax home.

Multiple Work Locations

If you work in more than one location, your tax home is your main place of business. To determine this, consider:

- the total time you spend in each place
- the level of your business activity in each place, and
- the amount of income you earn from each place.

EXAMPLE: Lee, a dentist, has his own dental office in Houston, Texas. In addition, he works in his father's dental office in Dallas, Texas. He spends three weeks a month in Houston and one week in Dallas. He makes $150,000 per year from his Houston practice and $50,000 per year from his work in Dallas. Houston—where he spends more time and makes more money—is his tax home.

No Main Place of Business

Some people have no main place of business—for example, a sales-person who is always on the road, traveling from sales contact to sales contact. In this event, your home (main residence) can qualify as your tax home, as long as you:

- perform part of your business there and live at home while doing business in that area
- have living expenses at your home that you must duplicate because your business requires you to travel away from home, and
- satisfy one of the following three requirements:
  - You have not abandoned the area where your home is located—that is, you work in the area or have other contacts there.

- You have family living at the home.
- You often live in the home yourself.

EXAMPLE: Ruth is a liquor salesperson whose territory includes the entire southern United States. She has a home in Miami, Florida, where her mother lives. Ruth's sales territory includes Florida. She uses her home for her business when making sales in the Miami area and lives in it when making sales calls in the area. She spends about 12 weeks a year at home and is on the road the rest of the time. Ruth's Miami home is her tax home because she satisfies all three factors listed above: (1) she does business in the Miami area and stays in her Miami home when doing so; (2) she has duplicate living expenses; and (3) she has family living at the home.

Even if you satisfy only two of the three factors, your home may still qualify as your tax home, depending on all the facts and circumstances.

EXAMPLE: Assume that Ruth in the above example has the Northeast as her sales territory and does no work in the Miami area where her home is located. She fails the first factor but still satisfies the second two. Her Miami home would probably qualify as her tax home.

If you can satisfy none or only one of the three factors, you have no tax home. You are a transient for tax purposes. If you're a transient, you may not deduct any travel expenses, because you are never considered to be traveling away from home. Obviously, this is not a good situation to find yourself in, tax-wise.

EXAMPLE: James Henderson was a stage hand for a traveling ice skating show. He spent most of his time on the road, but spent two to three months a year living rent-free in his parent's home in Boise, Idaho. Both the IRS and the courts found that he was a transient for tax purposes because he failed to satisfy the first two of the three criteria listed above. Namely, he did no work in Boise and he had no home living expenses that he had to duplicate while on the road because he didn't pay rent to his parents. Thus, Henderson was not entitled to a tax deduction for his travel expenses. (*Henderson v. Commissioner*, 143 F.3d 497 (9th Cir. 1998).)

If you travel a lot for business, you should do everything you can to avoid being considered a transient. This means you must take steps to satisfy at least two of the three factors listed above. For example, James could avoid his transient status if he performed work in the Boise area, paid his parents for his room (thereby resulting in duplicate expenses), and spent more time at his parent's home.

Temporary Work Locations

You may regularly work at your tax home and also work at another location. It may not always be practical to return from this other location to your tax home at the end of each workday. Your overnight stays at these temporary work locations qualify as business travel as long as your work there is truly temporary—that is, it is reasonably expected to last no more than one year. If that is the case, your tax home does not change and you are considered to be away from home for the entire period you spend at the temporary work location.

> **EXAMPLE:** Betty is a self-employed sexual harassment educator. She works out of her home office in Chicago, Illinois. She is hired to conduct sexual harassment training and counseling for a large company in Indianapolis, Indiana. The job is expected to last three months. Betty's assignment is temporary, and Chicago remains her tax home. She may deduct the expenses she incurs traveling to and staying in Indianapolis.

On the other hand, if you reasonably expect your work at the other location to last more than one year, that location becomes your new tax home and you cannot deduct your travel expenses while there.

> **EXAMPLE:** Carl is a plumbing contractor whose place of business is Seattle, Washington. He is hired to install the plumbing in a new subdivision in Boise, Idaho, and the job is expected to take 18 months. Boise is now Carl's tax home, and he may not deduct his travel expenses while staying there.

If you go back to your tax home from a temporary work location on your days off, you are not considered away from home while you are in your hometown. You cannot deduct the cost of meals and lodging there. However, you can deduct your expenses, including meals and lodging, while traveling between your temporary work location and your tax home. You can claim these expenses up to the amount it would have cost you to stay at your temporary work location. In addition, if you keep your hotel room during your visit home, you can deduct that cost.

Your Trip Must Be for Business

Your trip must be primarily for business to be deductible, and you must have a business intent and purpose before leaving on the trip. You have a business purpose if the trip benefits your business in some way. Examples of business purposes include:

- finding new customers or markets for your products or services
- dealing with existing customers or clients
- learning new skills to help in your business
- contacting people who could help your business, such as potential investors, or
- checking out what the competition is doing.

For example, a taxpayer who manufactured and sold weightlifting equipment was entitled to deduct the cost of attending the summer Olympics in Rome because the purpose of the trip was to find new customers for his product line. (*Hoffman v. Commissioner*, 798 F.2d 784 (3d Cir. 1962).)

It's not sufficient merely to claim that you had a business purpose for your trip. You must be able to prove this by showing that you spent at least part of the time engaged in business activities while at your destination. Acceptable business activities include:

- visiting or working with existing or potential clients or customers
- attending trade shows or conventions, or
- attending professional seminars or business conventions where the agenda is clearly connected to your business.

On the other hand, business activities do not include:

- sightseeing

- recreational activities that you attend by yourself or with family or friends, or
- attending personal investment seminars or political events.

Use common sense when deciding whether to claim that a trip is for business. If you're audited, the IRS will likely question any trip that doesn't have some logical connection to your existing business.

Travel for a New Business or Location

You must actually be in business to have deductible business trips. Trips you make to investigate a potential new business or to actually start or acquire a new business are not currently deductible business travel expenses. However, they may be deductible as business start-up expenses, which means you can deduct up to $5,000 of these expenses the first year you're in business if your total start-up expenses are less than $50,000. (See Chapter 3 for more on start-up expenses.)

Their European Trip Was Not for Business

In 1984, Oliver Bentley and his foster son spent approximately $7,500 for an extensive European trip. When they got back, they tried to make money off their travel by attempting to arrange student tours to Europe. They contacted travel agents and distributed flyers, but the business never got off the ground. When Bentley did his taxes for the year, he took a $5,127 tax deduction for the trip, claiming it was primarily for this business. The IRS and tax court both disagreed. Bentley could not claim a business travel deduction because he did not have an existing business when he took the trip, and the costs of investigating a new business venture are not currently deductible. (*Bentley v. Commissioners*, TC Memo 1988-444.)

Travel as an Education Expense

You may deduct the cost of traveling to an educational activity directly related to your business. For example, a French translator can deduct the cost of traveling to France to attend formal French language classes.

However, you can't take a trip and claim that the travel itself constitutes a form of education and is therefore deductible. For example, a French translator who travels to France may not take a business travel deduction if the purpose of the trip is to see the sights and become familiar with French language and culture. (See Chapter 14 for more on education expenses.)

Visiting Business Colleagues

Visiting business colleagues or competitors may be a legitimate business purpose for a trip. But you can't just socialize with them. You must use your visit to learn new skills, check out what your competitors are doing, seek investors, or attempt to get new customers or clients.

What Travel Expenses Are Deductible

Subject to the limits covered in "How Much You Can Deduct," below, virtually all of your business travel expenses are deductible. These fall into two broad categories: your transportation expenses and the expenses you incur at your destination.

Transportation expenses are the costs of getting to and from your destination—for example:

- fares for airplanes, trains, or buses
- driving expenses, including car rentals
- shipping costs for your personal luggage or samples, displays, or other things you need for your business, and
- meals, beverages, and lodging expenses you incur while en route to your final destination.

If you drive your personal car to your destination, you may deduct your costs by using the standard mileage rate or deduct your actual expenses. You may also deduct your mileage while at your destination. (See Chapter 8 for more on deducting car expenses.)

You may also deduct the expenses you incur to stay alive (food and lodging) and do business while at your destination. Destination expenses include:

- hotel or other lodging expenses for business days
- 50% of meal and beverage expenses (see "How Much You Can Deduct," below)

- taxi, public transportation, and car rental expenses at your destination
- telephone, Internet, and fax expenses
- computer rental fees
- laundry and dry cleaning expenses, and
- tips you pay on any of the other costs.

You may deduct 50% of entertainment expenses if you incur them for business purposes. You can't deduct entertainment expenses for activities that you attend alone, because this solo entertainment obviously wouldn't be for business purposes. If you want to deduct the cost of a nightclub or ball game while on the road, be sure to take a business associate along. (See Chapter 10 for a detailed discussion of the special rules that apply to deductions for entertainment expenses.)

Traveling First Class or Steerage

To be deductible, business travel expenses must be ordinary and necessary. This means that the trip and the expenses you incur must be helpful and appropriate for your business, not necessarily indispensable. You may not deduct lavish or extravagant expenses, but the IRS gives you a great deal of leeway here. You may, if you wish, travel first class, stay at four-star hotels, and eat at expensive restaurants. On the other hand, you're also entitled to be a cheapskate—for example, you could stay with a friend or relative at your destination to save on hotel expenses and still deduct meals and other expenses.

Taking People With You

You may deduct the expenses you pay for a person who travels with you only if he or she:

- is your employee
- has a genuine business reason for going on the trip with you, and
- would otherwise be allowed to deduct the travel expenses.

These rules apply to your family as well to nonfamily members. This means you can deduct the expense of taking your spouse, child, or other relative only if the person is your employee and has a genuine business reason for going on a trip with you. Typing notes or assisting in entertaining customers is not enough to warrant a deduction; the work must be essential to your business. For example, if you hire your son as a salesperson for your product or service and he calls on prospective customers during the trip, both your expenses and his are deductible.

However, this doesn't mean that you can't take any deductions at all when you travel with your family. You may still deduct your business expenses as if you were traveling alone—and you don't have to reduce your deductions, even if others get a free ride with you. For example, if you drive to your destination, you can deduct the entire cost of the drive, even if your family rides along with you. Similarly, you can deduct the full cost of a single hotel room even if you obtain a larger, more expensive room for your whole family.

> **EXAMPLE:** Yamiko travels from New Orleans to Sydney, Australia, for her landscape design business. She takes her husband and young son with her. The total airfare expense for her and her family is $2,500. She may deduct the cost of a single ticket: $1,000. She spends $250 per night for a two-bedroom hotel suite in Sydney. She may deduct the cost of a single room for one person: $100 per night.

How Much You Can Deduct

If you spend all of your time at your destination on business, you may deduct 100% your expenses (except meal expenses, which are only 50% deductible—see "50% Limit on Meal Expenses," below). However, things are more complicated if you mix business and pleasure. Different rules apply to your transportation expenses and the expenses you incur while at your destination ("destination expenses").

Reimbursement for Business Travel Expenses

If a client or customer reimburses you for all or part of your business travel expenses, you get no deduction for the amount of the reimbursement—the client gets the deduction. However, you don't have to count the amounts you're paid as business income.

EXAMPLE: Clarence, a lawyer, travels from Philadelphia to Nashville, Tennessee, to try a case for his client, Acme Corporation. He stays two weeks and incurs $5,000 in travel expenses. He bills Acme for this amount and receives the reimbursement. Clarence may not deduct the cost of the trip. Acme may deduct the $5,000 as a business expense. Clarence need not report the $5,000 reimbursement from Acme as business income.

Travel Within the United States

Business travel within the United States is subject to an all-or-nothing rule: You may deduct 100% of your transportation expenses only if you spend more than half of your time on business activities while at your destination. If you spend more time on personal activities than on business, you get no transportation deduction. In other words, your business days must outnumber your personal days. You may also deduct the destination expenses you incur on the days you do business. Expenses incurred on personal days at your destination are nondeductible personal expenses. (See "Calculating Time Spent on Business," below, for the rules used to determine what constitutes a business day.)

EXAMPLE: Tom works in Atlanta. He takes the train for a business trip to New Orleans. He spends six days in New Orleans, where he spends all his time on business and spends $400 for his hotel, meals, and other living expenses. On the way home, he stops in Mobile for three days to visit his parents and spends $100 for lodging and meals there. His round-trip train fare is $250. Tom's trip consisted of six business days and three personal days, so he spent more than half of the trip on business. He can deduct 100% of his train fare and the entire $400 he spent while on business in New Orleans. He may not, however, deduct the $100 he spent while visiting his parents. His total deduction for the trip is $650.

If your trip is primarily a vacation—that is, you spend over half of your time on personal activities—the entire cost of the trip is a nondeductible personal expense. However, you may deduct any expenses you have while at your destination that are directly related to your business. This includes such things as phone calls or faxes to your office or the cost of renting a computer for business work. It doesn't include transportation, lodging, or food.

EXAMPLE: Tom (from the above example) spends two days in New Orleans on business and seven days visiting his parents in Mobile. His entire trip is a nondeductible personal expense. However, while in New Orleans he spends $50 on long distance phone calls to his office—this expense is deductible.

As long as your trip is primarily for business, you can add a vacation to the end of the trip, make a side trip purely for fun, or go to the theater and still deduct your entire airfare. What you spend while having fun is not deductible, but you can deduct all of your business and transportation expenses.

EXAMPLE: Bill flies to Miami for a four-day business meeting. He spends three extra days in Miami swimming and enjoying the sights. Because he spent over half his time on business—four days out of seven—the cost of his flight is entirely deductible, as are his hotel and meal costs during the business meeting. He may not deduct his hotel, meal, or other expenses during his vacation days.

Travel Outside the United States

Travel outside the United States is subject to more flexible rules than travel within the country. The rules for deducting your transportation expenses depend on how long you stay at your destination.

Trips of Up to Seven Days

If you travel outside the United States for no more than seven days, you can deduct 100% of your airfare or other transportation expenses, as long as you spend part of the time on business. You can spend a majority of your time on personal activities, as long as you spend at least some time on business. Seven days means seven consecutive days, not counting the day you leave but counting the day you return to the United States. You may also deduct the destination expenses you incur on the days you do business. (See "Calculating Time Spent on Business," below, for the rules used to determine what constitutes a business day.)

> **EXAMPLE:** Billie flies from Portland, Oregon, to Vancouver, Canada. She spends four days sightseeing in Vancouver and one day visiting suppliers for her import-export business. She may deduct 100% of her airfare, but she can deduct her lodging, meal, and other expenses from her stay in Vancouver only for the one day she did business.

Trips for More Than Seven Days

The IRS does not want to subsidize foreign vacations, so more stringent rules apply if your foreign trip lasts more than one week. For these longer trips, the magic number is 75%: If you spend more than 75% of your time on business at your foreign destination, you can deduct what it would have cost to make the trip if you had not engaged in any personal activities. This means you may deduct 100% of your airfare or other transportation expense, plus your living expenses while you were on business and any other business-related expenses.

> **EXAMPLE:** Sean flies from Boston to Dublin, Ireland. He spends one day sightseeing and nine days in business meetings. He has spent 90% of his time on business, so he may deduct 100% of his airfare to Dublin and all of the living and other expenses he

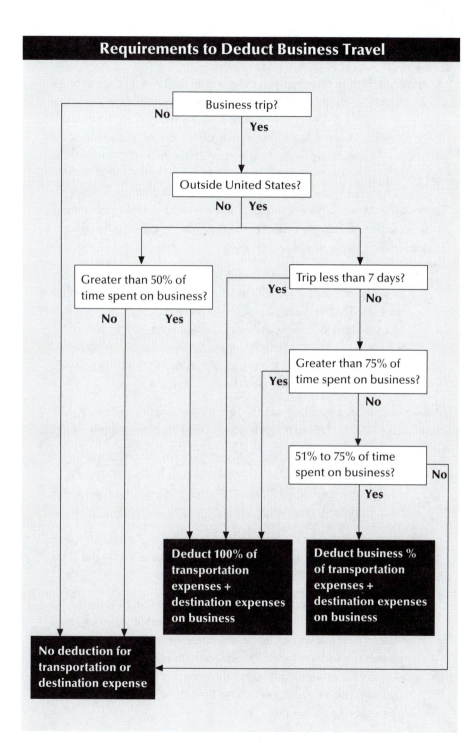

Requirements to Deduct Business Travel

What Is Foreign Travel?

Different deduction rules apply to travel within the United States and foreign travel, so it's important to know which is which. For IRS purposes, foreign travel means travel outside of the United States. Thus, for example, a trip to Puerto Rico would be a foreign trip, even though it is a United States possession. Travel outside the United States does not include travel from one point in the United States to another point in the U.S.

If you travel by plane, train, or other public transportation, any place in the United States where your plane or other means of transportation makes a scheduled stop is a point in the U.S. Your foreign trip begins at the last scheduled stop in the United States.

> **EXAMPLE:** Ben flies from Chicago to Miami, changes planes, and then flies to Puerto Rico. The flight from Chicago to Miami is within the United States, so the domestic travel rules apply. The flight from Miami to Puerto Rico is outside the United States, so the foreign travel rules apply. Ben then returns to Chicago on a nonstop flight from Puerto Rico. All of the return trip is outside the United States, because there are no scheduled stops in the U.S.

If you travel by private car to a foreign destination, the portion of the trip that is within the United States is governed by the domestic travel rules.

> **EXAMPLE:** Bart travels by car from Denver to Mexico City and returns. His travel to and from the U.S. border back to Denver is travel within the United States. The foreign travel rules apply only to the portion of his trip inside Mexico.

If you travel by private airplane, any trip (or portion of a trip) for which both takeoff and landing are in the United States is travel within the United States, even if part of the flight is over a foreign country.

> **EXAMPLE:** Brenda flies her private plane nonstop from Seattle to Juneau, Alaska. Because she took off and landed in the United States, the trip is within the United States for tax purposes—even though she had to fly over Canada on the way to Juneau. However, if she makes a scheduled stop in Vancouver, Canada, both legs of the flight are considered travel outside the United States and are subject to the foreign travel rules.

incurred during the nine days he was in Dublin on business. He may not deduct any of his expenses (including hotel) for the day he spent sightseeing.

If you spend more than 50%—but less than 75%—of your time on business, you can deduct only the business percentage of your transportation and other costs. You figure out this percentage by counting the number of business days and the number of personal days to come up with a fraction. The number of business days is the numerator (top number), and the total number of days away from home is the denominator (bottom number). For ease in determining the dollar amount of your deduction, you can convert this fraction into a percentage.

> **EXAMPLE:** Sam flies from Las Vegas to London, where he spends six days on business and four days sightseeing. He spent 6/10 of his total time away from home on business. The fraction 6/10 converts to 60% (6 ÷ 10 = 0.60). He therefore spent 60% of his time on business. He can deduct 60% of his travel costs—that is, 60% of his round-trip airfare, hotel, and other expenses. The trip cost him $3,000, so he gets an $1,800 deduction.

If you spend less than 51% of your time on business on foreign travel that lasts more than seven days, you cannot deduct any of your costs.

Side Trips

Expenses you incur if you stop at a nonbusiness (personal) destination en route to, or returning from, your business destination are not deductible. For example, if you stop for three vacation days in Paris on your way to a weeklong business meeting in Bangladesh, you may not deduct your expenses from your Paris stay.

Determining how much of your airfare or other transportation costs are deductible when you make side trips is a three-step process:

1. You must determine the percentage of the time you spent on vacation.
2. You multiply this vacation percentage by what it would have cost you to fly round trip from your vacation destination to the United States.

3. You subtract this amount from your total airfare expense to arrive at your deductible airfare expense.

EXAMPLE: Jason lives in New York. On May 5, he flew to Paris to attend a business conference that began that same day. The conference ended on May 14. That evening, he flew from Paris to Dublin to visit friends until May 21, when he flew directly home to New York. The entire trip lasted 18 days, 11 of which were business days (the nine days in Paris and the two travel days) and seven of which were vacation days. He spent 39% of his time on vacation (7/18 = 39%). His total airfare was $2,000. Round-trip airfare from New York to Dublin would have been $1,000. To determine his deductible airfare, he multiplies $1,000 by 39% and then subtracts this amount from his $2,000 airfare expense: 1,000 x 39% = 390; $2,000 − $390 = $1,610. His deductible airfare expense is $1,610.

Conventions

Your travel to, and stay at, a convention is deductible in the same manner as any other business trip, as long as you satisfy the following rules.

Conventions Within North America

You may deduct the expense of attending a convention in North America if your attendance benefits your business. You may not, however, deduct any expenses for your family.

How do you know if a convention benefits your business? Look at the convention agenda or program (and be sure to save a copy). The agenda does not have to specifically address what you do in your business, but it must be sufficiently related to show that your attendance was for business purposes. Examples of conventions that don't benefit your business include those for investment, political, or social purposes.

You probably learned in school that North America consists of the United States, Canada, and Mexico. However, for convention expense purposes, North America includes much of the Caribbean and many other great vacation destinations, including:

- American Samoa
- Baker Island

- Barbados
- Bermuda
- Canada
- Costa Rica
- Dominica
- Dominican Republic
- Grenada
- Guam
- Guyana
- Honduras
- Howland Island
- Jamaica
- Jarvis Island
- Johnston Island
- Kingman Reef
- Marshall Islands
- Mexico
- Micronesia
- Midway Islands
- Northern Mariana Islands
- Palau
- Palmyra
- Puerto Rico
- Saint Lucia
- Trinidad and Tobago
- United States (the 50 states and Washington, DC)
- U.S. Virgin Islands, and
- Wake Island.

Foreign Conventions

More stringent rules apply if you attend a convention outside of North America (as defined above). You can take a deduction for a foreign convention only if both the following are true:

- The convention is directly related to your business (rather than merely benefiting it).
- It's as reasonable for the convention to be held outside of North America as in North America.

To determine if it's reasonable to hold the convention outside of North America, the IRS looks at the purposes of the meeting and the sponsoring group, the activities at the convention, where the sponsors live, and where other meetings have been or will be held.

As a general rule, if you want a tax deduction, avoid attending a convention outside of North America unless there is a darn good reason for holding it there. For example, it would be hard to justify holding a convention for New York plumbing contractors in Tahiti. On the other hand, it would probably be okay for a meeting of European and American brain surgeons to be held in Paris.

Travel by Ship

You can deduct travel by ship if a convention or other business event is conducted on board a ship, or if you use a ship as a means of transportation to a business destination. The following additional rules apply to travel by sea.

Shipboard Conventions and Seminars

Forget about getting a tax deduction for a pure pleasure cruise. You may, however, be able to deduct part of the cost of a cruise if you attend a business convention, seminars, or similar meetings directly related to your business while on board. Personal investment or financial planning seminars don't qualify.

But there is a major restriction: You must travel on a U.S.-registered ship that stops only in ports in the United States or its possessions, such as Puerto Rico or the U.S. Virgin Islands. If a cruise sponsor promises you'll be able to deduct your trip, investigate carefully to make sure it meets these requirements.

If you go on a cruise that is deductible, you must file a signed note with your tax return from the meeting or seminar sponsor listing the business meetings scheduled each day aboard ship and certifying how many hours you spent in attendance. Make sure to get this statement from the meeting sponsor. Your annual deduction for attending conventions, seminars, or similar meetings on ships is limited to $2,000.

Transportation by Ship

You can get a deduction if you use an ocean liner, cruise ship, or other means of water travel solely as a means of transportation to a business destination. This isn't very common these days, but it can be done. In this event, your deduction for each travel day is limited to an amount equal to twice the highest amount federal workers are paid each day (called the per diem rate) for their living expenses while traveling inside the U.S. on government business. You can find the latest rates in IRS Publication 1542, *Per Diem Rates*.

> **EXAMPLE:** In 2005, Caroline, a self-employed travel agent, travels by ocean liner from New York to London. Her expense for the six-day cruise is $5,000. However, she may deduct only twice the highest federal per diem amount for each day of the cruise. This amount is $259, so she can only deduct $518 per day. Caroline's deduction for the cruise cannot exceed $3,108 (6 days x $518 = $3,108).

In addition, if your bill includes separately stated amounts for meals and entertainment while on the ship, you can deduct only 50% of these expenses. For example, if Caroline's bill showed that she was charged $2,000 for food and entertainment while on the trip, she could deduct only $1,000.

Does this mean you can take a long pleasure cruise to a business destination and get a deduction for each day? No—the regular foreign travel rules apply to ship travel. A foreign trip that lasts more than 14 days is deductible only if you spend more than half of the time on business.

> **EXAMPLE:** Marcia embarks on a 30-day cruise from Los Angeles to Tokyo, where she attends a three-day business conference. She then flies back to Los Angeles. Her entire trip took 34 days, three of which were for business. Because she spent less than 50% of her time on business, the entire trip is a nondeductible personal expense.

Calculating Time Spent on Business

To calculate how much time you spend on business while on a business trip, you must compare the number of days you spend on business with the days you spend on personal activities. All of the following are considered business days:

- Any day in which you work for more than four hours.
- Any day when you must be at a particular place for your business—for example, to attend a business meeting—even if you spend most of the day on personal activities.
- Any day when you spend more than four hours on business travel—travel time begins when you leave home and ends when you reach your hotel, or vice versa.
- Any day when you drive 300 miles for business (you can average your mileage). For example, if you drive 1,500 miles to your destination in five days, you may claim five 300-mile days, even if you drove 500 miles on one of the days and 100 miles on another.
- Any day when your travel and work time together exceeds four hours.
- Any day when you are prevented from working because of circumstances beyond your control—for example, a transit strike or terrorist act.
- Any day sandwiched between two work days if it would have cost more to go home than to stay where you are—this rule can let you count weekends as business days.

EXAMPLE: Mike, a self-employed inventor who hates flying, travels by car from his home in Reno, Nevada, to Cleveland, Ohio, for a meeting with a potential investor concerning his latest invention: diapers for pet birds. He makes the 2,100-mile drive in six days, arriving in Cleveland on Saturday night. He has his meeting with the investor for one hour on Monday. The investor is intrigued with Mike's idea but wants him to flesh out his business plan. Mike works on this for five hours on Tuesday and three hours on Wednesday, spending the rest of his time resting and sightseeing. He has his second investor meeting on Thursday, which lasts two hours. He sightsees the rest of the day and then drives straight home on Friday. Mike's trip consisted of 15 business days: 11 travel days, one sandwiched day (the Sunday before his first meeting), two meeting days, and one day when he worked more than four hours. He had one personal day: the day when he spent only three hours working.

Be sure to keep track of your time while you're away. You can do this by making simple notes on your calendar or travel diary. (See Chapter 15 for a detailed discussion of record keeping while traveling.)

50% Limit on Meal Expenses

The IRS figures that whether you're at home or away on a business trip, you have to eat. Because home meals ordinarily aren't deductible, the IRS won't let you deduct all of your food expenses while traveling. Instead, you can deduct only 50% of your meal expenses while on a business trip. There are two ways to calculate your meal expense deduction: You can keep track of your actual expenses or use a daily rate set by the federal government.

Deducting Actual Meal Expenses

If you use the actual expense method, you must keep track of what you spend on meals (including tips and tax) en route to and at your business destination. When you do your taxes, you add these amounts together and deduct half of the total.

> **EXAMPLE:** Frank goes on a business trip from Santa Fe, New Mexico, to Reno, Nevada. He gets there by car. On the way, he spends $200 for meals. While in Reno, he spends another $200. His total meal expense for the trip is $400. He may deduct half of this amount, or $200.

If you combine a business trip with a vacation, you may deduct only those meals you eat while on business—for example, meals you eat while attending business meetings or doing other business-related work. Meals that are part of business entertainment are subject to the rules on entertainment expenses covered in Chapter 10.

You do not necessarily have to keep all your receipts for your business meals, but you need to keep careful track of what you spend, and you should be able to prove that the meal was for business. See Chapter 15 for a detailed discussion of record keeping for meal expenses.

Using the Standard Meal Allowance

When you use the actual expense method, you must keep track of what you spend for each meal, which can be a lot of work. So the IRS provides an alternative method of deducting meals: Instead of deducting your actual expenses, you can deduct a set amount for each day of your business trip. This amount is called the standard meal allowance. It covers your expenses for business meals, beverages, tax, and tips. The amount of the allowance varies depending on where and when you travel.

Standard Meal Allowance Can't Be Used by Some Employees

The standard meal allowance may not be used by an employer to reimburse an employee for travel expenses if the employee:

- owns more than 10% of the stock in an incorporated business, or
- is a close relative of a 10% or more owner—a brother, sister, parent, spouse, grandparent, or other lineal ancestor or descendent.

In these instances, the employee must deduct actual meal expenses for business-related travel to be reimbursed by the employer. Thus, if you've incorporated your business and work as its employee, you must keep track of what you spend on meals when you travel for business and are reimbursed for your expenses by your corporation. (See "Reimbursing Employees for Business-Related Expenditures" in Chapter 11 for a detailed discussion.)

The good thing about the standard meal allowance is that you don't need to keep track of how much you spend for meals and tips. You only need to keep records to prove the time, place, and business purpose of your travel. (See Chapter 10 for more on meal and entertainment expenses.)

The bad thing about the standard meal allowance is that it is based on what federal workers are allowed to charge for meals while traveling and is therefore relatively modest. In 2006, the daily rates for domestic travel ranged from $39 per day for travel in the least expensive areas to up to $64 for high-cost areas, which includes most major cities. While it is possible to eat on $51 per day in places like New York City or San Francisco, you won't have a very good time. If you use the standard meal allowance and spend more than the allowance, you get no deduction for the overage.

The rates are generally higher for travel outside the continental United States—that is, Alaska, Hawaii, and foreign countries. For example, in 2006 the allowance for London, England, was $173 and $168 for Tokyo, Japan. In contrast, travelers to Baghdad were permitted only $11 per day; it's apparently very cheap to eat in Baghdad.

The standard meal allowance includes $3 per day for incidental expenses—tips you pay to porters, bellhops, maids, and transportation workers. If you wish, you can use the actual expense method for your meal costs and the $3 incidental expense rate for your tips. However, you'd have to be a pretty stingy tipper for this amount to be adequate.

The standard meal allowance is revised each year. You can find the current rates for travel within the United States on the Internet at www .gsa.gov (look for the link to "Per Diem Rates" in the "Featured Topics" section) or in IRS Publication 1542. The rates for foreign travel are set by the U.S. State Department and can be found at www.state.gov/m/a/als/ prdm. When you look at these rate listings, you'll see several categories of numbers. You want the "M & IE Rate"—short for meals and incidental expenses. Rates are also provided for lodging, but these don't apply to nongovernmental travelers.

You can only claim the standard meal allowance for business days. If you travel to more than one location in one day, use the rate in effect for the area where you spend the night. You are allowed to deduct 50% of the standard meal allowance from your taxes as a business expense.

> **EXAMPLE:** Art travels from Los Angeles to Chicago for a three-day business conference. Chicago is a high-cost locality, so the daily

meal and incidental expense rate (M&IE) is $64. Art figures his deduction by multiplying the daily rate by five and multiplying this by 50%: 5 days x $64 = $320; $320 x 50% = $160.

If you use the standard meal allowance, you must use it for all of the business trips you take during the year. You can't use it for some trips and then use the actual expense method for others. For example, you can't use the standard allowance when you go to an inexpensive destination and the actual expense method when you go to a pricey one.

Because the standard meal allowance is so small, it's better to use it only if you travel exclusively to low-cost areas or if you are simply unable or unwilling to keep track of what you actually spend for meals.

You Don't Have to Spend Your Whole Allowance

When you use the standard meal allowance, you get to deduct the whole amount, regardless of what you spend. If you spend more than the daily allowance, you are limited to the allowance amount. But if you spend less, you still get to deduct the full allowance amount. For example, if you travel to New York City and live on bread and water, you may still deduct $32 for each business day. This strategy will not only save you money, you'll lose weight as well.

Maximizing Your Business Travel Deductions

Here are some simple strategies you can use to maximize your business travel deductions.

Plan Ahead

Plan your itinerary carefully before you leave to make sure your trip qualifies as a business trip. For example, if you're traveling within the United States, you must spend more than half of your time on business for your transportation to be deductible. If you know you're going to spend three days on business, arrange to spend no more than two days on personal activities so this rule is satisfied. If you're traveling overseas for more than 14 days, you'll have to spend at least 75% of your time on business to deduct your transportation—you may be able to do this by using strategies to maximize your business days. (See "Maximize Your Business Days," below.)

Make a Paper Trail

If are audited by the IRS, there is a good chance you will be questioned about business travel deductions. Of course, you'll need to have records showing what you spent for your trips. (See Chapter 15 for a detailed discussion on record keeping.) However, you'll also need documents proving that your trip was for your existing business. You can do this by:

- making a note in your calendar or daily planner of every business meeting you attend or other business-related work you do—be sure to note the time you spend on each business activity
- obtaining and saving business cards from anyone you meet while on business
- noting in your calendar or daily planner the names of all the people you meet for business on your trip
- keeping the program or agenda from a convention or training seminar you attend, as well as any notes you made
- after you return, sending thank-you notes to the business contacts you met on your trips—be sure to keep copies, and
- keeping copies of business-related correspondence or emails you sent or received before the trip.

Maximize Your Business Days

If you mix business with pleasure on your trip, you have to make sure that you have enough business days to deduct your transportation costs. You'll need to spend more than 50% of your days on business on domestic trips and more than 75% for foreign trips of more than 14 days.

You don't have to work all day for that day to count as a business day: Any day in which you work at least four hours is a business day, even if you goof off the rest of time. The day will count as a business day for purposes of determining whether your transportation expenses are deductible, and you can deduct your lodging, meal, and other expenses during the day, even though you only worked four hours.

You can easily maximize your business days by taking advantage of this rule. For example, you can:

- work no more than four hours in any one day whenever possible
- spread your business over several days—for example, if you need to be present at three meetings, try to spread them over two or three days instead of one, and
- avoid using the fastest form of transportation to your business destination—travel days count as business days, so you'll add business days to your trip if you drive instead of fly. Remember, there's no law that says you have to take the quickest means of transportation to your destination.

Take Advantage of the Sandwich Day Rule

IRS rules provide that days when you do no business-related work count as business days when they are sandwiched between workdays, as long as it was cheaper to spend that day away than to go back home for the off days. If you work on Friday and Monday, this rule allows you to count the weekend as business days, even though you did no work.

> **EXAMPLE:** Kim flies from Houston to Honolulu, Hawaii, for a business convention. She arrives on Wednesday and returns the following Wednesday. She does not attend any convention activities during the weekend and goes to the beach instead. Nevertheless, because it was cheaper for her to stay in Hawaii than to fly back to Houston just for the weekend and fly back to Hawaii, she may count Saturday and Sunday as business days. This means she can deduct her lodging and meal expenses for those days (but not the cost of renting a surfboard).

How to Deduct Travel Expenses

How you deduct your travel expenses depends on how your business is legally organized. If you're a sole proprietor, you deduct your expenses on your personal tax return, However, if your business is an LLC or partnership, your expenses may have to be deducted on its own return, not your personal tax return. If your business is a corporation, any personal deduction will be limited.

Sole Proprietors

If you're a sole proprietor, you will list your travel expenses on Schedule C, *Profit or Loss From Business.* Travel expenses other than meals are listed on line 24a. Meals are listed on lines 24b-d. You list the full amount of meal expenses, but only deduct 50% of the total.

Partnerships and LLCs

If your business is organized as an LLC or partnership, it will ordinarily be taxed as a partnership. Your business can reimburse you for your travel expenses and then deduct them on its tax return; or, in some cases, you can deduct them on your own return.

You're Reimbursed for Your Expenses

Unless one very important exception noted below applies, you'll have to seek reimbursement for your deductible travel expenses from your business. The amount of the reimbursement is not taxable income to you, provided you comply with all required record-keeping rules for car expenses, and the reimbursement is made under an accountable plan. Basically, this requires that you submit all your documentation to the business in a timely manner and return any excess payments. Accountable plans are covered in detail in Chapter 11. The amount of the reimbursed travel expenses is listed on the partnership's tax return (Form 1065) and reduces its taxable profit for the year.

> **EXAMPLE:** Rick, co-owner of a construction business organized as an LLC, flies from Chicago to St. Paul to attend a two-day seminar on marketing for construction contractors. He incurs $1,500 in travel expenses. He keeps careful track of all of his expenses. After he gets back, he submits a request for reimbursement from the LLC, along with an expense report and all required receipts. The LLC pays him the $1,500. This money is not taxable income to Rick and the LLC may list it on its tax return as a business expense.

You Take a Personal Deduction for Your Expenses

The exception to the reimbursement rule permits you to deduct your car expenses on your personal tax return. But this is allowed only if: (1) a written partnership agreement or LLC operating agreement provides that the expense will *not* be reimbursed by the partnership or LLC, or (2) your business has an established routine business of not reimbursing the expense. Absent such a written statement or business, *no personal deduction may be taken*. Reimbursement from the partnership or LLC must be sought instead. If you take a personal deduction for your car expenses, your business does not list them on its tax return and they do not reduce your business's profits. But they will reduce your taxable income. (See Chapter 11.)

You deduct your unreimbursed car expenses (and any other unreimbursed business expenses) on IRS Schedule E (Part II) and attach it to your personal tax return. Don't use Schedule C. You must attach a separate schedule to Schedule E listing the car and other business expenses you're deducting.

> **EXAMPLE:** Assume that Rick's LLC has a written policy that all the company's owners must personally pay for their own travel expenses. Instead of seeking reimbursement, Rick lists his $1,500 travel expense on his own tax return, Schedule E, reducing his taxable income by that amount. The LLC does not list the expense on its return, thus it does not reduce the business's income.

Corporations

If your business is legally organized as a corporation (whether a C or S corporation), you will ordinarily be its employee. Special rules govern all business expense deductions by employees. Your best option is to have your corporation reimburse you for your travel expenses. This process is the same as for LLC and partnerships described above. If you comply with all the documentation rules for car expenses and accountable plan requirements, your corporation gets to deduct the expense on its tax return and you don't have to count the reimbursement as income. If you fail to follow the rules, any reimbursements must be treated as employee income subject to tax (but you may deduct your expenses as described below).

If your corporation won't reimburse you for your travel expenses you may deduct them on your personal tax return. However, this is best avoided because employees can deduct unreimbursed employee expenses only as miscellaneous itemized deductions on Form 1040, Schedule A. Thus, they are deductible only if an employee itemizes his or her deductions and only to the extent that these deductions, along with any other miscellaneous itemized deductions, exceed 2% of the employee's adjusted gross income. Additional deduction limits are imposed on higher income employees—in 2006, single employees earning more than $150,500, and married employees filing jointly with income over $225,750. For more information, see IRS Publication 17, *Your Federal Income Tax.*

Travel Expenses Reimbursed by Clients or Customers

Business owners who travel while performing services for a client or customer often have their expenses reimbursed by the client. You need not include such reimbursements in your income if you provide an adequate accounting of the expenses to your client and comply with the accountable plan rules. Basically, this requires that you submit all your documentation to the client in a timely manner, and return any excess payments. Accountable plans are covered in detail in Chapter 11. Record-keeping rules for long distance travel are covered in Chapter 15.

> **EXAMPLE:** Farley, an architect, incurs $5,000 in travel expenses while working on a new shopping center for a client. He keeps complete and accurate records of his expenses which he provides to his client who reimburses him the $5,000. Farley need not include the $5,000 in his income for the year. Farley's client may deduct the reimbursement as a business expense.

If you do not adequately account to your client for these expenses, you must include any reimbursements or allowances in your income, and they should also be included in any 1099-MISC form the client is required to provide the IRS reporting how much you were paid (see Chapter 11). The client can still deduct the reimbursement as compensation paid to you. You may deduct the expenses on your own return, but you'll need documentation to back them up in the event of an audit.

■

Chapter 10

Meal and Entertainment Expenses

Business isn't done only in an office. Some of your most important business meetings, client contacts, and marketing efforts may take place at restaurants, golf courses, or sporting events. The tax law recognizes this and permits you to deduct part of the cost of business-related entertainment. However, because many taxpayers have abused this deduction in the past, the IRS has imposed strict rules limiting the types of entertainment expenses you can deduct and the size of the deduction.

What Is Business Entertainment?

You may deduct only half of the total amount you spend on business entertainment activities. Because ordinary and necessary business activities are usually fully deductible, it's important to be able to distinguish between regular business activities and entertainment.

The basic rule is that entertainment involves something fun, such as:

- dining out
- going to a nightclub
- attending a sporting event
- going to a concert, a movie, or the theater
- visiting a vacation spot (a ski area or beach resort, for example), or
- taking a hunting, yachting, or fishing trip.

Although eating out might fall into other categories of business operating expenses depending on the circumstances, it is by far the number one business entertainment expense.

Activities That Aren't Entertainment

Activities you perform as a regular part of your business are not entertainment. This is true even though these same activities might constitute entertainment for others. For example, the cost of going to the theater would not be entertainment for a professional theater critic. But if a salesperson invited a client to the theater, the outing would constitute entertainment. The critic could deduct 100% of the cost of theater tickets, while the salesperson could deduct only 50% (provided all the other requirements are met).

Entertainment does not include activities that are for business purposes only and don't involve any fun or amusement, such as:

- providing supper money to an employee working overtime
- paying for a hotel room used while traveling on business, or
- automobile expenses incurred while conducting business.

In addition, meals or other entertainment expenses related to advertising or promotions are not considered entertainment. As a rule, an expense for a meal or other entertainment item will qualify as advertising if you make it available to the general public—for example, if a wine merchant holds wine tastings where he provides customers with free wine and food to promote his business, the costs of the events would not be considered entertainment expenses. These kinds of advertising and promotion costs are fully deductible business operating expenses. (See Chapter 4 for more about business expenses.)

Meals Can Be Travel or Entertainment

A meal can be a travel expense or an entertainment expense, or both. The distinction won't affect how much you can deduct: Both travel (overnight) and entertainment expenses are only 50% deductible. But different rules apply to the two categories.

A meal is a travel expense if you eat out of necessity while away on a business trip. For example, any meal you eat alone while on the road for business is a travel expense. On the other hand, a meal is an entertainment expense if you treat a client, customer, or other business associate and the purpose of the meal is to benefit your business. A meal is both a travel and an entertainment expense if you treat a client or other business associate to a meal while on the road. However, you may only deduct this cost once—whether you choose to do it as an entertainment or a travel expense, only 50% of the cost is deductible.

Who You Can Entertain

You must be with one or more people who can benefit your business in some way to claim an entertainment expense. This could include current or potential:

- customers
- clients
- suppliers

- employees (see Chapter 11 for special tax rules for employees)
- independent contractors
- agents
- partners, or
- professional advisers.

This list includes almost anyone you're likely to meet for business reasons. Although you can invite family members or friends along, you can't deduct the costs of entertaining them, except in certain limited situations.

Deducting Entertainment Expenses

Entertainment expenses, like all business operating expenses, are deductible only if they are ordinary and necessary. This means that the entertainment expense must be common, helpful, and appropriate for your business. Taxpayers used to have to show only that the entertainment wasn't purely for fun and that it benefited their business in some way. This standard was so easy to satisfy that the IRS imposed additional requirements for deducting these expenses.

Before the IRS made the standard tougher, you could deduct ordinary and necessary entertainment expenses even if business was never discussed. For example, you could deduct the cost of taking a client to a restaurant, even if you spent the whole time drinking martinis and talking about sports (the infamous "three-martini lunch"). This is no longer the case—now you must discuss business with one or more business associates either before, during, or after the entertainment if you want to claim an entertainment deduction (subject to one exception; see "Entertainment in Clear Business Settings," below).

Who's going to know? The IRS doesn't have spies lurking about in restaurants, theaters, or other places of entertainment, so it has no way of knowing whether you really discuss business with a client or other business associate. You're pretty much on the honor system here. However, be aware that if you're audited, the IRS closely scrutinizes this deduction, because many taxpayers cheat when they take it. You'll also have to comply with stringent record-keeping requirements. (See Chapter 15 for more on record keeping.)

Business Discussions Before or After Entertainment

The easiest way to get a deduction for entertainment is to discuss business before or after the activity. To meet this requirement, the discussion must be "associated" with your business—that is, it must have a clear business purpose, such as developing new business or encouraging existing business relationships. You don't, however, have to expect to get a specific business benefit from the discussion. Your business discussion can involve planning, advice, or simply exchanging useful information with a business associate.

You automatically satisfy the business discussion requirement if you attend a business-related convention or meeting to further your business. Business activities—not socializing—must be the main purpose for the convention. Save a copy of the program or agenda to prove this.

Generally, the entertainment should occur on the same day as the business discussion. However, if your business guests are from out of town, the entertainment can occur the day before or the day after the business talk.

> **EXAMPLE:** Mary, the buyer for a large department store chain, travels from Chicago to New York City to meet with Kim, a dress designer, to look at Kim's fall dress line. Mary arrives on Tuesday evening and Kim treats her to dinner at a nice restaurant that night. The following morning, Mary goes to Kim's office to look at her dresses and discuss buying some. Kim can deduct the dinner they had the night before as an entertainment expense.

You can get a deduction even if the entertainment occurs in a place like a nightclub, theater, or loud sports arena where it's difficult or impossible to talk business. This is because your business discussions occur before or after the entertainment, so the IRS won't be scrutinizing whether or not you actually could have talked business during your entertainment activity.

> **EXAMPLE:** Following lengthy contract negotiations at a prospective client's office, you take the client to a baseball game to unwind. The cost of the tickets is a deductible business expense.

The entertainment can last longer than your business discussions, as long as you don't spend just a small fraction of your total time on business. Thus, it's not sufficient simply to ask an associate, "How's business?" You must have a substantial discussion. Also, your business-related discussions don't have to be face to face—they can occur over the telephone or even by email.

Business Discussions During Meals

Another way you can deduct entertainment expenses is to discuss business during a meal at a restaurant. To get the deduction, you must show all of the following:

- The main purpose of the combined business discussion and meal was the active conduct of business—you don't have to spend the entire time talking business, but the main character of the meal must be business.
- You did in fact have a business meeting, negotiation, discussion, or other bona fide business transaction with your guest or guests during the meal.
- You expect to get income or some other *specific business benefit* in the future from your discussions during the meal—thus, for example, a casual conversation where the subject of business comes up won't do; you have to have a specific business goal in mind.

> **EXAMPLE:** Ivan, a self-employed consultant, has had ongoing email discussions with a prospective client who is interested in hiring him. Ivan thinks he'll be able to close the deal and get a contract signed in a face-to-face meeting. He chooses a lunch meeting because it's more informal and the prospective client will like getting a free lunch. He treats the client to a $40 lunch at a nice restaurant. During the lunch, they finalize the terms of a contract for Ivan's consulting services and come to a handshake agreement. This meal clearly led to a specific business benefit for Ivan, so he can deduct half of the cost as an entertainment expense.

You don't necessarily have to close a deal, sign a contract, or otherwise obtain a specific business benefit to get a deduction. But you do have to have a reasonable expectation that you can get some specific business benefit through your discussions at the meal—for example, to make progress toward new business, sales of your product, or investment in your business.

No Deductions for Business Discussions During Other Kinds of Entertainment

As a general rule, you can't get a business entertainment deduction by claiming that you discussed business during an entertainment activity other than a meal. In the IRS's view, it's usually not possible to engage in serious business discussions at entertainment venues other than restaurants because of the distractions. Examples of places the IRS would probably find not conducive to serious talk include:

- nightclubs, theaters, or sporting events
- cocktail parties or other large social gatherings
- hunting or fishing trips
- yachting or other pleasure boat outings, or
- group gatherings at a cocktail lounge, golf club, athletic club, or vacation resort that includes people who are not business associates.

This means, for example, that you usually can't claim that you discussed business during a golf game, even if your foursome consists of you and three business associates. In the IRS's view, golfers are unable to play and talk business at the same time. On the other hand, you could have a business discussion before or after a golf game—for example, in the clubhouse. This might seem ridiculous, but it is the rule.

Entertaining at Home

The cost of entertaining at your home is deductible if it meets either of the above two tests. However, the IRS will be more likely to believe that you discussed business during home entertainment if only a small number of people are involved—for example, if you have a quiet dinner party. A larger gathering—a cocktail party, for example—will probably only qualify as an entertainment expense if you have business discussions before or after the event. (For example, you sign a business contract with a client during the afternoon and invite him to your house for a large party with your business associates and family.) You can't, however, deduct the costs of inviting nonbusiness guests to your house. (See "Who You Can Entertain," above.)

No Deduction for Lawyer's Birthday Parties

Every year, Joseph Flaig, a successful personal injury lawyer, held birthday parties for himself. He rented a banquet hall and invited over 1,000 people, including present and former clients and insurance adjusters. The guests were treated to a buffet dinner where champagne was served and an orchestra played dance music. Flaig claimed the $5,000 to $7,000 he spent on these parties was a deductible business entertainment expense because he engaged in brief chit-chat with clients and potential clients and occasionally had them sign legal documents. The IRS and tax court disagreed. They concluded that the contacts Flaig had with clients at his parties were too insignificant to qualify as business discussions. The parties were primarily personal and social in nature, and therefore not deductible as entertainment expenses. (*Flaig v. Commissioner*, TC Memo 1984-150.)

Entertainment in Clear Business Settings

An exception to the general rule that you must discuss business before, during, or after entertainment is when the entertainment occurs in a clear business setting. For example, this exception applies to:

- the price of renting a hospitality room at a convention where you display or discuss your business products
- entertainment that is mainly a price rebate on the sale of your products—for example, a restaurant owner provides a free meal to a loyal customer, or

- entertainment that occurs under circumstances where there is no meaningful personal relationship between you and the people you entertained—for example, you entertain local business or civic leaders at the opening of a new hotel to get business publicity, rather than to form business relationships with them.

Calculating Your Deduction

Most expenses you incur for business entertainment are deductible, including meals (with beverages, tax, and tips), your transportation expenses (including parking), tickets to entertainment or sporting events, catering costs of parties, cover charges for admission to night clubs, and rent paid for a room where you hold a dinner or cocktail party.

You are allowed to deduct only 50% of your entertainment expenses. If you spend $50 for a meal in a restaurant, you can deduct $25. You must, however, keep track of everything you spend and report the entire amount on your tax return. The only exception to the 50% rule is transportation expenses, which are 100% deductible.

If you have a single bill or receipt that includes some business entertainment as well as other expenses (such as lodging or transportation), you must allocate the expense between the cost of the entertainment and the cost of the other services. For example, if your hotel bill covers meals as well as lodging, you'll have to make a reasonable estimate of the portion that covers meals. It's best to try and avoid this hassle by getting a separate bill for your deductible entertainment.

Expenses Must Be Reasonable

Your entertainment expenses must be reasonable—the IRS won't let you deduct entertainment expenses that it considers lavish or extravagant. There is no dollar limit on what is reasonable; nor are you necessarily barred from entertaining at deluxe restaurants, hotels, nightclubs, or resorts.

Whether your expenses will be considered reasonable depends on the particular facts and circumstances—for example, a $250 expense for dinner with a client and two business associates at a fancy restaurant would probably be considered reasonable if you closed a substantial business deal during the meal. Because there are no concrete guidelines, you have to use common sense.

Going "Dutch"

You can only deduct entertainment expenses if you pay for the activity. If a client picks up the tab, you obviously get no deduction. If you split the expense, you must subtract what it would have normally cost you for the meal from the amount you actually paid, and then deduct 50% of that total. For example, if you pay $20 for lunch and you usually pay only $5, you can deduct 50% of $15, or $7.50.

If you go Dutch a lot and are worried that the IRS might challenge your deductions, you can save your grocery bills or receipts from eating out for a month to show what you usually spend. You don't need to keep track of which grocery items you eat for each meal. Instead, the IRS assumes that 50% of your total grocery receipts are for dinner, 30% for lunch, and 20% for breakfast.

Expenses You Can't Deduct

There are certain expenses that you are prohibited from deducting as entertainment.

Entertainment Facilities

You may not deduct the cost of buying, leasing, or maintaining an entertainment facility such as a yacht, swimming pool, tennis court, hunting camp, fishing lodge, bowling alley, car, airplane, hotel suite, apartment, or home in a vacation resort. These entertainment facilities are not considered deductible business assets.

Expenses of Nonbusiness Guests

You may not deduct the cost of entertaining people who are not business associates. If you entertain business and nonbusiness guests at an event, you must divide your entertainment expenses between the two and deduct only the business part.

> **EXAMPLE:** You take three business associates and six friends to dinner. Because there were ten people at dinner, including you, and

only four were business-related, 40% of this expense qualifies as business entertainment. If you spend $200 for the dinner, only $80 would be deductible. And because entertainment expenses are only 50% deductible, your total deduction for the event is $40.

Ordinarily, you cannot deduct the cost of entertaining your spouse or the spouse of a business associate. However, there is an exception: You can deduct these costs if you can show that you had a clear business purpose (rather than a personal or social purpose) in having the spouse or spouses join in.

> **EXAMPLE:** You take a customer visiting from out of town to dinner with his wife. The customer's wife joins you because it's impractical (not to mention impolite) to have dinner with the customer and not include his wife. Your spouse joins the party because the customer's spouse is present. You may deduct the cost of dinner for both spouses.

Club Dues and Membership Fees

In the good old days, you could deduct dues for belonging to a country club or other club where business associates gathered. This is no longer possible. The IRS says you cannot deduct dues (including initiation fees) for membership in any club if one of the principal purposes of the club is to:

- conduct entertainment activities for members, or
- provide entertainment facilities for members to use.

Thus, you cannot deduct dues paid to country clubs, golf and athletic clubs, airline clubs, hotel clubs, or clubs operated to provide members with meals. However, you can deduct other expenses you incur to entertain a business associate at a club.

> **EXAMPLE:** Jack, the owner of a chain of dry cleaners, is a member of the Golden Bear Golf Club in Columbus, Ohio. His annual membership dues are $10,000. One night Jack invites a competitor to dinner at the club's dining room, where they discuss Jack buying him out. Jack pays $100 for the dinner. Jack's $10,000 annual dues are not deductible, but his costs for the dinner are.

You can deduct dues to join business-related tax-exempt organizations or civic organizations as long as the organization's primary purpose isn't to provide entertainment. Examples include organizations like the Kiwanis or Rotary Club, business leagues, chambers of commerce, real estate boards, trade associations, and professional associations such as a medical or bar association.

Entertainment Tickets

You can deduct only the face value of an entertainment ticket, even if you paid a higher price for it. For example, you cannot deduct service fees that you pay to ticket agencies or brokers or any amount over the face value of tickets that you buy from scalpers. However, you can deduct the entire amount you pay for a ticket if it's for an amateur sporting event run by volunteers to benefit a charity.

Ordinarily, you or an employee must be present at an entertainment activity to claim it as a business entertainment expense. This is not the case, however, with entertainment tickets. You can give tickets to clients or other business associates rather than attending the event yourself and still get a deduction. If you don't go to the event, you have the option of treating the tickets as a gift. You can get a bigger deduction this way sometimes. Gifts of up to $25 are 100% deductible (see Chapter 14 for more on deducting gifts), so with tickets that cost less than $50, you get a bigger deduction if you treat them as a gift. If they cost more, treat them as an entertainment expense.

> **EXAMPLE:** You pay $40 to a scalper for a ticket to a college basketball game that has a face value of only $30. You give the ticket to a client but don't attend the game yourself. By treating the ticket as a gift, you may deduct $25 of the expense. If you treated it as an entertainment expense, your deduction would be limited to 50% of $30, or $15. However, if you paid $100 for a ticket with a $60 face value, you would be better off treating it as an entertainment expense. This way you would be able to deduct 50% of $60, or $30. If you treated the ticket as a gift, your deduction would be limited to $25.

You may also deduct the cost of season tickets at a sports arena or theater. But, if you rent a skybox or other private luxury box, your deduction is limited to the cost of a regular nonluxury box seat. The cost of season tickets must be allocated to each separate event.

> **EXAMPLE:** Jim, an investment counselor, spends $5,000 for two season tickets to his local professional football team. The tickets entitle him and a guest to attend 16 games. He must allocate the cost game by game. If, during the course of the football season. he ends up giving tickets for eight games to clients and uses the others for himself and his wife, he may deduct 50% of the total cost as a business entertainment expense.

Reimbursed Expenses

If a client or customer reimburses you for entertainment expenses, you don't need to count the reimbursement that you receive as income as long as you give the client an adequate accounting of your expenses and comply with the accountable plan rules. Basically, this requires that you submit all your documentation to the client in a timely manner and return any excess payments. Accountable plans are covered in detail in Chapter 11.

If you comply with the rules, the client gets to deduct 50% of the expenses and you get 100% of your expenses paid for by somebody else. This is a lot better then getting only a 50% entertainment expense deduction. The reimbursement should not be listed by the client on any Form 1099-MISC a client is required to send to the IRS showing the amount paid to you for your services during the year.

> **EXAMPLE:** Philip, a self-employed private detective, takes several people out to lunch to discuss the theft of trade secrets from a biotechnology firm. He bills his client $200 for the lunches and provides all the proper documentation. The client reimburses Philip $200. Philip gets no deduction for the lunches, but he also doesn't have to include the $200 reimbursement in his income for the year; his client may deduct 50% of the expense as a business entertainment expense.

On the other hand, if you don't properly document your expenses and obtain reimbursement from your client, you must report the amount as income on your tax return, and the client should also include it in the Form 1099-MISC it submits to the IRS. You can still deduct the cost as a business entertainment expense on your own tax return, but your deduction will be subject to the 50% limit. The client can deduct the reimbursement as compensation paid to you. The client's deduction is not subject to the 50% limit because the payment is classified as compensation, not reimbursement of entertainment expenses.

> **EXAMPLE:** Assume that Philip from the above example fails to make an adequate accounting of his meal expenses to his client, but the client still reimburses him for the full $200. The client may deduct the entire $200, and must include this amount in the 1099-MISC form it provides the IRS reporting how much it paid Philip during the year. Philip must include the $200 as income on his tax return and pay tax on it. He may list the $200 as an entertainment expense on his personal tax return, but his deduction is limited to $100.

Clearly, it's better tax-wise to get your clients to reimburse you for entertainment expenses and keep careful track of the costs.

Meals for Employees

Ordinarily, meal and entertainment expenses for your employees are only 50% deductible, just like your own meal and entertainment expenses. However, you or your business may take a 100% deduction for employee meals:

- provided as part of a company recreational or social activity—for example, a picnic for your employees
- provided on business premises for your convenience—for example, you provide lunch because your employees must remain in the office to be available to work, or
- if the cost is included as part of the employee's compensation and reported as such on his or her W-2.

Reporting Entertainment Expenses on Your Tax Return

How you report your entertainment expenses on your tax return depends on how your business is organized and how you pay for the entertainment.

Sole Proprietors

If you're a sole proprietor, you must list your entertainment expenses on Schedule C, *Profit or Loss From Business*. The schedule contains a line just for this deduction. You list the total amount and then subtract from it the portion that is not deductible: 50%.

Partnerships, LLCs, and LLPs

If you've formed a partnership, LLC, or LLP, entertainment expenses can be paid from your business's bank account or by using a business credit card, or they can be paid by you from your personal funds or by using your personal credit card.

Expenses paid with partnership, LLC, or LLP funds are listed on the information return the entity files with the IRS. Your share of these and all other deductions for your entity pass through and are deducted on your individual tax return on Schedule E.

If you pay for entertainment expenses from your personal funds or credit card and you are reimbursed by your business entity, the expense is handled as if the entity paid it. You do not include the amount of the reimbursement in your income for the year.

If you personally pay for entertainment expenses and are not reimbursed by your business entity, you may directly deduct the expenses on your personal tax return by listing them on Schedule E. They are not included in your business entity's information return.

Corporations

If you've formed a C corporation and the corporation pays for your entertainment expenses, the corporation deducts the expenses on its own tax return. If you've formed an S corporation that pays your expenses, the tax reporting is the same as for a partnership or LLC.

Things are more complicated if you personally pay for entertainment expenses, because usually you will be your corporation's employee and special rules apply to expenses paid by employees. (See Chapter 11.)

Listing Meal and Entertainment Expenses on Tax Returns

Unlike Schedule C filed by sole proprietors, tax returns filed by partnerships, LLCs, LLPs, and corporations do not contain a specific line to report the amount of deductible entertainment expenses. Instead, you list them as "meals and entertainment" on a separate "Other Expenses" schedule.

Be careful never to lump together expenses for meals and entertainment with other expenses, such as those for business travel, lodging, or continuing education. Some taxpayers put all these expenses into a single expense category called "travel and entertainment." This is a mistake because, while meal and entertainment expenses are only 50% deductible, expenses for business travel, lodging, and continuing education are 100% deductible. Both your financial statements and tax returns should use separate expense categories for "travel and lodging," "continuing education," "employee benefits," and "meals and entertainment."

Chapter 11

Hiring Workers

T his chapter is about the host of tax rules that apply to businesses that hire people to help them, whether as employees or as independent contractors. These rules apply when you hire strangers or family members, or when your incorporated business hires you.

Employees Versus Independent Contractors

As far as the IRS is concerned, there are only two types of people you can hire to help in your business: employees and independent contractors. It's very important to understand the difference between the two, because the tax rules are very different for each. If you hire an employee, you become subject to a wide array of state and federal tax requirements. You must withhold taxes from your employee's pay, and you must pay other taxes yourself. You must also comply with complex and burdensome bookkeeping and reporting requirements. If you hire an independent contractor, none of these requirements applies. Tax deductions for businesses that hire employees and independent contractors differ as well.

Independent contractors (ICs) go by a variety of names: self-employed, freelancers, free agents, consultants, entrepreneurs, or business owners. What they all have in common is that they are people who are in business for themselves. Employees work for someone else's business.

Initially, it's up to you to determine whether any person you hire is an employee or an IC. However, your decision about how to classify a worker is subject to review by various government agencies, including:

- the IRS
- your state's tax department
- your state's unemployment compensation insurance agency, and
- your state's workers' compensation insurance agency.

These agencies are mostly interested in whether you have classified workers as independent contractors when you should have classified them as employees. The reason is that you must pay money to each of these agencies for employees, but not for independent contractors. The more workers are classified as employees, the more money flows into the agencies' coffers. In the case of taxing agencies, employers must withhold tax from employees' paychecks and hand it over to the government; ICs pay their own taxes, which means the government must wait longer to get its money and faces the possibility that ICs won't declare their income or will otherwise cheat on their taxes. An agency that determines that you misclassified an employee as an IC may impose back taxes, fines, and penalties.

Scrutinizing agencies use various tests to determine whether a worker is an IC or an employee. The determining factor is usually whether you have the right to control the worker. If you have the right to direct and control the way a worker performs—both as to the final results and the details of when, where, and how the work is done—then the worker is your employee. On the other hand, if your control is limited to accepting or rejecting the final results the worker achieves, then that person is an IC.

An employer may not always exercise its right of control. For example, if an employee is experienced and well trained, the employer may not feel the need to closely supervise him or her. But the employer still maintains the right to do so at any time.

> **EXAMPLE:** Mary takes a job as a hamburger cook at the local AcmeBurger. AcmeBurger personnel carefully train her in how to make an AcmeBurger hamburger—including the type and amount of ingredients to use, the temperature at which the hamburger should be cooked, and so forth.
>
> Once Mary starts work, AcmeBurger managers closely supervise how she does her job. Virtually every aspect of Mary's behavior on the job is under AcmeBurger control, including what time she arrives at and leaves work, when she takes her lunch break, what she wears, and the sequence of tasks she must perform. If Mary proves to be an able and conscientious worker, her supervisors may choose not to look over her shoulder very often. But they have the right to do so at any time. Mary is AcmeBurger's employee.

In contrast, a worker is an independent contractor if the hiring firm does not have the right to control the person on the job. Because the worker is an independent businessperson not solely dependent on you (the hiring party) for a living, your control is limited to accepting or rejecting the final results the IC achieves.

EXAMPLE: AcmeBurger develops a serious plumbing problem. AcmeBurger does not have any plumbers on its staff, so it hires Plumbing by Jake, an independent plumbing repair business owned by Jake. Jake looks at the problem and gives an estimate of how much it will cost to fix it. The manager agrees to hire him, and Jake and his assistant commence work. Jake is an independent contractor.

In a relationship of this kind where Jake is clearly running his own business, it's virtually certain that AcmeBurger does not have the right to control the way Jake performs his plumbing services. Its control is limited to accepting or rejecting the final result. If AcmeBurger doesn't like the work Jake has done, it can refuse to pay him.

The difficulty in applying the right of control test is determining whether you have the right to control a worker you hire. Government auditors can't look into your mind to see if you are controlling a worker. They rely instead on indirect or circumstantial evidence indicating control or lack of it—for example, whether you provide a worker with tools and equipment, where the work is performed, how the worker is paid, and whether you can fire the worker. The following chart shows the primary factors used by the IRS and most other government agencies to determine if you have the right to control a worker.

Part-Timers and Temps Can Be Employees

Don't think that a person you hire to work part time or for a short period must be an IC. People who work for you only temporarily or part time are your employees if you have the right to control the way they work.

For a detailed discussion of the practical and legal issues hiring firms face when hiring ICs, see *Working With Independent Contractors*, by Stephen Fishman (Nolo).

IRS Test for Worker Status		
Behavioral Control	Workers will more likely be considered ICs if you: • do not give them instructions • do not provide them with training	Workers will more likely be considered employees if you: • give them instructions they must follow about how to do the work • give them detailed training
Financial Control	Workers will more likely be considered ICs if they: • have a significant investment in equipment and facilities • pay business or travel expenses themselves • make their services available to the public • are paid by the job • have opportunity for profit or loss	Workers will more likely be considered employees if: • you provide them with equipment and facilities free of charge • you reimburse their business or travel expenses • they make no effort to market their services to the public • you pay them by the hour or other unit of time • they have no opportunity for profit or loss—for example, because they're paid by the hour and have all expenses reimbursed
Relationship Between You and the Worker	Workers will more likely be considered ICs if they: • don't receive employee benefits such as health insurance • sign a client agreement with the hiring firm • can't quit or be fired at will • perform services that are not part of your regular business activities	Workers will more likely be considered employees if they: • receive employee benefits • have no written client agreement • can quit at any time without incurring any liability to you • can be fired at any time • perform services that are part of your core business

Tax Deductions for Employee Pay and Benefits

Hiring employees costs you money, but you may deduct most or all of what you pay them as a business expense. Thus, for example, if you pay an employee $50,000 per year in salary and benefits, you'll ordinarily get a $50,000 tax deduction. You should factor this into your calculations whenever you're thinking about hiring an employee or deciding how much to pay him.

Employee Pay

Employee pay may be in the form of salaries, sales commissions, bonuses, vacation allowances, sick pay (as long as it's not covered by insurance), or fringe benefits. For tax deduction purposes, it doesn't really matter how you measure or make the payments. The amounts you pay an employee may fall into any of the four basic categories of deductible business expenses:

- business operating expenses
- business start-up expenses
- long-term asset purchase expenses, or
- inventory costs.

The general rules for each of these types of expenses are discussed in other chapters. Let's see how employee pay can fall into each category.

Operating Expenses

Most of the time, amounts you pay employees to work in your business will be business operating expenses. These expenses are currently deductible as long as they are:

- ordinary and necessary
- reasonable in amount
- paid for services actually performed, and
- actually paid or incurred in the year the deduction is claimed (as shown by your payroll records).

An employee's services are ordinary and necessary if they are common, accepted, helpful, and appropriate for your business; they don't have to be indispensable. An employee's pay is reasonable if the amount is in the range of what other businesses would pay for similar services. These requirements usually won't pose a problem when you hire an employee to perform any legitimate business function.

> **EXAMPLE:** Ken, the owner of a coffee bar, hires Kim to work as a barista and pays her $2,000 per month—what baristas are typically paid in the area. Ken can deduct Kim's $2,000 monthly salary as a business operating expense. If Kim works a full year, Ken will get a $24,000 deduction.

Payments to employees for personal services are not deductible as business expenses.

> **EXAMPLE:** Ken hires Samantha to work as a live-in nanny for his three children. Samantha is Ken's employee, but her services are personal, not related to his business. Thus, Ken may not deduct her pay as a business expense.

Special rules apply if you hire family members to work in your business or hire yourself. ("Employing Your Family or Yourself," below.)

Start-Up Expenses

Employee compensation for services performed during the start-up phase of your business is a business start-up expense. It is not currently deductible, but you may deduct up to $5,000 in start-up expenses the first year you're in business, provided your expenses don't exceed $50,000. Any excess can be deducted over 180 months. (See Chapter 3 for more on deducting start-up expenses.)

> **EXAMPLE:** Michelle, a famous chef, hires Benjamin to work as her full-time personal assistant while she works to start up a new restaurant. Benjamin helps Michelle find and rent a space for the restaurant, hire and train employees, and deal with myriad other details involved in starting such a complex business. Benjamin worked for Michelle for four months before the restaurant opened for business. His salary during this start-up phase—$15,000—is a business start-up from which Michelle may deduct $5,000 the first

year she's in business and the remaining $10,000 over 180 months ($666 per calendar year).

Long-Term Asset Expenses

If you pay an employee to help purchase, transport, install, or improve a long-term asset, the payments are not business operating expenses. Instead, they are added to the basis (cost) of the asset. As such, you may either depreciate them over several years or (in most situations) currently deduct them under Section 179. (See Chapter 5 for more on deducting long-term assets.)

> **EXAMPLE:** John owns a fleet of 50 used delivery trucks. He employs Martha, a mechanic, to install new engines in the trucks. The engines are long-term asset purchases. What John pays Martha to install the engines is added to their purchase price to arrive at their value for tax purposes (their taxable basis). John can depreciate this amount over five years or deduct the entire amount in one year under Section 179 (in most situations).

Inventory Costs

If you hire an employee to help you manufacture products for sale to customers, the employee's compensation is not a regular business expense. Instead, it is considered part of the cost of the products. These products are inventory, the cost of which may be deducted only as each item is sold. (See Chapter 6 for more on inventory.)

> **EXAMPLE:** Richard owns a small factory that manufactures clothes hangers for sale to clothing companies. He pays his ten employees a total of $25,000 each month. He adds this cost to the other costs he incurs to produce the hangers (rent, materials, equipment, electricity, and so forth) to figure his total cost of goods sold. He deducts this amount from his gross income to determine his business's gross profit.

Payroll Taxes

Whenever you hire an employee, you become an unpaid tax collector for the government. You are required to withhold and pay both federal and state taxes for the worker. These taxes are called payroll taxes or employment taxes. Federal payroll taxes consist of:

- Social Security and Medicare taxes—also known as FICA
- unemployment taxes—also known as FUTA, and
- federal income taxes—also known as FITW.

You must periodically pay FICA, FUTA, and FITW to the IRS, either electronically or by making federal tax deposits at specified banks, which transmit the money to the IRS. You are entitled to deduct as a business expense payroll taxes that you pay yourself. You get no deductions for taxes you withhold from employees' pay.

Every year, employers must file IRS Form W-2, *Wage and Tax Statement*, for each of their workers. The form shows the IRS how much the worker was paid and how much tax was withheld.

 IRS Circular E, *Employer's Tax Guide*, provides detailed information on these requirements. You can get a free copy by calling the IRS at 800-TAX-FORM, by calling or visiting your local IRS office, or by downloading it from the IRS website at www.irs.gov.

Employer's FICA Contributions

FICA is an acronym for Federal Income Contributions Act, the law requiring employers and employees to pay Social Security and Medicare taxes. FICA consists of:

- a 12.4% Social Security tax on an employee's wages up to an annual ceiling or cap—in 2006, the cap was $94,200 per year, and
- a 2.9% Medicare tax on all employee wages paid.

This adds up to a 15.3% tax, up to the Social Security tax ceiling. Employers must pay half of this—7.65%—out of their own pockets. They must withhold the other half from their employees' pay. You are entitled to deduct as a business expense the portion of the tax that you pay yourself.

The ceiling for the Social Security tax changes annually. You can find out what the Social Security tax ceiling is for the current year from IRS Circular E, *Employer's Tax Guide*; the amount is printed right on the first page.

FUTA

FUTA is an acronym for the Federal Unemployment Tax Act, the law that establishes federal unemployment taxes. Most employers must pay both state and federal unemployment taxes. Even if you're exempt from the state tax, you may still have to pay the federal tax. Employers alone are responsible for FUTA—you may not collect or deduct it from employees' wages.

You must pay FUTA taxes if either of the following is true:

- You pay $1,500 or more to employees during any calendar quarter— that is, any three-month period beginning with January, April, July, or October.
- You had one or more employees for at least some part of a day in any 20 or more different weeks during the year. The weeks don't have to be consecutive, nor does it have to be the same employee each week.

Technically, the FUTA tax rate is 6.2%, but, in practice, you rarely pay this much. You are given a credit of 5.4% if you pay the applicable state unemployment tax in full and on time. This means that the actual FUTA tax rate is usually 0.8%. In 2006, the FUTA tax was assessed on the first $7,000 of an employee's annual wages. The FUTA tax, then, is usually $56 per year per employee. This amount is a deductible business expense.

FITW

FITW is an acronym for federal income tax withholding. You must calculate and withhold federal income taxes from your employees' paychecks. Employees are solely responsible for paying federal income taxes. Your only responsibility is to withhold the funds and remit them to the government. You get no deductions for FITW.

State Payroll Taxes

Employers in every state are required to pay and withhold state payroll taxes. These taxes include:

- state unemployment compensation taxes in all states
- state income tax withholding in most states, and
- state disability taxes in a few states.

Employers in every state are required to contribute to a state unemployment insurance fund. Employees make no contributions, except in

Alaska, New Jersey, Pennsylvania, and Rhode Island, where employers must withhold small employee contributions from employees' paychecks. The employer contributions are a deductible business expense.

If your payroll is very small—below $1,500 per calendar quarter—you probably won't have to pay unemployment compensation taxes. In most states, you must pay state unemployment taxes for employees if you're paying federal FUTA taxes. However, some states have more strict requirements. Contact your state labor department for the exact rules and payroll amounts.

All states except Alaska, Florida, Nevada, South Dakota, Texas, Washington, and Wyoming have income taxation. If your state has income taxes, you must withhold the applicable tax from your employees' paychecks and pay it to the state taxing authority. Each state has its own income tax withholding forms and procedures. Contact your state tax department for information. Of course, employers get no deductions for withholding their employees' state income taxes.

California, Hawaii, New Jersey, New York, and Rhode Island have state disability insurance that provides employees with coverage for injuries or illnesses that are not related to work. Employers in these states must withhold their employees' disability insurance contributions from their pay. Employers must also make their own contributions in Hawaii, New Jersey, and New York—these employer contributions are deductible.

In addition, subject to some important exceptions, employers in all states must provide their employees with workers' compensation insurance to cover work-related injuries. Workers' compensation is not a payroll tax. Employers must purchase a workers' compensation policy from a private insurer or state workers' compensation fund. Your worker's compensation insurance premiums are deductible as a business insurance expense. (See Chapter 14 for more on deducting business insurance.)

> ⚠️ **Employers in California must withhold for parental leave.** Employers in California are also required to withhold (as part of their disability program) for parental leave.

> **EXAMPLE:** Isaac hires Vendela to work in his Seattle bookshop at a salary of $2,000 per month. Isaac may deduct this amount as a business operating expense. In addition, he may deduct his payroll tax contributions on her behalf. These consist of a monthly

$153 FICA contribution (7.65% x $2,000 = $153), $56 annual FUTA contribution, and $1,200 annual Washington state unemployment contribution. Isaac must withhold $300 from Vendela's pay each month to cover her FICA and FITW taxes and send it to the IRS. He need not withhold state income taxes because Washington has no income tax. He gets no deduction for these withheld amounts. So Isaac's annual tax deduction for Vendela is $27,092 ($24,000 salary + $1,836 FICA contribution + $1,200 state unemployment insurance + $56 FUTA = $27,092).

Bookkeeping Expenses Are Deductible

Figuring out how much to withhold, doing the necessary record keeping, and filling out the required forms can be complicated. If you have a computer, computer accounting programs such as *QuickBooks* or *QuickPay* can help with all the calculations and print out your employees' checks and IRS forms. You can also hire a bookkeeper or payroll tax service to do the work. Amounts you pay a bookkeeper or payroll tax service are deductible business operating expenses. You can find these services in the phone book or on the Internet under payroll tax services. You can also find a list of payroll service providers on the IRS website at www.irs.gov.

Be aware, however, that even if you hire a payroll service, you remain personally liable if your payroll taxes are not paid on time. The IRS recommends that employers: (1) keep their company address on file with the IRS, rather than the address of the payroll service provider, so that the company will be contacted by the IRS if there are any problems; (2) require the payroll service provider to post a fiduciary bond in case it defaults on its obligation to pay any penalties and interest due to IRS deficiency notices; and (3) ask the service provider to enroll in and use the Electronic Federal Tax Payment System (EFTPS) so the employer can confirm payments made on its behalf.

Employee Fringe Benefits

There is no law that says you must provide your employees with any fringe benefits—not even health insurance (except in Hawaii and Massachusetts), sick pay, or vacation. However, the tax law encourages you to provide employee benefits by allowing you to deduct the cost as a business expense. (These expenses should be deducted as employee benefit expenses, not employee compensation.) Moreover, your employees do not have to treat the value of their fringe benefits as income on which they need pay tax. So you get a deduction, and your employees get tax-free goodies.

In contrast, if you're a business owner (a sole proprietor, partner in a partnership, 2% or more of an S corporation, or LLC member), you must include in your income and pay tax on the value of any fringe benefits your company provides to you—the only exception is for de minimis fringes.

Tax-free employee fringe benefits include:
- health insurance
- accident insurance
- Health Savings Accounts (see Chapter 13)
- dependent care assistance
- educational assistance
- group term life insurance coverage—limits apply based on the policy value
- qualified employee benefits plans, including profit-sharing plans, stock bonus plans, and money purchase plans
- employee stock options
- lodging on your business premises
- moving expense reimbursements
- achievement awards
- commuting benefits
- employee discounts on the goods or services you sell
- supplemental unemployment benefits
- de minimis (low-cost) fringe benefits such as low-value birthday or holiday gifts, event tickets, traditional awards (such as a retirement gift), other special occasion gifts, and coffee and soft drinks, and
- cafeteria plans that allow employees to choose among two or more benefits consisting of cash and qualified benefits.

Health insurance is by far the most important tax-free employee fringe benefit; it is discussed in detail in Chapter 13. See IRS Publication 15-B, *Employer's Guide to Fringe Benefits*, for more information on the other types of benefits.

Employees may also be supplied with working condition fringe benefits. These are property and services you provide to an employee so that the employee can perform his or her job. A working condition fringe benefit is tax-free to an employee to the extent the employee would be able to deduct the cost of the property or services as a business or depreciation expense if he or she had paid for it. If the employee uses the benefit 100% for work, it is tax-free. But the value of any personal use of a working condition fringe benefit must be included in the employee's compensation, and he or she must pay tax on it. The employee must meet any documentation requirements that apply to the deduction.

> **EXAMPLE:** Sam, the owner of a small architecture firm, leases a computer and gives it to his employee Paul so that he can perform design work at home. If Paul uses the computer 100% for his work, it is tax-free to him. But if he uses it only 50% of the time for work and 50% of the time for personal purposes, he would have to pay income tax on 50% of its value.

The value of the personal use is determined according to its fair market value.

> **EXAMPLE:** It cost Sam $200 a month to rent the computer he gave Paul. If Paul uses the computer 50% of the time for work and 50% of the time for nondeductible personal uses, he would have to add $100 per month to his taxable compensation.

One of the most common working condition fringe benefits is a company car. If an employee uses a company car part of the time for personal driving, the value of the personal use must be included in the employee's income. The employer determines how to value the use of a car, and there are several methods that may be used. The most common is for the employer to report a percentage of the car's annual lease value as determined by IRS tables. For a detailed discussion of these valuation rules, refer to IRS Publication 15-B.

Reimbursing Employees for Business-Related Expenditures

When you own a business, you generally pay all your business expenses yourself, including expenses you incur to enable your employees to do their work—for example, office space, tools, and equipment. However, there may be times when an employee must pay for a work-related expense. Most commonly, this occurs when an employee is driving, traveling, or entertaining while on the job. However, depending on the circumstances, an employee could end up paying for almost any work-related expense—for example, an employee might pay for office supplies or parking at a client's office.

All these employee payments have important tax consequences, whatever form they take. The rules discussed below apply whether the expenses are incurred by an employee who is not related to you or by an employee who is your spouse or child. They also apply to a business owner who has incorporated the business and works as its employee.

Accountable Plans

The best way to reimburse or otherwise pay your employees for any work-related expenses is to use an accountable plan. When you pay employees for their expenses under an accountable plan, two great things happen:

- You don't have to pay payroll taxes on the payments.
- The employees won't have to include the payments in their taxable income.

Moreover, the amounts you pay will be deductible by you, just like your other business expenses, subject to the same rules.

> **EXAMPLE:** The Acme Cement Co. decides that Manny, its top salesperson, should attend the Wonderful World of Cement convention in Las Vegas. Manny pays his expenses himself. When he gets back, he fully documents his expenses as required by

Acme's accountable plan. These amount to $2,000 for transportation and hotel and $1,000 in meal and entertainment expenses. Acme reimburses Manny $3,000. Acme may deduct as a business expense the entire $2,000 cost of Manny's flight and hotel and deduct 50% of the cost of the meals and entertainment. Manny need not count the $3,000 reimbursement as income (or pay taxes on it), and Acme need not include the amount on the W-2 form it files with the IRS reporting how much Manny was paid for the year. Moreover, Acme need not withhold income tax or pay any Social Security or Medicare taxes on the $3,000.

Requirements for an Accountable Plan

An accountable plan is an arrangement in which you agree to reimburse or advance employee expenses only if the employee:

- pays or incurs expenses that qualify as deductible business expenses for your business while performing services as your employee
- adequately accounts to you for the expenses within a reasonable period of time, and
- returns to you within a reasonable time any amounts received in excess of the actual expenses incurred.

These payments to employees can be made through advances, direct reimbursements, charges to a company credit card, or direct billings to the employer.

These strict rules are imposed to prevent employees from seeking reimbursement for personal expenses (or nonexistent phony expenses) under the guise that they were business expenses. Employees used to do this all the time to avoid paying income tax on the reimbursed amounts (employees must count employer reimbursements for their personal expenses as income, but not reimbursements for the employer's business expenses).

An accountable plan need not be in writing (although it's not a bad idea). All you need to do is set up procedures for your employees to follow that meet the requirements.

Employees Must Document Expenses

Your employees must give you the same documentation for a work-related expense that the IRS requires of you when you claim that expense for your business. This documentation should be provided within 60 days after the expense was incurred.

You need thorough documentation for car, travel, entertainment, and meal expenses—these are the expenses the IRS is really concerned about. (See Chapter 10 for more about deducting meal and entertainment expenses.) However, you can ease up on the documentation requirements if you pay employees a per diem (per day) allowance equal to or less than the per diem rates the federal government pays its workers while traveling. You can find these rates at www.gsa.gov (look for the link to "Per Diem Rates" in the "Featured Topics" section) or in IRS Publication 1542. If you use this method, the IRS will assume that the amounts for lodging, meals, and incidental expenses are accurate without any further documentation. The employee need only substantiate the time, place, and business purpose of the expense. The same holds true if you pay the standard mileage rate for an employee who uses a personal car for business. (See Chapter 8 for more about deducting car expenses.)

However, per diem rates may not be used for an employee who:

- owns more than 10% of the stock in an incorporated business, or
- is a close relative of a 10% or more owner—a brother, sister, parent, spouse, grandparent, or other lineal ancestor or descendent.

In these instances, the employee must keep track of the actual cost of all business-related expenses that he or she wants to get reimbursed for by the employer. Any per diem rate reimbursement for an owner or owner's relative must be counted as taxable wages for the employee.

The documentation requirements are less onerous for other types of expenses. Nevertheless, the employer must still document the amount of money spent and show that it was for your business. For example, an employee who pays for a repair to his office computer out of his own pocket should save the receipt and write "repair of office computer" or something similar to show the business purpose of the payment. It's not sufficient for an employee to submit an expense report with vague categories or descriptions such as "travel" or "miscellaneous business expenses."

Returning Excess Payments

Employees who are advanced or reimbursed more than they actually spent for business expenses must return the excess payments to the employer within a reasonable time. The IRS says a reasonable time is 120 days after an expense is incurred. Any amounts not returned are treated as taxable wages for the employee and must be added to the employee's income for tax purposes. This means that you, the employer, must pay payroll tax on those amounts.

> **EXAMPLE:** You give your employee a $1,000 advance to cover her expenses for a short business trip. When she gets back, she gives you an expense report and documentation showing she only spent $900 for business while on the trip. If she doesn't return the extra $100 within 120 days after the trip, it will be considered wages for tax purposes and you'll have to pay payroll tax on the amount.

Unaccountable Plans

Any payments you make to employees for business-related expenses that do not comply with the accountable plan rule are deemed to be made under an unaccountable plan. These payments are considered to be employee wages, which means all of the following:

- The employee must report the payments as income on her tax return and pay tax on them.
- The employee may deduct the expenses—but only as a miscellaneous itemized deduction. (See "Unreimbursed Employee Expenses," below.)
- You (the employer) may deduct the payments as wages paid to an employee.
- You (the employer) must withhold the employee's income taxes and share of Social Security and Medicare taxes from the payments.
- You (the employer) must pay the employer's 7.65% share of the employee's Social Security and Medicare taxes on the payments.

This is a tax disaster for the employee and not a good result for the employer, either, because you will have to pay Social Security and Medicare tax that you could have avoided if the payments had been made under an accountable plan.

Unreimbursed Employee Expenses

Unless you've agreed to do so, you have no legal obligation to reimburse or pay employees for job-related expenses they incur. Employees are entitled to deduct from their own income ordinary and necessary expenses arising from their employment that are not reimbursed by their employers. In this event, you (the employer) get no deduction, because you haven't paid for the expense.

> ⚠️ **Some states require reimbursement.** Check with your state's labor department to find out the rules for reimbursing employee expenses. You might find that you are legally required to repay employees, rather than letting your employees deduct the expenses on their own tax returns. In California, for example, employers must reimburse employees for all expenses or losses they incur as a direct consequence of carrying out their job duties. (Cal. Labor Code § 2802.)

Employees may deduct essentially the same expenses as business owners, subject to some special rules. For example, there are special deduction rules for employee home office expenses (see Chapter 7), and employees who use the actual expense method for car expenses may not deduct car loan interest.

However, it's much better for the employees to be reimbursed by the employer under an accountable plan and let the employer take the deduction. Why? Because employees can deduct unreimbursed employee expenses only if the employee itemizes his or her deductions and only to the extent these deductions, along with the employee's other miscellaneous itemized deductions, exceed 2% of his adjusted gross income. Adjusted gross income (AGI) is the employee's total income, minus deductions for IRA and pension contributions and a few other deductions (shown on Form 1040, line 35). Moreover, if an employee's AGI exceeds $149,950, the deductible amount is reduced by 3% of the excess (this figure is adjusted each year for inflation).

These rules apply to all employees, including family members who work as your employees, and to you, if you've incorporated your business and work as its employee.

EXAMPLE: Eric has formed a regular C corporation for his consulting business and works as its sole employee. During 2006, he drives his own car 10,000 miles for his business. He pays all his car-related expenses out of his own pocket and does not seek reimbursement from his corporation. He may deduct his business mileage as an unreimbursed employee business expense on his individual tax return. However, he must keep track of his actual car expenses instead of using the standard mileage rate. His actual expenses are $5,000. He may deduct this amount to the extent that it, and his other miscellaneous itemized deductions, exceeds 2% of his adjusted gross income. Eric's AGI for the year was $100,000, and he had no other miscellaneous itemized deductions, so he may only deduct his $5,000 car expense to the extent it exceeds $2,000 (2% x $100,000 = $2,000). Thus, he may only deduct $3,000 of his $5,000 car expense.

An employee's unreimbursed expenses must be listed on IRS Schedule A, Form 1040, as a miscellaneous itemized deduction. Employees must also file IRS Form 2106 reporting the amount of the expenses.

Employing Your Family or Yourself

Whoever said "never hire your relatives" must never have read the tax code. The tax law promotes family togetherness by making it highly advantageous for small business owners to hire their spouses or children. If you're single and have no children, you're out of luck.

Employing Your Children

Believe it or not, your children can be a great tax savings device. If you hire your children as employees to do legitimate work in your business, you may deduct their salaries from your business income as a business expense. Your child will have to pay tax on the salary only to the extent it exceeds the standard deduction amount for the year: $5,150 in 2006. Moreover, if your child is under 18, you won't have to withhold or pay any FICA (Social Security or Medicare) tax on the salary (subject to a couple of exceptions).

These rules allow you to shift part of your business income from your own tax bracket to your child's bracket, which should be much lower than yours (unless you earn little or no income). This can result in substantial tax savings.

The following chart shows the federal income tax brackets for 2006. A child need only pay a 10% tax on taxable income up to $7,550—taxable income means total income minus the standard deduction. Thus, a child could earn up to $12,700 and pay only a 10% income tax. In contrast, if you were married and file jointly, you'd have to pay a 15% federal income tax on taxable income between $15,101 and $61,300, and a 25% tax on taxable income from $61,301 to $123,700. You'd also have to pay a 15.3% Social Security and Medicare tax (up to an annual ceiling), which your child under the age of 18 need not pay.

2006 Federal Personal Income Tax Brackets		
Tax Bracket	**Income If Single**	**Income If Married Filing Jointly**
10%	Up to $7,550	Up to $15,100
15%	$7,551 to $30,650	$15,101 to $61,300
25%	$30,651 to $74,200	$61,301 to $123,700
28%	$74,201 to $154,800	$123,701 to $188,450
33%	$154,801 to $336,550	$188,451 to $336,550
35%	All over $336,550	All over $336,550

EXAMPLE: Carol hires Mark, her 16-year-old son, to perform computer inputting services for her medical record transcription business, which she owns as a sole proprietor. He works ten hours per week and she pays him $20 per hour (the going rate for such work). Over the course of a year, she pays him a total of $9,000. She need not pay FICA tax for Mark because he's under 18. When she does her taxes for the year, she may deduct his $9,000 salary from her business income as a business expense. Mark pays tax only on the portion of his income that exceeds the $5,150 standard deduction—so he pays federal income tax only on $3,850 of his $9,000 salary. With such a small amount of income, he is in the lowest federal income tax bracket: 10%. He pays $385 in federal income tax for the year. Had Carol not hired Mark and done the work herself, she would have lost her $9,000 deduction and had to pay income tax and self-employment taxes on this amount—a 40% tax in her tax bracket (25% federal income tax + 15.3% self-employment tax = 40%). Thus, she would have had to pay an additional $3,600 in federal taxes. Depending on the state where Carol lives, she likely would have had to pay a state income tax as well.

What About Child Labor Laws?

You're probably aware that certain types of child labor are illegal under federal and state law. However, these laws generally don't apply to children under 16 who are employed by their parents, unless the child is employed in mining, manufacturing, or a hazardous occupation. Hazardous occupations include driving a motor vehicle; being an outside helper on a motor vehicle; and operating various power-driven machines, including machines for woodworking, metal forming, sawing, and baking; or roofing, wrecking, excavation, demolition, and shipbreaking operations.

A child who is at least 16 may be employed in any nonhazardous occupation. Children at least 17 years of age may spend up to 20% of their time driving cars and trucks weighing less than 6,000 pounds as part of their job if they have licenses and no tickets, drive only in daylight hours, and go no more than 30 miles from home. They may not perform dangerous driving maneuvers (such as towing) or do regular route deliveries. For detailed information, see the Department of Labor website (www.dol.gov).

No Payroll Taxes

As mentioned above, one of the advantages of hiring your child is that you need not pay FICA taxes for your child under the age of 18 who works in your trade or business, or your partnership if it's owned solely by you and your spouse.

EXAMPLE: Lisa, a 16-year-old, makes deliveries for her mother's mail order business, which is operated as a sole proprietorship. Although Lisa is her mother's employee, her mother need not pay FICA taxes on her salary until she turns 18.

Moreover, you need not pay federal unemployment (FUTA) taxes for services performed by your child who is under 21 years old.

However, these rules do not apply—and you must pay both FICA and FUTA—if you hire your child to work for:

- your corporation, or
- your partnership, unless all the partners are parents of the child.

EXAMPLE: Ron works in a computer repair business that is co-owned by his mother and her partner, Ralph, who is no relation to the family. FICA and FUTA taxes must be paid for Ron because he is working for a partnership and not all of the partners are his parents.

No Withholding

In addition, if your child has no unearned income (for example, interest or dividend income), you must withhold income taxes from your child's pay only if it exceeds the standard deduction for the year. The standard deduction was $5,150 in 2006 and is adjusted every year for inflation. Children who are paid less than this amount need not pay any income taxes on their earnings.

EXAMPLE: Connie, a 15-year-old girl, is paid $4,000 a year to help out in her parent's bakery shop. She has no income from interest or any other unearned income. Her parents need not withhold income taxes from Connie's salary because she has no unearned income and her salary was less than the standard deduction amount for the year.

However, you must withhold income taxes if your child has more than $250 in unearned income for the year and her total income exceeds $850 (in 2006).

EXAMPLE: If Connie (from the above example) is paid $4,000 in salary and has $500 in interest income, her parents must withhold income taxes from her salary because she has more than $250 in unearned income and her total income for the year was more than $850.

Employing Your Spouse

You don't get the benefits of income shifting when you employ your spouse in your business, because your income is combined when you file a joint tax return. You'll also have to pay FICA taxes on your spouse's wages, so you get no savings there, either. However, you need not pay FUTA tax if you employ your spouse in your unincorporated business. This tax is usually only $56 per year, so this is not much of a savings.

The real advantage of hiring your spouse is in the realm of employee benefits. You can provide your spouse with any or all of the employee benefits discussed in "Tax Deductions for Employee Pay and Benefits," above. You'll get a tax deduction for the cost of the benefit, and your spouse doesn't have to declare the benefit as income, provided the IRS requirements are satisfied. This is a particularly valuable tool for health insurance—you can give your spouse health insurance coverage as an employee benefit. (See Chapter 13 for a detailed discussion.)

Another benefit of hiring your spouse is that you can both go on business trips and deduct the cost as a business expense, as long as your spouse's presence was necessary (for your business, not for you personally).

If you work at an outside office or other workspace, there is no law that says your spouse must work there too. After all, having your spouse spend all day with you at your office might constitute too much togetherness. Fortunately, your spouse can work at home—for example, by doing accounting, collections, or marketing work for the family business. All these activities can easily be conducted from a home office.

Having your spouse work at home has tax benefits as well. If you set up a home office for your spouse that is used exclusively for business purposes, you'll get a home office deduction. Your spouse has no outside office, so the home office will easily pass the convenience of the employer test. (See Chapter 7.) Moreover, you can depreciate or deduct under Section 179 the cost of office furniture, computers, additional phone lines, copiers, fax machines, and other business equipment you buy for your spouse's use on the job.

Rules to Follow When Employing Your Family

The IRS is well aware of the tax benefits of hiring a child or spouse, so it's on the lookout for taxpayers who claim the benefit without really having their family members work in their businesses. If the IRS concludes that your children or spouse aren't really employees, you'll lose your tax deductions for their salary and benefits. And they'll have to pay tax on their benefits. To avoid this, you should follow these simple rules.

Rule 1: Your Child or Spouse Must Be a Real Employee

First of all, your child or spouse must be a bona fide employee. Their work must be ordinary and necessary for your business, and their pay must be for services actually performed. Their services don't have to be indispensable, only common, accepted, helpful, and appropriate for your business. Any real work for your business can qualify—for example, you could employ your child or spouse to clean your office, answer the phone, stuff envelopes, input date, or make deliveries (a child may only make deliveries by foot or bicycle, not by car; see "Employing Your Children," above). You get no business deductions when you pay your child for personal services, such as babysitting or mowing your lawn at home. On the other hand, money you pay for yard work performed on business property could be deductible as a business expense.

The IRS won't believe that an extremely young child is a legitimate employee. How young is too young? The IRS has accepted that a seven-year-old child may be an employee (see "Hardworking Seven-Year-Old Was Parents' Employee," below) but probably won't believe that children younger than seven are performing any useful work for your business.

Junior's Timesheet

Date	Time In	Time Out	Total Work Time	Services Performed
1/9/04	3:30 pm	5:30 pm	2 hours	copying, some filing
1/14/04	3:30 pm	5:00 pm	1 1/2 hours	printed out bills and prepared for them for mailing
1/15/04	3:45 pm	5:15 pm	1 1/2 hours	copying and filing
1/24/04	10:00 am	3:00 pm	5 hours	answered phones
1/30/04	3:30 pm	5:30 pm	2 hours	copying, filing
?1/04	10:00 am	2:00 pm	4 hours	cleaned office

Hardworking Seven-Year-Old Was Parents' Employee

Walt and Dorothy Eller owned three trailer parks and a small strip mall in Northern California. They hired their three children, ages seven, 11, and 12, to perform various services for their businesses including pool maintenance, landscaping, reading gas and electric meters, delivering leaflets and messages to tenants, answering phones, making minor repairs, and sweeping and cleaning trailer pads and parking lots. The children worked after school, on weekends, and during their summer vacations. The Ellers paid their children a total of $5,200; $4,200; and $8,400 over a three-year period and deducted the amounts as business expenses. The IRS tried to disallow the deductions, claiming that the children's pay was excessive. The court allowed most of the deductions, noting that these hardworking children performed essential services for their parents' businesses. The court found that the seven-year-old was a bona fide employee but ruled that he should earn somewhat less than his older brother and sister because 11- and 12-year-old children can generally handle greater responsibility and perform greater services than seven-year-old children. Thus, while the older siblings could reasonably be paid $5,700 for their services over the three years in question, the seven-year-old could only reasonably be paid $4,000. (*Eller v. Commissioner*, 77 TC 934 (1981).)

Rule 2: Compensation Must Be Reasonable

When you hire your children, it is advantageous (tax-wise) to pay them as much as possible. That way, you can shift as much of your income as possible to your children, who are probably in a much lower income tax bracket. Conversely, you want to pay your spouse as little as possible, since you get no benefits from income shifting. This is because you and your spouse are in the same income tax bracket (assuming you file a joint return, as the vast majority of married people do). Moreover, your spouse will have to pay a 7.65% Social Security tax on his or her salary—an amount that is not tax deductible. (As your spouse's employer, you'll have to pay employment taxes on your spouse's salary as well, but these taxes are deductible business expenses.) The absolute minimum you can pay your spouse is the minimum wage in your area.

However, you can't just pay any amount you choose: Your spouse's and/or your child's total compensation must be reasonable. Total compensation means the sum of the salary plus all the fringe benefits you provide your spouse, including health insurance and medical expense reimbursements, if any. This is determined by comparing the amount paid with the value of the services performed. You should have no problem as long as you pay no more than what you'd pay a stranger for the same work—don't try paying your child $100 per hour for office cleaning just to get a big tax deduction. Find out what workers performing similar services in your area are being paid. For example, if you plan to hire your teenager to do computer inputting, call an employment agency or temp agency in your area to see what these workers are being paid.

To prove how much you paid (and that you actually paid it), you should pay your child or spouse by check, not cash. Do this once or twice a month as you would for any other employee. The funds should be deposited in a bank account in your child's or spouse's name. Your child's bank account may be a trust account.

Rule 3: Comply With Legal Requirements for Employers

You must comply with most of the same legal requirements when you hire a child or spouse as you do when you hire a stranger.

- **At the time you hire.** When you first hire your child or spouse, you must fill out IRS Form W-4. You, the employer, use it to determine how much tax you must withhold from the employee's salary. A child who is exempt from withholding should write "exempt" in the space provided and complete and sign the rest of the form. You must also complete U.S. Citizenship and Immigration Services (USCIS) Form I-9, *Employment Eligibility Verification*, verifying that the employee is a U.S. citizen or is otherwise eligible to work in the U.S. Keep both forms. You must also record your employee's Social Security number. If your child doesn't have a number, you must apply for one. In addition, you, the employer, must have an Employment Identification Number (EIN). If you don't have one, you may obtain it by filing IRS Form SS-4.

- **Every payday.** You'll need to withhold income tax from your child's pay only if exceeds a specified amount. ("Employing Your Children," above.) You don't need to withhold FICA taxes for children younger than 18. You must withhold income tax and FICA for your spouse, but not FUTA tax. If the amounts withheld, plus the employer's share of payroll taxes, exceed $2,500 during a calendar quarter, you must deposit the amounts monthly by making federal tax deposits at specified banks or electronically depositing them with the IRS.

- **Every calendar quarter.** If you withhold tax from your child's or spouse's pay, you must deposit it with the IRS or a specified bank. If you deposit more than $1,000 a year, you must file Form 941, *Employer's Quarterly Federal Tax Return*, with the IRS showing how much the employee was paid during the quarter and how much tax you withheld and deposited. If you need to deposit less than $2,500 during a calendar quarter, you can make your payment along with the Form 941 instead of paying monthly. Starting in 2006, employers with total employment tax liability of $1,000 or less may file employment tax returns once a year instead of quarterly. Use new IRS Form 944, *Employer's Annual Federal Tax Return*. You should be notified by the IRS if you're eligible to file Form 944. If you haven't been notified but believe you qualify to file Form 944, call the IRS at 800-829-0115.

- **Each year.** By January 31 of each year, you must complete and give to your employee a copy of IRS Form W-2, showing how much you paid the employee and how much tax was withheld. You must also file copies with the IRS and the Social Security Administration by February 28. You must include IRS Form W-3 with the copy you file with the Social Security Administration. If your child is exempt from withholding, a new W-4 form must be completed each year.

You must also file Form 940 or Form 940-EZ, *Employer's Annual Federal Unemployment (FUTA) Tax Return.* The due date is January 31; however, if you deposited all of the FUTA tax when due, you have ten additional days to file. You must file a Form 940 for your child even though you are not required to withhold any unemployment taxes from his or her pay. If your child is your only employee, enter his or her wages as "exempt" from unemployment tax.

IRS Circular E, *Employer's Tax Guide*, and Publication 929, *Tax Rules for Children and Dependents*, provide detailed information on these requirements. You can get free copies by calling the IRS at 800-TAX-FORM, by calling or visiting your local IRS office, or by downloading them from the IRS website at www.irs.gov.

Employing Yourself

If you are a sole proprietor, partner in a partnership, or member of a limited liability company (LLC) taxed as a partnership (as most are), you are not an employee of your business. You are a business owner. However, if you have incorporated your business, whether as a regular C corporation or an S corporation, you must be an employee of your corporation if you actively work in the business. In effect, you will be employing yourself. This has important tax consequences.

Your Company Must Pay Payroll Taxes

Your incorporated business must treat you just like any other employee for tax purposes. This means it must withhold income and FICA taxes from your pay and pay half of your FICA tax itself. It must also pay FUTA taxes for you. It gets a tax deduction for its contributions, the same as any other employer. (See "Tax Deductions for Employee Pay and Benefits," above.) Your corporation—not you personally—must pay these payroll taxes.

You can't avoid having your corporation pay payroll taxes by working for free. You must pay yourself at least a reasonable salary—what similar companies pay for the same services.

Tax Deductions for Your Salary and Benefits

When you're an employee, your salary is deductible by your incorporated business as a business expense. However, you must pay income tax on your salary, so there is no real tax savings.

But being an employee can have an upside. You'll be eligible for all of the tax-advantaged employee benefits discussed in "Tax Deductions for Employee Pay and Benefits," above. This means your corporation can provide you with benefits like health insurance and deduct the expense. (See Chapter 13 for more on deducting medical expenses.) If your corporation is a regular C corporation, you won't have to pay income tax on the value of your employee benefits. However, most employees of S corporations must pay tax on their employee benefits, so you probably won't get a tax benefit. The only exception is for employees of an S corporation who own less than 2% of the corporate stock. It isn't likely you'll have this little stock in your own S corporation.

You Can't Deduct Business Owner's "Draws"

If you're a business owner—sole proprietor, partner, or LLC member— you do not pay yourself a salary, as you do when you are employed by your incorporated business. If you want money from your business, you simply withdraw it from your business bank account. This is called a "draw." Because you are not an employee of your business, your draws are not employee compensation and are not deductible as a business expense.

Your Employee Expenses

You have a couple of options for dealing with expenses you incur while working for your corporation—for example, when you travel on company business.

From a tax standpoint, the best option is to have your corporation reimburse you for your expenses. Whether you've formed a C or an S corporation, the rules regarding reimbursement of employee expenses, discussed above, apply to you. If you comply with the requirements for an accountable plan, your corporation gets to deduct the expense and you don't have to count the reimbursement as income to you. If you fail to follow the rules, any reimbursements must be treated as employee income subject to tax.

Another option is simply to pay the expenses yourself and forgo reimbursement from your corporation. This is not a good idea, however—as an employee, you may deduct work-related expenses only to the extent they exceed 2% of your adjusted gross income. (See "Reimbursing Employees for Business-Related Expenditures," above.)

Tax Deductions When You Hire Independent Contractors

As far as tax deductions are concerned, hiring independent contractors is very simple. Most of the time, the amounts you pay to an IC to perform services for your business will be deductible as business operating expenses. These expenses are deductible as long as they are ordinary, necessary, and reasonable in amount.

> **EXAMPLE:** Emily, a graphic designer, hires Don, an attorney, to sue a client who failed to pay her. He collects $5,000, and she pays him $1,500 of this amount. The $1,500 is an ordinary and necessary business operating expense—Emily may deduct it from her business income for the year.

Of course, you get no business deduction if you hire an IC to perform personal services.

> **EXAMPLE:** Emily pays lawyer Don $2,000 to write her personal will. This is a personal expense. Emily cannot deduct the $2,000 from her business income.

If you hire an IC to perform services on your behalf in the start-up phase of your business, to manufacture inventory, or as part of a long-term asset purchase, the rules for those types of expense must be followed. (See "Tax Deductions for Employee Pay and Benefits," above.)

EXAMPLE: Don hires Ralph, a business broker, to help him find a good bakery shop to buy. After a long search, Ralph finds the right shop and Don buys it for $200,000. He pays Ralph a $12,000 broker's fee. This fee is a business start-up expense, from which Don may deduct $5,000 during the first year he's in business and the remaining $7,000 over the first 180 months he's in business.

No Deductions for IC's Taxes

When you hire an independent contractor, you don't have to withhold or pay any state or federal payroll taxes on the IC's behalf. Therefore, you get no deductions for the IC's taxes; the IC is responsible for paying them.

However, if you pay an unincorporated IC $600 or more during the year for business-related services, you must:

- file IRS Form 1099-MISC telling the IRS how much you paid the IC, and
- obtain the IC's taxpayer identification number.

The IRS may impose a $100 fine if you fail to file a Form 1099 when required. But, far more serious, you'll be subject to severe penalties if the IRS later audits you and determines that you misclassified the worker.

If you're not sure whether you must file a Form 1099-MISC for a worker, go ahead and file one. You lose nothing by doing so and will save yourself the consequences of not filing if you were legally required to do so.

For a detailed discussion of how to file a 1099 form and the consequences of not filing one, see *Working With Independent Contractors*, by Stephen Fishman (Nolo).

Paying Independent Contractor's Expenses

Independent contractors often incur expenses while performing services for their clients—for example, for travel, photocopying, phone calls, or materials. Many ICs want their clients to separately reimburse them for such expenses. The best practice is not to do this. It's better to pay ICs enough so they can cover their own expenses, rather than paying them less and having them bill you separately for expenses. This is because ICs who pay their own expenses are less likely to be viewed as your employee by the IRS or other government agencies.

However, it's customary in some businesses and professions for the client to reimburse the IC for expenses. For example, a lawyer who handles a business lawsuit will usually seek reimbursement for expenses such as photocopying, court reporters, and travel. If this is the case, you may pay these reimbursements.

When you reimburse an IC for a business-related expense, you, not the IC, get the deduction for the expense. Unless the IC fails to follow the adequate accounting rules discussed below, you should not include the amount of the reimbursement on the 1099 form you must file with the IRS reporting how much you paid the IC. The reimbursement is not considered income for the IC. Make sure to require ICs to document expenses with receipts, and save them in case the IRS questions the payments.

Adequate Accounting for Travel and Entertainment Expenses

To make an adequate accounting of travel and entertainment expenses, an IC must comply with all three record-keeping rules applicable to business owners and employees. (See Chapter 15 for more on record keeping.) You are required to save these records. The IRS is particularly suspicious of travel, meal, and entertainment expenses, so there are special documentation requirements for these. You are not required to save the IC's expense records except for records for entertainment expenses. You may deduct the IC's travel, entertainment, and meal expenses as your own business expenses for these items. (But remember that meal and entertainment expenses are only 50% deductible.) You do not include the amount of the reimbursement you pay the IC on the Form 1099 you file with the IRS reporting how much you paid the IC.

> **EXAMPLE:** Tim hires Mary, a self-employed marketing consultant, to help him increase his business's sales. In the course of her work, Mary incurs $1,000 in meal and entertainment expenses while meeting potential customers. She makes an adequate accounting of these expenses and Tim reimburses her the $1,000. Tim may deduct

50% of the $1,000 as a meal and entertainment expense for his business; Mary gets no deduction. When Tim fills out the 1099 form reporting to the IRS how much he paid Mary, he does not include the $1,000.

No Adequate Accounting for Travel and Entertainment Expenses

If an IC doesn't properly document travel, meal, or entertainment expenses, you do not have to keep records of these items. You may reimburse the IC for the expenses and deduct the full amount as IC payments, provided they are ordinary, necessary, and reasonable in amount. You are not deducting these expenses as travel, meal, or entertainment expenses, so the 50% limit on deducting meal and entertainment costs does not apply. However, you must include the amount of the reimbursement as income paid to the IC on the IC's 1099 form. Clearly, you are better off if the IC doesn't adequately account for travel, meal, and entertainment expenses—but the IC is worse off, because he'll have to pay tax on the reimbursements.

> **EXAMPLE:** Assume that Mary (from the example above) incurs $1,000 in meal and entertainment expenses but fails to adequately account to Tim. Tim reimburses her the $1,000 anyway. Tim may deduct the full $1,000 as a payment to Mary for her IC services. Tim must include the $1,000 as a payment to Mary when he fills out her 1099 form, and Mary must pay tax on the money. She may deduct the expenses as business expenses on her own tax return, but her meal and entertainment expenses will be subject to the 50% limit. Moreover, she'll need to have adequate documentation to back up the deductions if she is audited by the IRS.

Chapter 12

Retirement Deductions

W hen you own your own business, it's up to you to establish and fund your own pension plan to supplement the Social Security benefits you'll receive when you retire. The tax law helps you do this by providing tax deductions and other income tax benefits for your retirement account contributions and earnings.

This chapter provides a general overview of the retirement plan choices you have as a small business owner. Choosing what type of account to establish is just as important as deciding what to invest in once you open your account—if not more so. Once you set up your retirement account, you can always change your investments within the account with little or no difficulty. But changing the type of retirement account you have may prove difficult and costly. So it's best to spend some time up front learning about your choices and deciding which plan will best meet your needs.

For additional information on the tax aspects of retirement, see:
- *Lower Your Taxes In Seven Steps,* by Stephen Fishman (Nolo)
- *Creating Your Own Retirement Plan,* by Twila Slesnick and John C. Suttle (Nolo)
- IRS Publication 560, *Retirement Plans for the Small Business,* and
- IRS Publication 590, *Individual Retirement Accounts.*
  Two easy-to-understand guides on retirement investing are:
- *Get a Life: You Don't Need a Million to Retire Well,* by Ralph Warner (Nolo), and
- *Investing for Dummies,* by Eric Tyson (IDG Books).

You should get professional help with your plan if you have employees (other than a spouse). Having employees makes it much more complicated to set up a retirement plan. (See "Having Employees Complicates Matters— Tremendously," below). Because of the many complex issues raised by having employees, any business owner with employees should turn to a professional consultant for help in choosing, establishing, and administering a retirement plan.

Why You Need a Retirement Plan (or Plans)

In all likelihood, you will receive Social Security benefits when you retire. However, Social Security will probably cover only half of your needs when you retire—possibly less, depending upon your retirement lifestyle. You'll need to make up this shortfall with your own retirement investments.

When it comes to saving for retirement, small business owners are better off than employees of most companies. This is because the federal government allows small businesses to set up retirement accounts specifically designed for small business owners. These accounts provide enormous tax benefits that are intended to maximize the amount of money you can save during your working years for your retirement years. The amount you are allowed to contribute each year to your retirement account depends upon the type of account you establish and how much money you earn. If your business doesn't earn money, you won't be able to make any contributions—you must have income to fund retirement accounts.

The two biggest benefits that most of these plans provide—tax deductions for plan contributions and tax deferral on investment earnings—are discussed in more detail below.

How Much Money Will You Need When You Retire?

How much money you'll need when you retire depends on many factors, including your lifestyle. You could need anywhere from 50% to 100% of the amount you were earning while you were employed. The average is about 70% to 80% of preretirement earnings.

Tax Deduction

Retirement accounts that comply with IRS requirements are called "tax qualified."

You can deduct the amount you contribute to a tax-qualified retirement account from your income taxes (except for Roth IRAs). If you are a sole proprietor, partner in a partnership, or LLC member, you can deduct from your personal income contributions you make to a retirement account. If you have incorporated your business, the corporation can deduct as a business expense contributions that it makes on your behalf. Either way, you or your business gets a substantial income tax savings with these contributions.

EXAMPLE: Art, a sole proprietor, contributes $10,000 this year to a qualified retirement account. He can deduct the entire amount from his personal income taxes. Because Art is in the 28% tax bracket, he saves $2,800 in income taxes for the year (28% x $10,000), and he has also saved $10,000 toward his retirement.

Tax Deferral

In addition to the tax deduction you receive for putting money into a retirement account, there is another tremendous tax benefit to retirement accounts: tax deferral. When you earn money on an investment, you usually must pay taxes on those earnings in the same year that you earn the money. For example, you must pay taxes on the interest you earn on a savings account or certificate of deposit in the year when the interest accrues. And when you sell an investment at a profit, you must pay income tax in that year on the gain you receive. For example, you must pay tax on the profit you earn from selling stock in the year that you sell the stock.

A different rule applies, however, for earnings you receive from a tax-qualified retirement account. You do not pay taxes on investment earnings from retirement accounts until you withdraw the funds. Because most people withdraw these funds at retirement, they are often in a lower income tax bracket when they pay tax on these earnings. This can result in substantial tax savings for people who would have had to pay higher taxes on these earnings if they paid as the earnings accumulated.

EXAMPLE: Bill and Brian both invest in the same mutual fund. Bill has a taxable individual account, while Brian invests through a tax-deferred retirement account. They each invest $5,000 per year. They earn 8% on their investments each year and pay income tax at the 28% rate. At the end of 30 years, Brian has $566,416. Bill only has $272,869. Reason: Bill had to pay income taxes on the interest his investments earned each year, while Brian's interest accrued tax-free because he invested through a retirement account. Brian must pay tax on his earnings only when he withdraws the money (but he'll have to pay a penalty tax if he makes withdrawals before age 59½, subject to certain exceptions).

The following chart compares the annual growth of a tax-deferred account and a taxable account.

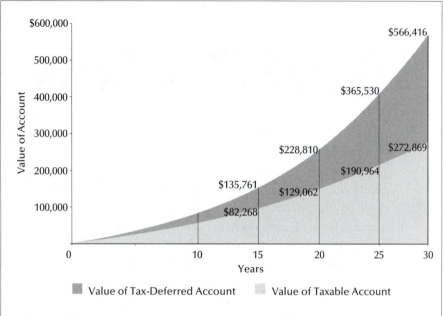

Assumptions:
- Investments earn 8% annually.
- $5,000 is invested annually in the tax-deferred account.
- $3,600 (what's left after $5,000 is taxed at 28%) is invested annually in the non-tax-deferred account.
- Income on the non-tax-deferred account is taxed annually at 28%, and recipient does not pay state income tax.

Retirement accounts have restrictions on withdrawals. The tax deferral benefits you receive by putting your money in a retirement account come at a price: You're not supposed to withdraw the money until you are 59½ years old; and, after you turn 70½, you must withdraw a certain minimum amount each year and pay tax on it. Stiff penalties are imposed if you fail to follow these rules. So, if you aren't prepared to give up your right to use this money freely, you should think about a taxable account instead where there are no restrictions on your use of your money. You should also consider a Roth IRA or Roth 401(k)—you can withdraw your contributions to these accounts (but not earnings) at any time without penalty (see below).

For detailed guidance on distributions from retirement accounts, refer to *IRAs, 401(k)s & Other Retirement Plans: Taking Your Money Out*, by Twila Slesnick and John C. Suttle (Nolo).

Having Employees Complicates Matters—Tremendously

If you own your own business and have no employees (other than your spouse), you can probably choose, establish, and administer your own retirement plan with little or no assistance. The instant you add employees to the mix, however, virtually every aspect of your plan becomes more complex. This is primarily due to something called nondiscrimination rules. These rules are designed to ensure that your retirement plan benefits all employees, not just you. In general, the law's prohibit you from doing the following:

- making disproportionately large contributions for some plan participants (like yourself) and not for others
- unfairly excluding certain employees from participating in the plan, and
- unfairly withholding benefits from former employees or their beneficiaries.

If the IRS finds the plan to be discriminatory at any time (usually during an audit), the plan could be disqualified—that is, determined not to satisfy IRS rules. If this happens, you and your employees will owe income tax and probably penalties, as well.

Having employees also increases the plan's reporting requirements. You must provide employees with a summary of the terms of the plan, notification of any changes you make, and an annual report of contributions. And you must file an annual tax return. Because of all the complex issues raised by having employees, any business owner with employees (other than a spouse) should seek professional help when creating a retirement plan.

Individual Retirement Accounts—IRAs

The simplest type of tax-deferred retirement account is the individual retirement account, or IRA. An IRA is a retirement account established by an individual, not a business. You can have an IRA whether you're a business owner or an employee in someone else's business. Moreover, you can establish an IRA for yourself as an individual and also set up one or more of the other types of retirement plans discussed below, which are just for businesses.

An IRA is a trust or custodial account set up for the benefit of an individual or his or her beneficiaries. The trustee or custodian administers the account. The trustee can be a bank, mutual fund, brokerage firm, or other financial institution (such as an insurance company).

IRAs are extremely easy to set up and administer. You need a written IRA agreement but don't need to file any tax forms with the IRS. The financial institution you use to set up your account will usually ask you to complete IRS Form 5305, *Individual Retirement Trust Account*, which serves as an IRA agreement and meets all of the IRS requirements. Keep the form in your records—you don't file it with the IRS.

Most financial institutions offer an array of IRA accounts that provide for different types of investments. You can invest your IRA money in just about anything: stocks, bonds, mutual funds, treasury bills and notes, and bank certificates of deposit. However, you can't invest in collectibles such as art, antiques, stamps, or other personal property.

You can establish as many IRA accounts as you want, but there is a maximum combined amount of money you can contribute to all of your IRA accounts each year. This amount goes up every year through 2008 as shown in the chart below. After 2008, the limit will be adjusted each year for inflation in $500 increments.

There are different limits for workers who are at least 50 years old. Anyone at least 50 years old at the end of the year can make increased annual contributions of $500 per year in 2006, and $1,000 per year thereafter. This rule is intended to allow older people to catch up with younger folks, who will have more years to make contributions at the higher levels.

Annual IRA Contribution Limits		
Tax Year	Under Age 50	Aged 50 or Over
2006-2007	$4,000	$5,000
2008 and later	$5,000	$6,000

If you are married, you can double the contribution limits. For example, a married couple in 2006 can contribute up to $4,000 per spouse into their IRAs, or a total of $8,000. This is true even if one spouse isn't working. To take advantage of doubling, you must file a joint tax return, and the working spouse must earn at least as much as the combined IRA contribution.

Traditional IRAs

There are two different types of IRAs that you can choose from:

- traditional IRAs, and
- Roth IRAs.

Traditional IRAs have been around since 1974. Anybody who has earned income (income from a job, business, or alimony) can have a traditional IRA. As stated above, you can deduct your annual contributions to your IRA from your taxable income. If neither you nor your spouse (if you have one) has another retirement plan, you may deduct your contributions no matter how high your income is.

However, there are income limits on your deductions if you (or your spouse, if you have one) are covered by another retirement plan. For these purposes, being covered by another plan means you have one of the self-employed plans described below (or your or your spouse is covered by an employer plan).

If you're a single taxpayer with a retirement plan, your deductions start to phase out when your modified adjusted gross income exceeds $50,000. Your modified adjusted income is your adjusted gross income before it is reduced by your IRA contributions and certain other more unusual items. Things are bit more complicated if you're married and file your taxes jointly, because each spouse's IRA contribution is separate. The phase-out begins once the spouse's joint modified AGI exceeds $80,000 if they both have other retirement plans. If only one spouse is covered by a retirement plan, the phase-out begins at $80,000 for the covered spouse and $150,000 for the uncovered spouse.

If your income is in the phase-out range, you can use an online calculator at www.choosetosave.org/calculators to determine how much you may deduct.

You can still contribute to an IRA even if you can't take a deduction. This is called a nondeductible IRA. Your money will grow in the account tax free; and, when you make withdrawals, you'll only have to pay tax on your account earnings, not the amount of your contributions (which have already been taxed). However, figuring out how much is taxable and how much is tax free can be a big accounting headache.

You may not make any more contributions to a traditional IRA after you reach age 70½. Moreover, you'll have to start making distributions from the account after you reach that age.

There are time restrictions on when you can (and when you must) withdraw money from your IRA. You are not supposed to withdraw any money from your IRA until you reach age 59½, unless you die or become disabled. And you must begin to withdraw your money by April 1 of the year after the year you turn 70. Once you start withdrawing money from your IRA, the amount you withdraw will be included in your regular income for income tax purposes.

As a general rule, if you make early withdrawals, you must pay regular income tax on the amount you take out, plus a 10% federal tax penalty. There are some exceptions to this early withdrawal penalty (for example, if you withdraw money to purchase a first home or pay educational expenses, the penalty doesn't apply—subject to dollar limits). To learn about these and other exceptions in detail, see *IRAs, 401(k)s & Other Retirement Plans: Taking Your Money Out*, by Twila Slesnick and John Suttle (Nolo).

Roth IRAs

Like traditional IRAs, Roth IRAs are tax-deferred and allow your retirement savings to grow without any tax burden. Unlike traditional IRAs, however, your contributions to Roth IRAs are not tax-deductible. Instead, you get to withdraw your money from the account tax-free when you retire.

Once you have established your account, your ability to contribute to it will be affected by changes in your income level. If you are single and your income reaches $95,000, your ability to contribute to your Roth IRA will begin to phase out. Once your income reaches $110,000, you will no longer be able to make contributions. If you are married and filing a joint return with your spouse, your ability to contribute to your account will start to phase out when your income reaches $150,000, and you will be prohibited from making any contributions at all when your income reaches $160,000.

You can withdraw the money you contributed to a Roth IRA penalty-free anytime—you already paid tax on it so the government doesn't care. But the earnings on your investments in a Roth IRA are a different matter. You can't withdraw these until after five years. Early withdrawals of your earnings are subject to income tax and early distribution penalties. You are not, however, required to make withdrawals when you reach age 70½. Because Roth IRA withdrawals are tax-free, the government doesn't care if you leave your money in your account indefinitely. However, your money will be tax-free on withdrawal only if you leave it in your Roth IRA for at least five years.

Is the Roth IRA a good deal? If your tax rate when you retire is higher than your tax rate before retirement, you'll probably be better off with a Roth IRA than a traditional IRA because you won't have to pay tax on your withdrawals at the higher rates. The opposite is true if your taxes go down when you retire. The catch is that nobody can know for sure what their tax rate will be when they retire. You can find several online calculators that will help you compare your results with a Roth IRA versus traditional IRA at www.choosetosave.org/calculators. Much more information on Roth IRAs can be found at www.rothira.com.

Roth IRA Conversions

If the Roth IRA sounds attractive to you, and you already have a traditional IRA, you may convert it to a Roth IRA. This can vastly increase the amount of money in your Roth IRA. Until the year 2010, you may do such a conversion only if your modified AGI is under $100,000. Starting in 2010, anyone will be allowed to convert to a Roth IRA, no matter what their income.

However, when you convert to a Roth, you'll have to pay income tax on the amount of the conversion. For example, if you convert $20,000 from your traditional IRA to a Roth IRA, you'll have to add $20,000 to your taxable income for the year. If you were in the 25% bracket, this would add $5,000 to your income taxes. (If you convert in 2010, you can pay the tax over two years instead of one.) One way to keep these taxes down is to convert only a portion of your traditional IRAs into a Roth each year for several years instead of doing it all at once.

Whether a Roth conversion is a good idea or not depends on many factors including your age, your current tax rate, and your tax rate upon retirement. You can find an online calculator at http://dinkytown.com/java/RothTransfer.html that allows you to compare the results when you convert to a Roth versus leaving your traditional IRAs alone.

Employer IRAs

You can establish an employer IRA as long as you are in business and earn a profit. You don't have to have employees working for you, and it doesn't matter how your business is organized: You can be a sole proprietor, partner in a partnership, member of a limited liability company, or owner of a regular or S corporation.

The great advantage of employer IRAs is that you can contribute more than you can with traditional IRAs and Roth IRAs, both of which have lower annual contribution limits. And as long as you meet the requirements for establishing an employer IRA, you can have this type of IRA in addition to one or more individual IRAs.

There are two kinds of employer IRAs to choose from: SEP-IRAs and SIMPLE IRAs.

SEP-IRAs

SEP-IRAs are designed for the self-employed. Any person who receives self-employment income from providing a service can establish a SEP-IRA. It doesn't matter whether you work full time or part time. You can even have a SEP-IRA if you are covered by a retirement plan at a full-time employee job.

A SEP-IRA is a simplified employee pension. It's very similar to an IRA, except that you can contribute more money under this plan. Instead of being limited to a $4,000 to $5,000 annual contribution in 2005–2007, you can invest up to 20% of your net profit from self-employment every year, up to a maximum of $44,000 a year in 2006. You don't have to make contributions every year, and your contributions can vary from year to year. As with IRAs, you can invest your money in almost anything (stocks, bonds, notes, mutual funds).

You can deduct your contributions to SEP-IRAs from your income taxes, and the interest on your SEP-IRA investments accrues tax-free until you withdraw the money. Withdrawals from SEP-IRAs are subject to the same rules that apply to traditional IRAs. This means that if you withdraw your money from your SEP-IRA before you reach age 59½, you'll have to pay a 10% tax penalty plus regular income taxes on your withdrawal, unless an exception applies. And you must begin to withdraw your money by April 1 of the year after the year you turn 70.

SIMPLE IRAs

Self-employed people and companies with fewer than 100 employees can set up SIMPLE IRAs. If you establish a SIMPLE IRA, you are not allowed to have any other retirement plans for your business (although you may still have an individual IRA). SIMPLE IRAs are easy to set up and administer and will enable you to make larger annual contributions than a SEP or Keogh plan if you earn less than $10,000 per year from your business.

SIMPLE IRAs may only be established by an employer on behalf of its employees. If you are a sole proprietor, you are deemed to employ yourself for these purposes and may establish a SIMPLE IRA in your own name as the employer. If you are a partner in a partnership, LLC member, or owner of an incorporated business, the SIMPLE-IRA must be established by your business, not you personally.

Contributions to SIMPLE IRAs are divided into two parts. You may contribute:

- up to 100% of your net income from your business up to an annual limit—the contribution limit is $10,000 for 2006 ($12,500 if you were born before 1955), and
- a matching contribution which can equal 3% of your net business income.

If you're an employee of your incorporated business, your first contribution (called a salary reduction contribution) comes from your salary, and the matching contribution is paid by your business.

The limits on contributions to SIMPLE IRAs might seem very low, but they could work to your advantage if you earn a small income from your business—for example, if you only work at it part time. This is because you can contribute an amount equal to 100% of your earnings, up to the $10,000 or $12,500 limits. Thus, for example, if your net earnings are only $10,000, you could contribute the entire amount (plus a 3% employer contribution). You can't do this with any of the other plans because their percentage limits are much lower. For example, you may contribute only 20% of your net self-employment income to a SEP-IRA or Keogh, so you would be limited to a $2,000 contribution if you had a $10,000 profit.

The money in a SIMPLE IRA can be invested like any other IRA. Withdrawals from SIMPLE IRAs are subject to the same rules as traditional IRAs, with one big exception: Early withdrawals from SIMPLE IRAs are subject to a 25% tax penalty if the withdrawal is made within two years after the date you first contributed to your account. Other early withdrawals are subject to a 10% penalty, the same as traditional IRAs, unless an exception applies.

Keogh Plans

Keogh plans—named after the Congressman who sponsored the legislation that created them—are only for business owners who are sole proprietors, partners in partnerships, or LLC members. You can't have a Keogh if you incorporate your business.

Keoghs require more paperwork to set up than employer IRAs, but they also offer more options: You can contribute more to these plans and still get an income tax deduction for your contributions.

Types of Keogh Plans

There are two basic types of Keogh plans:

- defined contribution plans, in which benefits are based on the amount contributed to and accumulated in the plan, and
- defined benefit plans, which provide for a set benefit upon retirement.

There are two types of defined contribution plans: profit-sharing plans and money purchase plans. These plans can be used separately or in tandem with one other.

Setting Up a Keogh Plan

As with individual IRAs and employer IRAs, you can set up a Keogh plan at most banks, brokerage houses, mutual funds, and other financial institutions, as well as trade or professional organizations. You can also choose among a huge array of investments for your money.

To set up your plan, you must adopt a written Keogh plan and set up a trust or custodial account with your plan provider to invest your funds. Your plan provider will ordinarily have an IRS-approved master or prototype Keogh plan for you to sign. You can also have a special plan drawn up for you, but this is expensive and unnecessary for most small business owners.

Profit-Sharing Plans

You can contribute up to 20% of your net self-employment income to a profit-sharing Keogh plan, up to a maximum of $44,000 per year in 2006. You can contribute any amount up to the limit each year or not contribute at all.

Money Purchase Plans

In a money purchase plan, you contribute a fixed percentage of your net self-employment earnings every year. You decide how much to contribute each year. Make sure you will be able to afford the contributions each year because you can't skip them, even if your business earns no profit for the year. In return for giving up flexibility, you can contribute a higher percentage of your earnings with a money purchase plan: 25% of your net self-employment earnings, up to a maximum of $44,000 per year (the same maximum amount as the profit-sharing plan).

Withdrawing Your Money

You may begin to withdraw your money from your Keogh plan after you reach age 59½. If you have a profit-sharing plan, early withdrawals are permitted without penalty in cases of financial hardship, if you become disabled, or if you have to pay health expenses in excess of 7.5% of your adjusted gross income. If you have a money purchase plan, early withdrawals are permitted if you become disabled, leave your business after you turn 55, or make child support or alimony payments from the plan under a court order. Otherwise, early withdrawals from profit-sharing and money purchase Keogh plans are subject to a 10% penalty.

Solo 401(k) Plans

Most people have heard of 401(k) plans—they are retirement plans established by businesses for their employees. 401(k)s are a type of profit-sharing plan in which a business's employees make plan contributions from their salaries and the business makes a matching contribution. These plans are complex to establish and administer and are generally used only by larger businesses. Until recently, self-employed people and businesses without employees rarely used them, because they offered no benefit over other profit-sharing plans that are much easier to set up and run.

However, things have changed. Now, any business owner who has no employees (other than a spouse) can establish a solo self-employed 401(k) plan (also called a one-person or individual 401(k)). Solo 401(k) plans are designed specifically for business owners without employees.

Solo 401(k) plans have the following advantages over other retirement plans:

- You can make very large contributions—as much as 20% of your net profit from self-employment, plus an elective deferral contribution of up to $15,000 in 2006. The maximum contribution per year is $44,000 in 2006 (the same maximum amount as for profit-sharing and money purchase plans discussed in "Keogh Plans," above). Business owners over 50 may make additional catch-up contributions of up to $5,000 per year that are not counted towards the $44,000 limit.

- You can borrow up to $50,000 from your solo 401(k) plan, as long as you repay the loan within five years (you cannot borrow from a traditional IRA, Roth IRA, SEP-IRA, or SIMPLE IRA).

As with other plans, you must pay a 10% penalty tax on withdrawals you make before age 59½, but you may make penalty-free early withdrawals for reasons of personal hardship (defined as an "immediate financial need" that can't be met any other way).

You can set up a solo 401(k) plan at most banks, brokerage houses, mutual funds, and other financial institutions and invest the money in a variety of ways. You must adopt a written plan and set up a trust or custodial account with your plan provider to invest your funds. Financial institutions that offer solo 401(k) plans have preapproved ready-made plans that you can use.

⚠ **Beware of retirement account deadlines.** If you want to establish any of the retirement accounts discussed in this chapter and take a tax deduction for the year, you must meet specific deadlines. The deadlines vary according to the type of account you set up, as shown in the following chart. Once you establish your account, you have until the due date of your tax return for the year (April 15 of the following year, plus any filing extensions) to contribute to your account and take a deduction.

Retirement Account Deadlines	
Plan Type	Deadline for Establishing Plan
Traditional IRA	Due date of tax return (April 15 plus extensions)
Roth IRA	Due date of tax return (April 15 plus extensions)
SEP-IRA	Due date of tax return (April 15 plus extensions)
SIMPLE IRA	October 1
Keogh Profit Sharing Plan	December 31
Keogh Money Purchase Plan	December 31
Keogh Defined Benefit Plan	December 31
401(k) Plan	December 31

Chapter 13

Medical Expenses

When you own your own business, you must pay for your own health insurance and other medical expenses—you don't have an employer to pay all or part of these costs for you. As we all know, the cost of health insurance keeps going up. However, business owners have an advantage that most others don't have with regard to these rising health care costs: They can deduct many of their health insurance costs from their taxes. In addition, you may be able to deduct a wide variety of uninsured medical expenses, including nonprescription medications, acupuncture, and eyeglasses. Finally, there is an entirely new way to pay for health care expenses that went into effect in 2004—the Health Savings Account (HSAs). HSAs represent the most radical change in health care financing in the last 50 years and can be a real boon for many small business owners.

The Personal Deduction for Medical Expenses

All taxpayers—whether or not they own a business—are entitled to a personal income tax deduction for medical and dental expenses for themselves and their dependents. Eligible expenses include both health insurance premiums and out-of-pocket expenses not covered by insurance. However, there are two significant limitations on the deduction, which make it virtually useless (unusable) for most taxpayers.

In order to take the personal deduction, you must comply with both of the following requirements:

- You must itemize your deductions on IRS Schedule A. (You can itemize deductions only if all of your itemized deductions exceed the standard deduction for the year: $10,300 for joint returns and $5,150 for single returns in 2006.)
- You can deduct only the amount of your medical and dental expenses that is more than 7.5% of your adjusted gross income (AGI). (Your AGI is your net business income and other taxable income, minus deductions for retirement contributions and one-half of your self-employment taxes, plus a few other items (as shown at the bottom of your Form 1040).)

EXAMPLE: Al is a self-employed interior decorator whose adjusted gross income for 2006 is $80,000. He pays $350 per month for health insurance for himself and his wife. He spends another $2,000 in out-of-pocket medical and dental expenses for the year. Al may deduct his medical expenses only if all of his itemized deductions exceed the $10,300 standard deductions for the year. If they do exceed the standard deduction, his personal medical expense deduction is limited to the amount he paid that's more than $6,000 (7.5% x $80,000 = $6,000). Because he paid a total of $6,200 in medical expenses for the year, his deduction is limited to $200.

As you can see, unless your medical expenses are substantial, the 7.5% limitation eats up most or all of your deduction. The more money you make, the less you can deduct. For this reason, most business owners need to look elsewhere for meaningful medical expense deductions.

Deducting Health Insurance Premiums

Health insurance premiums are the largest medical expense most people pay. There are several ways that business owners can deduct these premiums.

Personal Income Tax Deduction for the Self-Employed

Self-employed people are allowed to deduct health insurance premiums (including dental and long-term care coverage) for themselves, their spouses, and their dependents. Sole proprietors, partners in partnerships, LLC members, and S corporation shareholders who own more than 2% of the company stock can use this deduction. Basically, any business owner, other than the owner of a regular C corporation, can take this deduction. And you get the deduction whether you purchase your health insurance policy as an individual or have your business obtain it. It's important to understand, however, that this is not a business deduction. It is a special personal deduction for the self-employed. The deduction applies to your federal, state, and local income taxes, but not to self-employment taxes.

Self-Employment Tax Primer

Self-employment taxes are the Social Security and Medicare taxes that business owners must pay. They consist of a 12.4% Social Security tax and a 2.9% Medicare tax, for a total tax of 15.3%. The tax is paid on self-employment income, which is your net income from your business, not including deductions for retirement contributions. The Social Security tax is subject to an income ceiling that is adjusted each year for inflation. In 2006, the ceiling was $94,200 in self-employment income. Self-employed people who earn more than the ceiling amount pay only the 2.9% Medicare tax on the excess. If you earn more than the ceiling, being able to deduct your health insurance costs from your self-employment income will not give you a very significant tax savings, because you would have had to pay only a 2.9% tax on that income.

EXAMPLE: Kim is a sole proprietor who pays $10,000 each year for health insurance for herself, her husband, and her three children. Her business earned a $70,000 profit for the year. She may deduct her $10,000 annual health insurance expense from her gross income for federal and state income tax purposes. Her combined federal and state income tax rate is 30%, so she saves $3,000 in income taxes (30% x $10,000 = $3,000). She may not deduct her premiums from her income when she figures her self-employment taxes—in other words, she must pay the 15.3% self-employment tax on her full $70,000 business profit.

Business Income Limitation

There is a significant limitation on the health insurance deduction for the self-employed: You may deduct only as much as you earn from your business. If your business earns no money or incurs a loss, you get no deduction. Thus, for example, if Kim from the above example earned only $3,000 in profit from her business, her self-employed deduction would be limited to that amount; she wouldn't be able to deduct the remaining $7,000 in premiums she paid for the year.

If your business is organized as an S corporation, your deduction is limited to the amount of wages you are paid by your corporation.

If you have more than one business, you cannot combine the income from all your businesses for purposes of the income limit. You may only use the income from a single business you designate to be the health insurance plan sponsor.

Designating Your Plan Sponsor

If you purchase your health insurance plan in the name of one of your businesses, that business will be the sponsor. However, the IRS says you may purchase your health coverage in your own name and still get the self-employed health insurance deduction. (IRC Chief Counsel Memo 200524001.) This may be advantageous because it allows you to pick which of your businesses will be the sponsor at the start of each year. Obviously, you should pick the business you think will earn the most money that year.

Moreover, if you have more than one business, you can have one purchase medical insurance and the other purchase dental insurance and deduct 100% of the premiums for each policy subject to the income limits discussed above. This will be helpful if no single business earns enough income for you to deduct both policies through one business.

> **EXAMPLE:** Robert is a sole proprietor medical doctor who has a sideline business running a medical lab. He purchases a medical insurance policy for himself and his family with his medical practice as the sponsor. He also purchases a dental insurance plan with his lab business as the sponsor. He may deduct 100% of the premiums for each policy, subject to the income limits.

No Other Health Insurance Coverage

You may not take the self-employed health insurance deduction if you are eligible to participate in a health insurance plan maintained by your employer or your spouse's employer. This rule applies separately to plans that provide long-term care insurance and those that do not. Thus, for example, if your spouse has employer-provided health insurance that does not include long-term care, you may purchase your own long-term care policy and deduct the premiums.

Tax Reporting

Because the self-employed health insurance deduction is a personal deduction, you take this deduction directly on your Form 1040 (it does not go on your Schedule C if you're a sole proprietor). If you itemize your deductions and do not claim 100% of your self-employed health insurance costs on your Form 1040, you may include the rest with all other medical expenses on Schedule A, subject to the 7.5% limit. You would have to do this, for example, if your health insurance premiums exceed your business income.

Deducting Health Insurance as a Business Expense

You can deduct health insurance costs as a currently deductible business expense if your business pays them on behalf of an employee. The benefit to treating these costs as a business expense is that you can deduct them from your business income for tax purposes. The premiums are an employee fringe benefit and are not taxable income for the employee. Thus, if you are an employee of your business, you can have your business pay your health insurance premiums and then deduct the cost as a business expense, reducing both your income and your self-employment taxes.

> **EXAMPLE:** Mona, a sole proprietor data miner, hires Milt to work as an employee in her business. She pays $250 per month to provide Milt with health insurance. The payments are a business expense that she can deduct from her business income. Milt need not count the value of the insurance as income or pay any tax on it. Mona deducts her $3,000 annual payments for Milt's insurance from her business income for both income tax and self-employment tax purposes. The $3,000 deduction saves her $750 in income taxes (she's in the 25% income tax bracket; 25% x $3,000 = $750). She also saves $459 in self-employment taxes (15.3% x $3,000 = $459).

Sole Proprietors, LLCs, S Corporations, Partnerships, and LLPs

Unfortunately, if (like the majority of small business owners) you are a sole proprietor, partner in a partnership, LLC member, or S corporation shareholder with over 2% of the company stock, you cannot be an employee of your own business for health insurance purposes. If your partnership, LLC, or S corporation buys health insurance on your behalf, it may deduct the cost as a business expense, but it must also add the amount to your taxable income.

If your business is organized as a partnership or LLC, the premiums are ordinarily treated as a guaranteed payment. The business lists the payment on the Schedule K-1 it provides the IRS and you showing your income from the business. You'll then have to pay income and self-employment tax on the amount.

You can still take the self-employed health insurance tax deduction discussed above, which will effectively wipe out the extra income tax you had to pay. But the self-employed health insurance deduction is a personal deduction, not a business deduction, and thus does not reduce your business income for self-employment tax purposes.

> **EXAMPLE:** Jim is a co-owner of a consulting firm organized as an LLC. The firm spends $10,000 for health insurance for Jim. It treats the money as a guaranteed payment and lists it as income to Jim on the K-1 form it provides the IRS. The LLC gets to deduct the payment as a business expense. Jim must pay income and self-employment tax on the $10,000. However, he may also deduct the $10,000 from his income tax as a personal deduction using the self-employed health insurance deduction. The net result is that Jim only pays self-employment tax on the $10,000. The same result would have been achieved if Jim had purchased his health insurance himself.

Partnerships, LLCs, and LLPs can avoid having to report health insurance payments as income if they don't take a tax deduction for them. This will have the same tax result and make things simpler.

If your business is an S corporation, the insurance costs are added to your employee compensation and are deducted as such by the corporation. However, you only have to pay income tax on the amount, not employment taxes. Again, you can take the self-employed health insurance deduction and wipe out the extra income tax you had to pay.

C Corporations

If your business is organized as a C corporation, you ordinarily will work as its employee and will be entitled to the full menu of tax-free employee fringe benefits, including health insurance. This means the corporation can purchase health insurance for you, deduct the cost as a business expense, and not have to include the cost in your employee compensation. Your health insurance is completely tax-free.

If you want to convert your health insurance premiums to a tax-free fringe benefit and you don't have a C corporation, you must form one to run your business and have the corporation hire you as its employee. You can do this even if you're running a one-person business.

As an employee of a C corporation, you must be paid a salary, and your corporation must pay Social Security and Medicare taxes on your behalf. Your corporation deducts your health insurance premiums from its taxes—you don't deduct them from your personal taxes. Because you own the corporation, you get the benefit from the deduction.

There are disadvantages to incorporating, however. Incorporating costs money, you'll have to comply with more burdensome bookkeeping requirements, and you will have a more complex tax return. You'll also have to pay state and federal unemployment taxes for yourself—a tax you don't need to pay if you're not an employee of your business. And, depending on your state's requirements, you may have to provide yourself with workers' compensation coverage.

Because your health insurance is 100% deductible from your income taxes, it may not be worthwhile to incorporate just to save on Social Security and Medicare taxes. This is particularly true if your employee income would substantially exceed the 12.4% Social Security tax ceiling: $94,200 in 2006. If you're in this situation, think about obtaining a Health Savings Account instead. (See "Adopting a Medical Reimbursement Plan," below.)

Disability Insurance

Disability insurance pays a monthly benefit to employees who are unable to work due to sickness or injury. You may provide disability insurance to your employees, including your spouse, as an employee benefit and deduct the premiums as a business expense. If your business is a C corporation, it may deduct disability payments made for you, its employee. However, any employees who collect disability benefits must include them in their taxable income.

Employing Your Spouse

If you're a sole proprietor or have formed an entity other than an S corporation to run your business, there's another way you can deduct health insurance costs as a business expense: Hire your spouse to work in your business as an employee and provide him or her with health insurance. The insurance should be purchased in the name of the spouse/employee, not in the employer's name. The policy can cover your spouse, you, your children, and other dependents as well. Then you can deduct the cost of the health insurance as a business expense.

> **EXAMPLE:** Joe is a self-employed optometrist. He hires his wife, Martha, to work as his employee assistant. He pays her $25,000 per year and provides her with a health insurance policy covering both of them and their two children. The annual policy premiums are $5,000. Joe may deduct the $5,000 as a business expense for his optometry practice, listing it as an expense on his Schedule C. He gets to deduct the $5,000 not only from his $80,000 income for income tax purposes, but also from his self-employment income. His federal and state income tax rate is 40%, so he saves $2,000 in income tax. The self-employment tax is a 15.3% tax (up to the Social Security tax ceiling: $94,200 in 2006), so Joe saves $765 in self-employment taxes.

If you do this and you're self-employed, *you should not* take the health insurance deduction for self-employed people discussed above. You're better off tax-wise deducting all your health insurance premiums as a business expense, because a business deduction reduces the amount of your income subject to self-employment taxes. The self-employed health insurance deduction is a personal deduction, not a business deduction, and thus does not reduce your business income for self-employment tax purposes.

There are a couple of catches to this deduction. This method ordinarily doesn't work if you have an S corporation because your spouse is deemed to be a shareholder of the corporation along with you and can't also be a corporate employee In addition, your spouse must be a bona fide employee. In other words, he or she must do real work in your business, you must pay applicable payroll taxes, and you must otherwise treat your spouse like any other employee. (See Chapter 11 for a detailed discussion.)

You'll probably want to pay your spouse as low a salary as possible, because both of you will have to pay Social Security and Medicare taxes on that salary (but not on employee benefits like health insurance and medical expense reimbursements). You should, however, regularly pay your spouse at least some cash wages, or the IRS could claim your spouse is not a real employee. You can make the cash wages a relatively small part of your spouse's total compensation—wages plus fringe benefits like your medical reimbursement plan.

No matter how you pay your spouse, his or her total compensation must be reasonable—that is, you can't pay more than your spouse's services are worth. For example, you can't pay your spouse at a rate of $100 per hour for simple clerical work. Total compensation means the sum of the salary plus all the fringe benefits you pay your spouse, including health insurance and medical expense reimbursements, if any. (See "Adopting a Medical Reimbursement Plan," below.)

> **EXAMPLE:** Tina's husband, Tim, works part time as a helper in her wedding photography business. Tina calls a couple of employment agencies and learns that other wedding photography businesses in the area pay helpers like Tim about $10 per hour, so she decides to pay him at this rate. Tim will work 500 hours per year (10 hours per week, 50 weeks per year), so his total compensation should be about $5,000 (500 hours x $10/hr. = $5,000). Tina wants to provide Tim with a health insurance policy covering him and his family

(including Tina) and a medical reimbursement plan. She would like to purchase a health insurance policy for $7,500 per year, but she knows she can't justify this expense, since Tim's total annual compensation can't be more than about $5,000. Instead, Tina has her business provide Tim with $3,500 worth of health insurance, $500 of medical reimbursements, and $1,000 in salary. Tina and Tim must pay a 15.3% tax on his $1,000 in wages. But Tina gets to deduct the wages and the $4,000 in health insurance and medical reimbursement costs as a business expense. This saves her (and Tim) $1,500 in federal and state taxes for the year.

Your Spouse May Not Be Your Partner

A marriage may be a partnership, but you can't be partners with your spouse in your business and also claim he or she is your employee for purposes of health insurance deductions. If your spouse co-owns the business with you, he or she is treated as self-employed—not an employee—for purposes of health insurance. You and your spouse are co-owners if you file partnership returns for your business (IRS Form 1065) listing him or her as a partner, or if your spouse has made a substantial financial investment in your business with the spouse's own money.

Of course, if you're single, you won't be able to hire a spouse to take advantage of this method for turning health insurance costs into a business expense. However, if you're a single parent, you could hire your child and deduct the cost of your child's health insurance as a business expense. But your child's policy cannot also cover you or other family members.

Adopting a Medical Reimbursement Plan

Health insurance usually doesn't cover all your medical expenses. For example, it doesn't cover preexisting conditions or deductibles or co-payments—that is, amounts you must pay yourself before your insurance coverage kicks in. Many costs aren't covered at all, including ongoing physical therapy, fertility treatment, and optometric care. As a result, the average American pays about $900 a year in out-of-pocket health-related expenses. One way to deduct these expenses is to establish a medical reimbursement plan. Another way is to use a Health Savings Account (discussed below).

What Is a Medical Reimbursement Plan?

A medical reimbursement plan is an arrangement under which an employer reimburses its employees for health or dental expenses. These plans are usually self-funded—that is, the employer pays the expenses out of its own pocket, not through insurance.

Why would an employer do this? One good reason is that the reimbursements are tax deductible business expenses for the employer. Also, the employee doesn't have to include the reimbursements as taxable income (as long as the employee has not taken a deduction for these amounts as a personal medical expense).

So how does this help you? Again, your spouse (if you have one) comes to the rescue. You can hire your spouse as your employee and provide him or her with a medical reimbursement plan. The plan may cover not only your spouse, but also you, your children, and other dependents. This allows your business to reimburse your and your family's out-of-pocket medical expenses and deduct the amounts as a business expense. And you need not include the reimbursements in your own taxable income. The IRS has ruled that this is perfectly legal. (Tax Advice Memo 9409006.)

> **EXAMPLE:** Jennifer has her own public relations business. She hires her husband Paul to work as her part-time employee assistant. She establishes a medical reimbursement plan covering Paul, herself, and their young child. Paul spends $6,000 on medical expenses. Jennifer reimburses Paul for the $6,000 as provided by their plan. Jennifer may deduct the $6,000 from her business income for the year, meaning she pays neither income nor self-employment tax on that amount. Paul need not include the $6,000 in his income—it's tax-free to him. The deduction saves Jennifer and Paul $2,000 in taxes for the year.

⚠ **Your spouse must be a legitimate employee.** Your spouse must be a legitimate employee for your medical reimbursement plan to pass muster with the IRS. You can't simply hire your spouse on paper—he or she must do real work in your business. If you can't prove your wife is a legitimate employee, the IRS will disallow your deductions in the event of an audit. If you're audited, the IRS will be particularly suspicious if your spouse is your only employee.

> **EXAMPLE:** Mr. Haeder, a sole proprietor attorney who practiced law in his home, claimed that he hired his wife as his employee to answer the telephone, greet visitors, type legal papers, and clean his office. Mrs. Haeder had no employment contract or set work schedule, did not maintain any time records, and did not directly or regularly receive a salary. Instead, Mr. Haeder paid her the maximum amount she could deduct as an IRA contribution. Annually, he transferred money in his brokerage account to an IRA in his wife's name. For all but one of the years eventually audited by the IRS, no W-2 was issued to Mrs. Haeder. Mr. Haeder sponsored a medical reimbursement plan that covered out-of-pocket expenses for his wife, her children, and her spouse—that is, himself. Mrs. Haeder submitted bills for out-of-pocket medical expenses to her husband, which he reimbursed and attempted to deduct as business expenses. The IRS determined Mr. Haeder was not entitled to deduct the reimbursements under the medical reimbursement plan, because Mrs. Haeder was not a bona fide employee. The tax court agreed, finding that there was no credible evidence that Mrs. Haeder performed any services other than those reasonably expected of a family member. (Haeder v. Commissioner, TC Memo 2001-7.)

Again, the medical expense reimbursement plan deduction is available only to your employees, not to you (the business owner). The only way you can qualify as an employee is if your business is a C corporation. (See "Deducting Health Insurance as a Business Expense," above.) However, if you don't have a spouse to employ, you could employ your child and provide him or her with a reimbursement plan. But the plan may not cover you or any other family members.

What Expenses May Be Reimbursed?

One of the great things about medical reimbursement plans is that they can be used to reimburse employees for a wide variety of health-related expenses. Indeed, deductible medical expenses include any expense for the diagnosis, cure, mitigation, treatment, or prevention of disease, or any expense paid to affect the structure or function of the human body. (IRS Reg. 1.213.1(e).)

This includes, of course, premiums in health and accident insurance and health insurance deductibles and copayments. But it also includes expenses for acupuncture, chiropractors, eyeglasses and contact lenses, dental treatment, laser eye surgery, psychiatric care, and treatment for learning disabilities. (See "Withdrawing HSA Funds," below, for a list of expenses that can and cannot be deducted.) You can draft your plan to include only those expenses you wish to reimburse. Presumably, though, you'd want to include as many expenses as possible if the plan covers only your spouse, yourself, and your family.

In addition, the IRS ruled in 2003 that a medical expense reimbursement plan may include reimbursements for employee expenses for nonprescription medicines and drugs. (Rev. Rul. 2003-102.) Any over-the-counter drug or medicine is covered except for dietary supplements and other items that are used only for general health, not for specific medical problems. Thus, for example, reimbursements may be provided for nonprescription antacids, allergy medicines, pain relievers, and cold medicines. So, if you have a medical reimbursement plan, you can even get a tax deduction for aspirin! (You can't deduct nonprescription drugs under the personal medical expense deduction discussed above.)

Plan Requirements

If you decide to adopt a medical expense reimbursement plan, the plan must be in writing, it may not discriminate in favor of highly compensated employees, and it must reimburse employees only for medical expenses that are not paid for by insurance.

The nondiscrimination rule will affect you only if you have employees other than your spouse or children. If you do, a medical reimbursement plan may be too expensive for you, because you'll

have to provide coverage to nonfamily members as well. A plan is nondiscriminatory under IRS rules if it:
- covers at least 70% of all employees
- covers at least 80% of all employees eligible to benefit from the plan, provided that 70% or more of all employees are eligible, or
- is found to be nondiscriminatory by the IRS based on the facts and circumstances.

EXAMPLE: Jim employs 12 people in his printing company. Two work only 20 hours per week. To be nondiscriminatory, Jim's medical expense reimbursement plan must cover 80% of his ten employees eligible to participate—in other words, he must cover eight of his ten full-time employees.

However, the plan may exclude employees who:
- work fewer than 25 hours a week
- are not yet 25 years old
- work for you fewer than seven months in a year, or
- have worked for you less than three years.

If a plan is found to be discriminatory by the IRS, all or part of the medical benefits paid to highly compensated employees under the plan will be taxable to the employee. Highly compensated employees include:
- anyone among the top 25% highest-paid employees
- the five highest-paid corporate officers (if your business is incorporated), and
- shareholders who own more than 10% of the corporation stock.

How to Establish a Plan

If a medical expense reimbursement plan sounds attractive to you, you should act to establish one as early in the year as possible, because it only applies to medical expenses incurred after the date the plan is adopted. (Rev. Rul. 2002-58.) Forget about using a plan to reimburse your spouse or yourself for expenses you have already incurred. If you do, the reimbursement must be added to your spouse's income for tax purposes and income, and you must pay employment tax on it.

12 Steps to Audit-Proof Your Medical Reimbursement Plan

Your medical reimbursement plan is subject to attack by the IRS if it doesn't look like a legitimate business expense. Your spouse must be a real employee, you must treat him or her as such, and you must manage your plan in a businesslike manner.

1. Have your spouse sign a written employment agreement specifying his or her duties and work hours.

2. Adopt a written medical reimbursement plan for your business.

3. Use timesheets to keep track of the hours your spouse works.

4. Make sure your spouse's total compensation is reasonable.

5. Have your spouse open a separate bank account to use when he or she pays medical expenses or receives reimbursements from your business.

6. Comply with all payroll tax, unemployment insurance, and workers' compensation requirements for your spouse-employee.

7. Reimburse your spouse for covered expenses by check from a separate business bank account or pay the health care provider directly from your business account. Make a notation on the check that the payment is made under your medical reimbursement plan.

8. Never pay your spouse in cash.

9. Have your spouse submit all bills to be reimbursed or paid by your business at least twice a year, or monthly or quarterly if you prefer. Keep all documentation showing the nature and amounts of the medical expenses paid for by your plan—receipts, cancelled checks, and so on, to show that you didn't reimburse your spouse too much and that the payments were for legitimate business expenses.

10. Don't pay for expenses incurred before the date you adopted your plan.

11. If you have employees other than your spouse, make sure you meet the nondiscrimination requirements.

12. Claim your deduction on the correct tax form:
    - sole proprietors—Schedule C, line 14, "Employee benefit programs"
    - LLCs and partnerships—Form 1065, line 19, "Employee benefit programs"
    - C corporations—Form 1120, Line 25, "Employee Benefit Programs."

A written medical reimbursement plan must be drawn up and adopted by your business. If your business is incorporated, the plan should be adopted by a corporate resolution approved by the corporation's board of directors. You can find a form for this purpose in *The Corporate Records Handbook*, by Anthony Mancuso (Nolo).

Sample Plan

A sample medical expense reimbursement plan is provided below. It's self-explanatory, except that you need to decide certain components as described below.

Eligibility

If you have employees other than your spouse (or think you may have them in the future), you must decide whether to place limitations on which employees may be covered by your plan. You may cover all your employees or exclude certain classes of employees as described in "Plan Requirements," above. It's up to you. But, be careful about whom you exclude from your plan—make sure you don't eliminate your spouse. For example, if your plan excludes all employees who work fewer than 25 hours per week, your spouse will have to work at least 25 hours to qualify for your plan. If your spouse will only work 15 hours per week, your plan should exclude only those employees who work fewer than 15 hours.

Dollar Limits

You also have the option of placing an annual dollar limit on the reimbursements you'll make. If your spouse is your only employee, you probably won't want a limit. But, if you have other employees—or may have them in the future—a limit may be advisable.

Claims Submission

Finally, you must decide how often the employee must submit claims for reimbursement. Twice a year is fine, but you can make it more frequent if you wish.

Medical Expense Reimbursement Plan

Effective _____ [date], _____

[your business name] ("Employer") will reimburse all eligible employees for medical expenses incurred by themselves and their dependents, subject to the conditions and limitations set forth below.

Uninsured Expenses

Employer will reimburse eligible employees and their dependents only for medical expenses that are not covered by health or accident insurance.

Medical Expenses Defined

Medical expenses are those expenses defined by Internal Revenue Code § 213(d). They consist of any expense for the diagnosis, cure, mitigation, treatment, or prevention of disease; or any expense paid to affect the structure or function of the human body. Medical expenses include both prescription and nonprescription drugs and medicines.

Dependent Defined

Dependent is defined by IRC § 152. It includes any member of an eligible employee's family for whom the employee and his or her spouse provides more than half of the financial support.

Eligibility

(Choose Alternative A or B.)

Alternative A:

The plan shall be open to all employees.

Alternative B:

The plan shall be open to all employees who:

[Check applicable boxes—you may check any number]

☐ work more than _____ *[specify—25 hrs/week is maximum]* hours per week

☐ are at least _____ *[specify—25 years old is maximum]* years of age

☐ have completed _____ *[specify—3 years is maximum]* years of service with Employer

☐ work _____ *[specify—7 months is maximum]* months per year

Limitation (*Optional*)

Employer shall reimburse any eligible employee no more than _____ [*dollar amount*] in any calendar year for medical expenses.

Submission of Claims

Any eligible employee seeking reimbursement under this Plan shall submit to Employer, [*choose one*] ☐ monthly, ☐ quarterly ☐ at least twice a year on _____ [date] and _____ [date], all bills for medical care, including those for accident or health insurance. Such bills and other claims for reimbursement shall be verified by Employer prior to reimbursement. Employer, in its sole discretion, may terminate the employee's right to reimbursement if the employee fails to comply.

Direct Payments

At its option, Employer may pay all or part of a covered employee's medical expenses directly, instead of making reimbursements to the employee. Such a direct payment shall relieve Employer of all further liability for the expense.

Termination

Employer may terminate this Plan at any time. Medical expenses incurred prior to the date of termination shall be reimbursed by Employer. Employer is under no obligation to provide advance notice of termination.

Benefits Not Taxable

Employer intends that the benefits under this Plan shall qualify under IRC § 105 so as to be excludable from the gross income of the employees covered by the Plan.

_____   _____

Employer's Signature   Date

_____   _____

Employee's Signature   Date

Health Savings Accounts

Another tax-advantaged method of buying health insurance has been available since 2004: Health Savings Accounts (HSAs). HSAs can save you taxes, but they're not for everybody.

What Are Health Savings Accounts?

The HSA concept is very simple: Instead of relying on health insurance to pay small or routine medical expenses, you pay them yourself. To help you do this, you establish a Health Savings Account with a health insurance company, bank, or other financial institution. Your contributions to the account are tax deductible, and you don't have to pay tax on the interest or other money you earn on the money in your account. You can withdraw the money in your HSA to pay almost any kind of health-related expense, and you don't have to pay any tax on these withdrawals.

In case you or a family member gets really sick, you must also obtain a health insurance policy with a high deductible—at least $1,050 for individuals, $2,100 for families. The money in your HSA can be used to pay this large deductible and any copayments you're required to make.

Using an HSA can save you money in two ways:

- You'll get a tax deduction for the money you deposit in your account.
- The premiums for your high-deductible health insurance policy should be much lower than those for traditional comprehensive coverage policies or HMO coverage (perhaps as much as 40% lower).

Establishing Your HSA

To participate in the HSA program, you need two things:

- a high-deductible health plan that qualifies under the HSA rules, and
- an HSA account.

HSA-Qualified Plans

You can't have an HSA if you're covered by health insurance other than a high-deductible HSA plan—for example, if your spouse has family coverage for you from his or her job. So you may have to change your existing coverage. However, you may get your own HSA if you are not covered by your spouse's health insurance. In addition, people eligible to receive Medicare may not participate in the HSA program.

You need to obtain a bare-bones high-deductible health plan that meets the HSA criteria (is "HSA-qualified"). You may obtain coverage from an HMO, PPO, or traditional plan. If the coverage is for yourself only, your plan must have a $1,050 minimum annual deductible. If the coverage is for yourself and your family, your plan must have a $2,100 minimum deductible.

In the case of families, the deductible must apply to the entire family, not each family member separately. With such a per-family deductible, expenses incurred by each family member accumulate and are credited toward the one family deductible—for example, a family of four would meet the $2,100 deductible if $525 in medical expense were paid for each family member during the year (4 x $525 = $2,100). This is a unique feature of the HSA program.

You can have a deductible that is larger than the minimum amount if you wish. However, keep in mind that there are limits on how much money you can contribute to your HSA account each year. To be on the safe side, you don't want your deductible to exceed these limits, or your account may not have enough money in it to cover the deductible if you become seriously ill—particularly if you develop a chronic illness that will require payments year after year. In 2006, the maximum annual contribution to an HSA is $2,700 for individuals and $5,450 for families. These amounts will be adjusted each year for inflation.

Special Rule for Preventive Care

A special rule permits high-deductible health plans to provide coverage for preventive health care without the insured first satisfying the minimum annual deductible. Preventive is care that doesn't treat a preexisting condition. It includes, but is not limited to:

- periodic health evaluations, including tests and diagnostic procedures ordered in connection with routine examinations, such as annual physicals
- routine prenatal and well-child care
- child and adult immunizations
- tobacco cessation programs
- obesity weight-loss programs, and
- health screening services. (IRS Notice 2004-23.)

For example, your plan can pay for your annual physical even though you have not met the annual deductible.

Your plan must also have a cap on the annual out-of-pocket payments you must make each year. Out-of-pocket payments include deductibles, copayments, and other amounts (other than insurance premiums) you must pay for covered benefits under your health plan. As you can see from the following chart, the maximum annual out-of-pocket payments that your insurer can require are $5,250 for individuals and $10,500 for families.

HSA Deductibles and Out-of-Pocket Caps		
Type of Coverage	Minimum Annual Deductible	Maximum Annual Out-of-Pocket Payments
Self only	$1,050	$5,250
Family	$2,100	$10,500

In addition, your health insurance plan must be "HSA-qualified." To become qualified, the insurer must agree to participate in the HSA program and give the roster of enrolled participants to the IRS. If your insurer fails to report to the IRS that you are enrolled in an HSA-qualified insurance plan, the IRS will not permit you to deduct your HSA contributions.

HSA-qualified health insurance policies should be clearly labeled as such on the cover page or declaration page of the policy. It might be possible to convert a high-deductible health insurance policy you already have to an HSA-qualified health insurance policy; ask your health insurer for details.

You'll be able to obtain an HSA qualifying health plan from health insurers that participate in the program. The following websites contain directories and contact information for insurers providing HSAs: www.hsainsider.com and www.hsafinder.com. The U.S. Treasury has an informative website on HSAs at www.treas.gov/offices/public-affairs/hsa. You can also contact your present health insurer.

The premiums you pay for an HSA-qualified health plan are deductible to the same extent as any other health insurance premiums. This means that, if you're self-employed, you may deduct your entire premium from your federal income tax as a special personal deduction.

You can also deduct your contribution if your business is an LLC or partnership or if you've formed an S corporation. If your partnership or LLC makes the contribution for you, it must be reported as a distribution to you on your Schedule K-1. You still get the self-employed health insurance deduction but will have to pay tax on the distribution if it exceeds your basis (the value of your investment) in your LLC or partnership. Contributions by an S corporation to a shareholder-employee's HSA are treated as guaranteed payments. The S corporation may deduct them, but they must be included in the shareholder-employee's gross income and are subject to income tax. (IRS Notice 2005-8.)

If you've formed a C corporation and work as its employee, your corporation can make a contribution to your HSA and deduct the amount as employee compensation. The contribution is not taxable to you. ("HSAs for Employees," below.)

HSA Account

Once you have an HSA-qualified health insurance policy, you may open your HSA account. An HSA must be established with a trustee. The HSA trustee keeps track of your deposits and withdrawals, produces annual statements, and reports your HSA deposits to the IRS.

Any person, insurance company, bank, or financial institution already approved by the IRS to be a trustee or custodian of an IRA is approved automatically to serve as an HSA trustee. Others may apply for approval under IRS procedures for HSAs.

Health insurers can administer both the health plan and the HSA. However, you don't have to have your HSA administered by your insurer. You can establish an HSA with banks, insurance companies, mutual funds, or other financial institutions offering HSA products.

Whoever administers your account will usually give you a checkbook or debit card to use to withdraw funds from the account. You can also make withdrawals by mail or in person.

Look at the plans offered by several companies to see which offers the best deal. Compare the fees charged to set up the account, as well as any other charges (some companies may charge an annual service fee, for example). Ask about special promotions and discounts. And find out how the account is invested.

Making Contributions to Your HSA

When you have your HSA-qualified health plan and HSA account, you can start making contributions to your account. There is no minimum amount you are required to contribute each year; you may contribute nothing if you wish. If your business is a corporation, partnership, or LLC, you don't have to make all the contributions to your HSA from your personal funds. All or part of your annual contribution can be paid for by your business from its funds. But, as described in the following section, this changes how the contributions are deducted.

There are maximum limits on how much you may contribute each year:

- If you have individual coverage, the maximum you may contribute to your HSA each year is the amount of your annual deductible or $2,700, whichever is less.
- If you have family coverage, the maximum you may contribute to your HSA each year is the amount of your annual deductible or $5,450, whichever is less.

These maximums are for 2006. They will be adjusted for inflation each year.

EXAMPLE 1: Elvira has an individual HSA-qualified policy with a $1,500 deductible. She may contribute up to $1,500 each year to her HSA account.

EXAMPLE 2: Jim has a family health policy with a $6,000 deductible. He may contribute up to $5,450 each year.

Catch-Up Contributions

Individuals who are 55 to 65 years old can make additional optional tax-free catch-up contributions to their HSA accounts of up to $700 in 2006, gradually increasing to $1,000 by 2009 (see the following chart). This rule is intended to compensate for the fact that older folks won't have as many years to fund their accounts as younger taxpayers. If you're in this age group, it's wise to make these contributions if you can afford them, so your HSA account will have enough money to pay for future health expenses.

Year	Maximum Annual Catch-Up Contribution
2006	$700
2007	$800
2008	$900
2009 and later	$1,000

Deducting HSA Contributions

The amounts you contribute each year to your HSA account, up to the annual limit, are deductible from your federal income taxes. This is a personal deduction you take on the first page of your IRS Form 1040. It is deducted from your gross income, just like a business deduction. (See Chapter 1 for more on calculating deductions.) This means you get the full deduction whether or not you itemize your personal deductions.

EXAMPLE: Martin, a self-employed blacksmith, establishes an HSA for himself and his family with a $2,500 deductible. Every year, he contributes the maximum amount to his HSA account: $2,500. Since he is in the 25% federal income tax bracket, this saves him $625 in federal income tax each year.

Where to Invest Your HSA Contributions

The contributions you make to your HSA account may be invested just like IRA contributions. You can invest in almost anything: money market accounts, bank certificates of deposit, stocks, bonds, mutual funds, Treasury bills, and notes. However, you can't invest in collectibles such as art, antiques, postage stamps, or other personal property. Most HSA funds are invested in money market accounts and certificates of deposit.

Every year, you may roll over up to $500 of unused funds in your HSA into an Individual Retirement Account (IRA) without paying tax on the money.

Deducting HSA Contributions

The amounts contributed each year to HSA accounts, up to the annual limit, are deductible from federal income taxes.

Individual Contributions

You can deduct HSA contributions made with your personal funds as a personal deduction on the first page of your IRS Form 1040. You deduct the amount from your gross income, just like a business deduction. This means you get the full deduction whether or not you itemize your personal deductions.

> **EXAMPLE:** Martin, an actuary, establishes an HSA for himself and his family with a $2,100 deductible. Every year, he contributes the maximum amount to his HSA account: $2,700. Because he is in the 25% federal income tax bracket, this saves him $675 in federal income tax each year.

Contributions by Your Business

If your business is a partnership or LLC and it makes an HSA contribution for you as a distribution of partnership or LLC funds, it is reported as a cash distribution to you on your Schedule K-1 (Form 1065). You may take a personal deduction for the HSA contribution on your tax return

(IRS Form 1040) and the contribution is not subject to income or self-employment taxes.

However, the tax result is very different if the contribution is made as a guaranteed payment to the partner or LLC member. A guaranteed payment is like a salary paid to a partner or LLC member for services performed for the partnership or LLC. The amount of a guaranteed payment is determined without reference to the partnership's or LLC's income. The partnership or LLC deducts the guaranteed payment on its return and lists it as a guaranteed payment to you on your Schedule K-1 (Form 1065). You must pay income and self-employment tax on the amount. You may take a personal income tax deduction on your Form 1040 for the HSA contribution.

Contributions by an S corporation to a shareholder-employee's HSA are treated as wages subject to income tax, but they normally are not subject to employment taxes. The shareholder can deduct the contribution on his or her personal tax return (IRS Form 1040) as an HSA contribution.

If you've formed a C corporation and work as its employee, your corporation can make a contribution to your HSA and deduct the amount as employee compensation. The contribution is not taxable to you. However, if you have other employees, similar contributions must be made to their HSAs. You may also make contributions from your own fund.

Withdrawing HSA Funds

If you or a family member needs health care, you can withdraw money from your HSA to pay your deductible or any other medical expenses. You pay no federal tax on HSA withdrawals used to pay qualified medical expenses. Qualified medical expenses are broadly defined to include many types of expenses ordinarily not covered by health insurance—for example, dental or optometric care. This is one of the great advantages of the HSA program over traditional health insurance. (The lists in "What HSA Funds Can Be Used For," below, show the type of health expenses that can and cannot be paid with an HSA.)

No Approval Required

HSA participants need not obtain advance approval from their HSA trustee (whether their insurer or someone else) that an expense is a qualified medical expense before they withdraw funds from their accounts. You make that determination yourself. You should keep records of your medical expenses to show that your withdrawals were for qualified medical expenses and are therefore excludable from your gross income.

> **EXAMPLE:** Jane, a self-employed consultant and single mother, obtains family health insurance coverage with a $2,500 deductible. She sets up an HSA at her bank and deposits $2,500 every year for three years. She deducts each contribution from her gross income for the year for income tax purposes. Jane pays no taxes on the interest she earns on the money in her account, which is invested in a money market fund. By the end of three years, she has $7,750 in the account. Jane becomes ill after the third year and is hospitalized. She withdraws $2,000 from her HSA to pay her deductible. She also withdraws $3,000 to pay for speech therapy for her son, which is not covered by her health insurance. She pays no federal tax on these withdrawals.

However, you may not use HSA funds to purchase nonprescription medications. The only way to deduct these is to hire your spouse and establish a medical reimbursement plan. (See "Adopting a Medical Reimbursement Plan," above.)

Tax-Free Withdrawals

If you withdraw funds from your HSA to use for something other than qualified medical expenses, you must pay the regular income tax on the withdrawal plus a 10% penalty. For example, if you were in the 25% federal income tax bracket, you'd have to pay a 35% tax on your nonqualified withdrawals.

Once you reach the age of 65 or become disabled, you can withdraw your HSA funds for any reason without penalty. If you use the money for nonmedical expenses, you will have to pay regular income tax on the withdrawals. When you die, the money in your HSA account is transferred to the beneficiary you've named for the account. The transfer is tax-free if the beneficiary is your surviving spouse. Other transfers are taxable.

If you elect to leave the HSA program, you can continue to keep your HSA account and withdraw money from it tax-free for health care expenses. However, you won't be able to make any additional contributions to the account.

What HSA Funds Can Be Used For

Health insurance ordinarily may not be purchased with HSA funds. However, there are three exceptions to this general rule. HSA funds can be used to pay for:

- a health plan during any period of continuation coverage required under any federal law—for example, when you are terminated from your job and purchase continuing health insurance coverage from your employer's health insurer, which the insurer is legally required to make available to you under COBRA
- long-term health care insurance, or
- health insurance premiums you pay while you are receiving unemployment compensation.

You can use HSA funds to pay for the following health expenses:

- abdominal supports
- abortion
- acupuncture
- air conditioner (when necessary for relief from an allergy or for difficulty in breathing)
- alcoholism treatment
- ambulance
- arch supports
- artificial limbs
- birth control pills (by prescription)
- blood tests
- blood transfusions
- braces
- breast reconstruction surgery
- cardiographs
- chiropractor

- Christian Science Practitioner
- contact lenses
- contraceptive devices (by prescription)
- convalescent home (for medical treatment only)
- crutches
- dental treatment
- dentures
- dermatologist
- diagnostic fees
- diathermy
- drug addiction therapy
- elastic hosiery (prescription)
- eyeglasses
- fees paid to health institute prescribed by a doctor
- fertility treatment
- fluoridation unit
- guide dog
- healing services
- hearing aids and batteries
- hospital bills
- hydrotherapy
- insulin treatments
- lab tests
- laser eye surgery
- lead paint removal
- legal fees to authorize treatment for mental illness
- lodging while away from home for outpatient care
- medical conference expenses (only if the conference concerns the chronic illness of yourself, your spouse, or a dependent)
- metabolism tests
- neurologist
- nursing (including board and meals)
- nursing home
- obstetrician
- operating room costs
- ophthalmologist
- optician

- optometrist
- oral surgery
- organ transplant (including donor's expenses)
- orthopedic shoes
- orthopedist
- osteopath
- oxygen and oxygen equipment
- pediatrician
- physician
- physiotherapist
- podiatrist
- postnatal treatments
- practical nurse for medical services
- prenatal care
- prescription medicines
- psychiatrist
- psychoanalyst
- psychologist
- radium therapy
- sex therapy
- special education costs for the handicapped
- splints
- sterilization
- stop-smoking programs (not including nonprescription drugs)
- surgeon
- telephone or TV equipment to assist the hard-of-hearing
- therapy equipment
- transportation expenses to obtain health care
- ultraviolet ray treatment
- vaccines
- vitamins (if prescribed)
- weight-loss program (only if it is a treatment for a specific disease diagnosed by a doctor—for example, obesity; cost of reduced-calorie foods is not deductible)
- wheelchair
- x-rays.

HSA funds cannot be used to pay for the following health-related expenses:

- advance payment for services to be rendered next year
- athletic club membership
- bottled water
- child care for a healthy child
- commuting expenses of a disabled person
- cosmetic surgery and procedures
- cosmetics, hygiene products, and similar items
- diaper service
- domestic help
- funeral, cremation, or burial expenses
- health programs offered by resort hotels, health clubs, and gyms
- illegal operations and treatments
- illegally procured drugs
- maternity clothes
- nutritional supplements (unless recommended by a medical practitioner to treat a specific illness diagnosed by a doctor)
- nonprescription medication
- premiums for life insurance, income protection, disability, loss of limbs, sight, or similar benefits
- Scientology counseling
- social activities
- specially designed car for the handicapped other than an autoette or special equipment
- swimming pool or swimming lessons
- travel for general health improvement
- tuition and travel expenses to send a child to a particular school
- veterinary fees.

Are HSAs a Good Deal?

Should you get an HSA? It depends. HSAs appear to be a very good deal if you're young or in good health and don't go to the doctor often or take many expensive medications. You can purchase a health plan with a high deductible, pay substantially lower premiums, and have the security of knowing you can dip into your HSA if you get sick and have to pay the deductible or other uncovered medical expenses.

Comparing Health Costs for a Typical Family

The Joneses are a family of three whose health care costs are equal to the national average. They pay $650 per month for traditional health insurance. Their policy has a $500-per-person deductible and an out-of-pocket expense cap of $1,500. They incur $1,200 in uninsured medical and dental expenses each year.

Let's compare their annual health expenses if they switch to an HSA-qualified insurance plan with a $4,500 family deductible. Let's assume their high-deductible policy costs $400 per month and they put the $250 they save on insurance premiums each month into their HSA account. They use the money in their HSA account to pay their annual $1,200 in uninsured health expenses. Let's also assume that the breadwinner in this family is self-employed and qualifies for the self-employed health insurance deduction and that the family is in the 25% federal income tax bracket.

	Traditional Health Plan	HSA Health Plan
Annual health insurance premiums	$ 7,800	$ 4,800
Annual HSA contribution	0	3,000
Annual amount spent on uninsured health costs	1,200	1,200
Total annual expenses	9,000	9,000
HSA account balance on December 31	0	1,800
Tax savings from HSA contribution	0	750
Tax savings from self-employed health insurance deduction	1,950	1,200
Net cost	$ 7,050	$ 5,250

If you don't tap into the money, it will keep accumulating free of taxes. You also get the benefit of deducting your HSA contributions from your income taxes. And you can use your HSA funds to pay for many health-related expenses that aren't covered by traditional health insurance.

If you enjoy good health while you have your HSA and don't have to make many withdrawals, you may end up with a substantial amount in your account that you can withdraw without penalty for any purpose once you turn 65. Unlike all other existing tax-advantaged savings or retirement accounts, HSAs provide a tax break when funds are deposited and when they are withdrawn. No other account provides both a "front end" and a "back end" tax break. With IRAs, for example, you must pay tax either when you deposit or when you withdraw your money. This feature can make your HSA an extremely lucrative tax shelter—a kind of super IRA.

On the other hand, HSAs are not for everybody. You could be better off with traditional comprehensive health insurance if you or a member of your family has substantial medical expenses. When you are in this situation, you'll likely end up spending all or most of your HSA contributions each year and earn little or no interest on your account (but you'll still get a deduction for your contributions). Of course, whether traditional health insurance is better than an HSA depends on its cost, including the deductibles and copayments you must make. In addition, depending on your medical history and where you live, the cost of an HSA-qualified health insurance plan may be too great to make the program cost-effective for you. However, if your choice is an HSA or nothing, get an HSA.

HSAs for Employees

Employers may provide HSAs to their employees. Any business, no matter how small, may participate in the HSA program. The employer purchases an HSA-qualified health plan for its employees, and they establish their own individual HSA accounts. The employer may pay all or part of its employees' insurance premiums and make contributions to their HSA accounts. Employees may also make their own contributions to their individual accounts. The combined annual contributions of the employer and employee may not exceed the limits listed above.

HSAs are portable when an employee changes employers. Contributions and earnings belong to the account holder, not the employer. Employers are required to report amounts contributed to an HSA on the employee's Form W-2.

Health insurance payments and HSA contributions made by businesses on behalf of their employees are currently deductible business expenses. The employees do not have to report employer contributions to their HSA accounts as income. You deduct them on the "Employee benefit programs" line of your business income tax return. If you're filing Schedule C, this is on Part II, line 14.

If you've formed a C corporation and work as its employee, your corporation may establish an HSA on your behalf and deduct its contributions on its own tax return. The contributions are not taxable to you, but you get no personal deduction for them. You do get a deduction, however, if you make contributions to your HSA account from your personal funds. You can't do this if you have an S corporation, LLC, or partnership, because owners of these entities are not considered employees for employment benefit purposes.

Hiring Your Spouse

If you're a sole proprietor or have formed any business entity other than an S corporation, you may hire your spouse as your employee and have your business pay for an HSA-qualified family health plan for your spouse, you, and your children and other dependents. Your spouse then establishes an HSA, which your business may fully fund each year. The money your business spends for your spouse's health insurance premiums and to fund the HSA is a fully deductible business expense. This allows you to reduce both your income and your self-employment taxes. (See "Personal Income Tax Deductions for the Self-Employed," above.)

Nondiscrimination Rules

If you have employees other than yourself, your spouse, or other family members, you'll need to comply with nondiscrimination rules—that is, you'll have to make comparable HSA contributions for all employees with HSA-qualified health coverage during the year. Contributions are considered comparable if they are either of the same amount or the same percentage of the deductible under the plan. The rule is applied separately to employees who work fewer than 30 hours per week. Employers who do not comply with these rules are subject to a 35% excise tax.

Archer Medical Savings Accounts

Starting in 1997, Congress began a pilot program that allowed self-employed people and companies with 50 or fewer employees to establish Archer Medical Savings Accounts (MSAs). Archer MSAs were very similar to HSAs; they were a way for Congress to try out the health savings account concept. However, very few self-employed people and businesses have elected to establish MSAs. If you are one of the few with an Archer MSA, you may roll it over into an HSA without paying taxes on the money. Ask your insurer or Archer MSA trustee about this.

Tax Reporting for HSAs

You must report to the IRS each year how much you deposit to and withdraw from your HSA. You make the report using IRS Form 8889, *Health Savings Accounts*. You'll also be required to keep a record of the name and address of each person or company whom you pay with funds from your HSA

Chapter 14

Additional Deductions

T his chapter looks at some of the most common deductible operating expenses that small businesses incur. These are costs that a business is likely to incur in the normal course of running its operations, such as advertising expenses, insurance, and legal fees. You can deduct these costs as business operating expenses as long as they are ordinary, necessary, and reasonable in amount and meet the additional requirements discussed below.

Advertising

Almost any type of business-related advertising is a currently deductible business operating expense. You can deduct advertising to sell a particular product or service, to help establish good will for your business, or just to get your business known. Advertising includes expenses for:
- business cards
- brochures
- advertisements in the local Yellow Pages
- newspaper and magazine advertisements
- trade publication advertisements
- catalogues
- radio and television advertisements
- advertisements on the Internet
- fees you pay to advertising and public relations agencies
- billboards
- package design costs, and
- signs and display racks.

However, advertising to influence government legislation is never deductible. And help wanted ads you place to recruit workers are not advertising costs, but you can deduct them as ordinary and necessary business operating expenses.

Good Will Advertising

If it relates to business you reasonably expect to gain in the future, you can usually deduct the cost of institutional or "good will" advertising meant to keep your name before the public. Examples of good will advertsing include:

- advertisements that encourage people to contribute to charities, such as the Red Cross or similar causes
- having your business sponsor a little league baseball team, bowling team, or golf tournament
- giving away product samples, and
- holding contests and giving away prizes—for example, a car dealer can deduct the cost of giving a car away.

In one case, the tax court even allowed a gas station owner to deduct the cost of providing free beer to customers as an advertising expense. The court stated that a small business owner "can offer free beer to beer lovers" to improve business. (*Sullivan v. Commissioner*, TC Memo 1982-150).)

However, you can't deduct time and labor that you give away as an advertising expense, even though doing so promotes good will. You must actually spend money to have an advertising expense. For example, a lawyer who does pro bono work for indigent clients to advertise his law practice may not deduct the cost of his services as an advertising expense.

Giveaway Items

Giveaway items that you use to publicize your business (such as pens, coffee cups, T-shirts, refrigerator magnets, calendars, tote bags, and key chains) are deductible. However, you are not allowed to deduct more than $25 in business gifts to any one person each year. This limitation applies to advertising giveaway items unless they:

- cost $4 or less
- have your name clearly and permanently imprinted on them, and
- are one of a number of identical items you distribute widely.

EXAMPLE 1: Acme Press orders 1,000 ballpoint pens with its name and company logo printed on them and distributes them at book fairs, bookstores, and conventions. Each pen costs $1. The pens do not count toward the $25 gift limit. Acme may deduct the entire $1,000 expense for the pens.

EXAMPLE 2: Acme buys a $200 fountain pen and gives it to its best-selling author. The pen is a business gift to an individual, so Acme can deduct only $25 of the cost.

Signs, display racks, and other promotional materials that you give away to other businesses to use on their premises do not count as gifts.

Business Websites

The cost of a business website is a deductible business expense. You can use the site to take orders from customers or just to publicize the products or services your business sells. You can deduct the cost of designing the site and maintaining it—for example, the monthly charge you pay to an Internet access provider.

Permanent Signs

Signs that have a useful life of less than one year—for example, paper or cardboard signs—are currently deductible as business operating expenses. However, a permanent metal or plastic sign that has a useful life of more than one year is a long-term business asset, which you cannot currently deduct as a business operating expense. Instead, you must either depreciate the cost over several years or deduct it in one year under Section 179. (See Chapter 5 for more on deducting long-term assets.)

Business Bad Debts

Business bad debts are debts that arise from your business activities, such as:
- lending money for a business purpose
- selling inventory on credit, or
- guaranteeing business-related loans.

You can currently deduct business bad debts as a business operating expense when they become wholly or partly worthless. However, to claim the deduction, you must incur an actual loss of money or have previously included the amount of the debt as income on your tax return. Because of this limitation, many small businesses are unable to deduct bad debts.

Three Requirements to Deduct Bad Debts

Three requirements must be satisfied to deduct a business bad debt as a business operating expense:

- You must have a bona fide business debt.
- The debt must be wholly or partly worthless.
- You must have suffered an economic loss from the debt.

A Bona Fide Business Debt

A bona fide debt exists when someone has a legal obligation to pay you a sum of money—for example, you sell goods or merchandise to a customer on credit. A bona fide debt also exists if there is written evidence to support it—for example, a signed promissory note or other writing stating the amount of the debt, when it is due, and the interest rate (if any). An oral promise to pay may also be legally enforceable but would be looked upon with suspicion by the IRS.

A business debt is a debt that is created or acquired in the course of your business or becomes worthless as part of your business. Your primary motive for incurring the debt must be business-related. Debts taken on for personal or investment purposes are not business debts. (Remember, investing is not a business; see Chapter 1.)

> **EXAMPLE 1:** Mark, an advertising agent, lends $10,000 to his brother-in-law, Scott, to invest in his bird diaper invention. Mark will get 25% of the profits if the invention proves successful. This is an investment, not a business debt.

> **EXAMPLE 2:** Mark lends $10,000 to one of his best business clients to keep the client's business running. Because the main reason for the loan was business-related (to keep his client in business so he will continue as a client), the debt is a business debt.

A Worthless Debt

A debt must be wholly or partly worthless to be deductible. A debt becomes worthless when there is no longer any chance that the amount owed will be paid back to you. You don't have to wait until a debt is due to determine that it is worthless, and you don't have to go to court to try to collect it. You just have to be able to show that you have taken reasonable steps to try to collect the debt or that collection efforts would be futile. For example:

- You've made repeated collection efforts that have proven unsuccessful.
- The debtor has filed for bankruptcy or already been through bankruptcy and had all or part of the debt discharged (forgiven) by the bankruptcy court.
- You've learned that the debtor has gone out of business, gone broke, died, or disappeared.

Keep all documentation that shows a debt is worthless, such as copies of unpaid invoices, collection letters you've sent the debtor, logs of collection calls you've made, bankruptcy notices, and credit reports.

You must deduct the entire amount of a bad debt in the year it becomes totally worthless. If only part of a business debt becomes worthless—for example, you received a partial payment before the debt became uncollectible—you can deduct the unpaid portion that year, or you can wait until the following year to deduct it. For example, if you think you might get paid more the next year, you can wait and see what your final bad debt amount is before you deduct it.

An Economic Loss

You are not automatically entitled to deduct a debt because the obligation has become worthless. To get a deduction, you must have suffered an economic loss. According to the IRS, you have a loss only when you:

- have already reported as business income the amount you were supposed to be paid
- paid out cash, or
- made credit sales of inventory that were not paid for.

These rules make it impossible to deduct some types of business debts.

Types of Bad Debts

There are many different types of business debts that small businesses can incur. The sections that follow discuss some of the more common ones.

Sales of Services

Unfortunately, if you're a cash basis taxpayer who sells services to your clients (like many small businesses), you can't claim a bad debt deduction if a client fails to pay you. As a cash basis taxpayer, you don't report income until you actually receive it. As a result, you don't have an economic loss (in the eyes of the IRS) when a client fails to pay.

> **EXAMPLE:** Bill, a self-employed consultant, works 50 hours for a client and bills the client $2,500. The client never pays. Bill is a cash basis taxpayer, so he doesn't report the $2,500 as income, because he never received it. As far as the IRS is concerned, Bill has no economic loss and cannot deduct the $2,500 the client failed to pay.

The IRS strictly enforces this rule (harsh as it may seem). Absent the rule, the IRS fears that businesses will inflate the value of their services in order to get a larger deduction.

Accrual basis taxpayers, on the other hand, report sales as income in the year the sales are made—not the year payment is received. These taxpayers can take a bad debt deduction if a client fails to pay for services rendered, because they have already reported the money due as income. Therefore, accrual taxpayers have an economic loss when their services are not paid for.

> **EXAMPLE:** Acme Consulting Co. bills a client $10,000 for consulting services it performed during the year. Because Acme is an accrual basis taxpayer, it characterizes the $10,000 as income on its books and includes this amount in its gross income in the year in which it billed for the services, even though Acme hasn't actually received payment. The client later files for bankruptcy, and the debt becomes worthless. Acme may take a business bad debt deduction to wipe out the $10,000 in income it previously charged on its books.

There's no point in trying to switch from cash basis to the accrual method to deduct bad debts. The accrual method doesn't result in lower taxes—the bad debt deduction merely wipes out a sale that was previously reported as income.

Refer to Chapter 15 for a detailed discussion of the cash basis and accrual accounting methods.

Credit Sales of Inventory

Most deductible business bad debts result from credit sales of inventory to customers. If you sell goods on credit to a customer and are not paid, you get a deduction whether you are an accrual or cash basis taxpayer. You deduct the cost of the inventory at the end of the year to determine the cost of goods sold for the year. (See Chapter 6 for more about deducting inventory.)

Cash Loans

Whether you are a cash or accrual basis taxpayer, cash loans you make for a business purpose are deductible as bad debts in the year they become worthless.

> **EXAMPLE:** John, an advertising agent, loaned $10,000 to one of his best business clients to keep the client's business running. The client later went bankrupt and could not repay him. John may deduct the $10,000 as a business bad debt.

Business Loan Guarantees

If you guarantee a debt that becomes worthless, it qualifies as a business bad debt only if you:

- made the guarantee in the course of your business
- have a legal duty to pay the debt
- made the guarantee before the debt became worthless, and
- received reasonable consideration (compensation) for the guarantee—you meet this requirement if the guarantee is for a good faith business purpose or according to normal business practices.

> **EXAMPLE:** Jane owns Jane's Dress Co. She guaranteed payment of a $20,000 note for Elegant Fashions, a dress outlet. Elegant Fashions is one of Jane's largest clients. Elegant later filed for bankruptcy and defaulted on the loan. Jane had to make full payment to the bank.

She can take a business bad debt deduction, because her guarantee was made for a good faith business purpose—her desire to retain one of her better clients and keep a sales outlet.

Loans or Guarantees to Your Corporation

If your business is incorporated, you cannot take a bad debt deduction for a loan to your corporation if the loan is actually a contribution to capital—that is, part of your investment in the business. You must be careful to treat a loan to your corporation in the same way that you treat a loan made to a business in which you have no ownership interest. You should have a signed promissory note from your corporation setting forth:

- the loan amount
- the interest rate—which should be a reasonable rate
- the due date, and
- a repayment schedule.

If you are a principal shareholder in a small corporation, you'll often be asked to personally guarantee corporate loans and other extensions of credit. Creditors do this because they want to be able to go after your personal assets if they can't collect from your corporation. If you end up having to make good on your guarantee and can't get repaid from your corporation, you will have a bad debt. You can deduct this bad debt as a business debt if your dominant motive for making the loan or guarantee was to protect your employment status and ensure your continuing receipt of a salary. If your primary motive was to protect your investment in the corporation, the debt is a personal debt. The IRS is more likely to think you are protecting your investment if you receive little or no salary from the corporation or your salary is not a major source of your overall income.

> **EXAMPLE:** Andre is employed by, and the sole shareholder of, Andre's Fashions, Inc. The corporation pays Andre a $75,000 annual salary, which is his sole source of income. Andre's Fashion applies for a $50,000 bank loan. Before approving the loan, the bank requires Andre to personally guarantee payment of the loan. Andre's Fashions defaults on the loan and Andre has to make full

payment to the bank from his personal funds. Andre is entitled to a business bad debt deduction because his primary motive for guaranteeing the loan was to protect his job with his corporation, not to protect his investment in the corporation.

Personal Debts

The fact that a debt doesn't arise from your business doesn't mean it's not deductible. Bona fide personal debts that become worthless are deductible as *short-term capital losses*. This means they can be deducted only to offset any capital gains you received from the sale of capital assets during the year. (Capital assets include items such as real estate, stocks, and bonds.) Your total deduction for personal debts is limited to $3,000 per year. Any loss in excess of this limit may be carried over to future years to offset future capital gains. Unlike business bad debts, personal debts are deductible only if they become wholly worthless.

Casualty Losses

Casualty losses are damage to property caused by fire, theft, vandalism, earthquake, storm, floods, terrorism, or some other "sudden, unexpected, or unusual event." There must be some external force involved for a loss to be a casualty loss. Thus, you get no deduction if you simply lose or misplace property or it breaks or wears out over time.

You may take a deduction for casualty losses to business property if, and only to the extent that, the loss is not covered by insurance. Thus, if the loss is fully covered, you'll get no deduction.

Amount of Deduction

How much you may deduct depends on whether the property involved was stolen or completely destroyed or only partially destroyed. However, you must always reduce your casualty losses by the amount of any insurance proceeds you actually receive or reasonably expect to receive. If more than one item was stolen or wholly or partly destroyed, you must figure your deduction separately for each and then add them all together.

Total Loss

If the property is stolen or completely destroyed, your deduction is figured as follows: Adjusted Basis – Salvage Value – Insurance Proceeds = Casualty Loss. (Your adjusted basis is the property's original cost, plus the value of any improvements, minus any deductions you took for depreciation or Section 179 expensing—see Chapter 5.) Obviously, if an item is stolen, there will be no salvage value.

> **EXAMPLE:** Sean's business computer is stolen from his apartment by a burglar. The computer cost $2,000. Sean has taken no tax deductions for it because he purchased it only two months ago, so his adjusted basis is $2,000. Sean is a renter and has no insurance covering the loss. Sean's casualty loss is $2,000. ($2,000 Adjusted Basis – $0 Salvage Value – $0 Insurance Proceeds = $2,000.)

Partial Loss

If the property is only partly destroyed, your casualty loss deduction is the lesser of the decrease in the property's fair market value or its adjusted basis, reduced by any insurance you receive or expect to receive.

> **EXAMPLE:** Assume that Sean's computer from the example above is partly destroyed due to a small fire in his home. Its fair market value in its partly damaged state is $500. Since he spent $2,000 for it, the decrease in its fair market value is $1,500. The computer's adjusted basis is $2,000. He received no insurance proceeds. Thus, his casualty loss is $1,500.

Inventory

You don't have to treat damage to or loss of inventory as a casualty loss. Instead, you may deduct it on your Schedule C as part of the cost of your goods sold. (See Chapter 6 for a detailed discussion of inventory.) This is advantageous because it reduces your income for self-employment tax purposes, which casualty losses do not. However, if you do this, you must include any insurance proceeds you receive for the inventory loss in your gross income for the year.

Personal Property

You can deduct casualty losses to personal property—that is, property you don't use for your business—from your income tax as an itemized personal deduction, but the deduction is severely limited: You can deduct only the amount of the loss that exceeds 10% of your adjusted gross income for the year. This greatly limits or eliminates many casualty loss deductions. To add insult to injury, you must also subtract $100 from each casualty or theft you suffered during the year.

> **EXAMPLE:** Ken's suffers $5,000 in losses to his personal property when a fire strikes his home. His adjusted gross income for the year is $75,000. He can deduct only that portion of his loss that exceeds $7,500 (10% x $75,000 = $7,500). He lost $5,000, so he gets no deduction.

 These limits don't apply to casualty losses to personal property caused by Hurricane Katrina. For more information, refer to IRS Publication 4492, *Information for Taxpayers Affected by Hurricanes Katrina, Rita, and Wilma.*

Damage to Your Home Office

If you take the home office deduction, you may deduct losses due to damage to or destruction of your home office as part of your deduction. However, your loss is reduced by any insurance proceeds you receive or expect to receive.

You can deduct casualty losses that affect your entire house as an indirect home office expense. The amount of your deduction is based on your home office use percentage.

> **EXAMPLE:** Dana's home is completely destroyed by a fire. Her fire insurance only covered 80% of her loss. Her home office took up 20% of her home. She can deduct 20% of her total casualty loss as an indirect home office deduction.

You can fully deduct casualty losses that affect only your home office—for example, if only your home office is burned in a fire—as direct home office expenses. However, you can't deduct as a business expense casualty losses that don't affect your home office at all—for example, if your kitchen is destroyed by fire.

If the loss involves business property that is in your home office but is not part of your home—for example, a burglar steals your home office computer—it's not part of the home office deduction.

See Chapter 7 for a detailed discussion of the home office deduction.

Tax Reporting

You report casualty losses to business property on part B of IRS Form 4684, *Casualties and Thefts*, and then transfer the deductible casualty loss to Form 4797, *Sales of Business Property*, and the first page of your Form 1040. The amount of your deductible casualty loss is subtracted from your adjusted gross income for the year. However, casualty losses are not deducted from your self-employment income for Social Security and Medicare tax purposes. These reporting requirements are different from the reporting for other deductions covered in this chapter, which are reported on IRS Schedule C, Form 1040.

Partnerships, S corporations, and LLCs must also fill out Form 4797. The amount of the loss is taken into account when calculating the entity's total business income for the year. This amount is reported on the entity's information tax return (Form 1065 for partnerships and LLCs; Form 1120S for S corporations). C corporations deduct their casualty losses on their own tax returns (Form 1120).

If you take a casualty loss as part of your home office deduction, you must include it on Form 8829, *Expenses for Business Use of Your Home.*

Casualty Gains

In some cases, the insurance reimbursement you receive will exceed the value of the property that is stolen or destroyed. In this event, you have a casualty gain, not a deductible loss.

> **EXAMPLE:** Jeanette's laptop computer is stolen from her car. She has computer insurance covering the loss. Her insurer pays her $1,500. Jeanette paid $2,500 for the computer but deducted the entire amount in one year under Section 179; thus, her adjusted basis is 0. As a result, she has a $1,500 gain ($0 Adjusted Basis + $1,500 Insurance Proceeds = $1,500 Casualty Gain).

If you have a gain, you might have to pay tax on it. If you owned the property one year or more, the gain is a capital gain taxed at capital gains rates. Gains on property owned less than one year are taxed at ordinary income tax rates. However, you can defer any taxes you owe to a later year (or even indefinitely) by buying property to replace your loss within certain time limits.

Charitable Contributions

If you are a sole proprietor, partner in a partnership, LLC member, or S corporation shareholder, the IRS treats any charitable contributions your business makes as a personal contribution by you and your co-owners. As such, the contributions are not business expenses—you can deduct them only as a personal charitable contribution. You may deduct these contributions only if you itemize deductions on your personal tax return; they are subject to certain income limitations.

Charitable contributions are treated very differently for C corporations. C corporations can deduct charitable deductions as a business expense on their own corporate tax returns. If a C corporation contributes inventory to a public charity or operating foundation that uses the items to care for the needy or infants, it may add 50% of the difference between the inventory's tax basis (cost) and fair market value (up to twice the basis) to the deduction amount. This makes inventory contributions particularly attractive for C corporations.

> **EXAMPLE:** Acme Corporation manufactured 1,000 widgets in 2006 that it was unable to sell. It cost Acme $1,000 to manufacture the widgets—this is their basis. They have a fair market value of $1,500. Acme decides to donate the widgets to a local hospital. Its charitable deduction is equal to the fair market value of the widgets ($1,500), plus 50% of the difference between the widgets' fair market value and their basis ($1,500 – $1,000 = $500; $500 x 50% = $250). Thus, Acme's total deduction is $1,750 ($1,500 + $250 = $1,750).

In contrast, if a business that is not a C corporation donates inventory to a charity, the deduction is limited to the fair market value of the inventory on the date it is donated, reduced by any gain that would have been realized if the property had been sold at its fair market value instead of being donated.

> **EXAMPLE:** Barbee, the owner of a crafts store, donates unsold inventory to a nursing home. The fair market value of the inventory is $1,000. Barbee spent $500 to acquire the inventory, so she would have had a $500 gain had she sold it at its fair market value. Her charitable deduction must be reduced by the amount of this gain, so she gets only a $500 deduction.

There are several organizations that specialize in facilitating charitable donations of unsold inventory by corporations, including the National Association for Exchange of Industrial Resources (NAEIR) at www.naeir.org.

Clothing

You can deduct the cost of clothing if:
- it is essential for your business
- it is not suitable for ordinary street wear, and
- you don't wear the clothing outside of business.

Thus, for example, you may deduct the cost of uniforms or special work clothes not suitable for personal wear, such as nurse's uniforms, theatrical costumes, and special sanitary clothing or clothing with a company logo. But clothing that you can wear on the street is not deductible—for example, you can't deduct the cost of business suits. Courts have also disallowed deductions for a tennis pro outfit and a house painting uniform because both of these could be worn on the street. If your clothing is deductible, you may also deduct the cost of dry cleaning and other care.

Rock Musician Could Only Deduct Flashy Stage Clothing

Don Teschner, a musician in Rod Stewart's band, attempted to deduct as a business expense various items of stage clothing, including silk boxers, leather pants, men's underwear, hats, and a vest. The tax court rejected out of hand any deduction for the silk boxers and underwear, declaring that underwear clearly could not qualify as a business expense. The majority of the remaining clothes were likewise not deductible because they could be adapted for street wear. However, there were some items that the court deemed too "flashy" or "loud" to be acceptable for ordinary wear and it allowed Teschner a $200 deduction for them. The moral: Wear "loud" clothes on stage if you're a rock musician and want a tax deduction. (*Teschner v. Commissioner*, TC Memo 1997–498.)

Dues and Subscriptions

Dues you pay to professional, business, and civic organizations are deductible business expenses, as long as the organization's main purpose is not to provide entertainment facilities to members. This includes dues paid to:

- bar associations, medical associations, and other professional organizations

- trade associations, local chambers of commerce, real estate boards, and business leagues, and
- civic or public service organizations, such as a Rotary or Lions club.

You get no deduction for dues you pay to belong to other types of social, business, or recreational clubs—for example, country clubs or athletic clubs. (See Chapter 10.) For this reason, it's best not to use the word "dues" on your tax return, because the IRS may question the expense. Use other words to describe the deduction—for example, if you're deducting membership dues for a trade organization, list the expense as "trade association membership fees."

You may deduct subscriptions to professional, technical, and trade journals that deal with your business field as a business expense.

Education Expenses

You can deduct your expenses for business-related education—for example, a college course or seminar. You can also deduct the cost of attending a convention or professional meeting as an education expense. To qualify for an education deduction, you must be able to show that the education:

- maintains or improves skills required in your business, or
- is required by law or regulation to maintain your professional status.

EXAMPLE 1: Herb owns a repair shop for electronic equipment. The bulk of his business is television repairs, but he occasionally fixes disc players. To keep up with the latest technical changes, he takes a special course at a local trade school to learn how to repair disc players. Because the course maintains and improves skills required in his business, he can deduct the cost of the course.

EXAMPLE 2: Sue is a self-employed attorney. Every year, she is required by law to attend 12 hours of continuing education to keep her status as an active member of the state bar. The legal seminars she attends to satisfy this requirement are deductible education expenses.

Deductible education expenses include tuition, fees, books, and other learning materials. They also include transportation and travel (see below). You may also deduct expenses you pay to educate or train your employees.

Starting a New Business

You cannot currently deduct education expenses you incur to qualify for a *new* business or profession. For example, courts have held that IRS agents could not deduct the cost of going to law school, because a law degree would qualify them for a new business—being a lawyer (*Jeffrey L. Weiler*, 54 TC 398 (1970).) On the other hand, a practicing dentist was allowed to deduct the cost of being educated in orthodontia, because becoming an orthodontist did not constitute the practice of a new business or profession for a dentist. (Rev. Rul. 74-78.)

Minimum Educational Requirements

You cannot deduct the cost required to meet the minimum or basic level educational requirements for a business or profession. Thus, for example, you can't deduct the expense of going to law school or medical school.

Traveling for Education

Local transportation expenses paid to get to and from a deductible educational activity are deductible. This includes transportation between either your home or business and the educational activity. Going to or from home to an educational activity does not constitute nondeductible commuting. If you drive, you may deduct your actual expenses or use the standard mileage rate. (See Chapter 8 for more on deducting car expenses.)

There's no law that says you must take your education courses as close to home as possible. You may travel outside your geographic area for education, even if the same or a similar educational activity is available near your home or place of business. Companies and groups that sponsor educational events are well aware of this rule and take advantage of it by offering courses and seminars at resorts and other enjoyable vacation spots such as Hawaii and California. Deductible travel expenses may include airfare or other transportation, lodging, and meals. (See Chapter 10 for more about travel expenses.)

You cannot claim travel itself as an education deduction. You must travel to some sort of educational activity. For example, an architect could not deduct the cost of a trip to Paris because he studied the local architecture while he was there—but he could deduct a trip to Paris to attend a seminar on French architecture.

Lifetime Learning Credit

Instead of taking a tax deduction for your business-related education expenses, you may qualify for the lifetime learning credit. A tax credit is a dollar-for-dollar reduction in your tax liability, so it's even better than a tax deduction.

The lifetime learning credit can by used to help pay for any undergraduate or graduate level education, including nondegree education to acquire or improve job skills (for example a continuing education course). If you qualify, your credit equals 20% of the first $10,000 of postsecondary tuition and fees you pay during the year, for a maximum credit of $2,000 per tax return. However, the credit is phased out and then eliminated at the certain income levels: It begins to go down if your modified adjusted gross income is over $45,000 ($90,000 for a joint return) and you cannot claim the credit at all if your MAGI is over $55,000 ($110,000 for a joint return).

You can take this credit not only for yourself, but for a dependent child (or children) for whom you claim a tax exemption, or your spouse as well (if you file jointly). And it can be taken any number of times. However, you can't take the credit if you've already deducted the education cost as a business expense.

> **EXAMPLE:** Bill, a self-employed real estate broker with a $40,000 AGI, spends $2,000 on continuing real estate education courses during 2006. He may take a $400 lifetime learning credit (20% x $2,000 = $400).

Gifts

If you give someone a gift for business purposes, your business expense deduction is limited to $25 per person per year. Any amount over the $25 limit is not deductible. If this amount seems awfully low, that's because it was established in 1954!

> **EXAMPLE:** Lisa, a self-employed marketing consultant, gives a $200 Christmas gift to her best client. She may deduct $25 of the cost.

A gift to a member of a customer's family is treated as a gift to the customer, unless you have a legitimate nonbusiness connection to the family member. If you and your spouse both give gifts, you are treated as one taxpayer—it doesn't matter if you work together or have separate businesses.

The $25 limit applies only to gifts to individuals. It doesn't apply if you give a gift to an entire company, unless the gift is intended for a particular person or group of people within the company. Such company-wide gifts are deductible in any amount, as long as they are reasonable.

> **EXAMPLE:** Bob sells products to the Acme Company. Just before Christmas, he drops off a $100 cheese basket at the company's reception area for all of Acme's employees. He also delivers an identical basket to Acme's president. The first basket left in the reception area is a company-wide gift, not subject to the $25 limit. The basket for Acme's president is a personal gift and therefore is subject to the limit.

Insurance for Your Business

You can deduct the premiums you pay for any insurance you buy for your business as a business operating expense. This includes:
- medical insurance for your employees (see Chapter 13)
- fire, theft, and flood insurance for business property
- credit insurance that covers losses from business debts
- liability insurance

- professional malpractice insurance—for example, medical or legal malpractice insurance
- workers' compensation insurance you are required by state law to provide your employees (if you are an employee of an S corporation, the corporation can deduct workers' comp payments made on your behalf, but they must be included in your employee wages)
- business interruption insurance
- life insurance covering a corporation's officers and directors if you are not a direct beneficiary under the policy, and
- unemployment insurance contributions (either as insurance costs or business taxes, depending on how they are characterized by your state's laws).

Homeowners' Insurance for Your Home Office

If you have a home office and qualify for the home office deduction, you may deduct the home office percentage of your homeowners' or renters' insurance premiums. For example, if your home office takes up 20% of your home, you may deduct 20% of the premiums. You can deduct 100% of any special coverage that you add to your homeowners' or renters' policy for your home office and/or business property. For example, if you add an endorsement to your policy to cover business property, you can deduct 100% of the cost.

Car Insurance

If you use the actual expense method to deduct your car expenses, you can deduct the cost of insurance that covers liability, damages, and other losses for vehicles used in your business as a business expense. If you use a vehicle only for business, you can deduct 100% of your insurance costs. If you operate a vehicle for both business and personal use, you can deduct only the part of the insurance premiums that applies to the business use of your vehicle. For example, if you use a car 60% for business and 40% for personal reasons, you can deduct 60% of your insurance costs. (See Chapter 8.)

If you use the standard mileage rate to deduct your car expenses, you get no separate deduction for insurance. Your insurance costs are included in the standard rate. (See Chapter 8.)

Interest on Business Loans

Interest you pay on business loans is usually a currently deductible business expense. It makes no difference whether you pay the interest on a bank loan, personal loan, credit card, line of credit, car loan, or real estate mortgage. Nor does it matter whether the collateral you used to get the loan was business or personal property. If you use the money for business, the interest you pay to get that money is a deductible business expense. It's how you use the money that counts, not how you get it. Borrowed money is used for business when you buy something with the money that's deductible as a business expense.

> **EXAMPLE:** Max, the sole proprietor owner of a small construction company, borrows $50,000 from the bank to buy new construction equipment. He pays 6% interest on the loan. His annual interest expense is deductible on his Schedule C, Form 1040, because it is a business loan.

Your deduction begins only when you spend the borrowed funds for business purposes. You get no business deduction for interest you pay on money that you keep in the bank. Money in the bank is considered an investment—at best, you might be able to deduct the interest you pay on the money as an investment expense. (See "Deducting Investment Interest," below.)

How to Eliminate Nondeductible Personal Interest

Because interest on money you borrow for personal purposes—like buying clothes or taking vacations—is not deductible, you should avoid paying this type of interest whenever possible. If you own a business, you can do this by borrowing money to pay your business expense and then using the money your business earns to pay off your personal debt. By doing this, you "replace" your nondeductible personal interest expense with deductible business expenses.

Home Offices

If you are a homeowner and take the home office deduction, you can deduct the home office percentage of your home mortgage interest as a business expense. (See Chapter 7 for a detailed discussion of the home office deduction.)

Car Loans

If you use your car for business, you can deduct the interest that you pay on your car loan as an interest expense. You can take this deduction whether you deduct your car expenses using the actual expense method or the standard mileage rate, because the standard mileage rate was not intended to encompass interest on a car loan.

If you use your car only for business, you can deduct all of the interest you pay. If you use it for both business and personal reasons, you can deduct the business percentage of the interest. For example, if you use your car 60% of the time for business, you can deduct 60% of the interest you pay on your car loan.

Loans to Buy a Business

If you borrow money to buy an interest in an S corporation, partnership, or LLC, it's wise to seek an accountant's help to figure out how to deduct the interest on your loan. It must be allocated among the company's assets and, depending on what assets the business owns, the interest might be deductible as a business expense or an investment expense, which is more limited. (See "Deducting Investment Interest," below.)

Interest on money you borrow to buy stock in a C corporation is always treated as investment interest. This is true even if the corporation is small (also called "closely held") and its stock is not publicly traded.

Loans From Relatives and Friends

If you borrow money from a relative or friend and use it for business purposes, you may deduct the interest you pay on the loan as a business expense. However, the IRS is very suspicious of loans between family members and friends. You need to carefully document these transactions.

Treat the loan like any other business loan: sign a promissory note, pay a reasonable rate of interest, and follow a repayment schedule. Keep your cancelled loan payment checks to prove you really paid the interest.

Interest You Can't Deduct

You can't deduct interest:

- on loans used for personal purposes
- on debts your business doesn't owe
- on overdue taxes (only C corporations can deduct this interest)
- that you pay with funds borrowed from the original lender through a second loan (but you can deduct the interest once you start making payments on the new loan)
- that you prepay if you're a cash basis taxpayer (but you may deduct it the next year)
- on money borrowed to pay taxes or fund retirement plans, or
- on loans of more than $50,000 that are borrowed on a life insurance policy on yourself or another owner or employee of your business.

Points and other loan origination fees that you pay to get a mortgage on business property are not deductible business expenses. You must add these costs to the cost of the building and deduct them over time using depreciation. The same is true for interest on construction loans if you are in the business of building houses or other real property. Manufacturers of substantial amounts of goods—defined as goods worth $1 million or more, with an estimated production period of more than one year—must also depreciate the interest on money borrowed to produce their goods.

Deducting Investment Interest

Investing is not a business, so you get no business expense deduction for interest that you pay on money borrowed to make personal investments. You may take a personal deduction for investment interest, but you may not deduct more than your net annual income from your investments. Any amount that you can't deduct in the current year can be carried over to the next year and deducted then.

EXAMPLE: Donald borrows $10,000 on his credit card to invest in the stock market. The interest he pays on the debt is deductible as an itemized personal deduction he lists on his Schedule A, Form 1040. He cannot deduct more than he earned during the year from his investments.

Get Separate Credit Cards for Your Business and Car Expenses

If you use the same credit card for your business and nonbusiness expenses, you are theoretically entitled to a business deduction for the credit card interest on your business expenses. However, you'll have a very difficult time calculating exactly how much of the interest you pay is for business expenses. To avoid this problem, use a separate credit card for business. This can be a special business credit card, but it doesn't have to be. You can simply designate one of your ordinary credit cards for business use. If you drive for business and use the actual expense method to take your deduction, it's a good idea to use another credit card just for car expenses. This will make it much easier to keep track of what you spend on your car.

Always pay your personal credit cards first, because you can't deduct the interest you pay on those costs.

Keeping Track of Borrowed Money

As mentioned above, you may deduct interest on borrowed money only if you use the money for business purposes. But if you deposit the money in a bank account that you use to pay both business and personal bills, how do you know what you spent the money on?

EXAMPLE: Linda borrows $10,000 from the bank and deposits it in her checking account. The account already contains $5,000. Over the next several months, she writes checks to pay for food, her mortgage, personal clothing, the rent on her office, and office furniture and a computer for her business. How does Linda know whether the money she borrowed was used for her business expenses or personal expenses?

As you might expect, the IRS has plenty of rules to deal with this problem.

30-Day Rule

If you buy something for your business within 30 days of borrowing money, the IRS presumes that the payment was made from those loan proceeds (up to the amount of the loan proceeds). This is true regardless of the method or bank account you use to pay the business expense. If you receive the loan proceeds in cash, you can treat the payment as made on the date you receive the cash instead of the date you actually make the payment.

> **EXAMPLE:** Frank gets a loan of $1,000 on August 4 and receives the proceeds in cash. Frank deposits $1,500 in his bank account on August 18 and on August 28 writes a check on the account for a business expense. Also, Frank deposits his paycheck and other loan proceeds into the account and pays his bills from the account during the same period. Regardless of these other transactions, Frank can treat $1,000 of the deposit he made on August 18 as being paid on August 4 from the loan proceeds. In addition, Frank can treat the business expense he paid on August 28 as made from the $1,000 loan proceeds deposited in the account.

Allocation Rules

If you don't satisfy the 30-day rule, special allocation rules determine how loan proceeds deposited in a bank account were spent for tax purposes. Generally, the IRS will assume that loan proceeds were used (spent) before:

* any unborrowed amounts held in the same account, and
* any amounts deposited after the loan proceeds.

> **EXAMPLE:** On January 9, Edith opened a checking account, depositing a $5,000 bank loan and $1,000 in unborrowed money. On February 13, Edith takes $1,000 from the account for personal

purposes. On February 15, she takes out $5,000 to buy equipment for her business. Edith must treat the $1,000 used for personal purposes as made from the loan proceeds, leaving only $4,000 of the loan in the account for tax purposes. As a result, she may deduct as a business expense the interest she pays on only $4,000 of the $5,000 she used to buy the business equipment.

It's easy to avoid having to deal with these complex allocation rules: If you think you'll need to keep borrowed money in the bank for more than 30 days before you spend it on your business, place it in a separate account.

Legal and Professional Services

You can deduct fees that you pay to attorneys, accountants, consultants, and other professionals as business expenses if the fees are paid for work related to your business.

> **EXAMPLE:** Ira, a freelance writer, hires attorney Jake to represent him in a libel suit. The legal fees Ira pays Jake are a deductible business expense.

Legal and professional fees that you pay for personal purposes generally are not deductible. For example, you can't deduct the legal fees you incur if you get divorced or you sue someone for a traffic accident injury. Nor are the fees that you pay to write your will deductible, even if the will covers business property that you own.

Buying Long-Term Property

If you pay legal or other fees in the course of buying long-term business property, you must add the amount of the fee to the tax basis (cost) of the property. You may deduct this cost over several years through depreciation or deduct it in one year under IRC Section 179. (See Chapter 5 for more on depreciation.)

Starting a Business

Legal and accounting fees that you pay to start a business are deductible only as business start-up expenses. You can deduct $5,000 of start-up expenses the first year you're in business and any amounts over $5,000 over 180 months. The same holds true for incorporation fees or fees that you pay to form a partnership or LLC. (See Chapter 3 for more or start-up expenses.)

Accounting Fees

You can deduct any accounting fees that you pay for your business as a deductible business expense—for example, fees you pay an accountant to set up or keep your business books, prepare your business tax return, or give you tax advice for your business.

Self-employed taxpayers may deduct the cost of having an accountant or other tax professional complete the business portion of their tax returns—Schedule C and other business tax forms—but they cannot deduct the time the preparer spends on the personal part of their returns. If you are self-employed and pay a tax preparer to complete your Form 1040 income tax return, make sure that you get an itemized bill showing the portion of the tax preparation fee allocated to preparing your Schedule C (and any other business tax forms attached to your Form 1040).

Taxes and Licenses

Most taxes that you pay in the course of your business are deductible.

Income Taxes

Federal income taxes that you pay on your business income are not deductible. However, a corporation or partnership can deduct state or local income taxes it pays. Individuals may deduct state and local income taxes only as an itemized deduction on Schedule A, Form 1040. This is a personal, not a business, deduction. However, an individual can deduct state tax on gross business income as a business expense—for example, Michigan has a Single Business Tax of 2% on business gross receipts over $250,000. This tax is a federally deductible business operating expense. Of course, you can't deduct state taxes from your income for state income tax purposes.

Self-Employment Taxes

If you are a sole proprietor, partner in a partnership, or LLC member, you may deduct one-half of your self-employment taxes from your total net business income. This deduction reduces the amount of income on which you must pay personal income tax. It's an adjustment to gross income, not a business deduction. You don't list it on your Schedule C; instead, you take it on page one of your Form 1040.

The self-employment tax is a 15.3% tax, so your deduction is equal to 7.65% of your income. To figure out your income after taking this deduction, multiply your net business income by 92.35% or .9235.

> **EXAMPLE:** Billie, a self-employed consultant, earned $70,000 from her business and had $20,000 in business expenses. Her net business income was $50,000. She multiplies this amount by .9235 to determine her net self-employment income, which is $46,175. This is the amount on which Billie must pay federal income tax.

This deduction is intended to help ease the tax burden on the self-employed.

Employment Taxes

If you have employees, you must pay half of their Social Security and Medicare taxes from your own funds and withhold the other half from their pay. These taxes consist of a 12.4% Social Security tax, up to an annual salary cap ($94,200 in 2006), and a 2.9% Medicare tax on all employees' pay. You may deduct half of this amount as a business expense. You should treat the taxes you withhold from your employees' pay as wages paid to your employees on your tax return.

> **EXAMPLE:** You pay your employee $18,000 a year. However, after you withhold employment taxes, your employee receives $14,500. You also pay an additional $1,500 in employment taxes from your

own funds. You should deduct the full $18,000 salary as employee wages and deduct the $1,500 as employment taxes paid.

Sales Taxes

You may not deduct state and local sales taxes on your goods and services that you are required to collect from the buyer and turn over to your state or local government. Do not include these taxes in gross receipts or sales.

However, you may deduct sales taxes that you pay when you purchase goods or services for your business. The amount of the tax is added to the cost of the goods or services for purposes of your deduction for the item.

> **EXAMPLE:** Jean, a self-employed carpenter, buys $100 worth of nails from the local hardware store. She had to pay $7.50 in state and local sales taxes on the purchase. She may take a $107.50 deduction for the nails. She claims the deduction on her Schedule C as a purchase of supplies.

If you buy a long-term business asset, the sales taxes must be added to its basis (cost) for purposes of depreciation or expensing under IRC Section 179.

> **EXAMPLE:** Jean buys a $2,000 power saw for her carpentry business. She pays $150 in state and local sales tax. The saw has a useful life of more than one year and is therefore a long-term business asset for tax purposes. She can't currently deduct the cost as a business operating expense. Instead, Jean must depreciate the cost over several years or expense the cost (deduct the full cost in one year) under Section 179. The total cost to be depreciated or expensed is $2,150.

Real Property Taxes

You can deduct your current year's state and local property taxes on business real property as business expenses. However, if you prepay the next year's property taxes, you may not deduct the prepaid amount until the following year.

Home Offices

The only real property most small business people own is their home. If you are a homeowner and take the home office deduction, you may deduct the home office percentage of your property taxes. However, as a homeowner, you are entitled to deduct all of your mortgage interest and property taxes, regardless of whether you have a home office. Taking the home office deduction won't increase your income tax deductions for your property taxes, but it will allow you to deduct them from your income for the purpose of calculating your self-employment taxes. You'll save $153 in self-employment taxes for every $1,000 in property taxes you deduct (15.3% self-employment tax x $1,000 = $153).

> **EXAMPLE:** Suzy uses 20% of her three-bedroom Tulsa home as a home office. She pays $10,000 per year in mortgage interest and property taxes. By taking the home office deduction, she gets to deduct this amount from her income for self-employment tax purposes, which saves her $1,530.

Charges for Services

Water bills, sewer charges, and other service charges assessed against your business property are not real estate taxes, but they are deductible as business expenses. If you have a home office, you can deduct your home office percentage of these items.

However, real estate taxes imposed to fund specific local benefits such as streets, sewer lines, and water mains are not deductible as business expenses. Because these benefits increase the value of your property, you should add what you pay for them to the tax basis (cost for tax purposes) of your property.

Buying and Selling Real Estate

When real estate is sold, the real estate taxes must be divided between the buyer and seller according to how many days of the tax year each held ownership of the property. You'll usually find information on this in the settlement statement you receive at the property closing.

Other Taxes

Other deductible taxes include:

- excise taxes—for example, Hawaii imposes a general excise tax on businesses ranging from .5% to 4% of gross receipts
- state unemployment compensation taxes or state disability contributions
- corporate franchise taxes
- occupational taxes charged at a flat rate by your city or county for the privilege of doing business, and
- state and local taxes on personal property—for example, equipment or machinery that you use in your business.

You can deduct taxes on gasoline, diesel fuel, and other motor fuels that you use in your business. However, these taxes are usually included as part of the cost of the fuel. For this reason, you usually do not deduct these taxes separately on your return. However, you may be entitled to a tax credit for federal excise tax that you pay on fuels used for certain purposes—for example, farming or off-highway business use. See IRS Publication 378, *Fuel Tax Credits and Refunds* (available from the IRS website at www.irs.gov).

License Fees

License fees imposed on your business by your local or state government are deductible business expenses.

Domestic Production Activities

A brand-new business tax deduction came into effect in 2005: the domestic production activities deduction (IRC § 199.) This deduction is intended to give a tax break to businesses that hire employees to produce goods or engage in certain other manufacturing or production activities within the United States, rather than farming out the work overseas. It's very complicated, so we give only a brief overview of how the deduction works.

Activities That Qualify for the Deduction

Domestic production activities consist of:

- Any sale, lease, rental, license, exchange, or other disposition of tangible personal property, computer software, or sound recordings that you manufactured, produced, grew, or extracted, in whole or in significant part, within the United States.
- Construction performed in the United States—including both new buildings and substantial renovations of existing buildings. However, rental income from real property isn't eligible for the deduction.
- Engineering or architectural services performed in the United States for construction projects in the United States.
- Films and videos you produced if at least 50% of the production work was performed in the United States. (Sexually explicit films and videos are excluded.)
- Electricity, natural gas, or potable water you produced in the United States.

The first category mentioned above—the tangible personal property category—is by far the broadest and most inclusive category. If you produce any tangible personal property "in significant part" in the United States and later dispose of it by sale or otherwise in the course of your business, you may be entitled to a deduction. According to the IRS, "significant part" means that the labor and overhead incurred in the United States was at least 20% of the total cost of the property. (IRS Notice 2005-14.)

Tangible personal property is any tangible property other than land, buildings, and structural components of buildings, including:

- clothing
- goods
- food
- books
- magazines
- newspapers
- production machinery
- printing presses
- transportation and office equipment

- testing equipment
- display racks and shelves
- neon and other signs
- hydraulic car lifts, and
- automatic vending machines.

Many businesses other than traditional manufacturers fall under this broad definition. Almost any activity relating to manufacturing, producing, growing, extracting, installing, developing, improving, or creating tangible personal property qualifies for the deduction. This includes making tangible property from new or raw material, or by combining or assembling two or more articles.

> **EXAMPLE:** Barbee owns a crafts business. She has two employees who make leather belts from raw leather Barbee purchases. The belts qualify as tangible personal property produced in significant part in the United States. Barbee's activity qualifies for the domestic production deduction.

Excluded Activities

Design and development costs, including packaging, labeling, and minor assembly operations, are not domestic production activities. Also not included is personal property you lease, license, or rent to a person related to you. The deduction also does not apply to income derived from the sale of food and beverages you prepare at a retail establishment.

Tangible Personal Property Mixed With Services

If you produce tangible personal property as a part of a service you provide customers, you can still obtain the deduction. But you must separately allocate the income you earn from your service and from your production activities. Only the production activity income qualifies for the deduction. However, an exception applies if you earn less than 5% of your gross receipts from providing a service.

EXAMPLE: Marcus is a doctor with his own practice, but he also runs a medical lab that performs medical tests. The work his lab does qualifies as a domestic production activity, but the medical services he provides his patients do not. If his income from the lab is more than 5% of his total gross income, Marcus must separately allocate the income he receives from the lab and from his medical practice. Only the lab income can qualify for the domestic production activities deduction.

Amount of Deduction

For 2006, the deduction is 3% of the income you earn from your domestic production activities. Income means your gross receipts from a production activity reduced by the cost of goods sold and related expenses, including the cost of production and a portion of your indirect expenses such as rent. The deduction will increase in later years as shown in the following chart.

Year	Deduction for Domestic Production Activities
2005-2006	3%
2007-2009	6%
2010 and later	9%

Limits on the Deduction

The domestic production activities deduction is intended to encourage businesses to hire more employees in the United States and, thereby, benefit the American public. Thus, a business can qualify for the deduction only if it has employees. For example, if you have a one-person business and do all the work yourself or use independent contractors to do the work you don't do, you get no deduction, because you have no employees.

Whether a person is an employee is determined according to common law rules. Under these rules, anyone you have the right to control on the job is your employee. People who work for you that you don't control are independent contractors, not employees. (See Chapter 11.)

If you have employees, you can get the deduction if you meet all the other requirements. However, it cannot exceed 50% of the total wages you paid to employees engaged in domestic production activities. For example, if your total annual payroll is $100,000, your total domestic production activities deduction is limited to $50,000. Obviously, you can increase your deduction limit if you hire more employees instead of doing work yourself or hiring independent contactors. However, the value of the deduction may not justify the increased expense of having employees.

There is one more significant limitation on the deduction: It may not exceed your adjusted gross income if you're a sole proprietor or the owner of an LLC, partnership, or S corporation. If you own a C corporation, the deduction may not exceed the corporation's taxable income. Thus, businesses that don't earn a profit and pay no taxes get no domestic production activities deduction.

If you want to take this deduction, seek guidance from a tax professional. It may increase your bookkeeping and accounting burdens. It could also subject you to the uniform capitalization rules. (IRC § 263A.) These rules prevent you from taking a current business deduction for the direct, and some indirect, costs incurred in production activities. Thus, for example, you could be prohibited from currently deducting all or part of your labor and overhead costs. Instead, you recover the costs through depreciation, amortization, or deducting the cost of goods sold when you sell or otherwise dispose of the property. This can take much longer than obtaining a current deduction.

Chapter 15

Record Keeping and Accounting

W hen you incur business expenses, you get tax deductions and save money on your taxes. But those deductions are only as good as the records you keep to back them up.

This is what Alton Williams, a schoolteacher with a sideline business selling new and used books, found out when he was audited by the IRS. Over a four-year period, he claimed over $70,000 in business deductions and inventory costs from his business. Unfortunately, he had no records or receipts tracking these expenses. His excuse: "A receipt is something I never thought I would actually need." The auditor reduced his deductions for each year by 50% to 70%, and Williams ended up owing the IRS almost $10,000. (*Williams v. Commissioner*, 67 TC Memo 2185 (1994).)

Any expense you forget to deduct, or lose after an IRS audit because you can't back it up, costs you dearly. Every $100 in unclaimed deductions costs the average midlevel-income person (in a 25% tax bracket) $43 in additional federal and state income and self-employment taxes.

Luckily, it's not difficult to keep records of your business expenses. In this chapter, we'll show you how to document your expenditures so you won't end up losing your hard-earned business deductions.

Basic Record Keeping for Tax Deductions

This section explains how to set up a basic system for keeping track of your deductible expenses. All you need is:

- a business checking account
- an appointment book
- an expense journal, and
- supporting documents, such as receipts.

This system will get you started—it is by no means everything you'll need for your business record keeping. For example, every business must keep track of its income. If you make or sell merchandise, you will have to also keep inventory records. And if you have employees, you must create and keep a number of records, including payroll tax records, withholding records, and employment tax returns.

 For an excellent overall guide to small business bookkeeping, refer to *Small Time Operator*, by Bernard B. Kamoroff (Bell Springs Press).

Business Checkbook and Credit Cards

One of the first things you should do (if you haven't done it already) is to set up a separate checking account for your business. Your business checkbook will serve as your basic source of information for recording your business expenses and income. Deposit all your business receipts (checks you receive from clients, for example) into the account and make all business-related payments by check from the account. Don't use your business account to pay for personal expenses or your personal account to pay for business items.

A separate business checkbook is legally required if you've formed a corporation, partnership, or LLC. Keeping a separate business account is not legally required if you're a sole proprietor, but it will provide these important benefits:

- It will be much easier for you to keep track of your business income and expenses if you pay them from a separate account.
- Your business account will clearly separate your personal and business finances; this will prove very helpful if you're audited by the IRS.
- Your business account will help convince the IRS that you are running a business and not engaged in a hobby. Hobbyists don't generally have separate bank accounts for their hobbies. This is a huge benefit if you incur losses from your business, because losses from hobbies are not fully deductible. (See Chapter 2 for more on the hobby loss rule.)

Setting Up Your Bank Account

Your business checking account should be in your business name. If you're a sole proprietor, this can be your own name. If you've formed a corporation, partnership, or limited liability company, the account should be in your corporate, partnership, or company name.

You don't need to open your business checking account at the same bank where you have your personal checking account. Shop around and open your account with the bank that offers you the best services at the lowest price.

If you're doing business under your own name, consider opening up a second account in that name and using it solely for your business instead of a separate business account. You'll usually pay less for a personal account than for a business account.

If you're a sole proprietor doing business under an assumed name, you'll likely have to give your bank a copy of your fictitious business name statement.

If you've incorporated your business, call your bank and ask what documentation is required to open the account. You will probably need to show the bank a corporate resolution authorizing the opening of a bank account and showing the names of the people authorized to sign checks. Typically, you will also have to fill out, and impress your corporate seal on, a separate bank account authorization form provided by your bank. You will also need to have a federal employer identification number.

Similarly, if you've established a partnership or limited liability company, you'll likely have to show the bank a resolution authorizing the account.

You may also want to establish interest-bearing accounts for your business in which you place cash you don't immediately need. For example, you may decide to set up a business savings account or a money market mutual fund in your business name.

When You Write Checks

If you already keep an accurate, updated personal checkbook, do the same for your business checkbook. If, however, like many people, you tend to be lax in keeping up your checkbook, you're going to have to change your habits. Now that you're in business, you can't afford this kind of carelessness. Unless you write large numbers of business checks, maintaining your checkbook won't take much time.

When you write business checks, you may have to make some extra notations besides the date, number, amount of the check, and name of the person or company to which the check is written. If it's not clear from the name of the payee what a check is for, describe the business reason for the check—for example, the equipment or service you purchased.

You can use the register that comes with your checkbook and write in all this information manually, or you can use a computerized register. Either way works fine as long as the information is complete and up-to-date. (See "Records Required for Specific Expenses," below, to find out what information you need for various types of expenses.)

Don't Write Checks for Cash

Avoid writing checks payable to cash, because this makes it hard to tell whether you spent the money for a business purpose. Writing cash checks might lead to questions from the IRS if you're audited. If you must write a check for cash to pay a business expense, be sure to include the receipt for the cash payment in your records.

Use a Separate Credit Card for Business

Use a separate credit card for business expenses instead of putting both personal and business items on one card. Credit card interest for business purchases is 100% deductible, while interest for personal purchases is not deductible at all. (See Chapter 2.) Using a separate card for business purchases will make it much easier for you to keep track of how much interest you've paid for business purchases. The card doesn't have to be in your business name. It can just be one of your personal credit cards.

Appointment Book

The next item you need is an appointment book, day planner, tax diary, or calendar. You can find inexpensive ones in any stationery store. Many computerized calendars are available as well. However, a calendar completed by hand in ink will always be more convincing to the IRS than one you create on a computer, because it is very easy to forge or alter a computerized calendar.

Properly used, this humble item will:

- provide solid evidence that you are serious about making a profit from your business, and thereby avoid having the IRS claim that your activity is a hobby (see Chapter 2 for more on businesses versus hobbies).

- help show that the expenses you incur are for business, not personal purposes
- help verify entertainment, meal, and travel expenses
- enable you to use a sampling method to keep track of business mileage, instead of keeping track of every mile you drive all year (see "Records Required for Specific Expenses," below), and
- if you claim a home office deduction, help show that you use your office for business.

EXAMPLE: Tom, a self-employed advertising copywriter who worked out of his Florida home, kept a detailed appointment book. He devoted a page to each day, listing all of his business activities. He also kept a mileage log to record his business mileage. When he was audited by the IRS, the auditor picked out a trip from his mileage log at random and asked him the purpose of the trip. Tom looked at his appointment book entry for that day and was able to truthfully and credibly tell the auditor that the trip was to visit a client. The auditor accepted his explanation and the rest of his business mileage deductions.

Every day you work, you should write down in your appointment book (in ink):

- the name of every person you talk to for business
- the date, time, and place of every business meeting
- every place you go for business
- the amount of all travel, meal, and entertainment expenses that are below $75, and
- if you claim the home office deduction, the time you spend working in your office.

Here's a sample page from an appointment book for a self-employed real salesperson. (You'll find information in "Records Required for Specific Expenses," below, on what information you need to list for different types of expenses.)

Sunday	Monday	Tuesday	Wednesday	Thursday	Friday	Saturday
	1 Meeting with Earl Crowler	2	3 Show 111 Green St.	4 Answer phones	5 Sales Meeting	6
7 Open House 111 Green St.	8	9 Sales Meeting	10 Lunch Gibbons	11	12 Meeting Kim Mann	13 Prepare for open house— Green St.
14 Open House 222 Blue St.	15	16 Show Gibbon 222 Blue St.	17	18 Lunch Mortgage Broker	19 Sales Meeting	20
21 Open House 456 Main St.	22	23 Sales Meeting	24 Lunch Mortgage Broker	25 Breakfast Kiwanis Club	26 Sales Meeting	27
28 Open House 826 3rd St.	29 Continuing education seminar	30	31			

Expense Journal

You can track your expenses by creating what accountants call a chart of accounts—a listing by category of all your expenses. This will show what you buy for your business and how much you spent. It's very easy to do this. You can write your chart out on paper or you can set up a computer spreadsheet program, such as *Excel* or *Lotus*, to do it. Or, if you already have or would prefer to use a financial computer program such as *Quicken*, you can do that instead.

Creating a Paper Expense Journal

You can easily create an expense journal by using paper divided into columns or a professional multicolumn book you can get from any stationery or office supply store. These multicolumn pages are also called "ledger sheets." Get ledger sheets with at least 12 or 14 columns. Devote a separate column to each major category of expenses you have. Alternatively, you can purchase accounting record books with the expense categories already printed on them. These cost more, however, and may not offer categories that meet your needs.

To decide what your expense categories should be, sit down with your bills and receipts and sort them into categorized piles. IRS Schedule C, the tax form sole proprietors must use to list their expenses, contains categories of business expenses. These categories are a good place to start when you devise your own list, because you'll have to use the ones that apply to you when you complete your Schedule C for your taxes. The Schedule C categories include:

- advertising
- bad debts
- car and truck expenses
- commissions and fees
- depletion (rarely used by most small business)
- depreciation and Section 179 expense deductions
- employee benefit programs
- insurance (other than health)
- interest
- legal and professional services
- office expenses
- pension and profit-sharing plans
- rent or lease—vehicles, machinery, and equipment
- rent or lease—other business property
- repairs and maintenance
- supplies
- taxes and licenses
- travel
- meals and entertainment
- utilities, and
- wages.

The Schedule C list of business categories is by no means exclusive. (In fact, it used to contain more categories.) It just gives you an idea of how to break down your expenses. Depending on the nature of your business, you may not need all these categories or you might have others. For example, a graphic designer might have categories for printing and typesetting expenses, or a writer might have a category for agent fees.

You should always include a final category called Miscellaneous for various and sundry expenses that are not easily pigeonholed. However, you should use this category sparingly, to account for less than 10% of your total expenses. Unlike "travel" or "advertising," "miscellaneous" is not a type of business expense. It's just a place to lump together different types of expenses that don't fit into another category.

You can add or delete expense categories as you go along—for example, if you find your miscellaneous category contains many items for a particular type of expense, add it as an expense category. You don't need a category for automobile expenses, because these expenses require a different kind of documentation for tax purposes.

In separate columns, list the check number, date, and name of the person or company paid for each payment. If you pay by credit card or cash, indicate it in the check number column.

Once a month, go through your check register, credit card slips, receipts, and other expense records and record the required information for each transaction. Also, total the amounts for each category when you come to the end of the page and keep a running total of what you've spent for each category for the year to date.

The following example shows a portion of an expense journal.

Expense Journal

Date	Check No.	Transaction	Amount	Adver-tising	Outside Contractors	Utilities	Supplies	Rent	Travel	Equip-ment	Meals & Entertain-ment	Misc.
5/1	123	ABC Properties	500					500				
5/1	124	Office Warehouse	150				150					
5/10	VISA	Computer World	1,000							1,000		
5/15	VISA	Cafe Ole'	50								50	
5/16	Cash	Sam's Stationery	50				50					
5/18	125	Electric Co.	50			50						
5/30	126	Bill Carter	5,050		500							
Total This Page			2,300		500	50	200	500		1,000	50	
Total Year to Date			7,900	200	2,000	250	400	2,500	300	1,500	250	500

Using Computer Financial Programs

There are many computer programs designed to help people and businesses keep track of their finances. These range from relatively simple checkbook programs like *Quicken* to complex and sophisticated accounting programs like *QuickBooks Pro* and *MYOB*. You can use these in place of the handwritten ledger sheets or simple spreadsheets described above. However, you'll be better off using handwritten ledger sheets, which are easy to create and understand and simple to keep up to date, instead of a complicated computer program that you don't understand or use properly. So, if you're not prepared to invest the time to use a computer program correctly, don't use it!

We won't discuss how to use these programs in detail. You'll need to read the manual and/or tutorial that comes with the program you choose. There are also books that explain how to use them—for example, *Using Quicken in a Business*, by Stephen Nelson, CPA. (Redmond Technology Press).

Before You Purchase a Program

You don't want to spend your hard-earned money on a financial program only to discover that you don't like it. Before you purchase a program:

- talk to others in similar businesses to find out what they use— if they don't like a program, ask them why
- think carefully about how many features you need—the more complex the program, the harder it will be to learn and use it, and
- obtain a demo version you can try out for free to see if you like it—you can usually download one from the software company's website.

The simplest financial programs are those like *Quicken* and *MS Money* that work off of a computerized checkbook. When you buy something for your business, you write a check using the program. It automatically inputs the data into a computerized check register, and you print out the check using your computer (payments can also be made online). You'll have to input credit card and cash payments separately.

You create a list of expense categories just like you do when you create a ledger sheet or spreadsheet. Programs like *Quicken* come with preselected categories, but these are not adequate for many businesses, so you'll probably have to create your own. The expense category is automatically noted in your register when you write a check.

The program can then take this information and automatically create income and expense reports—that is, it will show you the amounts you've spent or earned for each category. This serves the same function as the expense journal. It can also create profit and loss statements. You can even import these amounts into tax preparation software, such as *TurboTax*, when it's time to do your income taxes.

Quicken or *MS Money* provides all the tools many small service businesses need. However, if your business involves selling goods or maintaining an inventory, or if you have employees, you'll need a more sophisticated program. Other programs (such as *MYOB Account Edge* and *Plus* by MYOB, *Peachtree Accounting* by Peachtree Software, and *QuickBooks* by Intuit) can accomplish more complex bookkeeping tasks, such as double-entry bookkeeping, tracking inventory, payroll, invoicing, handling accounts receivable, and maintaining fixed asset records.

Supporting Documents

The IRS lives by the maxim that "figures lie and liars figure." It knows very well that you can claim anything in your books and on your tax returns, because you create or complete them yourself. For this reason, the IRS requires that you have documents to support the deductions you claim on your tax return. In the absence of a supporting document, an IRS auditor may conclude that an item you claim as a business expense is really a personal expense, or that you never bought the item at all. Either way, your deduction will be disallowed.

The supporting documents you need depend on the type of deduction involved. However, at a minimum, every deduction should be supported by documentation showing what, how much, and who. That is, your supporting documents should show:

- what you purchased for your business
- how much you paid for it, and
- whom (or what company) you bought it from.

Additional record-keeping requirements must be met for deductions for local transportation, travel, entertainment, meal, and gift deductions, as well as for certain long-term assets that you buy for your business. ("Records Required for Specific Expenses," below, covers these rules.)

You can meet the what, how much, and who requirements by keeping the following types of documentation:

- canceled checks
- sales receipts
- account statements
- credit card sales slips
- invoices, or
- petty cash slips for small cash payments.

Keep your supporting documents in a safe place. If you don't have a lot of receipts and other documents to save, you can simply keep them all in a single folder. If you have a lot of supporting documents to save or are the type of person who likes to be extremely well organized, separate your documents by category—for example, income, travel expenses, or equipment purchases. You can use a separate file folder for each category or get an accordion file with multiple pockets.

Canceled Check + Receipt = Proof of Deduction

Manny, a self-employed photographer, buys a $500 digital camera for his business from the local electronics store. He writes a check for the amount and is given a receipt. How does he prove to the IRS that he has a $500 business expense?

Could Manny simply save his canceled check when it's returned from his bank? Many people carefully save all their canceled checks (some keep them for decades), apparently believing that a canceled check is all the proof they need to show that a purchase was a legitimate business expense. This is not the case. All a canceled check proves is that you spent money for something. It doesn't show what you bought. Of course, you can write a note on your check stating what you purchased, but why should the IRS believe what you write on your checks yourself?

MANNY FARBER
123 SHADY LANE
ANYTOWN, IL 12345

Date Feb. 1, 2007　　12-046780

Pay to the order of　Acme Camera Store　　$ 500.00

Five hundred and 100/100 ~～～～　Dollars

Piggy Bank
100 Main Street
Anytown, IL 12345

Memo　Digital Camera　　Manny Farber

⑆ 578000358⑆ 5355 ⑈ 05556 ⑈ 05555 ⑈

Does Manny's sales receipt prove he bought his camera for his business? Again, no. A sales receipt only proves that somebody purchased the item listed in the receipt. It does not show who purchased it. Again, you could write a note on the receipt stating that you bought the item. But you could easily lie. Indeed, for all the IRS knows, you could hang around stores and pick up receipts people throw away to give yourself tax deductions.

509257

CUSTOMER'S ORDER NO. 14601		DATE February 1, 2007					
NAME							
ADDRESS							
CITY, STATE, ZIP							
SOLD BY SF	CASH	C.O.D.	CHARGE	ON ACCT.	MDSE. RETD.	PAID OUT	

QUAN.		DESCRIPTION	PRICE	AMOUNT
1	1	Minolta Digital Camera	500	500
2				
3				
4				
5				
6				
7				
8				
9				
10				
11			Total	500
12				

RECEIVED BY

KEEP THIS SLIP FOR REFERENCE

However, when you put a canceled check together with a sales receipt (or an invoice, a cash register tape, or a similar document), you have concrete proof that you purchased the item listed in the receipt. The check proves that you bought something, and the receipt proves what that something is.

This doesn't necessarily prove that you bought the item for your business, but it's a good start. Often, the face of a receipt, the sales slip, or the payee's name on your canceled check will strongly indicate that the item you purchased was for your business. But if it's not clear, note what the purchase was for on the document. Such a note is not proof of how you used the item, but it will be helpful. For some types of items that you use for both business and personal purposes—cameras are one example—you might be required to keep careful records of your use. (See "Records Required for Specified Expenses," below.)

Credit Cards

Using a credit card is a great way to pay business expenses. The credit card slip will prove that you bought the item listed on the slip. You'll also have a monthly statement to back up your credit card slips. You should use a separate credit card for your business.

Account Statements

Sometimes, you'll need to use an account statement to prove an expense. Some banks no longer return canceled checks, or you may pay for something with an ATM card or another electronic funds transfer method. Moreover, you may not always have a credit card slip when you pay by credit card—for example, when you buy an item over the Internet. In these events, the IRS will accept an account statement as proof that you purchased the item. The chart below shows what type of information you need on an account statement.

Proving Payments With Bank Statements	
If payment is by:	**The statement must show:**
Check	Check number Amount Payee's name Date the check amount was posted to the account by the bank
Electronic funds transfer	Amount transferred Payee's name Date the amount transferred was posted to the account by the bank
Credit card	Amount charged Payee's name Transaction date

Records Required for Specific Expenses

The IRS is particularly suspicious of business deductions people take for local transportation, travel, meals, gift, and entertainment expenses. It knows that many people wildly inflate these deductions—either because they're dishonest or because they haven't kept good records and make estimates of how much they think they must have spent. For this reason, special record-keeping requirements apply to these deductions. Likewise, there are special requirements for long-term assets that can be used for both personal and business purposes. If you fail to comply with the requirements discussed below, the IRS may disallow the deduction, even if it was legitimate.

Automobile Mileage and Expense Records

If you use a car or other vehicle for business purposes other than just commuting to and from work, you're entitled to take a deduction for gas and other auto expenses. You can either deduct the actual cost of your gas and other expenses or take the standard rate deduction based on the number of business miles you drive. In 2006, the standard rate was 44.5 cents per mile. (See Chapter 8 for more on car expenses.)

Either way, you must keep a record of:

- your mileage
- the dates of your business trips
- the places you drove for business, and
- the business purpose for your trips.

The last three items are relatively easy to keep track of. You can record the information in your appointment book, calendar, or day planner. Or, you can record it in a mileage logbook—you can get one for a few dollars from any stationery store and stash it in your car glove compartment.

No Documentation Needed for Utilitarian Vehicles

All this documentation is not required for vehicles that ordinarily are not driven for personal use—for example, ambulances, hearses, trucks weighing more than 14,000 pounds, cement mixers, cranes, tractors, garbage trucks, dump trucks, forklifts, moving vans, and delivery trucks with seating only for the driver or seating only for the driver plus a folding jump seat. But you still need to keep track of your gas, repair, and other expenses.

Calculating your mileage takes more work. The IRS wants to know the total number of miles you drove during the year for business, commuting, and personal driving other than commuting. Commuting is travel from home to your office or other principal place of business. If you work from a home office, you'll have no commuting mileage. (See Chapter 8 for more on commuting and automobile expenses.) Personal miles other than commuting include all the driving you do other than from home to your office—for example, to the grocery store, on a personal vacation, or to visit friends or relatives.

Claiming a Car Is Used Solely for Business

If you use a car 100% for business, you don't need to keep track of your personal or commuting miles. However, you can successfully claim to use a car 100% for business only if you:

- work out of a tax deductible home office
- have at least two cars, and
- use one car just for business trips.

If you don't work from a home office, your trips from home to your outside office are nonbusiness commuting, so the car you take from home to your office is not used 100% for business, even if you drive it only for business after you get to your office and then drive straight home.

There are several ways to keep track of your mileage; some are easy, and some are a bit more complicated.

52-Week Mileage Book

The hardest way to track your mileage—and the way the IRS would like you to do it—is to keep track of every mile you drive every day, 52 weeks a year, using a mileage logbook or business diary. This means you'll list every trip you take, whether for business, commuting, or personal reasons. If you enjoy record keeping, go ahead and use this method. But there are easier ways.

Tracking Business Mileage

An easier way to keep track of your mileage is to record your mileage only when you use your car for business. Here's what to do:

- Obtain a mileage logbook and keep it in your car with a pen attached.
- Note your odometer reading in the logbook at beginning and end of every year that you use the car for business. (If you don't know your January 1 odometer reading for this year, you might be able to estimate it by looking at auto repair receipts that note your mileage.)

- Record your mileage and note the business purpose for the trip every time you use your car for business.
- Add up your business mileage when you get to the end of each page in the logbook. (This way, you'll have to add only the page totals at the end of the year instead of all the individual entries).
- If you commute to your office or other workplace, figure out how many miles you drive each way and note in your appointment book how many times you drive to the office each week.

Below is a portion of a page from a mileage logbook.

At the end of the year, your logbook will show the total business miles you drove during the year. You calculate the total miles you drove during the year by subtracting your January 1 odometer reading from your December 31 reading.

If you use the actual expense method, you must also calculate your percentage of business use of the car. You do this by dividing your business miles by your total miles.

Mileage Log

Date	Business Purpose	Odometer Reading Begin	End	Business Miles
5/1	Visit Art Andrews—potential client	10,111	10,196	85
5/4	Delivered documents to Bill James in Stockton	10,422	10,476	54
5/5	Picked up office supplies	10,479	10,489	10
5/8	Meeting—Acme Corp.—Sacramento	10,617	10,734	117
5/10	Lunch with Stu Smith—client	10,804	10,841	37
5/13	Meeting—Acme Corp.—Sacramento	10,987	11,004	117
5/15	Breakfast—Mary Moss—client	11,201	11,222	21
5/15	Lunch—Sam Simpson—potential client	11,222	11,247	25
5/15	Attend sales seminar—Hilton Hotel	11,247	11,301	54
5/17	Bank	11,399	11,408	8
5/18	Meeting—ABC Company	11,408	11,436	28
5/20	Sales presentation—Smith Bros. & Co.	11,544	11,589	55
Total				603

EXAMPLE: Yolanda, a self-employed salesperson, uses her car extensively for business. At the beginning of the year her odometer reading was 34,201 miles. On December 31, it was 58,907 miles. Her total mileage for the year was therefore 24,706. She recorded 62 business trips in her mileage logbook for a total of 9,280 miles. Her business use percentage of her car is 37% (9,290 ÷ 24,706 = .366). Yolanda commuted to her office every day, 50 weeks a year. She determined that her office was ten miles from her home. So Yolanda had 5,000 miles of commuting mileage for the year.

Record Your Mileage Electronically

If writing your mileage down in a paper mileage logbook seems too primitive, you can keep your records in electronic form with an electronic device such as a Palm device or computer. There is special software available for recording business mileage. However, be warned: Although the IRS's official policy is that electronic records are acceptable, many IRS auditors are old-fashioned. They like to see paper-and-ink mileage records because they are much harder to alter, forge, or create in a hurry than electronic records.

Sampling Method

There is an even easier way to track your mileage: use a sampling method. Under this method, you keep track of your business mileage for a sample portion of the year and use your figures for that period to extrapolate your business mileage for the whole year.

This method assumes that you drive about the same amount for business throughout the year. To back up this assumption, you must scrupulously keep an appointment book showing your business appointments all year long. If you don't want to keep an appointment book, don't use the sampling method.

Your sample period must be at least 90 days—for example, the first three months of the year. Alternatively, you may sample one week each month—for example, the first week of every month. You don't have to use the first three months of the year or the first week of every month; you could use any other three-month period or the second, third, or fourth week of every month. Use whatever works best—you want your sample period to be as representative as possible of the business travel you do throughout the year.

You must keep track of the total miles you drove during the year by taking odometer readings on January 1 and December 31 and deduct any atypical mileage before applying your sample results.

> **EXAMPLE:** Tom, a traveling salesman, uses the sample method to compute his mileage, keeping track of his business miles for the first three months of the year. He drove 6,000 miles during that time and had 4,000 business miles. His business use percentage of his car was 67%. From his January 1 and December 31 odometer readings, Tom knows he drove a total of 27,000 miles during the year. However, Tom drove to the Grand Canyon for vacation, so he deducts this 1,000 mile trip from his total. This leaves him with 26,000 total miles for the year. To calculate his total business miles, he multiplies the year-long total by the business use percentage of his car: 67% x 26,000 = 17,420. Tom claims 17,420 business miles on his tax return.

Keeping Track of Actual Expenses

If you take the deduction for your actual auto expenses instead of the standard rate (or are thinking about switching to this method), keep receipts for all of your auto-related expenses, including gasoline, oil, tires, repairs, and insurance. You don't need to include these expenses in your ledger sheets; just keep them in a folder or envelope. At tax time, add them up to determine how large your deduction will be if you use the actual expense method. Also add in the amount you're entitled to deduct for depreciation of your auto. (See Chapter 8 for more on calculating automobile deductions.)

Use a Credit Card for Gas

If you use the actual expense method for car expenses, use a credit card when you buy gas. It's best to designate a separate card for this purpose. The monthly statements you receive will serve as your gas receipts. If you pay cash for gas, you must either get a receipt or make a note of the amount in your mileage logbook.

Costs for business-related parking (other than at your office) and for tolls are separately deductible whether you use the standard rate or the actual expense method. Get and keep receipts for these expenses.

Entertainment, Meal, Travel, and Gift Expenses

Deductions for business-related entertainment, meals, and travel are a hot-button item for the IRS because they have been greatly abused by many taxpayers. You need to have more records for these expenses than for almost any others, and they will be closely scrutinized if you're audited.

Whenever you incur an expense for business-related entertainment, meals, gifts, or travel, you must document the following five facts:

- **The date.** The date the expense was incurred will usually be listed on a receipt or credit card slip; appointment books, day planners, and similar documents have the dates preprinted on each page, so entries on the appropriate page automatically date the expense.
- **The amount.** How much you spent, including tax and tip for meals.
- **The place.** The nature and place of the entertainment or meal will usually be shown by a receipt, or you can record it in an appointment book.
- **The business purpose.** Show that the expense was incurred for your business—for example, to obtain future business, encourage existing business relationships, and so on. What you need to show depends on whether the business conversation occurred before, during, or after entertainment or a meal. (See Chapter 10 for more on deducting meal expenses.)

- **The business relationship.** If entertainment or meals are involved, show the business relationship of people at the event—for example, list their names and occupations and any other information needed to establish their business relation to you.

The IRS does not require that you keep receipts, canceled checks, credit card slips, or any other supporting documents for entertainment, meal, gift, or travel expenses that cost less than $75. However, you must still document the five facts listed above. This exception does not apply to lodging—that is, hotel or similar costs—when you travel for business. You do need receipts for these expenses, even if they are less than $75.

> ⚠️ **The $75 rule applies only to travel, meals, gifts, and entertainment.** The rule that you don't need receipts for expenses less than $75 applies only to travel, gift, meal, and entertainment expenses. It does not apply to other types of business expenses. For example, if you go to the office supply store and buy $50 worth of supplies for your business and then spend $70 for lunch with a client, you need a receipt for the office supplies, but not the business lunch. If you find this rule hard to remember, simply keep all of your receipts.

All this record keeping is not as hard as it sounds. You can record the five facts you have to document in a variety of ways. The information doesn't have to be all in one place. Information that is shown on a receipt, canceled check, or other item need not be duplicated in a log, appointment book, calendar, or account book. Thus, for example, you can record the five facts with:

- a receipt, credit card slip, or similar document alone
- a receipt combined with an appointment book entry, or
- an appointment book entry alone (for expenses less than $75).

However you document your expense, you are supposed to do it in a timely manner. You don't need to record the details of every expense on the day you incur it. It is sufficient to record them on a weekly basis. However, if you're prone to forget details, it's best to get everything you need in writing within a day or two.

Receipt or Credit Card Slip Alone

An easy way to document an entertainment, gift, travel, or meal expense is to use your receipt, credit card slip, invoice, or bill. A receipt or credit

Proof Required for Travel, Entertainment, and Gift Deductions				
Records must show:	**Amount**	**Time**	**Place or Description**	**Business Purpose and Relationship**
Travel	Cost of each separate expense for travel, lodging, meals. Incidental expenses may be totaled in categories such as taxis, daily meals, and so on.	Dates you left and returned for each trip, and the number of days spent on business.	Name of city, town, or other destination.	Business purpose for the expense, or the benefit gained or expected to be gained.
Entertainment (including meals)	Cost of each separate expense. Incidental expenses such as taxis, telephones, etc. may be totaled on a daily basis.	Date of entertainment.	Name and address or location of place of entertainment. Type of entertainment, if not otherwise apparent. For entertainment directly before or after business discussion: date, place, nature, and duration.	Nature of business discussion or activity. Identities of people who took part in discussion and entertainment. Occupations or other information (such as names or titles) about the recipients that shows their business relationship to you. Proof you or your employee was present at business meal.
Gifts	Cost of gift.	Date of gift.	Description of gift.	Same as for Entertainment.

card slip will ordinarily contain the name and location of the place where the expense was incurred, the date, and the amount charged. Thus, three of the five facts you must document are taken care of. You just need to describe the business purpose and business relationship if entertainment or meals are involved. You can write this directly on your receipt or credit card slip.

```
         GREENS RESTAURANT
         FORT MASON, BLDG A
            SF, CA 94123
           (415)771-6222
                              05/26/2005
                                 6:35 PM
   Server: LES                     30005
   Table 28/1
   Guests: 2
                                    6.50
   Bowl of soup                    12.00
   Sampler                         19.75
   Filo                            21.00
   Ravioli
                                   59.25
   Sub Total                        5.04
   Tax
                                   64.29
   Total
                                  64.29
   Balance Due
                          $10.00 tip

   Lunch with Harold Lipshitz,
   president, Acme Technologies, Inc.
   Discussed signing contract for
   programming services.
```

EXAMPLE: Mary, a freelance computer programmer, has lunch with Harold, president of Acme Technologies, Inc., to discuss doing some programming work for Acme. Her restaurant bill shows the date, the name and location of the restaurant, the number of people served, and the amount of the expense. Mary just has to document the business purpose for the lunch and identify who it was with. She writes on the receipt: "Lunch with Harold Lipshitz, President, Acme Technologies, Inc. Discussed signing contract for programming services." All five facts Mary must prove to document her meal expense are on the receipt. This is all Mary needs. She need not duplicate the information elsewhere—for example, in an appointment book or day planner.

Receipt Plus Appointment Book

You can also document the five facts you need to record for an expense by combining the information on a receipt with entries in an appointment book, day planner, calendar, diary, or similar record.

> **EXAMPLE:** Assume that Mary from the above example saves her receipt from the restaurant where she had her business lunch. She writes nothing on the receipt. She still needs to document the five facts. Her receipt contains the date, name, and location of the restaurant, and the amount of the lunch. She records who the lunch was with and the business purpose by writing a note in her appointment book: "Lunch—Harold Lipshitz, President, Acme Technologies. Greens Restaurant. Discussed signing contract for programming services."

Appointment Book		
19 *Thursday*	*232/134*	
7		
8		
9		
10		
11		
12	Lunch—Harold Lipshitz, President, Acme Technologies. Greens Restaurant.	
1	Discussed signing contract for programming service.	
2		
3		
4		
5		
6		
20 *Friday*	*233/133*	
7		
8		

Appointment Book Alone

If your expense is for less than $75, you don't need to keep a receipt (unless the expense is for lodging). You may record the five facts in your appointment book, day planner, daily diary, or calendar, or on any other sheet of paper.

> **EXAMPLE:** Assume that Mary from the above examples doesn't keep her receipt from her lunch. Because lunch cost less than $75, she does not need it. Instead, she documents the five facts she needs to record in her appointment book. She writes: "Lunch—Greens Restaurant, with Harold Lipshitz, President, Acme Technologies, Inc. Discussed signing contract for programming services. $74." This short entry records the place of the lunch, who it was with, the business purpose, and the amount. She doesn't need to add the date because this is already shown by her appointment book.

Receipts to Keep	
Type of Expense	**Receipts to Save**
Travel	Airplane, train, or bus ticket stubs; travel agency receipts; rental car; and so on.
Meals	Meal check, credit card slip.
Lodging	Statement or bill from hotel or other lodging provider; your own written records for cleaning, laundry, telephone charges, tips, and other charges not shown separately on hotel statement.
Entertainment	Bill from entertainment provider; ticket stubs for sporting event, theatre, or other event; credit card slips.

Listed Property

Listed property refers to certain types of long-term business assets that can easily be used for personal as well as business purposes. Listed property includes:

- cars, boats, airplanes, motorcycles, and other vehicles
- computers
- cellular phones, and

- any other property generally used for entertainment, recreation, or amusement—for example, VCRs, cameras, and camcorders.

Because all listed property is long-term business property, it cannot be deducted like a business expense. Instead, you must depreciate it over several years or deduct it in one year under Section 179. (See Chapter 5 for more on deducting long-term assets.)

Special Record-Keeping Requirements

With listed property, the IRS fears that taxpayers might claim business deductions but really use the property for personal reasons instead. For this reason, you're required to document how you use listed property. Keep an appointment book, logbook, business diary, or calendar showing the dates, times, and reasons for which the property is used—both business and personal. You also can purchase logbooks for this purpose at stationery or office supply stores.

> **EXAMPLE:** Bill, an accountant, purchases a computer he uses 50% for business and 50% to play games. He must keep a log showing his business use of the computer. Following is a sample from one week in his log.

Usage Log for Personal Computer			
Date	Time of Business Use	Reason for Business Use	Time of Personal Use
5/1	4.5 hours	Prepared client tax returns	1.5 hours
5/2			3 hours
5/3	2 hours	Prepared client tax returns	
5/4			2 hours

Exception to Record-Keeping Rule for Computers

You usually have to document your use of listed property even if you use it 100% for business. However, there is an exception to this rule for computers: If you use a computer or computer peripheral (such as a printer) only for business and keep it at your business location, you need not comply with the record-keeping requirement. This includes computers that you keep at your home office if the office qualifies for the home office deduction. (See Chapter 7.)

> **EXAMPLE:** John, a freelance writer, works full time in his home office, which he uses exclusively for writing. The office is clearly his principal place of business and qualifies for the home office deduction. He buys a $4,000 computer for his office and uses it exclusively for his writing business. He does not have to keep records showing how he uses the computer.

This exception applies only to computers and computer peripheral equipment. It doesn't apply to other items such as calculators, copiers, fax machines, or typewriters.

How Long to Keep Records

You need to have copies of your tax returns and supporting documents available in case you are audited by the IRS or another taxing agency. You might also need them for other purposes—for example, to get a loan, mortgage, or insurance.

You should keep your records for as long as the IRS has to audit you after you file your returns for the year. These statutes of limitation range from three years to forever—they are listed in the table below.

To be on the safe side, you should keep your tax returns indefinitely. They usually don't take up much space, so this is not a big hardship. Your supporting documents probably take up more space. You should keep these for at least six years after you file your return. If you file a fraudulent return, keep your supporting documents indefinitely (if you have any). If you're audited, they will show that at least some of your deductions were legitimate. Keeping your records this long ensures that you'll have them available if the IRS decides to audit you.

Keep your long-term asset records for three years after the depreciable life of the asset ends. For example, keep records for five-year property (such as computers) for eight years.

You should keep your ledger sheets for as long as you're in business, because a potential buyer of your business might want to see them.

IRS Statutes of Limitations	
If:	**The limitations period is:**
You failed to pay all the tax due	3 years
You underreported your gross income for the year by more than 25%	6 years
You filed a fraudulent return	No limit
You did not file a return	No limit

What If You Don't Have Proper Tax Records?

Because you're human, you may not have kept all the records required to back up your tax deductions. Don't despair, all is not lost—you may be able to fall back on the *Cohan* rule. This rule (named after the Broadway entertainer George M. Cohan, involved in a tax case in the 1930s) is the taxpayer's best friend. The *Cohan* rule recognizes that all businesspeople must spend at least some money to stay in business and so must have had at least some deductible expenses, even if they don't have adequate records to back them up.

If you're audited and lack adequate records for a claimed deduction, the IRS can use the *Cohan* rule to make an estimate of how much you must have spent and allow you to deduct that amount. However, you must provide at least some credible evidence on which to base this estimate, such as receipts, canceled checks, notes in your appointment book, or other records. Moreover, the IRS will only allow you to deduct the least amount you must have spent, based on the records you provide. In addition, the *Cohan* rule cannot be used for travel, meal, entertainment, or gift expenses, or for listed property.

If an auditor claims you lack sufficient records to back up a deduction, you should always bring up the *Cohan* rule and argue that you should still get the deduction based on the records you do have. At best, you'll probably get only part of your claimed deductions. If the IRS auditor disallows your deductions entirely or doesn't give you as much as you think you deserve, you can appeal in court and bring up the *Cohan* rule again there. You might have more success with a judge. However, you

can't compel an IRS auditor or a court to apply the *Cohan* rule in your favor. Whether to apply the rule and how large a deduction to give you is within their discretion.

Reconstructing Tax Records

If you can show that you possessed adequate records at one time, but now lack them due to circumstances beyond your control, you may reconstruct your records for an IRS audit. Circumstances beyond your control would include acts of nature such as floods, fires, earthquakes, or theft. (Treas. Reg. 1.275.5(c)(5).) Loss of tax records while moving does not constitute circumstances beyond your control. Reconstructing records means you create brand-new records just for your audit or obtain other evidence to corroborate your deductions—for example, statements from people or companies from whom you purchased items for your business.

Accounting Methods

An accounting method is a set of rules used to determine when and how your income and expenses are reported. Accounting methods might sound like a rather dry subject, but your choice about how to account for your business expenses and income will have a huge impact on your tax deductions. You don't have to become as expert as a CPA. on this topic, but you should understand the basics.

You choose an accounting method when you file your first tax return. If you later want to change your accounting method, you must get IRS approval. The IRS requires some types of businesses to use the accrual method. If your business doesn't fall into this group, you are free to choose the method you want, as long as it clearly shows your income and expenses. If you operate two or more separate businesses, you can

use a different accounting method for each. (A business is separate for tax purposes only if you keep a separate set of books and records for it.)

There are two basic methods of accounting: cash basis and accrual basis. Any business can use the accrual method, but not all can use the cash method.

Personal and Business Accounting Methods May Differ

You can account for business and personal items using different accounting methods. For example, you can figure your business income under an accrual method, even if you use the cash method to figure personal items. Almost everyone uses the cash basis method of accounting for personal finances, so it can be convenient to continue to use it for personal items even if you want or are required to use the accrual method for your business.

Cash Method

The cash method is by far the simplest method. It is used by individuals who are not in business and by most small businesses that provide services and do not maintain inventory or offer credit. However, if you produce, purchase, or sell merchandise and keep an inventory, you might have to use the accrual method.

The cash method is based on this commonsense idea: You haven't earned income for tax purposes until you actually receive the money, and you haven't incurred an expense until you actually pay the money. Using the cash basis method, then, is like maintaining a checkbook. You record income only when the money is received and expenses only when they are actually paid. If you borrow money to pay business expenses, you incur an expense under the cash method only when you make payments on the loan.

The Cash Method of Paying Expenses

Although it's called the cash method, this method for paying business expenses includes payments by check, credit card, or electronic funds transfer, as well as by cash. If you pay by check, the amount is deemed paid during the year in which the check is drawn and mailed—for example, a check dated December 31, 2007 is considered paid during 2007 only if it has a December 31, 2007 postmark. If you're using a check to pay a substantial expense, you may wish to mail it by certified mail so you'll have proof of when it was mailed.

EXAMPLE 1: Helen, a marketing consultant, completes a market research report on September 1, 2007 but isn't paid by the client until February 1, 2008. Using the cash method, Helen records the payment in February 2008—when it's received.

EXAMPLE 2: On December 1, 2007, Helen goes to the Acme electronics store and buys a laser printer for her consulting business. She buys the item on credit from Acme—she's not required to make any payments until March 1, 2008. Helen does not record the expense until 2008, when she actually pays for the printer.

Constructive Receipt

Under the cash method, payments are "constructively received" when an amount is credited to your account or otherwise made available to you without restrictions. Constructive receipt is as good as actual receipt. If you authorize someone to be your agent and receive income for you, you are considered to have received it when your agent receives it.

EXAMPLE: Interest is credited to your business bank account in December 2007, but you do not withdraw it or enter it into your passbook until 2008. You must include the amount in gross business income for 2007, not 2008.

No Postponing Income

You cannot hold checks or other payments from one tax year to another to avoid paying tax on the income. You must report the income in the year the payment is received or made available to you without restriction.

> **EXAMPLE:** On December 1, 2007, Helen receives a $5,000 check from a client. She holds the check and doesn't cash it until January 10, 2008. She must still report the $5,000 as income for 2007, because she constructively received it that year.

No Prepayment of Expenses

The general rule is that you can't prepay expenses when you use the cash method—you can't hurry up the payment of expenses by paying them in advance. An expense you pay in advance can be deducted only in the year to which it applies.

> **EXAMPLE:** Helen pays $1,000 in 2007 for a business insurance policy that is effective for one year, beginning July 1st. She can deduct $500 in 2007 and $500 in 2008.

However, there is an important exception to the general rule, called the 12-month rule. Under this rule, you may deduct a prepaid expense in the current year if the expense is for a right or benefit that extends no longer than the earlier of:

- 12 months, or
- until the end of the tax year after the tax year in which you made the payment.

> **EXAMPLE 1:** You are a calendar year taxpayer and you pay $10,000 on July 1, 2007 for a business insurance policy that is effective for one year beginning July 1, 2007. The 12-month rule applies because the benefit you've paid for—a business insurance policy—extends only 12 months into the future. Therefore, the full $10,000 is deductible in 2007.

EXAMPLE 2: You are a calendar year taxpayer and you pay $3,000 in 2007 for a business insurance policy that is effective for three years, beginning July 1, 2007. This payment does not qualify for the 12-month rule because the benefit extends more than 12 months. Therefore, you must use the general rule: $500 is deductible in 2007; $1,000 is deductible in 2008; $1,000 is deductible in 2009; and $500 is deductible in 2010.

To use the 12-month rule, you must apply it when you first start using the cash method for your rental activity. You must get IRS approval if you haven't been using the rule and want to start doing so. Such approval is granted automatically upon filing IRS Form 3115.

Accrual Method

In accrual basis accounting, you report income or expenses as they are earned or incurred, rather than when they are actually collected or paid. With the accrual method, income is counted when a sale occurs and expenses are counted when you receive the goods or services. You don't have to wait until you see the money or actually pay money out of your checking account. The accrual method can be difficult to use because there are complex rules to determine when income or expenses are accrued.

When Expenses Are Incurred

Under the accrual method, you generally deduct a business expense when:

- you are legally obligated to pay the expense
- the amount you owe can be determined with reasonable accuracy, and
- you have received or used the property or services involved.

EXAMPLE: Bill, the owner of a welding shop, borrows $10,000 from his bank to help pay his business operating expenses. He signs a promissory note on December 15, 2007 and receives the money the same day but doesn't start making payments to the bank until the following January. Bill can deduct the expense in 2007 because on December 15, 2007 he became legally obligated to pay the expense by signing the note, the amount of the expense can be determined from the note, and he received the money that day.

Thus, when you use the accrual method, you can take a deduction for an expense you incur even if you don't actually pay for it until the following year. You can't do this under the cash basis method. There are obvious advantages to getting a tax deduction this year without actually having to shell out any money until a future year.

When Income Is Received

While the accrual method lets you deduct expenses that you haven't paid for yet, it also requires that you report as income payments you haven't yet received. Transactions are counted as income when an order is made, an item is delivered, or services are provided, regardless of when the money for them (receivables) is actually received or paid.

> **EXAMPLE:** Andrea operates a watch repair shop. She is hired to repair an antique watch and finishes the job on December 15, 2007. She bills the customer for $250, which she receives on January 20, 2008. Because she uses the accrual method of accounting, Andrea must count the $250 as income in December 2007, because that's when she earned the money by finishing the job. This income must be reported in her 2007 tax return even though she did not receive the money that year.

Businesses That Must Use the Accrual Method

Any business, however small, may use the accrual method. Some types of businesses are required to use it, including C corporations with average annual gross receipts exceeding $5 million and partnerships with average annual gross receipts exceeding $5 million that have C corporations as partners.

More important, you are usually required to use the accrual method if you produce, purchase, or sell merchandise and are required to maintain an inventory. (See Chapter 6 for more about deducting inventory.) However, there are two big exceptions.

Exception #1—Businesses that earn less than $1 million. Even if you deal in merchandise, you may use the cash basis method if your average annual gross receipts were $1 million or less for the three tax years ending with the prior tax year.

Exception #2—Some businesses that earn less than $10 million. Even if your business earns more than $1 million per year, you may use the cash basis method if your average annual gross receipts were $10 million or less for the three tax years ending with the prior tax year, and:

- your principal business is providing services
- your principal business is making or modifying personal property according to customers' specifications, or
- your business does not involve mining, manufacturing, wholesale or retail trade, or certain information services. (See IRS Publication 538, *Accounting Periods and Methods*, for more details.)

Which Is Better: Accrual or Cash Method Accounting?

There is no single best accounting method. Each method has its advantages and disadvantages. The cash basis method is much simpler to use and easier to understand. Because you don't report income until it's actually received, it's more advantageous than the accrual method if you're in a business in which you are paid slowly.

> **EXAMPLE:** Tom is a freelance writer who usually must wait months until he is paid for his articles by magazines and newspapers. He contracts with the *Podunk Review* to write an article about inventions created by people in jail. He is to be paid $1,000 within 60 days after the article is accepted. The article is accepted by the *Podunk Review* on September 1, 2007, but Tom doesn't receive his check until March 2008. If he used the accrual method, he would have to recognize the $1,000 as income for 2007, even though he didn't receive it that year. If he used the cash basis method, he wouldn't recognize the income until 2008, when he gets the check.

The accrual method is more complicated than the cash basis method and harder to use, but it shows the ebb and flow of business income and debts more accurately than the cash basis method. You get a truer picture of your net profits for any given time period with the accrual method, because income earned in one time period is accurately matched against the expenses for that period. Moreover, the accrual method is more advantageous than the cash basis method if you are paid promptly by your clients or customers, because you are allowed to deduct expenses when you incur them, not when you actually pay for them.

When you are paid promptly, the cash method's actual receipt rule is not important; and, using the accrual method, you may prepay business expenses in advance to offset the income you received for the year— something you can't do with the cash method.

> **EXAMPLE:** Dick is a consultant who makes his clients pay within 30 days. He received $100,000 in consulting income by December 1, 2007 and had no outstanding receivables. To offset his business income, he purchases $10,000 worth of business equipment on credit in December. He doesn't have to pay for the equipment until the end of January 2008, but he can still deduct the $10,000 from his 2007 business income because he uses the accrual method of accounting.

Obtaining IRS Permission to Change Your Accounting Method

You choose your accounting method by checking a box on your tax form when you file your tax return. Once you choose a method, you can't change it without getting permission from the IRS. Permission is granted automatically for many types of changes, including using the 12-month rule to deduct prepaid expenses. You must file IRS Form 3115, *Application for Change in Accounting Method,* with your tax return for the year you want to make the change (if the change is automatically granted).

Automatic approval can also be obtained to change to the cash method if you've been using the accrual method and come within one of the exceptions discussed above. However, changing your accounting method can have serious consequences, so consult a tax professional before doing so.

Tax Years

You are required to pay taxes for a 12-month period, also known as the tax year. Sole proprietors, partnerships, limited liability companies, S corporations, and personal service corporations are required to use the calendar year as their tax years—that is, January 1 through December 31.

However, there are exceptions that permit some small businesses to use a tax year that does not end in December (also known as a fiscal year). You need to get the IRS's permission to use a fiscal year. The IRS doesn't like businesses to use a fiscal year, but it might grant you permission if you can show a good business reason for it.

One good reason to use a fiscal year is that your business is seasonal. For example, if you earn most of your income in the spring and incur most of your expenses in the fall, a tax year ending in July or August might be better than a calendar tax year ending in December because the income and expenses on each tax return will be more closely related. To get permission to use a fiscal year, you must file IRS Form 8716, *Election to Have a Tax Year Other Than a Required Tax Year.* ∎

Chapter 16

Claiming Tax Deductions for Prior Years

S am, a self-employed consultant, used his car 60% for business last year. He paid $5,000 in interest on a loan for the vehicle. However, he failed to deduct any portion of the payments because he didn't realize that the business portion of car loan interest was deductible as a business expense. After reading this book, he realizes that he should have claimed the deduction on his last two tax returns. Had he done so, he would have saved thousands on his taxes. But what can he do now?

Fortunately, tax returns are not engraved in stone. If, like Sam, you realize that you failed to claim tax deductions which you were entitled to take, you may be able to amend your tax returns for those years and get the IRS to send you a refund check.

Reasons for Amending Your Tax Return

It's very common for taxpayers to file amended tax returns. Here are some reasons why you might want to amend a tax return:

- You forgot to take a deduction.
- You have a net operating loss for the year and want to apply it to prior years.
- You claimed a deduction which you were not entitled to take
- You entered incorrect information on your return.
- A retroactive change in the tax laws makes you eligible for an additional deduction.

You need not amend your return if you discover that you made a simple math error. These will be corrected by the IRS computers, and you'll be notified of the change by mail.

However, if you made a mistake in your favor, failed to report income, or took deductions which you were not entitled to take, amending your return may avoid all or some fines, interest, and penalties if you're later audited by the IRS.

⚠️ **Filing an amended return makes an audit more likely.** You don't have to file an amended return if you don't want to. Filing an amended tax return increases the chances that your tax return for the year involved will be audited by the IRS. Thus, it may not be worth doing unless you are entitled to a substantial refund. If you're not sure whether to amend, consult a tax professional for advice.

Net Operating Losses

Many owners pay out more for expenses than they take in as income. When a business's expenses for a tax year exceed its income, it has a "net operating loss" (NOL for short). Although it may not be pleasant to lose money over an entire year, an NOL has some important tax benefits: You can apply the NOL to reduce your taxable income from other sources for the same tax year—for example, income from a job, your spouse's income, or investment income. If you still have all or part of your NOL left over, you have the option of applying it to future tax years. This is called carrying a loss forward. You can carry the NOL forward for up to 20 years and use it to reduce your taxable income in the future.

Alternatively, you may apply the loss to past tax years by filing an amended return for those years. Ordinarily, you may elect to carry back the loss for the two years before the year you incurred the loss. However, if you had an NOL for 2001 or 2002, you may carry back the loss to five years before the NOL year. The loss is used to offset the taxable income for the earliest year first, and then applied to the next year(s). This will reduce the tax you had to pay for those years and result in a tax refund. This is called carrying a loss back.

As a general rule, it's advisable to carry a loss back, so you can get a quick refund from the IRS on your prior years' taxes. However, you may elect not to carry an NOL back if you paid no income tax in prior years, or if you expect your income to rise substantially in future years and you want to use your NOL in the future, when you'll be subject to a higher tax rate.

Need to know more about NOLs? Refer to IRS Publication 536, *Net Operating Losses*, for more information. You can download it from the IRS website at www.irs.gov or obtain a paper copy by calling the IRS at 800-TAX-FORM.

Retroactive Tax Laws

Sometimes, Congress or the IRS changes the tax laws or regulations and makes the change retroactive—that is, the change applies to returns filed some time before the change was made. If a retroactive change is more favorable to you than the laws that were in effect when you filed your return, you might be entitled to a refund for prior years.

House Sales After May 6, 1997

One important retroactive tax change involves the home office deduction. Under the tax law in effect before 2003, business owners who took the home office deduction often had to pay extra tax when they sold their homes. If they took a home office deduction for more than three of the five years before they sold their house, they had to pay capital gains tax on the profit from the home office portion of their home.

Fortunately, effective December 24, 2002, the IRS changed its regulations to eliminate this requirement. As long as you live in your home for at least two of the five years before you sell it, the profit you make on the sale—up to $250,000 for single taxpayers and $500,000 for married taxpayers filing jointly—is not taxable. (See Chapter 7 for more information on the home office deduction.) Moreover, the change was made retroactive to May 6, 1997. If you sold your house after this date and paid capital gains tax on the home office portion, and you meet the two-out-of-five-year requirement, you are entitled to a refund of the tax. You obtain your refund by filing an amended tax return for the year.

> **EXAMPLE:** Greta sold her house in July 2002 for a $50,000 profit. She used 20% of the space in her house as a home office for her business and took a home office deduction every year. When she did her taxes for 2002, she mistakenly paid a $2,000 capital gains tax on her profit from the house sale (20% x $50,000 = $10,000 x 20% = $2,000). Greta made the error because she didn't know the change in the tax law was retroactive. In 2006, she discovers her error, amends her 2002 tax return to eliminate the capital gains tax, and receives a refund from the IRS of the $2,000.

However, it may be too late for you to claim this refund, because there are limits on how far back you can go to amend your returns. See "Time Limits for Filing Amended Returns," below, for information on these time limits.

Bonus Depreciation

Another instance of a retroactive change in the tax laws involves bonus depreciation. In March 2002, Congress enacted a law allowing business owners to take an additional 30% (later increased to 50%) first-year depreciation deduction for business assets purchased after 9/11/01, the date of the attack on the World Trade Center. Not every taxpayer wanted to take bonus depreciation—it might not have been advantageous if you expected your income to go up substantially in future years, which would have placed you in a higher tax bracket and made the deductions you took in the future more valuable.

However, bonus depreciation applied automatically for tax years 2002 through 2004, unless you filed a statement with your tax return that you wished to opt out of the deduction. (See "Tax Reporting and Record Keeping for Section 179 and Depreciation," in Chapter 5) If you didn't take bonus depreciation but failed to file the statement opting out, you should file an amended tax return including such a statement. If you don't file the statement, the IRS will act as if you took a bonus depreciation deduction, even though you really didn't. This could result in your having to pay extra taxes if you sell long-term assets you purchased during 2002 to 2004. You must file your amendment within the six-month period described in "Section 179 Deductions," below. (Write "Filed pursuant to Section 301.9100-2" on the amended return.) Bonus depreciation ended on December 31, 2004.

Casualty Losses

There is a special rule for certain types of casualty losses: losses to business property caused by things like fire, floods, or earthquakes. If you suffer a loss to your business property due to a disaster that occurs in an area the president declares to be a disaster area, you have the option of deducting the loss from your previous year's taxes. You do this by filing an amended tax return for the year and deducting the amount of the loss from your taxable income for that year. This will reduce the taxes you had to pay for the year, and the IRS will send you a refund check for the difference. Alternatively, you can wait and deduct your loss from the current year's taxes. But if you want to get some money from the IRS quickly, you should file an amended return (unless you paid no tax the prior year). (See Chapter 14 for a detailed discussion of casualty losses.)

John Kerry Amends His Tax Return

In the midst of the 2004 presidential campaign, Senator John Kerry released his 2003 tax return to the public. A Texas CPA who analyzed the return discovered an error. Kerry and his wife had sold a rare Dutch painting they co-owned for $1,350,000. Kerry's share of the profit on the sale was $175,000. For some reason, his accountant thought this gain should be taxed at the 20% capital gains rate then in effect. However, this was clearly wrong. Kerry's profit should have been taxed at his 28% income tax rate, because the painting was not a capital asset. Soon after this was brought to his attention, Kerry filed an amended tax return for 2003 and paid an extra $11, 577 in income tax for the year.

Time Limits for Filing Amended Returns

Unfortunately, you can't wait forever to amend a tax return for a prior year. If you wait too long, you'll forever lose your right to file an amended return for the year, even if it means you'll be forced to give up a deduction for the year in which you were legally entitled to the deduction.

Three-Year Amendment Period

The general rule is that you can file an amended return until the later of:
- three years after the date you filed the original return (April 15 or later if you obtained an extension to file), or
- two years after the date you paid the tax, whichever is later.

Even if you filed your return for the year before April 15, it is deemed to be filed on that date for amendment purposes. For example, you have until April 15, 2008 to file an amended return for your 2004 taxes, which are deemed to have been filed on April 15, 2005 (even if you filed them earlier). The three-year period applies in most cases.

> **EXAMPLE:** Sam failed to claim a deduction for the interest he paid on a loan for a car he used in his business during 2005. He filed his 2005 taxes on April 1, 2006. How long does Sam have to amend his 2005 tax return to claim the deduction? Until April 15, 2009, three years after he is deemed to have filed his original tax return for 2005 (April 15, 2006). If he fails to meet the deadline, he loses his right to claim the deduction and obtain a tax refund.

However, if you obtain an extension of time to file your original return for the year involved, you may add that time to the three-year period. You can get an automatic extension of time to file your return until October 15.

> **EXAMPLE:** Assume that Sam from the above example obtained an extension of time to file his 2005 tax return to October 15, 2006. He would have until October 15, 2009 to amend his tax return for 2005.

Section 179 Deductions

There are two different rules for amending tax returns to claim or disclaim a Section 179 deduction. For the years 2002 through 2005, you may amend your return for Section 179 deductions in the same manner as other amendments (as described above). (IRS Reg. 1.179-5T.)

For tax years before 2002 and after 2005, amendments are much more difficult. You must file your amended return within six months after the due date for the return for the tax year involved, including any extensions of time you received. Because tax returns are ordinarily due on April 15, you must file your amended return by October 15 to claim a Section 179 deduction for the prior year, unless you received an extension of time to file your return.

EXAMPLE: Jill bought a $3,000 computer for her medical record transcription business during 2006. When she did her taxes for the year in early 2007, she thought she had to depreciate the computer's cost over five years. She took a depreciation deduction for the computer on her 2006 tax return. However, she learned later that she could have deducted the entire cost in one year using Section 179. She has until October 15, 2007 to file an amended 2006 return to claim the deduction. If she fails to do so, she loses the right to claim a Section 179 deduction for the property and must use depreciation instead.

Net Operating Losses

There are two ways to claim a refund of a prior year's taxes due to a later net operating loss: You can file IRS Form 1040X, *Amended U.S. Individual Income Tax Return,* within the usual three-year limitation period, or you can seek a quick refund by filing IRS Form 1045, *Application for Tentative Refund.* If you file Form 1045, the IRS is required to send your refund within 90 days. However, you must file Form 1045 within one year after the end of the year in which the NOL arose.

Bad Debts

In some instances, you may be able to deduct a business bad debt as a business operating expense. A debt doesn't become "bad" until it is clearly worthless. This may occur years after the loan was originally made. (See Chapter 14 for more on the requirements for deducting bad debts.) If you failed to claim a bad debt deduction on your original tax return for the year the debt became totally worthless, you have up to seven years to file an amended return listing the bad debt. However, the seven-year term applies only to debts that are completely worthless. If a debt is only partially worthless, you must amend your return within the usual three-year period.

Business Start-Up Expenses

If you want to deduct your business start-up expenses, you must file an election with the IRS on or before the date your first tax return is due after you start your business. For example, if your business begins in 2006, you must file the election with your 2006 tax return, due April 15, 2007 (or later if you receive an extension). If you miss this deadline, you have one last chance to make your election: You may file an amended return making the election within six months after the date your original return was due (April 15, or later if you got an extension). If you fail to do this, you will lose your right to deduct your start-up expenses and you'll have to treat them as capital expenses. (See Chapter 3 for a detailed discussion of deducting business start-up expenses.)

Should You File Your Amendment As Late as Possible?

The IRS ordinarily has only three years after a return is filed to audit the return. Filing a Form 1040X does not extend this period. Thus, if you file your Form 1040X near the end of the three-year period, the IRS will have very little time to audit your return for the year involved. As a result, it might accept your claim without auditing your return. However, it might also refuse to accept your 1040X unless you agree to extend the time it has to audit your return for the year.

How to Amend Your Return

If, like most small business owners, you are a sole proprietor, you amend your income tax return by filing IRS form 1040X, *Amended U.S. Individual Income Tax Return*. When you file Form 1040X to obtain a refund of taxes you've already paid, it is called a "claim for refund."

Filing an amended tax return is not terribly difficult. You can usually do it yourself, with or without the aid of a computer tax-preparation program. The heart of the form consists of three columns: A, B, and C. You record the relevant figures from your original tax return in Column

A; the corrected information is listed in Column C; and the difference between the two is listed in Column B. You must also provide a brief explanation for the changes. For example, Senator Kerry included the following explanation when he filed a Form 1040X to amend his 2003 taxes: "The tax on the one-half interest in the Adam Willerts painting was inadvertently calculated at the 20% rather than the 28% rate."

If you're amending your previous year's tax return and are entitled to an additional refund for that year, tax experts suggest that you wait until you receive your original refund check for that year. You can go ahead and cash the first refund check as soon as you receive it. Of course, you can file your amended return immediately if you were not entitled to a refund on your original return.

You must mail or hand deliver Form 1040X to the IRS. You can't file it electronically. If you mail it, send it by certified mail, with postal return receipt requested. This will let you know when the IRS received it. If you amend your returns for more than one year, mail each 1040X in a separate envelope. The 1040X instructions show where to mail the form.

You may also hand deliver the form to the IRS service center where you file your tax returns. If you do this, be sure to get a stamped copy as your filing receipt.

To obtain a refund due to an NOL, you may file either IRS Form 1045 alone, or along with Form 1040X. You can often get your refund faster by using Form 1045 alone. The calculations required to figure out how much you can deduct from your income in prior years can be complicated. Tax preparation programs like *TurboTax* aren't designed to handle net operating losses, so it's a good idea to get some help from a tax professional. Refer to IRS Publication 536, *Net Operating Losses*, for more information.

Don't forget your state tax returns. The IRS routinely shares information with states that impose income taxes (every state except Alaska, Florida, Nevada, South Dakota, Texas, Washington, and Wyoming). Thus, your state tax department will probably learn that you amended your federal tax return. For this reason, tax experts advise that you also amend your state tax returns for the years affected.

How the IRS Processes Refund Claims

The IRS doesn't like paying back money to taxpayers. When you file a Form 1040X, your tax return for that year will receive extra special attention. An IRS employee will pull your return and examine it and your 1040X to decide whether you're really entitled to a refund and, if so, how much. Your claim may be denied or accepted as filed, or the amended items may be audited. If a claim is audited, the procedures are almost the same as in the audit of a regular tax return. Moreover, the IRS has the option of extending the audit to your entire tax return, not just the amended items. Thus, *filing an amended tax return increases your chances of an audit.*

You should receive your refund, if you're entitled to one, in about 12 weeks. However, your refund may be reduced by amounts you owe for past-due child support, debts you owe to another federal agency, or past-due state income tax obligations. You will be notified if this happens.

If the IRS denies your claim, it must explain why—for example, because you filed it late. You have the right to appeal such a denial. For a detailed discussion of IRS appeals, refer to *Stand Up to the IRS*, by Frederick W. Daily (Nolo).

Chapter 17

Staying Out of Trouble With the IRS

ost taxpayers have at least some concern about the possibility of facing an IRS audit. You may be wondering how the IRS decides to audit, how likely it is that you'll be audited, and what you can do to avoid being one of the unlucky ones. This chapter explains IRS audits and provides tips and strategies that will help you avoid attracting the attention of the IRS—or come out of an audit unscathed, if you find yourself in the government's crosshairs.

Need more information on dealing with the IRS? For a detailed discussion of audits and other IRS procedures, see *Stand Up to the IRS*, by Frederick Daily (Nolo).

What Every Business Owner Needs to Know About the IRS

Just as you should never go into battle without knowing your enemy, you should never file a tax return without understanding what the IRS plans to do with it.

Anatomy of an Audit

You can claim any deductions you want to take on your tax return—after all, you (or your tax preparer) fill it out, not the government. However, all the deductions you claim are subject to review by the IRS. This review is called a tax audit. There are three types of audits: correspondence audits, office audits, and field audits.

- **Correspondence audits.** As the name indicates, correspondence audits are handled entirely by mail. These are the simplest, shortest, and most common type of IRS audit, usually involving a single issue. The IRS sends you written questions about a perceived problem, and may request additional information and/or documentation. If you don't provide satisfactory answers or information, you'll be assessed additional taxes. Correspondence audits are often used to question a business about unreported income—income the IRS knows the taxpayer received because an IRS Form 1099 listing the payment has been filed by a client or customer.

- **Office audits.** Office audits take place face to face with an IRS auditor at one of the 33 IRS district offices. These are more complex than correspondence audits, often involving more than one issue or more than one tax year. If you make less than $100,000 per year, this is the type of in-person audit you're likely to face.
- **Field audits.** The field audit is the most comprehensive IRS audit, conducted by an experienced revenue officer. In a field audit, the officer examines your finances, your business, your tax returns, and the records you used to create the returns. As the name implies, a field audit is normally conducted at the taxpayer's place of business; this allows the auditor to learn as much about your business as possible. Field audits are ordinarily reserved for taxpayers who earn a lot of money. You probably won't be subjected to one unless your business earns more than $100,000 per year.

How Small Business Owners Get in Trouble With the IRS

When auditing small business owners, the IRS is most concerned about whether you have:

- **Underreported your income.** Unlike employees who have their taxes withheld, business owners who are not employees have no withholding—and many opportunities to underreport how much they earned, particularly if they run a cash business.
- **Claimed tax deductions to which you were not entitled.** For example, you claimed that nondeductible personal expenses, such as a personal vacation, were deductible business expenses
- **Properly documented the amount of your deductions.** If you don't have the proper records to back up the amount of a deduction, the IRS may reduce it, either entirely or in part. Lack of documentation is the main reason small business owners lose deductions when they get audited.
- **Taken business deductions for a hobby.** If you continually lose money, or you are involved in a fun activity such as art, photography, crafts, or writing and don't earn profits every year, the auditor may also question whether you are really in business. If the IRS claims you are engaged in a hobby, you could lose every single deduction for the activity. (See Chapter 2 for more on the hobby loss rule.)

Records Available to Auditors

An IRS auditor is entitled to examine the business records you used to prepare your tax returns, including your books, check registers, canceled checks, and receipts. The auditor can also ask to see records supporting your business tax deductions, such as a mileage record if you took a deduction for business use of your car. The auditor can also get copies of your bank records, either from you or your bank, and check them to see whether your deposits match the income you reported on your tax return. If you deposited a lot more money than you reported earning, the auditor will assume that you didn't report all of your income, unless you can show that the deposits you didn't include in your tax return weren't income. For example, you might be able to show that they were loans, inheritances, or transfers from other accounts. This is why you need to keep good financial records.

The IRS: Clear and Present Danger or Phantom Menace?

A generation ago, the three letters Americans feared most were I-R-S. There was a simple reason for this: The IRS, the nation's tax police, enforced the tax laws like crazy. In 1963, an incredible 5.6% of all Americans had their tax returns audited. Everybody knew someone who had been audited. Jokes about IRS audits were a staple topic of nightclub comedians and cartoonists.

In 2004, only .62% of all Americans were audited, and an IRS audit was a relatively rare event. There are several reasons for the change:

- **A decline in the IRS workforce.** Between 1995 and 2004, the IRS workforce declined by 35%.
- **An increase in workload.** At the same time the IRS workforce was declining, its workload was increasing. Between 1995 and 2004, the number of returns filed increased 12%, reaching 174 million.
- **A new emphasis on taxpayer service, rather than enforcement.** Starting in the mid-1990s, the IRS began to emphasize taxpayer service rather than enforcement.
- **Legal changes.** Congress enacted new laws in 1998 that were intended to prevent perceived abuses by IRS agents and auditors. These new protections also made it more difficult for the IRS to go after tax cheats.

According to the IRS Oversight Board, the IRS does not have the resources to pursue at least $30 billion worth of known taxes that are incorrectly reported or not paid. In 2001, the nation's "tax gap"—the total inventory of taxes that are known and not paid—was estimated at between $312 and $353 billion.

Both the IRS and the Congress are aware of the IRS's enforcement problems and have taken some steps to ameliorate them. The IRS has received moderate budget increases in the past few years and has placed a renewed emphasis on enforcement. Staff has been shifted from performing service functions like answering taxpayer questions to doing audits. The precipitous decline in audit rates that began in the mid 1990s has been stopped, but audit rates remain at low levels. However, the IRS commissioner promises that audit rates will go up in the next few years, with small businesses one of the main targets. With huge federal budget deficits yawning as far as the eye can see, it seems likely that this is one government promise that will be kept.

Aggressive or Dishonest?

Given the relatively low audit rates in recent years, many tax experts say that this is a good time to be aggressive about taking tax deductions. In this context, "aggressive" means taking every deduction to which you might arguably be entitled. If a deduction falls into a gray area of law, you would decide the question in your favor. This is *tax avoidance*, which is perfectly legal.

However, being aggressive does not mean being dishonest—that is, taking phony deductions that you are clearly not entitled to take or falsely increasing the amount of the deductions to which you are entitled. This is *tax evasion*, which is a crime.

You Are a Prime IRS Target

Although the IRS is a troubled agency and audit rates are at or near all-time lows, hundreds of thousands of people still get audited every year. In 2005, the IRS audited 279,038 of the 9,094,637 tax returns filed by Schedule C filers—the category that includes most small business owners. Every year, the IRS releases statistics about who got audited the previous year. Here are the most recent available audit statistics.

IRS Audit Rates		
	2005 Audit Rate	**2004 Audit Rate**
Sole Proprietors		
Income under $25,000	3.68%	3.15%
$25,000 to $100,000	2.21%	1.47%
$100,000 and over	3.65%	1.86%
Partnerships	0.33%	0.26%
S Corporations	0.30%	0.19%
C Corporations		
Assets under $250,000	0.74%	0.18%
$250,000 to $1 million	0.96%	0.34%
$1 million to $5 million	1.02%	0.60%
$5 million to $10 million	2.67%	1.90%
Individuals (not in business)		
Income under $25,000	1.48%	1.26%
$25,000 to $50,000	0.60%	0.43%
$50,000 to $100,000	0.57%	0.44%
$100,000 and over	1.19%	1.39%

This chart shows that in 2005, 3.68% of sole proprietors earning less than $25,000 from their business were audited. Only corporations with assets worth more than $10 million were audited more often.

These statistics undoubtedly reflects the IRS's belief that sole proprietors habitually underreport their income, take deductions to which they are not entitled, or otherwise cheat on their taxes. The lesson these numbers teach is that you need to take the IRS seriously. This doesn't mean that you shouldn't take all the deductions you're legally entitled to take, but you should understand the rules and be able to back up the deductions you do take with proper records.

How Tax Returns Are Selected for Audits

It's useful to understand how tax returns are selected for audit by the IRS. (By the way, if you are audited, you are entitled to know why you were selected. You ordinarily have to ask to find out.)

DIF Scores

One way the IRS decides who to audit is by plugging the information from your tax return into a complex formula to calculate a "discriminate function" score (DIF). Returns with high DIFs have a far higher chance of being flagged for an audit, regardless of whether or not you have done anything obviously wrong. Anywhere from 25% to 60% of audited returns are selected this way. Because the DIF formula is out of date, fully one-third of audits conducted in recent years through the formula resulted in either no change or a tax refund. The IRS is in the process of revising the DIF formula to achieve better audit results. Exactly how the DIF is calculated is a closely guarded secret. Some of the known factors the formula takes into account are:

- **The nature of your business.** Businesses that deal with large amounts of cash are scrutinized more closely than those that don't.
- **Where you live.** Audit rates differ widely according to where you live. In 2000, for example, taxpayers in Southern California were almost five times more likely to be audited than taxpayers in Georgia. The IRS no longer releases information on audit rates by region, but according to the latest available data, the state with the highest audit rate is Nevada; other high-audit states include Alaska, California, and Colorado. Low-audit states include Illinois, Indiana, Iowa, Maryland, Massachusetts, Michigan, New York (not including Manhattan), Ohio, Pennsylvania, and West Virginia.
- **The amount of your deductions.** Returns with extremely large deductions in relation to income are more likely to be audited. For example, if your tax return shows that your business is earning $25,000, you are more likely to be audited if you claim $20,000 in deductions than if you claim $2,000.
- **Hot-button deductions.** Certain types of deductions have long been thought to be hot buttons for the IRS—especially auto, travel, and entertainment expenses. Casualty losses and bad debt deductions may also increase your DIF score. Some people believe

that claiming the home office deduction makes an audit more likely, but the IRS denies this.

- **Businesses that lose money.** Businesses that show losses are more likely to be audited, especially if the losses are recurring. The IRS may suspect that you must be making more money than you are reporting—otherwise, why would you stay in business?

- **Peculiar deductions.** Deductions that seem odd or out of character for your business could increase your DIF score—for example, a plumber who deducts the cost of foreign travel might raise a few eyebrows at the IRS.

- **How you organize your business.** Sole proprietors get higher DIF scores than businesses that are incorporated or owned by partnerships or limited liability companies. As a result, sole proprietors generally are most likely to be audited by the IRS. Partnerships and small C corporations are ten times less likely to be audited than sole proprietors.

IRS Matching Program

Whenever a client pays you $600 or more for your services during the year, it must report the payments to the IRS on IRS Form 1099. IRS computers match the information on 1099s with the amount of income reported on tax returns using Social Security and other identifying numbers. Discrepancies usually generate correspondence audits.

Groups Targeted for Audit

Every year, the IRS gives special attention to specific industries or groups of taxpayers that it believes to be tax cheats. Businesses that receive a lot of cash are a perennial audit favorite. Other IRS favorites include doctors, dentists, lawyers, CPAs, and salespeople.

The IRS also targets taxpayers who use certain tax shelters or have offshore bank accounts or trusts. But you don't have to be rich to be an audit target. The IRS also heavily audits low-income taxpayers who claim the earned income tax credit.

Tips and Referrals

You could also get audited as a result of a referral from another government agency, such as your state tax department. The IRS also receives tips from private citizens—for example, a former business partner or ex-spouse.

Bad Luck

A certain number of tax returns are randomly selected for audit every year. If you find yourself in this category, there's not much you can do about it. As long as you have adequate documentation to support your deductions, you should do just fine.

State Tax Audits Grow Increasingly Common

Although most people (and books) focus on IRS audits, audits by state income tax agencies are becoming increasingly common. Many states have increased fines and late-payment penalties. Others have adopted severe—and highly effective—punishments against delinquent taxpayers. For example, some states refuse to issue driver's licenses to people who owe back taxes. Others are hiring private tax collectors and publishing names of tax evaders online.

Ten Tips for Avoiding an Audit

Here are ten things you can do to minimize your chances of getting audited.

Tip #1: Be Neat, Thorough, and Exact

If you file by mail (as you should), submit a tax return that looks professional; this will help you avoid unwanted attention from the IRS. Your return shouldn't contain erasures or be difficult to read. Your math should be correct. Avoid round numbers on your return (like $100 or $5,000). This looks like you're making up the numbers instead of taking them from accurate records. You should include, and completely fill out, all necessary forms and schedules. Moreover, your state tax return should be consistent with your federal return. If you do your own taxes, using a tax-preparation computer program will help you produce an accurate return that looks professional.

Tip #2: Mail Your Return by Certified Mail

Mail your tax return by certified mail, return receipt requested. In case the IRS loses or misplaces your return, your receipt will prove that you submitted it. The IRS also accepts returns from four private delivery services: Airborne Express, DHL Worldwide Express, Federal Express, and United Parcel Service. Contact these companies for details on which of their service options qualify and how to get proof of timely filing.

Tip #3: Don't File Early

Unless you're owed a substantial refund, you shouldn't file your taxes early. The IRS generally has three years after April 15 to decide whether to audit your return. Filing early just gives the IRS more time to think about whether you should be audited. You can reduce your audit chances even more by getting an extension to file until August 15 or October 15 (the latest extension you can obtain). Note, however, that filing an extension does not extend the date by which you have to pay any taxes due for the prior year—these must be paid by April 15.

Tip #4: Don't File Electronically

The IRS would like all taxpayers to file their returns electronically— that is, by email. There is a good reason for this: It saves the agency substantial time and money. Every year, the IRS must hire thousands of temp workers to enter the numbers from millions of paper returns into its computer system. This is expensive, so the IRS only has about 40% of the data on paper returns transcribed. The paper returns are then sent to a warehouse where they are kept for six years and then destroyed. The IRS makes its audit decisions based on this transcribed data. By filing electronically, you give the IRS easy access to 100% of the data on your return instead of just 40%. Moreover, if you file electronically, you cannot add written explanations of any deductions the IRS might question (see Tip #6). No one can say for sure whether filing a paper return lessens your chance of an audit, but why make life easier for the IRS if you don't have to?

Tip #5: Form a Business Entity

The IRS audit rate statistics, discussed above, show that partnerships and small corporations are audited far less often than sole proprietors. In 2005, for example, the IRS audited 0.33% of partnerships, 0.30% of S corporations, and only 0.74% of regular C corporations with assets worth less than $250,000. In contrast, 3.68% of sole proprietors earning less than $25,000 were audited. The majority of small business owners are sole proprietors, but no law says they have to be. Incorporating your business or forming a limited liability company will greatly reduce your audit risk. However, you must balance this against the time and expense involved in forming a corporation or LLC and having to complete more complex tax returns. Moreover, in some states—most notably California—corporations and LLCs have to pay additional state taxes.

Tip #6: Explain Items the IRS Will Question

If your return contains an item that the IRS may question or that could increase the likelihood of an audit, include an explanation and documentation to prove everything is on the up and up. For example, if your return contains a substantial bad debt deduction, explain the circumstances showing that the debt is a legitimate business expense. This won't necessarily avoid an audit, but it may reduce your chances. Here's why: If the IRS computer gives your return a high DIF score, an IRS classifier screens it to see whether it warrants an audit. If your explanations look reasonable, the screener may decide you shouldn't be audited after all.

Tip #7: Avoid Ambiguous or General Expenses

Don't list expenses under vague categories such as "miscellaneous" or "general expense." Be specific. IRS Schedule C lists specific categories for the most common small business expenses. If an expense doesn't fall within one of these classifications, create a specific name for it.

Tip #8: Report All of Your Income

The IRS is convinced that self-employed people, including many home business owners, don't report all of their income. Finding such hidden income is a high priority. As mentioned above, IRS computers compare 1099 forms with tax returns to determine whether there are any discrepancies. Not all income business owners receive is reported to the IRS on Form 1099—for example, if you sell a product to customers rather than providing a service, your receipts will not be reported on Form 1099. However, if you are audited, the auditor may examine your bank records to see whether you received any unreported income.

Tip #9: Watch Your Income-to-Deduction Ratio

Back in the 1990s, a statistics professor named Amir D. Aczel got audited by the IRS. The experience proved so unpleasant that he decided to conduct a statistical study of how and why people get selected for IRS audits. He carefully examined more than 1,200 returns that were audited and reported his findings in a book (now out of print) called *How to Beat the IRS at Its Own Game* (Four Walls Eight Windows, 1995). He concluded that the key factor leading to an audit was the ratio of a taxpayer's expenses to his or her income.

According to Aczel, if your total business expenses amount to less than 52% of your gross business income, you are "not very likely" to be audited. If your business expenses are 52% to 63% of your business income, there is a "relatively high probability" that the IRS computer will tag you for an audit. Finally, if your expenses are more than 63% of your income, Aczel claims you are "certain to be computer tagged for audit." Of course, this doesn't necessarily mean that you *will* be audited. Less than 10% of returns that are computer tagged for audit are actually audited. But being tagged considerably increases the odds that you'll be audited.

Whether Aczel's precise numbers are correct or not is anyone's guess. However, his basic conclusion—that your income-to-deduction ratio is an important factor in determining whether you'll be audited—is undoubtedly true. (A former IRS commissioner admitted as much in a CNN interview in 1995.)

Tip #10: Beware of Abnormally Large Deductions

It is not just the total amount of your deductions that is important. Very large individual deductions can also increase your audit chances. How much is too much? It depends in part on the nature of your business. A $2,000 foreign travel deduction might look abnormal for a plumber, but not for a person in the import-export business.

Shown below are two charts from a 2004 Government Accountability Office report which show the dollar range for common deductions claimed by sole proprietors in 2001. The first chart shows expenses by sole proprietors who earned less than $25,000 from their businesses. Looking at this chart, you can see that in 2001, the business travel deduction ranged from a low of $20 (the amount claimed by taxpayers in the 1st percentile) to a high of $8,520 (the amount claimed by taxpayers in the 99th percentile). The average deduction (mean) was $1,200. The median deduction (half of the sample size claimed more than this number, while the other half claimed less) was $560. This tells you that if you claim a $15,000 travel deduction, the IRS will think something could be wrong. This does not necessarily mean you will get audited, but it increases your chances. Of course, if you're entitled to a $15,000 travel deduction, you should claim it. But be prepared to back it up with good documentation.

The other chart shows the amounts for the same deductions claimed in 2001 by sole proprietors who earned $25,000 to $100,000. As you'd expect, these amounts are somewhat higher than the deductions claimed by proprietors who earned less than $25,000. For example, the average home office deduction claimed by these taxpayers was $3,000.

These deductions were claimed back in 2001, so you must correct for inflation when using the charts today. In recent years, inflation has averaged between 2% and 3% per year. Therefore, you'd expect these deductions to be about 12% to 15% higher for sole proprietors in 2007.

Range of Expenses for Sole Proprietorships With Gross Income Less Than $25,000 (Tax Year 2001)

Expense category	Mean	1st	10th	Median	90th	99th
Advertising	$ 600	$ 10	$ 40	$ 220	$1,200	$5,290
Bad debts	1,700	10	50	300	2,020	18,480
Car/truck	2,300	30	190	1,420	5,480	12,530
Commissions	1,600	10	60	440	3,480	14,060
Depletion	1,400	0	70	770	2,850	6,060
Depreciation	2,000	20	130	950	4,560	17,150
Employee benefit programs	2,300	180	310	1,540	4,460	7,300
Insurance	800	20	100	460	1,780	4,830
Interest on mortgage	3,400	10	320	1,840	7,210	25,960
Interest on other business debt	1,800	10	70	480	2,830	11,770
Legal/professional services	400	20	50	160	680	3,790
Office	600	10	40	250	1,360	4,510
Pension/profit sharing plans	1,500	0	10	800	3,480	6,950
Rent on machinery/ equipment	1,800	10	100	750	4,810	9,120
Rent on other business property	2,800	30	200	1,990	6,170	13,970
Repairs	900	10	60	370	2,330	7,110
Supplies	1,100	10	70	500	2,710	8,410
Taxes	400	10	30	140	860	2,960
Travel	1,200	20	80	560	2,800	8,520
Meals/entertainment	500	10	30	200	1,140	3,560
Utilities	900	10	110	580	2,030	5,370
Wages	4,500	30	190	1,190	8,000	29,940
Other	2,200	10	110	860	4,480	16,320
Home office	1,800	40	280	1,120	3,900	10,130
All categories	$7,000	$ 60	$ 590	$4,400	$14,970	$36,260

Source: GAO analysis of IRS data

Range of Expenses for Sole Proprietorships With Gross Income From $25,000 to $100,000 (Tax Year 2001)						
Expense category	Mean	1st	10th	Median	90th	99th
Advertising	$1,600	$ 20	$ 80	$ 680	$4,290	$10,920
Bad debts	1,500	20	70	580	2,680	15,530
Car/truck	6,100	100	880	4,200	12,990	30,910
Commissions	5,200	20	140	1,670	13,910	51,330
Depletion	6,000	40	280	4,960	13,780	24,490
Depreciation	4,300	50	330	2,400	9,900	27,870
Employee benefit programs	2,700	90	160	1,830	6,890	10,500
Insurance	1,600	60	250	990	3,610	8,060
Interest on mortgage	4,100	30	410	2,190	9,020	32,400
Interest on other business debt	1,900	10	140	970	4,750	11,910
Legal/professional services	700	40	90	250	1,290	7,820
Office	1,300	20	100	580	3,020	10,150
Pension/profit sharing plans	3,100	0	100	1,170	9,020	10,440
Rent on machinery/ equipment	3,100	20	130	1,260	7,600	21,950
Rent on other business property	6,400	40	600	4,790	14,400	26,610
Repairs	2,200	30	110	900	5,700	18,250
Supplies	3,000	30	180	1,250	7,110	26,840
Taxes	1,000	10	50	400	2,540	7,520
Travel	2,300	30	140	1,070	5,490	17,930
Meals/entertainment	1,000	20	70	500	2,440	6,070
Utilities	2,100	60	370	1,500	4,400	11,690
Wages	10,500	100	750	6,640	26,160	48,090
Other	6,200	40	410	2,880	15,110	45,530
Home office	3,000	110	550	2,060	6,910	12,960
All categories	$26,200	$1,560	$ 7,240	$21,420	$51,140	$90,100

Source: GAO analysis of IRS data

Chapter 18

Help Beyond This Book

There are many resources available to supplement and explain more fully the tax information covered in this book. Many of these resources are free; others are reasonably priced. The more expensive tax publications for professionals are often available at public libraries or law libraries. And, a lot of tax information is available on the Internet.

If you have a question about a specific tax deduction or any other tax-related matter, you can:

- consult a secondary tax source
- review the tax law, or
- see a tax professional.

You can do these suggested steps in any order you wish. For example, you can see a tax professional right away instead of doing any research yourself. This will save you time but will cost you money.

Before you try to research tax law on your own, we recommend that you learn how to do legal research first. An excellent resource is *Legal Research: How to Find & Understand the Law*, by Stephen Elias and Susan Levinkind (Nolo), or you can go to Nolo's Legal Research Center at www.nolo.com.

Secondary Sources of Tax Information

Going straight to the tax code when you have a tax question is generally not the best approach. The tax code itself can be dry and difficult to decipher—particularly if you're trying to figure out how a particular law or rule applies to your situation. Instead of diving right into the code books, your best bet is to start with one of the many secondary sources that try to make the tax law more understandable. Unlike the primary sources listed in "Tax Publications," below, these sources are not the law itself or the IRS's official pronouncements on the law. Instead, they are interpretations and explanations of the law intended to make it more understandable. Often, you'll be able to find the answer to your question in one or more of these sources. You can also learn about topics not covered in this book—for example, what constitutes income for tax purposes, how to complete your tax returns, or how to deal with an IRS audit.

Information From the IRS

The IRS has made a huge effort to inform the public about the tax law, creating hundreds of informative publications, an excellent website, and a telephone answering service. However, unlike the regulations and rulings issued by the IRS, these secondary sources of information are for informational purposes only. They are not official IRS pronouncements, and the IRS is not legally bound by them.

Reading IRS publications is a useful way to obtain information on IRS procedures and to get the agency's view of the tax law. But keep in mind that these publications only present the IRS's interpretation of the law, which may be very one-sided and even contrary to court rulings. That's why you shouldn't rely exclusively on IRS publications for information.

IRS Website

The IRS has one of the most useful Internet websites of any federal government agency. Among other things, almost every IRS form and informational publication can be downloaded from the site. The Internet address is www.irs.gov.

The IRS website has a special section for small businesses and the self-employed (www.irs.gov/businesses/small/index.html). It includes:

- answers to basic tax questions and a calendar of tax deadlines
- online access to most IRS forms and information booklets
- industry-specific tax information for certain industries like construction and food service
- tips to avoid common tax problems
- announcements of new IRS policies and procedures of particular interest to small businesses
- links to court opinions and to rulings and regulations on specific industries
- links to non-IRS sites for general tax information, and
- links to helpful small business resources.

IRS Booklets and CD-ROM

The IRS publishes over 350 free booklets explaining the tax code, called IRS Publications ("Pubs," for short). Many of these publications are referenced in this book. Some are relatively easy to understand, others are incomprehensible or misleading. As with all IRS publications, they only present the IRS's interpretation of the tax laws—which may or may not be upheld by the federal courts.

You can download all of the booklets from the IRS website at www.irs.gov. You can also obtain free copies by calling 800-TAX-FORM (800-829-3676) or by contacting your local IRS office or sending an order form to the IRS.

IRS Telephone Information

The IRS offers a series of prerecorded tapes of information on various tax topics on a toll-free telephone service called TELETAX (800-829-4477). See IRS Publication 910 for a list of topics.

You can talk to an IRS representative on the telephone by calling 800-829-1040. (It is difficult to get though to someone from January through May.) Be sure to double check anything an IRS representative tells you over the phone—the IRS is notorious for giving misleading or outright wrong answers to taxpayers' questions, and the agency will not stand behind oral advice that turns out to be incorrect.

Free IRS Programs

In larger metropolitan areas, the IRS offers small business seminars on various topics, such as payroll tax reporting. You can ask questions at these half-day meetings, which are often held at schools or federal buildings. Call the IRS at 800-829-1040 to see if programs are offered near you and to get on the IRS small business mailing list. The IRS also has an online tax workshop for small businesses. It can be found at the online classroom on the IRS website. You can also order a free CD-ROM with a video presentation of the workshop through the IRS website.

Other Online Tax Resources

In addition to the IRS website, there are hundreds of privately created websites on the Internet that provide tax information and advice. Some of this information is good; some is execrable. A comprehensive collection of Web links about all aspects of taxation can be found at www.taxsites.com. Other useful tax Web link pages can be found at:

- www.willyancey.com/tax_internet.htm
- www.abanet.org/taxes

- www.natptax.com/tax_links.html
- www.el.com/elinks/taxes.

Some useful tax-related websites include:

- www.accountantsworld.com
- www.unclefed.com
- www.smbiz.com/sbwday.html
- http://aol.smartmoney.com/tax/filing
- www.taxguru.net.

Nolo's Website

Nolo maintains a website that is useful for small businesses and the self-employed. The site contains helpful articles, information about new legislation, book excerpts, and the Nolo catalogue. The site also includes a legal encyclopedia with specific information for businesspeople, as well as a legal research center you can use to find state and federal statutes, including the Internal Revenue Code. The Internet address is www.nolo.com.

Tax Publications

If you're a person who likes to read books, you'll be happy to know that there are enough books about tax law to fill a library. Tax publications vary from the broadly focused to the highly detailed. You can find answers to most tax questions in one or more of these resources.

Publications for the Nonexpert

There are many books (like this one) that attempt to make the tax law comprehensible to the average person. The best known are the paperback tax preparation books published every year. These books emphasize individual taxes but also have useful information for small businesses. Two of the best are:

- *The Ernst and Young Tax Guide* (John Wiley & Sons), and
- *J.K. Lasser's Your Income Tax* (John Wiley & Sons).

J.K. Lasser publishes other useful tax guides, many of which are targeted at small businesses. You can find a list of these publications at www.wiley.com/WileyCDA/Section/id-103210.html.

Tax guides designed for college courses can also be extremely helpful. Two good guides to all aspects of income taxes that are updated each year are:

- *Prentice Hall's Federal Taxation Comprehensive* (Prentice Hall), and
- *CCH Federal Taxation Comprehensive Topics* (Commerce Clearing House).

Nolo also publishes several books that deal with tax issues:

- *Home Business Tax Deductions: Keep What You Earn,* by Stephen Fishman (Nolo), emphasizes deductions for home businesses.
- *Tax Deductions for Professionals,* by Stephen Fishman (Nolo), covers deductions for those with professional practices, such as doctors, lawyers, architects, dentists, and others.
- *Lower Your Taxes in Seven Easy Steps,* by Stephen Fishman (Nolo), is a guide to tax planning for both business owners and non-owners.
- *Stand Up to the IRS*, by Frederick W. Daily (Nolo), explains how to handle an IRS audit.
- *Tax Savvy for Small Business*, by Frederick W. Daily (Nolo), provides an overview of the entire subject of taxation, geared to the small business owner.
- *Working With Independent Contractors*, by Stephen Fishman (Nolo), shows small businesses how to hire independent contractors without running afoul of the IRS or other government agencies.
- *Working for Yourself,* by Stephen Fishman (Nolo), covers the whole gamut of legal issues facing the one-person business.
- *Every Landlord's Tax Deduction Guide,* by Stephen Fishman (Nolo), provides detailed guidance on tax deductions for small residential landlords.
- *IRAs, 401(k)s & Other Retirement Plans*, by Twila Slesnick and John C. Suttle (Nolo), covers the tax implications of withdrawing funds from retirement accounts.
- *What Every Inventor Needs to Know About Business & Taxes*, by Stephen Fishman (Nolo), covers tax aspects of inventing.

Publications for Tax Professionals

Sometimes, you'll have a question you can't answer by looking at websites or tax publications for the layperson. In this event, you can consult one or more publications for tax professionals: accountants, CPAs, and attorneys. These are the most detailed and comprehensive secondary sources available.

There are six main publishing companies that publish reference materials for tax professionals:

- Business News Association (BNA); www.bna.com
- Commerce Clearing House (CCH); www.cch.com
- Klienrock Publishing; www.kleinrock.com
- Research Institute of America (RIA); www.riahome.com
- Tax Analysts; www.taxanalysts.com, and
- West Group; http://west.thomson.com.

These publishers produce an incredible volume of tax information, ranging from detailed analyses of the most arcane tax questions to brief, one-volume guides to the entire federal tax law. Among their publications are the following.

Tax services. These are highly detailed discussions of the tax law, organized by IRC section or topic and updated frequently—every week, or at least every month. The most authoritative is *The Law of Federal Income Taxation*, published by West Group (it's also called "Mertens" by tax professionals because it was originally edited by Jacob Mertens). Other tax services include the *United States Tax Reporter* (published by RIA) and *Standard Federal Tax Reporter* (published by CCH).

Tax treatises. Tax treatises provide in-depth, book-length treatments of a particular tax topic. Among the most useful are the Tax Management Portfolios, a series of paperback booklets published by BNA. If you're looking for information on a very precise tax issue, you might find what you need in a portfolio.

Tax citators. Tax citators summarize tax cases and compile and organize them by subject matter and IRC section. By using a citator, you can find all the tax cases that have addressed a specific tax topic. Both CCH and RIA publish citators.

Tax deskbooks. CCH publishes a well-known one-volume tax "deskbook" called the *Master Tax Guide* that provides an overview of the tax law. It's updated each year.

You can find a good discussion on how to use these tax materials in *West's Federal Tax Research* (South-Western College Publishing).

All of these publications are available in print form, on CD-ROMs, and on subscriber websites maintained by the publishers themselves or commercial databases (notably Westlaw and Lexis, subscriber databases containing legal information). As you might expect, they are generally very expensive. You can also find them in a law library, some large public libraries, or a tax professional's office.

Trade Association Publications

There are hundreds of trade associations and organizations representing every conceivable occupation—for example, the American Society of Home Inspectors, the Association of Independent Video and Filmmakers, and the Graphic Artists Guild. Most of these have specialized publications and newsletters that track tax issues of common interest. You can learn about specific tax issues in your industry that even your tax professional might not know about—perhaps a new case or IRS ruling. Also, you can often find speakers on tax topics at programs offered to members at conventions and trade shows.

If you don't know the name and address of an association relevant to your business, ask other businesspeople in your field. Or check out the *Encyclopedia of Associations* (Gale Research); it should be available at your public library. Also, many of these associations have websites on the Internet, so you may be able to find the one you want by doing an Internet search.

Tax Software

Today, millions of taxpayers use tax preparation software to complete their own income tax returns. The best-known programs are *TurboTax* and *TaxCut*. These programs contain most IRS tax forms, publications, and other tax guidance. Both have helpful websites at www.turbotax.com and www.taxcut.com.

The Tax Law

If you can't find an answer to your question in a secondary source, you might be able to find help in the tax law itself. Or, you may want to consult the tax law to verify (or clarify) what you've learned from secondary sources.

The "tax law" of the United States comes from several sources:
- the Internal Revenue Code
- IRS regulations
- court cases, and
- IRS rulings, interpretations, and tax advice.

Every branch of the federal government is involved in creating the tax law. The Internal Revenue Code is enacted by Congress (the legislative branch), IRS regulations and rulings are issued by the IRS (a department of the executive branch), and taxpayers may appeal the IRS's actions to the federal courts (the judicial branch).

The Tax Law Versus *War and Peace*	
	Number of pages
Internal Revenue Code	3,653
IRS Regulations	13,079
War and Peace, by Leo Tolstoy	1,444

Internal Revenue Code

The Internal Revenue Code (IRC) is the supreme tax law of the land. The IRC (also called "the code" or "the tax code") is written, and frequently rewritten, by Congress. The first tax code, adopted in 1913, contained 14 pages. Today, the tax code is more than 3,600 pages long.

The IRC is found in Title 26 of the United States Code (USC for short). The USC encompasses all of our federal laws. "Title" simply refers to the place within the massive USC where the IRC is found.

The entire tax code covers income taxes, Social Security taxes, excise taxes, estate and gift taxes, and tax procedure. It is organized by category and broken down into subtitles, chapters, subchapters, parts, subparts, sections, subsections, paragraphs, subparagraphs, and clauses. The income tax laws are in Chapter 1 of Subtitle A of the tax code. Most of the laws dealing with tax deductions are found in Parts VI and VII of Subchapter B of Chapter 1.

For our purposes, the most important thing to remember about the organization of the tax code is that each specific tax law is contained in a separate numbered section. For example, Section 179 covers first-year expensing of long-term business assets. For the sake of convenience, tax professionals will often refer to these numbered sections of the tax code.

> **EXAMPLE:** "IRC § 179(b)(4)(A)" means that this particular tax law is found in Title 26 of the USC (the Internal Revenue Code), Section 179, subsection b, paragraph 4, subparagraph A.

The tax code is published each year in a two-volume set (usually in paperback). You should be able to find it in the reference section of any public library. You can also purchase a set from various tax publishers, such as Commerce Clearing House and Research Institute of America. A complete set of the tax code costs over $80. You can also purchase a one-volume abridged version for much less. This will likely contain all the tax code provisions you'll want to refer to. The entire United State Code (including the IRC) is also available on CD-ROM from the Government Printing Office for under $40.

Fortunately, the IRC is available for free on the Internet. You can get to the entire IRC from Nolo's Legal Research Center—go to www.nolo.com. Portions are also available on the IRS website (www.irs.gov) and several other websites.

Make sure your tax code is current. The IRC is amended every year; in recent years, these amendments have made major changes to the law. Make sure that any copy of the IRC you use in your research is current.

IRS Regulations

Even though the Internal Revenue Code contains over 3,600 pages, it does not provide adequate guidance for every situation that arises in real life. To supplement the IRC, the IRS issues regulations, called "Treasury Regulations," "Regulations," or "Regs." Although written by the IRS, not

Congress, these regulations have almost the same authoritative weight as the tax code itself.

While the tax code is usually written in broad and general terms, the regulations get down and dirty, providing details about how tax code provisions are intended to operate in the real world. Regulations are slightly easier to read than the tax code on which they are based and often include examples that can be helpful. The regulations cover many (but not all) of the tax code provisions.

To see if a particular IRC section is supplemented by a regulation, start with the number of the IRC section. If there is a corresponding regulation, it will bear the same number, usually preceded by the number "1."

> **EXAMPLE:** "Reg. 1.179" refers to a Treasury regulation interpreting IRC Section 179.

The regulations are published in a multivolume set by the Government Printing Office and tax publishers such as CCH and RIA. These are available in law libraries and may also be found in some large public libraries. Many regulations can be downloaded from the IRS website.

Court Cases

When a dispute arises between a taxpayer and the IRS, the taxpayer may take the matter to federal court. The courts are the final arbiters of tax disputes. A court may overrule the IRS if the court concludes that the IRS applied the tax code in a manner contrary to the United States Constitution or differently from what Congress intended.

Tax disputes are tried in three different courts: a special tax court that handles only tax disputes, the regular federal trial courts (called U.S. District Courts), and the Court of Federal Claims. If either the taxpayer or the IRS doesn't like the result reached at trial, it may appeal to the federal appellate courts (called the U.S. Courts of Appeals), and even to the United States Supreme Court.

Decisions of these courts are published, along with explanations and discussions of the tax law. These court decisions provide valuable interpretations of the tax laws. Many, but not all, of these court interpretations are binding on the IRS. Thousands of court decisions dealing with tax law have been published, so chances are good that there is at least one decision on the issue that interests you.

To locate a published court decision, you must understand how to read a case citation. A citation provides the names of the people or companies involved on each side of the case, the volume of the legal publication (called a reporter) in which the case can be found, the page number on which it begins, and the year in which the case was decided. Here is an example of what a legal citation looks like: *Smith v. Jones*, 123 F.3d 456 (1995). Smith and Jones are the names of the people in the legal dispute. The case is reported in volume 123 of the Federal Reporter, Third Series, beginning on page 456; the court issued the decision in 1995.

Opinions by the federal district courts are in a series of reporters called the Federal Supplement, or F.Supp. Any case decided by a federal court of appeals is found in a series of books called the Federal Reporter. Older cases are contained in the first series of the Federal Reporter, or F. More recent cases are contained in the second or third series of the Federal Reporter, F.2d or F.3d. Cases decided by the U.S. Supreme Court are found in three publications: United States Reports (identified as U.S.), the Supreme Court Reporter (identified as S.Ct.), and the Supreme Court Reports, Lawyer's Edition (identified as L.Ed.). Supreme Court case citations often refer to all three publications.

Many, but not all, of these legal decisions are available free on the Internet. Tax court decisions and tax decisions from other courts from 1990 to date can be accessed for free at www.legalbitstream.com. Tax court decisions from 1999 to date can also be accessed at www. ustaxcourt.gov. The website www.findlaw.com contains links to all types of law-related websites. Virtually all legal decisions are available on the subscriber websites Lexis.com and Westlaw.com. You may be able to access these websites through a library or a tax professional's office.

Hard copies of published decisions by the United States Tax Court can be found in the Tax Court Reports, or TC, published by the U.S. Government Printing Office. Tax court decisions can also be found in a reporter called Tax Court Memorandum Decisions, or TCM, published by Commerce Clearing House, Inc. Decisions from all federal courts involving taxation can be found in a reporter called U.S. Tax Cases, or

USTC, published by Commerce Clearing House, Inc. These are available in law libraries.

For a detailed discussion of how to research court cases, see *Legal Research: How to Find & Understand the Law,* by Stephen Elias and Susan Levinkind (Nolo), or go to Nolo's Legal Research Center at www. nolo.com.

IRS Rulings, Interpretations, and Tax Advice

It might seem like the tax code, regulations, and court decisions would provide everything anyone ever wanted to know about tax law. But even more IRS guidance is available. The IRS publishes several types of statements (besides Regs) of its position on various tax matters. These pronouncements guide IRS personnel and taxpayers as to how the IRS will apply specific tax laws.

Unlike the tax code and regulations, these statements do not have the force of law. Rather, they are the IRS's own interpretation of the tax law, which is not necessarily binding on the courts (or on you, should you choose to challenge the IRS's interpretation in court). However, they give you a good idea of how the IRS would handle the situation involved.

Revenue Rulings

IRS Revenue Rulings (Rev. Rul.) are IRS announcements of how the tax law applies to a hypothetical set of facts. The IRS publishes over 100 of these rulings every year. These rulings represent the IRS's view of the tax law, and the IRS presumes that they are correct. If an auditor discovers that you have violated a revenue ruling, you will probably have to pay additional tax. On the other hand, if you can show an auditor that a revenue ruling supports your position, you probably won't have to pay more tax. If you have violated a revenue ruling, all is not necessarily lost. Revenue rulings are not binding on the courts, which can (and do) disregard them from time to time. Thus, it's possible you could win your case on appeal.

You can download free copies of all IRS Revenue Rulings from 1954 to date from www.taxlinks.com. Revenue rulings also appear in the weekly *Internal Revenue Cumulative Bulletin,* which is published by the U.S. Government Printing Office. Tax book publishers Prentice-Hall, Commerce Clearing House, and Research Institute of America also reprint IRS Revenue Rulings. They are indexed by IRC section and subject matter.

> **EXAMPLE:** "Rev. Rul. 03-41" refers to IRS Revenue Ruling number 41, issued in 2003.

Revenue Procedures

Revenue procedures ("Rev. Procs.") are IRS announcements dealing with procedural aspects of tax practice. Rev. Procs. are used primarily by tax return preparers. They often explain when and how to report tax items, such as how to claim a net operating loss on a tax form or return. Revenue procedures are contained in the weekly *Internal Revenue Cumulative Bulletin*, which you can find in larger public and law libraries, and also are reprinted by tax book publishers and on the IRS website. You can obtain free copies of many revenue procedures at www.legalbitstream.com.

> **EXAMPLE:** "Rev. Proc. 99-15" refers to a published Revenue Procedure number 15, issued in 1999.

Letter Rulings

IRS letter rulings are IRS answers to specific written questions from taxpayers about complex tax situations. The only person who is entitled to rely on the ruling as legal authority is the taxpayer to whom the ruling is addressed; even if you find yourself in a similar position, the IRS is not legally required to follow the guidance it gave in the letter. However, letter rulings offer valuable insight into the IRS's position on tax treatment of complex transactions. Since 1976, letter rulings have been made available to the general public. You can access free copies of many letter rulings at www.legalbitstream.com. They are also published by tax publishers.

> **EXAMPLE:** "Ltr. Ruling 9913043 (April 3, 1999)" refers to a letter ruling issued on April 3, 1999. The first two numbers of the seven-digit identifier show the year it was issued, the next two indicate the week of the year, and the last three show the ruling for that week.

Thus, this letter ruling was the 43rd issued during the 13th week of 1999.

IRS General Guidance

From time to time, the IRS gives general guidance and statements of policy in official "announcements" and "notices" similar to press releases. They appear in the weekly *Internal Revenue Cumulative Bulletin*. It doesn't usually pay to search IRS announcements or notices, because they are too broad to answer specific questions. You can access many of these for free at www.legalbitstream.com.

Internal Revenue Manual

The *Internal Revenue Manual* (IRM) is a series of handbooks that serve as guides to IRS employees on tax law and procedure. The IRM tells IRS employees (usually auditors or collectors) how specific tax code provisions should be enforced. The manual is available on the IRS website (www.irs.gov).

The IRM is revealing of IRS attitudes in certain areas—for example, Section 4.10.3 of the manual describes the techniques IRS auditors are supposed to use when they examine the depreciation deductions claimed by a business.

IRS Forms and Instructions

IRS forms are well known to us all, especially Form 1040, the annual personal income tax return. There are more than 650 other IRS forms, listed in Publication 676, *Catalog of Federal Tax Forms*. You can get them free at IRS offices or by calling 800-829-FORM or 800-829-1040. You can also download them from the IRS website at www.irs.gov. Many IRS forms come with instructions and explanations of the tax law.

Consulting a Tax Professional

You don't have to do your own tax research. There are hundreds of thousands of tax professionals (tax pros) in the United States ready and eager to help you—for a price. A tax pro can answer your questions, provide guidance to help you make key tax decisions, prepare your tax returns, and help you deal with the IRS if you get into tax trouble.

Types of Tax Pros

There are several different types of tax pros. They differ widely in training, experience, and cost:

- **Tax preparers.** As the name implies, tax preparers prepare tax returns. The largest tax preparation firm is H & R Block, but many mom-and-pop operations open for business in storefront offices during tax time. In most states, anybody can be a tax preparer; no licensing is required. Most tax preparers don't have the training or experience to handle taxes for businesses and, therefore, are probably not a wise choice. A 2006 study by the Government Accountability Office underscores this. Posing as taxpayers, GAO investigators visited 19 outlets of several unidentified commercial tax-preparation firms and asked them to prepare returns based on two hypothetical situations. The 19 preparers arrived at the correct refund amount only twice. The GAO said that several of the preparers gave very bad tax advice, particularly when it came to reporting business income.

- **Enrolled agents.** Enrolled agents (EAs) are tax advisers and preparers who are licensed by the IRS. They must have at least five years of experience or pass a difficult IRS test. They can represent taxpayers before the IRS and in administrative proceedings, circuit court, and, possibly, tax court, if they pass the appropriate tests. Enrolled agents are the least expensive of the true tax pros but are reliable for tax return preparation and more routine tax matters. They can be quite adequate for many small businesses.

- **Certified Public Accountants.** Certified public accountants (CPAs) are licensed and regulated by each state. They undergo lengthy training and must pass a comprehensive exam. CPAs represent the high end of the tax pro spectrum. In addition to preparing tax returns, they perform sophisticated accounting and tax work. CPAs are found in large national firms or in small local outfits. The large national firms are used primarily by large businesses. Some states also license public accountants. These are competent but are not as highly regarded as CPAs.

- **Tax attorneys.** Tax attorneys are lawyers who specialize in tax matters. The only time you'll ever need a tax attorney is if you get into serious trouble with the IRS or another tax agency and need legal representation before the IRS or in court. Some tax attorneys also give tax advice, but they are usually too expensive for small businesses. You're probably better off hiring a CPA if you need specialized tax help.

Finding a Tax Pro

The best way to find a tax pro is to obtain referrals from business associates, friends, or professional associations. If none of these sources can give you a suitable lead, try contacting the National Association of Enrolled Agents or one of its state affiliates. You can find a listing of affiliates at the NAEA website at www.naea.org. Local CPA societies can give you referrals to local CPAs. You can also find tax pros in the telephone book under "Accountants, Tax Return." Local bar associations can refer you to a tax attorney. Be aware that CPA societies and local bar associations refer from a list on a rotating basis, so you shouldn't construe a referral as a recommendation or certification of competence.

Your relationship with your tax pro will be one of your most important business relationships. Be picky about the person you choose. Talk with at least three tax pros before hiring one. You want a tax pro who takes the time to listen to you, answers your questions fully and in plain English, seems knowledgeable, and makes you feel comfortable. Make sure the tax pro works frequently with small businesses. It can also be helpful if the tax pro already has clients in businesses similar to yours. A tax pro already familiar with the tax problems posed by your type of business can often give you the best advice for the least money.

■

Index

Get the Latest in the Law

① **Nolo's Legal Updater**
We'll send you an email whenever a new edition of your book is published!
Sign up at **www.nolo.com/legalupdater**.

② **Updates at Nolo.com**
Check **www.nolo.com/update** to find recent changes in the law that
affect the current edition of your book.

③ **Nolo Customer Service**
To make sure that this edition of the book is the most recent one, call us at
800-728-3555 and ask one of our friendly customer service representatives
(7:00 am to 6:00 pm PST, weekdays only). Or find out at **www.nolo.com**.

④ **Complete the Registration & Comment Card ...**
... and we'll do the work for you! Just indicate your preferences below:

Registration & Comment Card

NAME   DATE

ADDRESS

CITY   STATE   ZIP

PHONE   EMAIL

COMMENTS

WAS THIS BOOK EASY TO USE?   (VERY EASY)   5   4   3   2   1   (VERY DIFFICULT)

☐ Yes, you can quote me in future Nolo promotional materials. *Please include phone number above.*

☐ Yes, send me **Nolo's Legal Updater** via email when a new edition of this book is available.

Yes, I want to sign up for the following email newsletters:

    ☐ **NoloBriefs** (monthly)
    ☐ **Nolo's Special Offer** (monthly)
    ☐ **Nolo's BizBriefs** (monthly)
    ☐ **Every Landlord's Quarterly** (four times a year)

☐ Yes, you can give my contact info to carefully selected
partners whose products may be of interest to me.

NOLO

DEDU 3.0